Sexology and Translation

In the series *Sexuality Studies*,
edited by Janice Irvine and Regina Kunzel

Also in this series:

Edited by Heike Bauer

Sexology and Translation

Cultural and Scientific Encounters
across the Modern World

TEMPLE UNIVERSITY PRESS
Philadelphia • Rome • Tokyo

TEMPLE UNIVERSITY PRESS
Philadelphia, Pennsylvania 19122
www.temple.edu/tempress

Library of Congress Cataloging-in-Publication Data

Sexology and translation : cultural and scientific encounters across
the modern world / edited by Heike Bauer.
    pages cm. — (Sexuality studies)
  Includes bibliographical references and index.
  ISBN 978-1-4399-1248-5 (hardback) — ISBN 978-1-4399-1249-2
(paper) — ISBN 978-1-4399-1250-8 (e-book)   1. Sex—Cross-cultural
studies.   2. Sexology—Cross-cultural studies.   I. Bauer, Heike.
  HQ16.S465 2015
  306.7—dc23

                                                    2015000678

Printed in the United States of America

9 8 7 6 5 4 3 2

Contents

A Note on Translation

The chapters included here discuss texts in Arabic, Chinese, French, German, Greek, Hebrew, Japanese, Latin, Russian, and Spanish as well as English. While their uses of translation vary, longer quotations have been generally rendered into English in the main text for ease of readability. Titles and shorter quotations are mostly given in the original language with the translation [in square brackets]. Some chapters also include parallel translations or other ways of working between languages. The notes allow readers to track down the original sources.

Acknowledgments

irst, thanks are due to the contributors who have brought to this project enthusiasm as well as their critical expertise. I am grateful to the Wellcome Trust for funding my "Sexology and Translation" symposium in 2012, thus initiating the scholarly dialogue that would inspire this collection. Thanks are also due to Birkbeck's Department of English and Humanities, and BiGS, Birkbeck's forum for gender and sexuality studies, which have supported the project intellectually and financially, and to the students in my option modules "Sexuality and Modernity" and "Disciplining Sex," who have engaged in many lively debates about the social and cultural politics of sexuality across the modern world. Chiara Beccalossi, Kirsti Bohata, Sean Brady, Carolyn Burdett, Laura Doan, Lisa Downing, Veronika Fuechtner, Natalia Gerodetti, Robert Gillett, Douglas Haynes, Joanne Leal, Churnjeet Mahn, Ofer Nur, Sasha Roseneil, Anna Katharina Schaffner, and Elizabeth Stephens have contributed to the shaping of this project. The astute anonymous reviewers have sharpened its focus. The completion of the manuscript was aided by Janet Francendese, the series editors, Janice Irvine and Regina Kunzel, and the production team at Temple University Press. As always, Diane Watt has been my precious first reader.

Sexology and Translation

Introduction

*Translation and the Global Histories
of Sexuality*

HEIKE BAUER

I s the emergence of modern sexuality a global phenomenon? *Sexology and
Translation* examines the shape and shaping of sexual ideas and related scientific practices and cultural representations in parts of Europe, Asia, the
Middle East, and South America between the late nineteenth century and
the period leading up to World War II. It brings together historians, literary
and cultural critics, and translation scholars who explore how the textual
and real encounters between an international band of writers, reformers,
and medical doctors shaped ideas about "sex" across the modern world. The
studies gathered here present original research and fresh conceptual insights
on the intersections between sexuality and modernity in a range of disciplinary, cultural, and (trans)national contexts. They focus on the translations
and mistranslations that occurred when bodies and desires were conceptualized in terms of "sex" and uncover hitherto unexplored avenues of exchange
between different contexts and the key figures that shaped sexual debates
during the inaugural period of the sexual science, 1880–1930s. While some
of the chapters reconsider the more familiar European archives of sexology
to reveal their affective development and debts to a wide range of cultural
and scientific debates, others explore the development of modern sex research and related cultural and political debates in Russia, China, Japan,
Egypt, Palestine, and Peru. Individually, these studies present new knowledge about the development of different national and transnational sexologies and their relationship to each other. Together they provide an important

corrective to the pervasive idea that sexuality is a "Western" construct that was transmitted around the world.

The collection shows that attention to translation—understood in the broadest sense as the dynamic process by which ideas are produced and transmitted—offers compelling new insights into how sexual ideas were formed in different contexts via a complex process of cultural negotiation. The Introduction draws out key findings that emerged out of the dialogue between scholars whose chapters examine the development of sexual sciences and discourses across the modern world. It contextualizes the research presented in the collection in relation to recent debates about the shape and methods of the history of sexuality and in so doing also addresses head-on some of the challenges that occur when distinct linguistic, disciplinary, and cultural contexts are brought into critical dialogue. *Sexology and Translation* extends understanding of how the intersections between national and transnational contexts, as well as the relationship between science and culture and discourse and experience, shaped modern sexuality. It substantively and theoretically reshapes existing scholarship on the histories of sexuality and modernity by demonstrating that the concept of "sexuality" was forged across the modern world at the intersections between science and culture via an intricate, and sometimes surprising, web of influences, disavowals, and allegiances that turned erotic desires, sexual acts, intimate relationships, and queer bodies into the contested markers of modernity.

Sexology (Re)Defined

One of the defining questions in critical studies of the formation of modern sexuality is what name to give the discursive, cultural, political, and medico-forensic fields in which sexuality gained shape. This collection uses the term "sexology" to describe the formation of a sustained, if not always systematic, scientific field of inquiry that emerged in the late nineteenth century and was dedicated to studying, theorizing, and sometimes "treating" sexual desires and bodies. But the term is also used here and elsewhere, often interchangeably, alongside other expressions such as "sexual science" and its Latin equivalent, *scientia sexualis*, as well as "sex research" and "sexual theory."[1] The multiplication of descriptors, which can also be found within the chapters in this collection, reflects the fact that the emergence of the modern subject of sex is defined by fluid boundaries that frequently blur the distinctions between science and culture. Recent research has emphasized this point. In contrast to early studies of sexology that focused specifically on its medico-scientific and political contexts, a growing body of scholarship is exploring the literary and subcultural dimensions of modern sexuality formation to show that "sexology" is as much a product of culture as it is a strictly medico-forensic praxis.[2]

While the history of sexology can no longer be called an emerging field—scholars have, after all, been excavating since at least the 1980s how sexuality was constructed, regulated, and lived in the past—it is fair to say that our understanding of it has been shaped by American and a selection of European perspectives.[3] By "us" I here mean primarily critics publishing in English and located in Anglo-American universities, although scholars based in others regions, especially perhaps in central Europe and Australia, have also made significant contributions to the field that has become known as the history of sexuality. Broadly speaking, it is fair to say that initially at least the history and historiography of sexology focused almost exclusively on (central) European and North American contexts.[4] The scholarly "rediscovery of sexology" in these regions, as Rita Felski has noted, "is largely due to the emergence of the gay rights movements of the 1960s and 1970s and a growing interest in constructing a history and tradition of same-sex desire."[5] It owes significant intellectual debts to the work of the French philosopher Michel Foucault. Foucault, whose three-part series of studies on *The History of Sexuality*, including *La volonté de savoir* (*The Will to Knowledge*, 1976), *L'usage des plaisirs* (*The Use of Pleasure*, 1984), and *Le souci de soi* (*The Care of the Self*, 1984), made sexuality central to the way in which the constructions of self and its location in modernity are understood.[6] Concerned with the relationship between power, discourse, and the subject, Foucault argued that the formation of a *scientia sexualis* in the late nineteenth century and the related emergence of a new vocabulary of sex (words such as "homosexuality" and "fetishism" were coined at the time) marks a distinct moment in the shaping of Western modernity, signaling a shift from religion to science and producing a modern sexual subject that is classified according to its desires and bodily acts. Rejecting grand narratives about linear progress, Foucault developed instead methods of historical research that are concerned with the excavation of "hidden" meanings and power structures (a method he called "archeology") and the deconstruction of how ideas and norms have come to be established over time (what he called "genealogy").

These methods have become hugely influential, including in studies that address the critical absences in Foucault's work such as his silence on issues of gender and race or his disregard of feelings, experience, and lived reality in historical analysis.[7] Only relatively recently, however, have critics also confronted what is arguably one of the most problematic yet pervasive features of Foucault's work: the distinction between a predominantly "Eastern" (or obsolete Roman) "*ars erotica*" and the "*scientia sexualis*" that according to Foucault characterizes "Western" modernity.[8] Critics such as Naoki Sakai have pointed out that in Foucault's work, "the notion of Western culture or its unity is never under suspicion," noting that his construction of an Eastern versus Western sexual binary encourages reductive, and often stereotypical, perspectives in cultural and historical research.[9] Yet what is still missing from the growing body of scholarship on the histories of sexuality in different parts of the world is a deeper understanding of the comparative, transnational, or global dimensions of modern sexology. *Sexology and Translation* addresses this gap. The studies gathered here track the emergence of sexual discourses and disciplines in different parts of the world, 1880–1930, expanding the definitions of sexology to include a wide range of cultural, scientific, and political phenomena to show that sexuality became a defining feature of global modernity.

Sexology across the Modern World: A Global History?

The geopolitical frameworks of modern sexuality are contested. Initially at least, histories of sexuality and modernity have tended to be framed specifically in relation to colonialism, reflecting the fact that both the discipline of sexology and the modern concept of sexuality emerged at that moment in the late nineteenth century when European colonialism violently expanded in Africa, Asia, and South America. This scholarship has shown that in Europe, as Ann Laura Stoler has noted, "the discursive and practical field in which nineteenth-century bourgeois sexuality emerged was situated on an imperial landscape where the cultural accoutrements of bourgeois distinction were partially shaped through contrasts forged in the politics and language of race."[10] The work of Stoler and other postcolonial historians has importantly turned attention to the implication of sexual discourses in colonialism to reveal both the racialized constructions of sexuality in Europe and the fact that, as Edward Said has influentially noted, a reductive sexualized deployment of the "Orient" underpins the very construction of "Western" civilization itself.[11] More recently, postcolonial scholars have scrutinized the problematic legacies of colonial conceptions of sexuality and their reemergence in contemporary political discourse. Jasbir Puar, for instance, has argued that in the twenty-first century sexual rights discourse has become part of the rhetorical arsenal by which certain states declare their own modernity and justify attacks on, and the oppression of, other peoples and territories.[12] At the same time, historians of sexuality have also begun to scrutinize the geopolitical frame of debate by turning attention to the histories of modern sexuality in different parts of the world including India, the country sometimes considered "the birthplace of sexology."[13] A new project led by Veronika Fuechtner and Douglas Haynes, for example, specifically explores the limits and possibilities of studying a "global history of sexuality 1880–1950," while the proliferating scholarship on the histories of sexuality in Asia, Africa, and South America continues to decenter the focus on Europe and North America, which dominated the history and historiography of sexuality in the twentieth century.[14]

How to discuss sexology in and across different cultural and geopolitical contexts without either essentializing or overemphasizing differences, and without perpetuating racist stereotypes and reductive ideas about the outward flow of ideas from a colonial center to its peripheries, remains one of the most important questions in debates about sexuality. This line of questioning is often pursued under the mantle of transnational studies, a concept that frames the intersections between gender, sexuality, race, and class in a broader global context by emphasizing that the exigencies of capitalism, rather than national boundaries, shape the conditions of human existence. Elizabeth Povinelli and George Chauncey Jr., writing in the late 1990s about what has become known as the "transnational turn" in sexuality studies, have defined the concept in terms of critical attention to "the dense, variegated traffic in cultural representations, people, and capital [that] increasingly characterizes the social life of people around the world."[15] Where much of the early focus on the transnational was on North American contexts— a focus that led Inderpal Grewal and Caren Kaplan to observe that while "the term *transnational* can address the asymmetries of the globalization process . . . it has already become so ubiquitous in cultural, literary and critical studies that much of its political valence seems to have become evacuated"—a recent explosion of scholarship on sexual subcultures and the histories of sexuality in Asia, Africa, Europe, and the Caribbean has complicated understanding of the transnational frameworks and the intersections between sexuality and modernity in different parts of the world.[16] Recent studies of sexology in Europe and North America have explored the complex circuits of exchange by which sexual ideas and politics were formed in these contexts.[17] New scholarship on the less frequently discussed regions of Europe as well as parts of Africa, Asia, and South America in turn has excavated diverse histories of sexuality in these regions of the world.[18] Together, these histories offer rich insights into culturally specific histories of sexuality and the synchronic emergence of modern sexuality within different national contexts.

Sexology and Translation builds on and expands this research by exploring how encounters between science and culture, and discourse and experience, shaped the emergence of modern sexual discourses and identities in Austria, China, Egypt, England, France, Germany, Japan, Palestine, Peru, and Russia. The collection deliberately uses the formulation *across the modern world*—in place of, say, transnational or global history—to define its scope. This is not to deny the usefulness of either of these perspectives but to emphasize that *how* we approach sexuality shapes our understanding of the intersections between local and global contingencies. The studies of the emergence of modern sexual discourses in a range of cultural contexts gathered here scrutinize the shapes and shaping of modern sexology from a range of angles. Some chapters explore how a cross-national flow of ideas and people shaped the traditional European centers of sexological research, while a chapter on Russia tracks the contested boundaries of Europe and their impact on sexological exchange. A cluster of studies on the histories of sexology in the Middle East, China, Japan, and Peru in turn examines the formation of modern sexual debates on the intersections between indigenous and transnational knowledges, thus making clear that the *scientia sexualis* was not only, as Foucault would have it, a Western phenomenon. By bringing together studies that track the connections and similarities between sexuality discourses in different cultural and national contexts, the collection pays attention to how ideas moved in and across different parts of the globe and intersected with culturally specific concerns along the way. It thus addresses debates about the national, transnational, and global histories of sexology even as it conceptualizes the emergence of a *scientia sexualis* in terms of dynamic movements that demonstrate that there are structural similarities in the way "sex" came to be spoken about across different parts of the world between the 1880s and the 1930s, a transformative period in history.

Describing this research as history that looks *across the modern world* aligns the collection with the concerns of queer studies. For the word "across"—which can be defined in terms such as "not straight," "askance," "at odds"—resonates with the "traversing" and "twisting" that, in Eve Kosofsky Sedgwick's famous observations, describes the meaning of "queer."[19] Yet the collection deliberately uses the expression "across" in place of the critically charged "queer" to indicate that while some of the chapters directly engage with concepts or methods associated with queer theory (both Chiang and Cryle, for instance, trace genealogies, while Bauer considers the affective shaping of sexology), all the studies included here move in critical directions that run against established narratives about the formations of a sexual science and its scope.[20] They look in different directions, glancing sideways, backward, and ahead as they explore the emergence of modern sexology and sexuality discourses.

Translation: A Critical Framework for the History of Sexuality

Translation provides a useful framework for discussing the emergence of sexual science and discourses in different parts of the world, including in terms of distinct cultural histories and their points of contact. Extending

Walter Benjamin's influential conceptualization of translation as the subject of cultural contingency, scholars have used the concept specifically to address issues of power, subjectivity, and cultural politics.[21] Susan Bassnett, in the most recent edition of her influential *Translation Studies*, sums up key points of debate when she writes that "the movement of peoples around the globe can be seen to mirror the very process of translation itself, for translation is not just the transfer of texts from one language into another, it is now rightly seen as a process of negotiation between texts and between cultures, a process during which all kinds of transactions take place mediated by the translator."[22] Bassnett's emphasis on negotiation, transaction, and the role of the translator draws together the insights gained by postcolonial critiques that have turned to translation to conceptualize the unequal distribution of power and its relationship to subjectivity and identity formation, and the findings of literary and cultural scholars who have argued that translation and translators play a central but often overlooked role in cultural production.[23] That translation also lends itself specifically to research on the history of sexuality is suggested by Naoki Sakai and Jon Solomon's argument that the violent institution of modernity can be understood in terms of a "biopolitics of translation."[24] They make the case for a "politically-informed discussion about the production of both social relations and humanistic knowledge [especially] in the context of anthropological difference inherited from colonialism," a discussion that challenges Foucault's Occidentalism and replaces it with a more nuanced understanding of the racialized processes by which bodies entered modernity.[25]

The collection expands the debates about translation to ask new questions about how bodies and desires came to be apprehended and politicized around the turn of the last century. How were sexual ideas formed? In what ways did national and transnational concerns shape the emergence of sexology in different parts of the modern world? How were the new sexual discourses received? Addressing these questions from a translation perspective reflects the historical context in which sexuality emerged. At the moment in time when debates about sexuality took hold in scientific, legal, political and cultural spheres, many of the experts and lay women and men involved in these debates could read more than one language, which enabled the rapid transmission and development of sexual writings. Works such as Richard von Krafft-Ebing's *Psychopathia Sexualis*, for instance, which was a key text in the emergence of European medico-forensic sexology, quickly gained influence in different cultural contexts despite the fact that it took half a dozen years before the German text was translated, first into English and soon into other languages including Japanese, Dutch, French, Russian, Hungarian, and Italian.[26] Krafft-Ebing published the first German edition in 1886, revising and enlarging it in a total of twelve editions published during his lifetime.

It was the tenth German edition that was first translated into English and published in the United States; a British edition soon followed that differed from the American translation in a number of ways, suggesting that it was Anglicized for the British market.[27] A number of contributors to this collection engage with different editions and translations of *Psychopathia Sexualis* and other sexological works. Sometimes they explicitly show that an understanding of publication history can offer substantive insights into the history of sexuality, while at other times the choice of edition reflects the current availabilities of texts. The individual chapters furthermore make clear that issues of language, as well as publication history, significantly shaped the field as both multilingualism and translation between languages was crucial in the development of modern sex research. The linguistic boundaries of sexology reflect the ties of modern sexuality to the unequal cultural politics of colonialism, as in some countries such as Peru the language of the colonizer became the language of modern sexuality. But they also indicate that sexuality was implicated in complex ways in the political and economic transformations of modernity, which enabled cross-cultural collaborations and the exchange of knowledges and ideas even as they also reinforced the inequalities put in place by colonialism.

While translation thus serves as a framework for analyzing how sexuality traveled across linguistic boundaries, and the politics of this process, it can also help to conceptualize the construction of sexual desires and bodies. Many of the studies included here explore specifically how observations of the body and its desires were translated into new knowledge formations and disciplinary practices. This research addresses one of the fundamental questions in the modern history of sexuality: why sexuality? Or, to phrase this differently, they consider afresh why erotic desires and sexual acts have gained such a prominent role in modern debates about politics, science, and individual and collective subject formations. Here attention to translation extends the focus of analysis beyond same-sex issues and the medico-forensic literatures that have become so central to the history and historiography of sexuality. Instead the chapters gathered in the collection explore a range of contexts in which sex was discussed. They reveal, for instance, that existing conceptions of intimacy such as "love" were transformed at the same time as sexual "perversions" entered the modern imagination. By focusing on the productive exchange between science, literature, and other cultural formations, this research furthermore makes clear that the sexual body was a highly problematic construct from the outset, concerned with a perceived sexual lack as well as excess, and with heterosexual as well as same-sex acts and desires. The collection thus broadens understanding of sexology to reveal that the conception of sexuality was tied in complex ways to norms about the modern human.

The diverse critical approaches to sexology and translation gathered here share a concern with movement. Looking across the modern world, they describe the processes of travel, transfer, transmission, and transformation that shape the formation of ideas, knowledges, and disciplinary formations and their dissemination and reception. This research challenges critics who have argued that bringing together such a proliferation of concepts and metaphors under the umbrella term "translation" reductively smooths over vital distinctions that exist between them. Instead it shows that translation provides a framework for critical debates that would otherwise run alongside each other. Doris Bachmann-Medick in her assessment of the "translational turn"—or the use of translation as an analytical concept across the humanities—has argued that the critical potential of translation lies in its ability to move "right across the disciplines as a new means of knowledge and a methodologically reflected analytical category."[28] The collection follows in her vein, making translation its focal point to bring together research that is methodologically and substantively wide-ranging. The project is prompted by the realization that while interdisciplinary, multidisciplinary, and cross-disciplinary approaches are feted in contemporary research in the humanities and social science, the dialogue between disciplines and fields of research is often fraught with the challenges of negotiating disciplinary conventions and following one-way trajectories that apply insights gained within one academic field to the study of another.

Sexology and Translation thus models a fostering of critical dialogue across literary and cultural studies, history, languages, and translation studies. Approaching the history of sexology from a translation perspective allows the contributors to maintain their disciplinary frameworks but also to develop comparative, transnational, and global perspectives. What emerges is less a single picture than a rough-edged mosaic of sexual modernity across the globe.

Navigating Sexology

The collection brings together studies of modern sexuality in Arabic-, Chinese-, English-, French-, German-, Hebrew-, Japanese-, Russian-, and Spanish-speaking contexts. They explore a wide range of sexual discourses, disciplines, and lives, employing approaches as diverse as Peter Cryle's close intellectual history of the concept of frigidity and Liat Kozma's social history of sex research in Egypt and Palestine. Some studies engage in the close reading of literary texts (such as Birgit Lang's study of Sacher-Masoch's novels; Jennifer Fraser's reading of Peruvian feminist fiction; and James Wilper's analysis of *The Intersexes*), while others explore sexual subcultures (Katie Sutton's work on the "third sex"; Heike Bauer's analysis of suicide and homosexual community) or the shaping of sexual science and discourses in Britain (as examined by Kate Fisher and Jana Funke), China (the chapters by Howard Chiang and Leon Rocha), Japan (analyzed by Michiko Suzuki), and Russia (the focus of Brian Baer's chapter). There are many other ways of grouping together this work and pointing out similarities and distinctions in approach, subject matter, and the conclusions drawn in these analyses of modern sexuality. For instance, given the focus of the collection, it might be productive to read the individual chapters in sections that reflect the different intellectual and political traditions that have shaped the debates about translation as a critical tool—its debts to deconstruction, psychoanalysis, postcolonial theory, and linguistics—and that address key critical debates about translation: how to deconstruct the meanings and cultural contingencies of texts and ideas (the focus of the studies by Chiang, Cryle, Lang, and Wilper); how to conceptualize the relationship between language and subjectivity (explored by Bauer, Fraser, and Sutton); how to articulate the processes of, and issues at stake in, cross-cultural encounters (examined here by Fisher and Funke, Kozma, Rocha, and Suzuki); and, finally, what the field of "translation studies" itself, concerned with the relationship between source texts and their translations, adds to historical research (the focus of Baer's chapter). However, the collection is structured in three parts, which, while by no means seeking to close down other ways of navigating through the material, deliberately aim to draw out the contribution made by the collection to the history of sexuality.

The three closely connected parts that make up *Sexology and Translation* speak to key debates in the field. Their scope and rationale is explained in detail in the section introductions. Briefly, Part I, "Conceptualizations," uses translation to explore key concepts in modern sexual discourse—frigidity, Darwinism, subjectivity, inversion—and considers what they can tell us about the intersections between scientific and literary culture in the shaping of modern sexuality. Part II, "Formations," which pays particular attention to the global networks that shaped modern sexology, discusses the translations of sexual ideas and practices into "national" sexologies in England, Russia, Egypt, Palestine, and China. And the final Part III, "Dis/Identifications," examines how sexological ideas were received by individual women and men, who in turn translated them into new political, disciplinary, and subcultural contexts. While there is clearly overlap between these sections, this structure nevertheless seeks to draw out the affinities as well as the distinctions and, sometimes, the contradictory findings of the diverse research gathered here.

Where earlier histories of sexology have focused specifically on same-sex histories, this collection finds a broader range of concerns relating to sexology as it explores the relationship between science and culture and between experts and "lay" people in the gendered development of modern sexual politics. Examining the range of experiences associated with sexuality and the political concerns that shape them, the chapters included here make clear that sexology was not just the business of men but that feminist activists and writers made a significant contribution to the emergence and popularization of sexual discourse—nowhere more so than in Peru, where, as Jennifer Fraser's chapter shows, feminist fiction rather than science was the primary space for the development of sexual ideas. Together, these studies reveal that sexual debates were closely tied in to issues of national politics and modern state formation, but that a material and conceptual traffic in ideas and people equally influenced the development of both national sexologies and transnational sexuality. Such an examination of the global translations of sexuality is thus much more than a project of tracing how certain ideas spread from a center to the margins. It is a way of asking new questions about the role of sexuality in shaping how the human came to be apprehended and politicized around the turn of the century. *Sexology and Translation* demonstrates that sexology was forged out of complex intersections between scientific and cultural debates across the modern world.

NOTES

1. Good overviews include Lucy Bland, *Banishing the Beast: Sexuality and the Early Feminists* (London: Penguin, 1995), 250–296; Joseph Bristow, *Sexuality*, 2nd ed. (New York: Routledge, 2011); Sally Ledger and Roger Luckhurst, eds., *The Fin de Siècle: A Reader in Cultural History c. 1880–1900* (Oxford: Oxford University Press, 2000), 291–312; Chris Waters, "Sexology," in *Palgrave Advances in the Modern History of Sexuality*, ed. Harry G. Cocks and Matt Houlbrook (Basingstoke, UK: Palgrave, 2005), 41–63; Chris White, ed., *Nineteenth-Century Writings on Homosexuality: A Sourcebook* (London: Routledge, 1999).

2. I have explored the cultural dimensions of sexology in *English Literary Sexology: Translations of Inversion, 1860–1930* (Basingstoke, UK: Palgrave Macmillan, 2009). See also Claudia Breger, "Feminine Masculinities: Scientific and Literary Representations of 'Female Inversion' at the Turn of the Twentieth Century," *Journal of the History of Sexuality* 14, no. 1–2 (2005): 76–106; the six-volume *Cultural History of Sexuality* produced under the general editorship of Julie Peakman (London: Berg, 2010); Anna Katharina Schaffner, *Modernism and Perversion: Sexual Deviance in Sexology and Literature, 1850–1930* (Basingstoke, UK: Palgrave Macmillan, 2012); Hugh Stevens and Caroline Howlett, eds., *Modernist Sexualities* (Manchester, UK: University of Manchester Press, 2000); Sarah Toulalan and Kate Fisher, eds., *The Routledge History of Sex and the Body, 1500 to the Present* (Abingdon, UK: Routledge, 2013).

3. Influential national and regional histories of sexuality include Matt Cook, *London and the Culture of Homosexuality, 1885–1914* (Cambridge: Cambridge University Press, 2003); John D'Emilio and Estelle B. Freedman, *Intimate Matters: A History of Sexuality in America* (New York: Harper and Row, 1988); Laura Doan, *Fashioning*

Sapphism: The Origins of a Modern English Lesbian Culture (New York: Columbia University Press, 2001); Lisa Duggan, *Sapphic Slashers: Sex, Violence, and American Modernity* (Durham, NC: Duke University Press, 2001); Dagmar Herzog, ed., *Sexuality and German Fascism* (Oxford: Berghahn, 2005); Janice M. Irvine, *Disorders of Desire: Sexuality and Gender in Modern American Sexology* (Philadelphia: Temple University Press, 2005); Frank Mort, *Dangerous Sexualities: Medico-Moral Politics in England since 1830* (London: Routledge and Kegan Paul, 1987); Harry Oosterhuis, *Stepchildren of Nature: Krafft-Ebing, Psychiatry, and the Making of Sexual Identity* (Chicago: University of Chicago Press, 2000); Vernon A. Rosario, *The Erotic Imagination: French Histories of Perversity* (Oxford: Oxford University Press, 1997); James D. Steakley, *The Homosexual Emancipation Movement in Germany* (Salem, NH: Ayer, 1975); Jennifer Terry, *An America Obsession: Science, Medicine, and Homosexuality in Modern Society* (Chicago: University of Chicago Press, 1999); Martha Vicinus, *Intimate Friends: Women Who Loved Women, 1778–1928* (Chicago: University of Chicago Press, 2004).

4. Next to the histories of sexuality mentioned previously, the following studies have helped define the field: Lucy Bland and Laura Doan, eds., *Sexology in Culture: Labelling Bodies and Desires* (Cambridge: Polity, 1998); Lawrence Birken, *Consuming Desire: Sexual Science and the Emergence of a Culture of Abundance, 1871–1914* (Ithaca, NY: Cornell University Press, 1988); George Chauncey Jr., "From Sexual Inversion to Homosexuality: Medicine and the Changing Conceptualisation of Female Deviance," *Salmagundi* 58–59 (1982–1983): 114–146; Carolyn J. Dean, *Sexuality and Modern Western Culture* (New York: Twayne, 1996); Martin B. Duberman, Martha Vicinus, and George Chauncey Jr., eds., *Hidden from History: Reclaiming the Gay and Lesbian Past* (New York: New American Library, 1989); Lisa Duggan, "From Instincts to Politics: Writing the History of Sexuality in the U.S.," *Journal of Sex Research* 27, no. 1 (1990): 95–109; Lesley Hall and Roy Porter, *The Facts of Life: The Creation of Sexual Knowledge in Britain, 1650–1950* (New Haven, CT: Yale University Press, 1995); David M. Halperin, *One Hundred Years of Homosexuality and Other Essays on Greek Love* (New York: Routledge, 1990); Thomas Laqueur, *Making Sex: Body and Gender from the Greeks to Freud* (Cambridge, MA: Harvard University Press, 1990); Vernon A. Rosario, ed., *Science and Homosexualities* (New York: Routledge, 1997); Jeffrey Weeks, *Sex, Politics and Society: The Regulation of Sexuality since 1800* (London: Longman, 1981).

5. Rita Felski, "Introduction," in Bland and Doan, *Sexology in Culture*, 4.

6. For a critical overview of Foucault's work, see Lisa Downing, *The Cambridge Introduction to Michel Foucault* (Cambridge: Cambridge University Press, 2008). This is the first work of this kind to pay attention to how issues of translation have shaped the Anglophone reception of Foucault.

7. Important interventions include Carolyn J. Dean, "The Productive Hypothesis: Foucault, Gender and the History of Sexuality," *History and Theory* 33, no. 3 (1994): 271–296; Joan Scott, "The Evidence of Experience," *Critical Inquiry* 17, no. 4 (1991): 773–797; and, more recently, Roderick Ferguson, *Aberrations in Black: Towards a Queer of Color Critique* (Minneapolis: University of Minnesota Press, 2004).

8. Michel Foucault, *The History of Sexuality*, vol. 1, *An Introduction*, trans. Robert Hurley (London: Penguin, 1990), 58. See Chapter 8 in this volume for a discussion of Foucault's changing views on this binary.

9. Naoki Sakai, "The Dislocation of the West," in *Traces 1: Spectres of the West and the Politics of Translation* (Hong Kong: Hong Kong University Press, 2001), 92. See also

Naoki Sakai and Jon Solomon's critique of Foucault's Occidentalism in *Translation, Biopolitics and Colonial Difference* (Hong Kong: Hong Kong University Press, 2006).

10. Ann Laura Stoler, *Race and the Education of Desire: Foucault's* History of Sexuality *and the Colonial Order of Things* (Durham, NC: Duke University Press, 2005).

11. Edward Said, *Orientalism* (London: Penguin, 1978). This field of research is vast. It ranges from early assessments of gender and colonialism such as Anne McClintock, *Imperial Leather: Race, Gender and Sexuality in Colonial Contest* (New York: Routledge, 1995), and inward-looking studies of how colonialism affected the colonizers, such as Ronald Hyman, *Empire and Sexuality: The British Experience* (Manchester, UK: Manchester University Press, 1990), to more recent critiques of the production of racialized sexual norms and their legacies, such as Ferguson's *Aberrations in Black*; Valerie Rohy, *Anachronism and Its Others: Sexuality, Race, Temporality* (New York: State University of New York Press, 2009); Siobhan B. Somerville, *Queering the Color Line: Race and the Invention of Homosexuality in American Culture* (Durham, NC: Duke University Press, 2000); Ann Laura Stoler, *Carnal Knowledge and Imperial Power: Race and the Intimate in Colonial Rule* (Berkeley: University of California Press, 2002); Sylvia Tamale, ed., *African Sexualities: A Reader* (Cape Town: Pambazuka, 2011); Omise'eke Natasha Tinsley, *Thiefing Sugar: Eroticism between Women in Caribbean Literature* (Durham, NC: Duke University Press, 2010).

12. Jasbir Puar, *Terrorist Assemblages: Homonationalism in Queer Times* (Durham, NC: Duke University Press, 2007); and her "Rethinking Homonationalism," *International Journal of Middle East Studies* 45 (2013): 336–339.

13. Veronika Fuechtner, "Indians, Jews and Sex: Magnus Hirschfeld and Indian Sexology", in *Imagining Germany, Imagining India: Essays in Asian-German Studies*, ed. Veronika Fuechtner and Mary Riehl (Rochester, NY: Camden House, 2013), 120.

14. Veronika Fuechtner, Douglas E. Haynes, and Ryan Jones, eds., *Towards a Global History of Sexual Science, 1880–1950* (forthcoming). See also notes 17 and 18 for recent studies of sexuality that expand the geopolitical boundaries of debate.

15. Elizabeth A. Povinelli and George Chauncey Jr., "Thinking Sexuality Transnationally: An Introduction," *GLQ: A Journal of Lesbian and Gay Studies* 5, no. 4 (1999): 442.

16. Inderpal Grewal and Caren Kaplan, "Global Identities: Theorizing Transnational Studies of Sexuality," *GLQ: A Journal of Lesbian and Gay Studies* 7, no. 4 (2001): 663.

17. Bauer, *English Literary Sexology*; Peter Cryle and Christopher Forth, eds., *Sexuality at the Fin de Siècle: The Makings of a "Central Problem"* (Newark: University of Delaware Press, 2008); Leila Rupp, *Sapphistries: A Global History of Love between Women* (New York: New York University Press, 2009); Schaffner, *Modernism and Perversion*.

18. While widely diverging in terms of approach and subject matter, the following studies decenter Anglo-American perspectives on sexuality and indicate the range of new scholarship in the field: Chiara Beccalossi, *Female Sexual Inversion: Same-Sex Desires in Italian and British Sexology, c. 1870–1920* (New York: Palgrave Macmillan, 2012); Pablo Ben, "Male Sexuality, the Popular Classes, and the State: Buenos Aires, 1880–1955" (Ph.D. diss., University of Chicago, 2009); Howard Chiang and Ari Larissa Heinrich, *Queer Sinophone Cultures* (London: Routledge, 2013); Alison Donnell, "Caribbean Queer: New Meetings of Place and the Possible in Shani Mootoo's Valmiki's Daughter," *Contemporary Women's Writing* 6, no. 3 (2012): 213–232; Sabine Frühstück,

Colonizing Sex: Sexology and Social Control in Modern Japan (Berkeley: University of California Press, 2003); Liat Kozma, *Policing Egyptian Women: Sex, Law and Medicine in Egypt 1850–1882* (Syracuse, NY: Syracuse University Press, 2011); Dan Healey, *Homosexual Desire in Revolutionary Russia: The Regulation of Sexual and Gender Dissent* (Chicago: University of Chicago Press, 2001); Jonathan D. Mackintosh, *Homosexuality and Manliness and Postwar Japan* (Abingdon, UK: Routledge, 2010); Fran Martin and Ari Larissa Heinrich, eds., *Embodied Modernities: Corporealities, Representation, and Chinese Cultures* (Honolulu: University of Hawai'i Press, 2006); Fran Martin, Peter A. Jackson, Mark McLelland, and Audrey Yue, eds., *AsiaPacifiQueer: Rethinking Genders and Sexualities* (Urbana: University of Illinois Press, 2008); Joanna Mizielinska and Robert Kulpa, eds., *De-Centring Western Sexualities: Central and Eastern European Perspectives* (Farnham, UK: Ashgate, 2011); Ishita Pande, *Medicine, Race and Liberalism in British Bengal: Symptoms of Empire* (New York: Routledge, 2012); Tse-Lan Sang, *The Emerging Lesbian: Female Same-Sex Desire in Modern China* (Chicago: University of Chicago Press, 2003); Michiko Suzuki, *Becoming Modern Women: Love and Female Identity in Prewar Japanese Literature and Culture* (Stanford, CA: Stanford University Press, 2010); Ruth Vanita, ed., *Queering India: Same-Sex Love and Eroticism in Indian Culture and Society* (New York: Routledge, 2002).

19. *Oxford English Dictionary*, 2nd ed., s.v. "across." Eve Kosofsky Sedgwick has famously pointed out that "queer" takes its name from a word whose "Indo-European root *twerkw* . . . also yields the German *queer* (traverse) [and] Latin *torquere* (to twist)." Eve Kosofsky Sedgwick, *Tendencies* (Durham, NC: Duke University Press, 1993), xii.

20. Recent works on the conceptual boundaries of queer history include Laura Doan, *Disturbing Practices: History, Sexuality, and Women's Experiences of Modern War* (Chicago: University of Chicago Press, 2013); Noreen Giffney, Michelle Sauer, and Diane Watt, eds., *The Lesbian Premodern* (New York: Palgrave Macmillan, 2011); Janet Halley and Andrew Parker, eds., *After Sex? On Writing since Queer Theory* (Durham, NC: Duke University Press, 2011).

21. Walter Benjamin, "Die Aufgabe des Übersetzers," in Walter Benjamin, *Gesammelte Schriften*, ed. Tillman Rexroth (Frankfurt: Suhrkamp, 1972), 4 (1): 9–21.

22. Susan Bassnett, *Translation Studies*, 4th ed. (Abingdon, UK: Routledge, 2014), 6.

23. See Emily Apter, *The Translation Zone: A New Comparative Literature* (Princeton, NJ: Princeton University Press, 2006); Homi Bhabha, *The Location of Culture* (New York: Routledge, 1994); Gayatri Spivak, "The Politics of Translation," in her *Outside in the Teaching Machine* (New York: Routledge, 1993), 179–200; Lawrence Venuti, *The Translator's Invisibility: A History of Translation*, 2nd ed. (Abingdon, UK: Routledge, 2008).

24. See Jon Solomon, "Translation, Violence, and the Heterolingual Intimacy," *eipcp* 9 (2007): n. 16, available at http://eipcp.net/transversal/1107/solomon/en/#_ftnref16.

25. Ibid.

26. Oosterhuis, *Stepchildren of Nature*, 275n54.

27. I have explored the publication history in *English Literary Sexology*, 30–31.

28. Doris Bachmann-Medick, "Introduction: The Translational Turn," *Translation Studies* 2, no. 1 (2009): 4.

I

Conceptualizations

How was the notion of modern "sexuality" developed? Words such as "homosexuality" and "fetishism" were coined in Europe in the late nineteenth century in debates about law and literature, medicine and modern state formation. While scholars have examined in some detail the discursive and related disciplinary transformations that occurred when the new vocabulary of (same-sex) sexuality and perversion emerged, we have still to gain a better understanding of the genealogies of these concepts, how they were received, and to what extent the "European" developments reflect or intersect with debates about sexuality in other parts of the world. The chapters in this opening part address these questions by exploring a series of key concepts in modern sexual discourse: frigidity, love, the third sex, and the intersections between homosexuality and sexology. Like other chapters in the collection, they understand translation as a dynamic process that allows us to grasp how ideas and discourses are formed and transmitted between languages, between scientific and cultural contexts, and between texts and audiences. But what distinguishes the studies in Part I is their specific attention to "conceptualization," or the processes by which ideas are formed and transmitted. The chapters gathered here explore in different ways the meanings, genealogies, and reception of words and discourses that came to define how "sex" was understood in modernity.

The first two chapters, by Peter Cryle and Birgit Lang, take issues of (mis)translation between linguistic, cultural, and disciplinary contexts as their analytical entry point for exploring key concepts in modern sexual discourse formation, concepts that have been somewhat sidelined in the critical focus on same-sex sexuality. Cryle's intellectual history of "frigidity" makes clear from the outset that the conceptualization of sexuality in modern Europe has a long history, a history that testifies to the existence of deeply entrenched, gendered assumptions about what constitutes an "appropriate" sexual body. While the language by which this "appropriateness" was declared may have changed from the "natural" to the "normal" during the nineteenth century, Cryle shows that concepts describing anxieties about bodies that "fail" to be sexual remained central to the development of a modern lexicon of sexuality. His analysis is based on texts written in French, German, Italian and Latin, which were produced, loosely, within the scientific realm. In contrast, Lang turns to the literary archive to track the emergence of a modern concept of "love" in German-speaking contexts. She explores how the Austrian novelist Leopold von Sacher-Masoch adapted the influential ideas of English biologist Charles Darwin in his novels and in so doing popularized evolutionary ideas about "sexual selection" as literary narratives about "love." Lang's chapter demonstrates that literature played a crucial if somewhat idiosyncratic role in the conceptualization of "modern love" in German-speaking areas, a "love" that was based on Darwinian ideals. It is a reminder that the history of sexuality is about a politics of intimacy and desire as much as it is the story of the medicalization and politicization of sexual acts.

The remaining chapters in Part I turn fresh attention to the conceptualization of bodies, desires, and identities that are today associated with same-sex sexuality. They employ translation as the critical framework for exploring how cultural and scientific discourses interact in the conceptualization of sexuality. Katie Sutton examines how sexological discourses about the "third sex", and related terms describing sex/gender expressions that run against contemporary conventions, were received in early twentieth-century Germany. She uses translation to conceptualize the relationship between sexological discourse and its audiences, specifically those subjects who identified in some way with (aspects of) the new sexual theories. If Sutton's work can thus also be read together with the chapters in Part III as a study of the "dis/identifications" that occurred when sexological ideas were encountered by people who in some ways saw themselves (mis)represented in these texts, it is included here for the insights it provides into the development of a concept—"the third sex"—that influentially represented sexual transgression as a form of gender transgression. In contrast Howard Chiang's chapter examines the intersection between sexual science and same-sex discourse in the emergence of what he calls "(homo)sexology" in modern China. His study speaks closely to debates about the formation of national sexologies, which are the focus of Part II of this collection; and it can be read as a contrast piece to Leon Rocha's argument that sexual science developed in two distinct trajectories in modern China. However, Chiang's work is included here for its genealogical attention to the conceptualizations of same-sex desire in modern Chinese culture. His chapter shows that sexual debates in the country were shaped by complex intersections between indigenous epistemologies and translations from European sexology, intersections that trouble assumptions about the significance of the flow of "European" ideas into China.

Together, then, the chapters in Part I extend the discursive as well as the geopolitical boundaries of existing histories of sexuality by demonstrating that "sexuality" is the product of complex intersections between cultural and scientific ideas and processes of transmission. The contexts they discuss differ considerably including geopolitically (Chiang's piece, for instance, is the only one to discuss a non-European context here; Sutton's chapter is the only one to focus on translations within one linguistic context), but also in terms of the archives they excavate (Cryle's genealogy, for example, is the only chapter not to discuss fiction in any detail). Yet what emerges when we read these chapters together is a sense that culturally distinct formations of modern sexuality developed in ways that were structurally similar. By framing the formation of sexual ideas and discourses in terms of translation, we gain a better understanding of the conceptualizations of sexuality. Attention to translation shows how certain ideas about sex were formed and transmitted out of a dialogue between scientific and cultural debates, personal interjections, and a complex process of negotiation between existing and new forms of knowledge and ideas. Traveling across linguistic and disciplinary contexts, this process describes how dispersed notions about human bodies and their desires gathered to become modern sexuality.

1

Translation as Lexical Invention

An Intellectual History of Frigiditas and Anaphrodisia

PETER CRYLE

In recent years, historians of sexuality have tended to become self-conscious about their use of the word "invention." Ian Hacking, in his pointed critique of the notion, spoke of "an early 1990s orgy of inventions."[1] He did so with the aim not of defending essentialism or naturalism against social constructionism, but of suggesting that while "the metaphor of social construction once had excellent shock value," it had "now become tired."[2] Histories that speak at every turn of invention and construction appear not to have the provocative force they had two decades ago. Historiographical fatigue is widespread. Moreover, that fatigue is not just a consequence of rhetorical insistence. Cultural and intellectual historians who advance behind these metaphors are venturing onto theoretically uncertain terrain. Surely they cannot mean to say that notions like homosexuality or indeed sexuality were expressly fabricated out of nothing by knowing agents at a particular point in history? There must have been antecedent notions or discursive material to hand that supported and enabled any process of "invention." To put it in theoretical terms informed by such thinkers as Michel Foucault and Jacques Derrida, whatever counted at the time as new must have already been available to thought, already inscribed in language and able to take shape as an object of knowledge. The notion must have been, in some sense, already thinkable and sayable. Reminding ourselves in this way that discursive antecedence is a prerequisite for change can only serve to dull any residual enthusiasm we might have had for a further "orgy of inventions." But we can be constrained by such awareness without being stymied by it. For while metaphors of invention and construction appear to have lost some of their vigor, the revisionist historical projects they served so well show no signs of decrepitude. We may simply have something to gain at this point in our endeavors by allowing other metaphors to come to the fore. And one candidate for this role has effectively been brought to our attention by the organizers of this collection. It is the metaphor of translation.

This chapter will pursue an interest in translation by considering a cluster of approximately equivalent terms in French and German related to the notion of frigidity. It will draw attention to the particular roles played by terms derived from Latin and Greek, arguing that derivation of this kind ought to be understood as a form of translation. There was, I intend to show, a long tradition inscribed in the Latin *frigiditas*, and I will point to the conceptual inertia that marked centuries of usage of the word. As if to undo the effects of such discursive antecedence, attempts were made in nineteenth-century medical talk to promote the use of the Greek-derived *anaphrodisia*, which did not carry the same historical baggage. That attempt had only limited success in France, and even less in the German-speaking world, where the Latin-derived term persisted alongside the Greek-Latin hybrid *anaesthesia sexualis*. Throughout the nineteenth century, medical writers tended to eschew vernacular terms such as *froideur* (coldness) in favor of more learned ones, although the vernacular term was occasionally called on to occupy a specific place in their discourse. In the early decades of the twentieth century, especially in German, there was marked disagreement about the underlying metaphor that ought to support the key term. Was it better to speak of coldness or of some deficiency? The psychoanalyst who had most to say about the topic simply turned away from classically derived terms and reverted to the vernacular, declaring that the disorder was quite imaginary in any case. No neologism ultimately prevailed. But something was achieved: my analysis will point to the function of classical-language derivation in providing a lexis of reference for an international community of scholars devoted to the study of psychosexuality.

Traductions/Translations

French distinguishes in a way that English does not between *traduction* (rendering into another language) and *translation* (carrying from one place to another). We can use French—and the slight difficulty of translating that distinction into English—as a way of refreshing our understanding of the notion. Historians of sexuality quite often seem to find themselves interrogating items in the long list of new psychosexual terms that appeared in the latter part of the nineteenth century, and I shall ask first of all whether the emergence of those terms might not be given a more precise history if we describe them not as inventions but as translations, or rather as both translations and inventions, *traductions* and *translations* at the same time, since to translate a term is always to nominate a new frame of reference for it. When we look back on the terminological proliferation of the nineteenth century, we find so many terms rederived from ancient Greek. "Homosexual" is a hybrid of Greek and Latin, but many terms were translated-and-invented—I am expressly hyphenating those two verbs—from the Greek. Think of "erotomania," "algolagnia," "pedophilia," "coprophilia," and the like. It is a contingent effect of modern education that historians today have greater difficulty reading these terms as translations, simply because, by contrast with humanists and scientists of the nineteenth century, we can no longer be counted on to have classical languages as a primary element of our education.

I shall say something, then, about how invention and translation from classical languages built the lexis of nineteenth-century psychosexuality. The sole example I shall consider, that of frigidity and its competitor terms, is an instructive one precisely because it is rather complicated—complicated by its very history. Unlike the terms I have just listed, the word "frigidity" was in no sense a new lexical plaything: it was loaded with a history of past usage in Latin. So while the word was, like the other psychosexual terms just mentioned, a learned neologism, it was an older neologism that had been around for centuries. Furthermore, it was drawn, not from the Greek favored by nineteenth-century medical writers, but from the Latin *frigiditas.* "Frigidity" and its variants existed in a number of European languages, being used in a range of fields extending from geography to medicine. According to the *Oxford English Dictionary* (OED), "frigidity" was used in English in the seventeenth century to refer to a "want of generative heat" and was associated with impotence. I have not done the detailed work of tracing its early modern usage in English, but I have done that work in French, and I indicate how the term became available in French for learned medical and juridical use before going on to describe how it was recycled and revised during the nineteenth and early twentieth centuries in both French and German.

For centuries, classical languages played a central role in medical education. Eighteenth-century doctors trained in medical faculties in France and elsewhere in Europe were required to read Hippocrates and Galen in the original Greek and Latin. That distinguished them from surgeon-barbers, who carried out practical operations, and from a large, indeterminate class of empirics, healers, and "operators" who were often referred to by faculty-trained doctors and others as charlatans. It is no coincidence that the name of this inferior class of healers was drawn from the Italian word *ciarlatano.* Charlatans pitched their services in the marketplace, as the Italian verb *ciarlare* implied. They did not deal in ancient languages. So when in the course of the nineteenth century, medicine built its professional prestige at the expense of popular medicine, a knowledge of classical languages continued to be available as an intellectual and rhetorical resource. One of the pioneers of such work in France was Philippe Pinel. Best known today for his practical impact on the treatment of patients in asylums, Pinel made a broader contribution that helped to shape French medicine for decades thereafter. He was a nosologist, and nosology, the classification of diseases, became something of a French specialty. Visiting American doctors in the first half of the nineteenth century even noted that their French colleagues seemed preoccupied with nosological description at the expense of therapy.[3] Pinel produced a multivolume text titled *Nosographie philosophique*. From the title onward, he drew on ancient Greek to produce and invent classificatory names for a great range of illnesses. This was high-minded work, but that did not prevent it from having a polemical purpose. In his introduction, Pinel condemned "the scientific jargon of humoral and popular medicine that circulates in the transactions of civil life."[4] Medicine based on the centuries-old theory of the humors was being relegated to the past, or so he hoped, and its "jargon" could now be actively displaced by the deployment of learned neologisms. For Pinel and his followers, "true medicine, the one that is founded on principles, consists far less in administering medication than it does in the deep knowledge of illnesses."[5]

Medico-Forensic Disorders

The increasing use of Greek terms in medical discourse provided the context in which a young Frenchman, Michel-Etienne Descourtilz, presented his 1814 doctoral thesis in medicine, republished in 1831 with the title *De l'impuissance et de la stérilité, ou Recherches sur l'anaphrodisie distinguée de l'agénésie* (On impotence and sterility, or research on anaphrodisia distinguished from agenesia).[6] The title itself told some of the story. It began with two Latinate terms, "impotence" and "sterility," displacing them with Greek ones that were approximate equivalents: "anaphrodisia" and "agenesia." The Greek terms translated the Latin ones, carrying across their meaning while leaving something behind. That was just as Descourtilz wanted it. In order to carry out his self-appointed task of "philosophical" analysis, he found it necessary to reject not only the terms "impotence" and "sterility" nominated in his title, but the very term "frigidity" that might otherwise have been taken to define his topic. "Anaphrodisia" properly named belonged in Pinel's nosology, as Descourtilz pointed out, in the category of "névrose aphroditique" (aphroditic neurosis).[7] Understood thus, anaphrodisia was "a genital syncope, or suspension of the sensations necessary for a perfect copulation."[8] It was not characterized by a lack of generative heat but by a pathological interruption of the ability to perform copulation in the requisite manner.

In setting aside *frigidité*, Descourtilz observed that the term was inappropriate because the disorder he was describing was not to be understood as a consequence of coldness.[9] The Greek term was to be preferred, it seems, because the Latin one owed too great a debt to the classical medicine of humors. According to the old view, some individuals were simply born with greater reserves of natural heat than others, and the consequences of that temperamental difference were failures of copulation and fertility. The notion of temperament had long given a quite material dimension to medicine of that kind, but its very basis was now being questioned in the name of a functional physiology. Another medical writer, Jacques-Louis Moreau de la Sarthe, had set the critical tone a decade earlier when he declared:

> Such is the idea of temperaments that people have in their minds when they are strangers to the new direction and progress of science devoted to the bodily economy [*organisation*] of man. But in the vocabulary of modern physiology, the word "temperament," which perhaps ought to be completely banned, is understood in a different acceptation. It is synonymous with "individual nature," which ought in fact to be the preferred term.[10]

To invent the term "anaphrodisia" was to leave behind the medicine of temperament and humor, displacing it with a Greek word in which the prefix "an-" signified simply the absence of aphroditic pleasure and not the presence of a congenital material quality. The neologism helped Descourtilz to hold a different perspective on the causes at work and to indicate a new orientation for therapy:

> That is why the expression *genital syncope* appears to us more appropriate than *venereal frigidity*. Most often, this temporary suspension of the genital functions is the result of a painful affection of the soul, or of excessively violent desires that are only temporary, and lead to the premature emission of seminal liquid.[11]

But *frigidité* and with it the Latin *frigiditas* carried an even older discursive mortgage. In addition to being used in humoral medicine, *frigiditas* had long been deployed as a medico-juridical term within the tradition of canon law. As early as the first half of the thirteenth century, Pope Gregory IX had produced a papal letter titled "De frigidis et maleficiatis" (On frigid people and those placed under spells). Frigidity had a titular role to play in this context because it was deemed to be the primary natural cause of impotence, alongside the supernatural cause of malefice. Impotence, whenever it persisted, drew the attention of canonists because it constituted an impediment to marriage and was potentially a reason for annulment. The leading authority in canon law from about the middle of the seventeenth century onward was the Roman Protomedico Paolo Zacchia. In his comprehensive *Quaestionum medico-legalium* (On medico-legal issues), the definitive edition of which was published in 1660, Zacchia gave a definition of *frigiditas*: "frigid people in the strict sense of the word are those who by reason of listlessness of the genitals resulting from a lack of natural heat, are impotent to engage in coitus."[12] This made frigidity and impotence into roughly equivalent notions insofar as they inhibited the consummation of marriage by the husband. Wives, on the other hand, were to be considered impotent only when the narrowness of their genital configuration presented an obstacle to copulation. Whether women might be frigid and suffering from genital listlessness was deemed by many canonists to be inconsequential. Zacchia, for his part, was of the opinion that women could indeed be frigid: they could have a shortage of seed, and be as frigid as any man.[13]

It would be a mistake to suppose that the canon law tradition, including the preoccupation with men as the key subjects of frigidity, was simply swept away during the eighteenth century by enlightenment thinking. Denis Diderot and Jean le Rond d'Alembert's great *Encyclopédie*, in an entry headed "frigidity," identified the term as a jurisprudential one and spoke of it much as Zacchia had:

> This disorder [*vice*] which constitutes in men an impediment justifying the annulment of marriage, is a lack of strength, a kind of feebleness [*imbécillité*] of temperament that is not brought on either by old age or by any passing sickness. It is the condition of an impotent man who does not ever have the necessary sensations to carry out his conjugal duty.[14]

A man who was "cold" (*froid*) in this way, the article went on, could not properly enter into a marriage contract. Women were specifically excluded from consideration here, "since *frigidity* in women is not a cause of impotence nor an impediment to marriage." Even the list of causes given in the *Encyclopédie* was an unvarying assertion of the canon law tradition: "Frigidity can arise from three different causes: by birth, by a chance event, or by malefice." The third cause may be particularly surprising in this now iconic place of enlightenment thinking: it shows that *frigidité* continued to act by association as a vehicle not only for the notion of temperament but even for that of malefice, the casting of spells. At the end of the encyclopedia article, the references given were to Gregory IX's thirteenth-century letter, to Zacchia, and to one of his most eminent canonist colleagues.[15] In the mid-eighteenth century, the canonist understanding of *frigiditas* remained largely uncontested.

And so it continued even into the early decades of the nineteenth century. A multivolume dictionary of the medical sciences published over the period 1812–1822 contained an article titled "Frigidité" in which that long-established neologism was allowed to stand alongside the vernacular *froideur* (coldness). It was not, the author stated, that the two terms had the same "absolute signification" but that they "refer to qualities of temperament and character that are closely analogous one to the other."[16] Moreover, the primary focus in this secular medical dictionary continued to be on coldness in men, even where conjugal duty within sacramental marriage was not at issue: "Frigidity is the condition of a person of one or the other sex, but principally man, who proves to be impotent and incapable of generation, and even of coitus."[17] By material logic, treatment of the condition called for the application of natural heat: "And so it is indeed the body's natural heat (not the morbid kind) that most favors love, or fights most effectively against the disorder [*vice*] of frigidity."[18]

This must have been the kind of talk that Descourtilz wanted to bring to an end. By constructing the object of his attention as "anaphrodisia," he was presumably seeking to free medicine of both ecclesial concerns and a preoccupation with temperament. Translation and neologism, rather than a more explicit polemic, were mobilized to do this work. By clearing the decks of old words attached to old habits of thinking, he hoped to achieve a better account of the etiology of the disorder along with greater nosological precision. But the contest against the established ways of thinking was not so easily won. The resources of nosological neologism and the perspective of scientific modernity were never such as to ensure that *frigiditas*, with its humoral and canonist inheritance, could be simply banished from the field of psychosexual pathology. The discursive power of progressive medical science was not such as to bring to a halt the conceptual inertia of discourses that had served for centuries to shape these objects of medical knowledge.

Coining Impotence and Sterility

When, in 1855, Félix Roubaud published a two-volume work on impotence and sterility, he claimed a place as the leading French authority on the question. But the topical nouns that organized his work were no more securely established in medical discourse than they had been when Descourtilz had published a quarter of a century earlier. Roubaud did not put Descourtilz's neologisms in the title of his book or in his chapter headings, although his analysis made some of the same points. It was helpful, he said, to distinguish clearly between (the absence of) pleasure and (the absence of) generation or reproduction, as Descourtilz had done already. But Roubaud took a further step by drawing on new research recently carried out in Germany. The physiologist Georg Kobelt had conducted experiments that showed female sexual organs to be active in copulation,[19] thereby allowing Roubaud to characterize such physiological activity as the normal condition of copulative sexual pleasure, describing inactivity as its pathological absence: "it has to be acknowledged that the absence of one or several conditions for normal coitus in woman constitutes a morbid or pathological state."[20] The key notion here was that of absence, and, in Roubaud's view, "frigidity" was not a helpful term for it. He was uncomfortable about the imprecision of recent attempts to use the term for that purpose:

> Meanwhile some authors, taking into account that passivity in coitus is not the normal [*physiologique*] state for women, made such passivity into a morbid entity that they referred to by the name of *frigidity*. But confusion immediately undid the gains made by this happy distinction because for some frigidity was understood to be the absence of venereal desires, whereas for others it stood for the absence of pleasure.[21]

Was this condition—as distinct from any quality of temperament—to be understood as an absence of desire or an absence of pleasure? Talk of "frigidity" had done nothing to clarify the matter, and Roubaud appeared to consider that using the term "anaphrodisia" would prove no more decisive. He did use Descourtilz's word from time to time, observing for example that "the inability to carry out coitus according to all the laws of nature" was "a variety of anaphrodisia."[22] Most often, however, he continued to talk of "frigidity," presumably because the very use of "frigidity" by his predecessors gave rise to the problems he wished to address.

But if "frigidity" was one of Roubaud's entrees into the subject, there can be no doubt about his determination to disqualify the term and remove it from specialized medical usage. In order to displace it, he put forward the word *impuissance* (impotence), intending thereby to name a disorder that could be considered common to women and to men. Roubaud was in many ways a progressive thinker, but if one takes a long view of the history of medical discourse on the topic, the reprise of that Latinate term *impuissance* might well be considered a regressive move. Zacchia and his canon law colleagues had long spoken of *impotentia*, distinguishing between *impotentia coeundi*, the incapacity to copulate, and *impotentia generandi*, the incapacity to reproduce. It had seemed to Descourtilz that the inclusion of both inabilities under the heading of "impotence" had regularly led medical thinkers to confuse frigidity with sterility, but Roubaud was more concerned with giving a (supposed) disorder occurring in women an equivalent and homologous place alongside one found in men. If men could be impotent for the purposes of normal copulation, so too could women. It followed from this insistence on physiological process that frigidity in women ought not to be thought of as a matter of individual constitution: "It would be a great mistake to think that an unfortunate [*mauvaise*] constitution is a cause of frigidity for woman."[23] There might perhaps be women who were naturally cold by temperament, but such cases were extremely rare.[24] So for clinical reasons there was little point in speaking of temperamental frigidity. And there were also compelling theoretical reasons for giving up the term, since its use led to nosological complications.

> Moreover, whatever acceptation was given to frigidity, the morbid condition I am describing, which *generally* does not result in sterility, was not identifiable [in earlier writers] as either impotence or sterility, but rather something separate. And the impossibility of finding a place for it in a methodical classification meant that it was cast into the category of neuroses [disorders without detectable lesions], as if the congenital or accidental absence of the clitoris, for example, a powerful cause of frigidity, could find a place in the category of nervous disorders.[25]

This was, inter alia, an allusion to Pinel's classification, adopted and quoted by Descourtilz. For Roubaud, "frigidity" was doubly archaic: it was disqualified by its association with temperament and by its failure to align with a newly developed physiology of female genital activity in coitus.

Pierre Garnier, who published a work on the same topic a quarter of a century later in 1882, took up a position that was antithetical to Roubaud's. Indeed, the orientation of Garnier's work appears to have been partly determined by that antithesis. A thoroughgoing conservative in medical matters, Garnier never missed an opportunity to contrast his own views with those of his well-known predecessor, seeming at some points to manufacture disagreement for its own sake. Garnier used both Latin and Greek neologisms to define his position, making the two work in parallel. He kept the term "frigidity," capitalizing it to mark its valorization and using it exclusively about women. The "moral impotence" (lack of desire) that occurred in "woman" rightly bore, in his view, the name of "frigidity": "Much more frequent in her case than physical impotence in view of the great importance to her of the moral element in love, it corresponds to anaphrodisia in man."[26] So the Latin word was for women and the Greek word for men, "frigidity" being favored for women precisely because it was less specific about physiology: "That is the secret of her inborn modesty, her reticence, her very impassiveness."[27] It had been a mistake—both medical and moral—on Roubaud's part to "look for the cause of this disorder in the simple material absence of the clitoris, or in its underdevelopment or insensitivity."[28] "The true focus of love in woman" could not be found "at such a low point."[29] Women might indeed be "impotent," as Roubaud had claimed, but it was inappropriate and disrespectful of their inherent nobility of feeling to call any venereal disorder from which they might suffer by the same name as that of men. Garnier sought in effect to lessen the claims of physiological medicine on the description and treatment of women's bodies. Frigidity could still be understood, he asserted, as temperament had once been. It was simply a matter of degree:

> Besides, it is by no means always a sickness or an infirmity, as most authors seem to think. Feminine frigidity has its degrees. No matter how habitual or essential it may be, it is never absolute. . . . It does not prevent a woman from marrying, never makes her sterile and allows her to be an excellent mother after all.[30]

Against Descourtilz and Roubaud, both medical progressives in their own way, Garnier was engaged in what might be characterized as reactionary invention. By this realignment of the key neologisms, he was retrieving and defending, more or less within medical discourse, a conception of femininity that was said to rise above functional accounts of genital (in)activity.

As it happened, neither Roubaud's nor Garnier's interventions, despite the vigor with which they were conducted, could be said to have brought about a change in general usage. If uptake is the key criterion for measuring the significance of a neologism, as it surely is, then it has to be said that *anaphrodisie* enjoyed only limited success in French. By the turn of the twentieth century, the term had almost entirely disappeared. Charles Féré, the leading French medical author on sexuality at the very end of the century, used the less specialized *anesthésie* (anesthesia) to refer to men and continued to use *frigiditas*, in Latin, referred to its canonist source, when speaking of women: "Zacchia has pointed out that *naturae frigiditas* [frigidity of nature] in woman is much more frequent than anaesthesia in man, and is often linked to a neuropathic condition. It often manifests itself as extreme slowness in the production of orgasm or responsiveness [*défaillances*]."[31] Neither Descourtilz's neologism nor Roubaud's one-sex physiological model were in play here. Zacchia had spoken of *impotentia* and *frigiditas* in both women and men. He had not used the Greek *anaesthesia* to refer to men, but in 1899, in Féré's work, women could still be held within the authority of Zacchia's

Latin, while men occupied a less constrained space marked out by a Greek neologism that had a wider range of possible uses.

Cross-National Currencies

The business of scientific neologism, successful or unsuccessful, was not of course limited to one country and one language. Indeed, the highest ambition of translation-and-invention, despite the limitations that tended to be imposed by national boundaries, must surely have been that an international scientific community should come into existence, and the use of classical neologisms made that more likely. In general, it would be a mistake even to suppose that French usage clung to Latinate terms while psychosexual writing in German used mainly Germanic ones. If we take the example of Richard von Krafft-Ebing's prestigious *Psychopathia Sexualis*, it is clear from the book's title that classical-language terms could play a significant role in writing on sexuality in German. As it happened, Krafft-Ebing used the German neologisms *Frigidität* and *Anaphrodisie* from time to time, appearing in fact to make no effective distinction between them. At one point in *Psychopathia Sexualis*, he used "Frigidität und Anaphrodisie" as a chapter heading, as if to ensure that both were included in his topic, referring to them as equivalent in the body of the chapter.[32]

The classical term preferred by Krafft-Ebing was another Greek-based neologism close to, but more specific than, the one used by Féré, who was in fact an attentive reader of his German-language colleagues. The term, actually a hybrid of Greek and Latin, was *anaesthesia sexualis*. Here the use of the negative prefix "an-," common to *anaphrodisia* and *anaesthesia*, seemed to have its own conceptual momentum since it appeared to entail a quite radical view of absent sexuality. Krafft-Ebing made a clearer distinction than any of his French predecessors or contemporaries between cerebral and physiological functions, and that was precisely what allowed him to describe *anaesthesia sexualis* as a pathological disjunction of the two: "Only those cases can be regarded as unquestionable examples of absence of sexual instinct dependent on cerebral causes, in which, in spite of generative organs normally developed and the performance of their functions (secretion of semen, menstruation), the corresponding emotions of sexual life are absolutely wanting."[33] The general cause of this condition, according to Krafft-Ebing, was degeneration. But while the effects of degeneration were held to be visible here and indeed almost everywhere, there was something quite particular about the "complete" absence of sexual feeling. It had to be considered a rarity: "These functionally sexless individuals are rare cases, and, indeed, always persons having degenerative effects, in whom other functional cerebral disturbances, states of psychical degeneration, and even anatomical signs of degeneration, may be observed."[34] There appears here to be a circular effect of meaning abetted by the choice of the term "anesthesia." It had been easy enough for Garnier and others before him to speak of "degrees of frigidity." Whenever coldness was considered a matter of humor or temperament, it could occur anywhere within a natural range of possibilities. But the logic of the prefix "an-" was more constraining. Certainly, to define a disorder by the complete absence of any sexual impulse was to mark a limit rarely encountered in clinical experience. It mattered greatly to Krafft-Ebing whether sexual pathologies were congenital or acquired, but as Heike Bauer noted in discussion of this point, the idea of *anaesthesia sexualis* threatened to trouble that distinction. While the focus of both canon law and humoral medicine had always been on congenital frigidity, Krafft-Ebing turned his attention, somewhat inconclusively, to "Erworbene Anaesthesie," acquired anesthesia. As he saw it, a range of causes, "organic and functional, psychical and somatic, central and peripheral," might result in "acquired diminution of sexual instinct, extending through all degrees to extinction."[35] Degrees there might still be, but the full realization of absence defined the tendency as such, and that absence could hardly ever be found in practice.

Krafft-Ebing did use "anaphrodisia" by itself, so to speak, when giving an account of "nymphomania." There was, he said, a condition in which lascivious desires were not accompanied by actual pleasure of any kind. "Neurasthenia of the genitals" might occur, resulting in "pollutions" and "erotic crises." But women suffering from this disorder could not find "full gratification . . . any more than those of their unfortunate fellow-sufferers who abandon themselves to men. This *anaphrodisia* explains to a large extent the persistence of the sexual affect, *i.e.*, that nymphomania which heaps crisis on crisis."[36] Far from restricting "anaphrodisia" to men, as Garnier had done, Krafft-Ebing was restricting its meaning in another way by using it specifically to refer to the absence of sexual gratification, even in the presence of strong desire. To refer to that condition as "frigidity" could only have seemed to him counterintuitive, not to say contradictory. There was presumably nothing to be gained in his view by recycling the old metaphor of coldness in an account of nymphomania. Genital insensitivity accompanied by strong desires needed to be given another name.

In talking about degrees of sexual anesthesia, Krafft-Ebing had occasion to refer to Zacchia's work, which clearly remained in play here for the purposes of reference just as it did for Féré. Krafft-Ebing declared, to translate his words as literally as possible: "A milder form of anesthesia is represented by Zacchia's *naturae frigidae*."[37] He meant that Zacchia's Latin category of natural disorder (in men and women) could be given a particular place within the wide range opened up by the more recent Greek neologism that he was now using. The translator of the English-language version of Krafft-Ebing's text published in 1998 struggled to render the discursive reference, offering only: "The frigid nature of *Zacchias* [in italics, as if to say that he did not know what kind of things Zacchias were] are examples of a milder form of anaesthesia."[38] It does seem that by the time this translation was being produced in the late twentieth century, Zacchia's work was no longer available to psychology or sexology. It had finally been left behind, much as Descourtilz might have wished when he published his views on the matter in 1831. What was not made clear to readers of the English translation of *Psychopathia Sexualis* is that Krafft-Ebing quite often used Latin terms taken from Zacchia to refer to an established, almost routine notion of frigidity. At one point, the English version says: "By nature he was very sensual, whilst his wife was very frigid."[39] The German original, translated more literally, says: "He characterized himself as very sensual by nature, whereas his wife was rather a *natura frigida*."[40] When Latin phrases drawn from Zacchia occur in the German text, the 1998 translation simply renders them into English, thereby jettisoning their historical discursive load. In another instance, Krafft-Ebing's *Frigiditas uxoris* (frigidity of the wife) becomes simply "female frigidity."[41]

Cold Women

The first full-length book to be devoted to the question of frigidity in women continued the lexical counterpoint of Latin and Greek that had gone on throughout the nineteenth century but did so rather differently. This was Otto Adler's *Die mangelhafte Geschlechtsempfindung des Weibes* (Deficient sexual sensation in woman), first published in 1904. The key expression in its title—*mangelhafte Geschlechtsempfindung*, deficient sexual sensation—was derived in the standard manner of German. At the outset, Adler presented a history of writings on his topic, which he was happy to identify as *anaesthesia sexualis*, subsuming under that term *fehlende Libido* (deficient libido), which he also called *Anaphrodisie*, thereby seeming to part company with Krafft-Ebing, and *fehlende Orgasmus* (deficient orgasm), which he also called *Dyspareunie*.[42] In the time-honored academic manner, Adler deplored the lack of writing on his topic, although he mentioned Krafft-Ebing and various other colleagues writing in German. The first person to have written on the subject, he said, was Paolo Zacchia, identifying him as the author of the term *natura frigida*.[43] Without mentioning Descourtilz and others who had made much the same objection when writing in French, Adler went on to explain why the German words *kalt* (cold) and *Kälte* (coldness), and the general notion they referred to, seemed to him inappropriate in this context. But he did not refer to humoral medicine and, having paid a small tribute to Zacchia, showed no preoccupation with any residual influence of canon law. He did, on the other hand, point toward the future, referring optimistically to the therapeutic prospects offered by the "Freudian school of psychoanalytical method."[44]

One of the most interesting things about Adler's book is his general attempt to move away from the metaphor of coldness, with its long history, and come closer to an economic model in which notional measures of sensitivity and satisfaction were to the fore. Deficiency could only ever be a matter of degree, whereas, despite what Garnier might have hoped or imagined, the notion of coldness always tended to appear more or less absolute.[45] That was why, said Adler, it was better to use *mangelhaft*: one should always speak of this disorder in terms of an economy of desires and pleasures. It was "not good" to speak of certain women as having "icy and cold natures," he said, all the while adding "*natura frigida*" in brackets as the classic term. Such women were in fact often excessively sensual.[46] Adler did not put an end to *frigiditas*, and did not even claim to do so, being content to speak of coldness for reasons of discursive convenience. He referred to one female patient, for example, as a "typical *natura frigida*."[47] But by the same token, he was effectively resisting the connotations of the prefix "an-," and doing so more resolutely, more explicitly than those who had preceded him, including Krafft-Ebing. There were, Adler insisted, no cases at all of absolute congenital sexual anesthesia.[48]

The general tendency of Adler's terminological translation-and-invention, in emphasizing matters of degree, was to describe varying sexual deficiency as it occurred across populations. At stake here was a shift from the natural as it was borne by Zacchia's ubiquitous term toward an understanding of greater and lesser deficiency as they were distributed across a range from normal to abnormal. Adler's intervention was rethinking and revising the tendency that had begun with the neologistic invention of *anaphrodisia*. He was finding a characteristically modern approach to this supposed disorder, referring rather hopefully to statistics that were not available, thus giving the topic an epidemiological dimension.[49] His assumption was that there must be cases at every point on the scale, except perhaps at absolute zero. Yet when Adler sought to characterize a particular patient, he resorted without fuss, as Krafft-Ebing had, to a "type" that continued to be identified using Zacchia's term. A female patient could thus be described as a "typische *natura frigida*."[50]

Twenty years or so after Adler, Wilhelm Stekel published a two-volume work on the topic that gave a striking inflection, and a conclusion of sorts, to the history of lexical invention that I have been examining here. As if to confirm that the metaphor of coldness would not go away despite the efforts of writers throughout the preceding century, Stekel presented a major work that eschewed neologisms and gave coldness pride of place in its Germanic title: *Die Geschlechtskälte der Frau* (Sexual coldness in woman).[51] He occasionally used Zacchia's key Latin term, *natura frigida*,[52] and referred to the Greek-based hybrid neologism that had become standard in German: *anaesthesia sexualis*. But for Stekel, by contrast with Adler and Krafft-Ebing, sexual anesthesia was not something so rare as to be effectively nonexistent: it was quite simply imaginary. Where Krafft-Ebing had drawn attention to a pathological disjunction of physical and mental activities in patients with apparent sexual anesthesia, Stekel posed as a matter of principle that the relation between the two was the key theoretical and practical issue. The mistake typically made in medical treatment was to suppose that the physical symptoms must point to an organic problem: "The account is difficult for the reason that psychic and physical disorders influence one another and may be found either isolated or combined so that the clinical picture of the resulting morbid condition becomes obscured, its psychogenesis is masked, and the disorder may be mistaken for something organic."[53]

Anesthesia, said Stekel, was not an organic phenomenon. It deserved to be treated as masking or denial: "Certain investigators still speak of complete sexual anaesthesia, or asexualism; on closer investigation such cases prove to be largely imaginary."[54] So, from Stekel's therapeutically oriented perspective, coldness and anesthesia were equivalent only because one imaginary notion was as unsound as another. It was less a matter of refining knowledge through lexical precision than of identifying and undoing the denial of "psychogenetic" factors. For that purpose, the oldest illusions were likely to be the most deeply ingrained, and thus the most in need of therapeutic resolution. More elaborate descriptions of the syndrome or fine nosological work would serve little purpose. In the long run, Stekel seemed to suppose, classical translation-and-invention had cured no one. Therapy needed to proceed by addressing and undoing a longstanding burden of false knowledge. He identified a certain kind of person as most in need of such treatment: "they refuse to recognize the masks under which their sexuality hides itself."[55] "The anaesthetic woman," in particular, was "merely a woman who has not discovered the form of sexual gratification which alone can be adequate in her case."[56] What lay ahead of the supposedly cold woman in treatment was the discovery of her possibilities for sexual gratification. What lay behind her, or might come to do so if treatment were successful, was a world of misapprehension in which talk about coldness, frigidity, anaphrodisia, and anesthesia held sway. Where sexologists had sought to refine and complexify their knowledge of sexual pathologies by narrow description and precise terminology, psychoanalysis as Stekel practiced it sought to do away with the mistaken ideas kept in play by any or all of those words.

Other terms besides "frigidity" would reward a study of derivation comparable to the one I have pursued here for "frigidity." One of those, already examined in the *longue durée* by Thomas Laqueur, is masturbation.[57] "Onanism," as Laqueur shows, was misderived from a biblical source. It came to the fore in the early modern period, playing a prominent role first in English and then in French and other European languages. Competing with it were a number of Latinate terms that held a place in a Catholic discourse about sin, notably *manustupratio*, from which the modern "masturbation" was derived. In place of the biblical and Latinate terms, early sexologists tended to prefer the Greek-derived "auto-eroticism," although the Latinate expression has finally prevailed in contemporary usage. "Orgasm" is another term worthy of study along the same lines, although it underwent a quite different set of transformations. It began as a medical term used by Hippocrates, *orgasmos*, to describe swelling or congestion as a morbid symptom. For most of the nineteenth century, it remained a learned neologistic synonym for "irritation" or arousal. Only in the last decade of the century did "orgasm" begin to be used with its modern meaning, which could be considered an inversion of its classical Greek sense. One of the first sexologists to use the term in this way was Albert Moll.[58] Moll was able to avoid the ambiguity occasioned by misconstrual of the Greek by using a pair of Latin-based neologisms. "Tumescenz" [tumescence] was close to the original sense of the Greek *orgasmos*, and "Detumescenz" [detumescence] to its emerging modern sense.[59]

The broad point about such histories of translation is that when new terms were being invented by early sexologists, translation from classical languages was a primary mode of terminological production, sometimes attended and eroded by complicated discursive histories.

NOTES

1. Ian Hacking, *The Social Construction of What?* (Cambridge, MA: Harvard University Press, 1999), 13.

2. Ibid., 35.

3. For a general discussion of American perceptions of French medicine of the time, see John Harley Warner, *Against the Spirit of System: The French Impulse in Nineteenth-Century American Medicine* (Princeton, NJ: Princeton University Press, 1998).

4. Philippe Pinel, *Nosographie philosophique, ou la méthode de l'analyse appliquée à la médecine* [Philosophical nosology, or the method of analysis applied to medicine], 4th ed. (Paris: Brosson, 1810), 1:1.

5. Ibid., 1:i–ii.

6. Michel-Etienne Descourtilz, *De l'impuissance et de la stérilité, ou Recherches sur l'anaphrodisie distinguée de l'agénésie: Ouvrage destiné aux personnes mariées qui ne peuvent avoir d'enfans* [On impotence and sterility, or research on anaphrodisia distinguished from agenesia: A work aimed at married people who cannot have children] (Paris: Masson et Yonet, 1831).

7. Descourtilz, *De l'impuissance et de la stérilité*, 6. He refers to order 3, genre 56 of Pinel's *Nosographie philosophique*, 2:111.

8. Ibid., 13.

9. Ibid., 14–15.

10. Jacques-Louis Moreau de la Sarthe, *Histoire naturelle de la femme suivie d'un traité d'hygiène appliquée à son régime physique et moral aux différentes époques de la vie* [A natural history of woman followed by a treatise on hygiene applied to her physical and moral regimen at different periods of her life] (Paris: Duprat, 1803), 413–414.

11. Descourtilz, *De l'impuissance et de la stérilité*, 14–15; original emphasis.

12. Paolo Zacchia, *Quaestionum medico-legalium: Tomus posterior, quo continentur liber nonus et decimus, necnon decisiones sacrae rotae romanae ad praedictas materias spectantes* [On medico-legal issues: The final tome, in which are contained books nine and ten, as well as decisions by the holy rota of Rome regarding the aforesaid matters] (Lugduni [Lyon]: Sumptibus Ioan. Ant. Huguetan, et Marciant, 1661), lib. 9, tit. 3, quaest. 2, 54.

13. Ibid., 69.

14. Denis Diderot et al., *Encyclopédie ou dictionnaire raisonné des sciences, des arts et des métiers* [Encyclopedia or ordered dictionary of sciences, arts, and crafts] (Stuttgart: Frommann, 1995) [facsimile reprint of the first edition of 1751–1780], art. "Frigidité."

15. Ibid.

16. *Dictionnaire des sciences médicales* [Dictionary of medical sciences] (Paris: Panckoucke, 1812–1822), 17:11.

17. Ibid.

18. Ibid., 17:14.

19. Georg Kobelt, *De l'appareil du sens génital des deux sexes dans l'espèce humaine et dans quelques mammifères, au point de vue anatomique et physiologique* [On the apparatus of the genital sense in the human species and some mammals, from the point of view of anatomy and physiology], trans. H. Kaula (Strasburg: Berger-Levrault, 1851).

20. Félix Roubaud, *Traité de l'impuissance et de la stérilité chez l'homme et chez la femme, comprenant les moyens recommandés pour y remédier* [A treatise on impotence and sterility in man and woman, including the recommended means for treating them] (Paris: Baillière, 1855), 2:450.

21. Ibid., 1:154–155; original emphasis.

22. Ibid., 1:155.

23. Ibid., 2:519.

24. Ibid., 2:521.

25. Ibid., 1:155; original emphasis.

26. Pierre Garnier, *L'impuissance physique et morale chez l'homme et la femme* [Physical and moral impotence in man and woman] (Paris: Garnier, 1882), 358.

27. Ibid.

28. Ibid.

29. Ibid.

30. Ibid., 507.

31. Charles Féré, *L'instinct sexuel: Evolution et dissolution* [Sexual instinct: Evolution and dissolution] (Paris: Alcan, 1899), 104–105.

32. See, for example, Richard von Krafft-Ebing, *Psychopathia Sexualis; mit besonderer Berücksichtigung der conträren Sexualempfindung: Eine medicinisch-gerichtliche*

Studie für Ärzte und Juristen. Zwoelfte, verbesserte und vermehrte Auflage [Psychopathia sexualis, with special reference to the antipathic sexual instinct: A medico-forensic study for doctors and jurists. A twelfth improved and expanded edition] (Stuttgart: Enke, 1903), 300. It seems odd in this regard that a recent English translation should title the chapter "Frigidity *or* Aphrodisia." See Richard von Krafft-Ebing, *Psychopathia Sexualis, with Especial Reference to the Antipathic Sexual Instinct: A Medico-Forensic Study,* trans. from the 12th German edition by Franklin S. Klaf (New York: Arcade, 1998), 263.

33. Krafft-Ebing, *Psychopathia Sexualis* [American ed.], 40.

34. Ibid.

35. Ibid., 45–46.

36. Ibid., 323; original emphasis.

37. Krafft-Ebing, *Psychopathia Sexualis* [German ed.], 58.

38. Krafft-Ebing, *Psychopathia Sexualis* [American ed.], 40.

39. Ibid., 182.

40. Krafft-Ebing, *Psychopathia Sexualis* [German ed.], 209.

41. Ibid., 297; Krafft-Ebing, *Psychopathia Sexualis* [American ed.], 262.

42. Otto Adler, *Die mangelhafte Geschlechtsempfindung des Weibes* [Deficient sexual sensation in woman], 3rd ed. (Berlin: Kornfeld, 1919), 2.

43. Ibid., 8.

44. Ibid., 8–9.

45. Ibid., 12.

46. Ibid., 90.

47. Ibid., 180.

48. Ibid., 155.

49. Ibid., 10.

50. Ibid., 180.

51. The original edition is Wilhelm Stekel, *Die Geschlechtskälte der Frau: Eine Psychopathologie des weiblichen Liebeslebens* [Sexual coldness in woman: A psychopathology of womanly love] (Berlin: Urban und Schwarzenberg, 1921).

52. See, for example, Wilhelm Stekel, *Disorders of the Instincts and the Emotions: The Parapathiac Disorders: Frigidity in Woman,* trans. James S. van Teslaar (New York: Boni and Liveright, 1926), 1:108.

53. Ibid., 1:1.

54. Ibid., 1:64.

55. Ibid., 1:64.

56. Ibid., 1:117.

57. See Thomas Laqueur, *Solitary Sex: A Cultural History of Masturbation* (New York: Zone Books, 2003).

58. See, for example, Albert Moll, *Untersuchungen über die Libido sexualis* [Investigations into *Libido sexualis*] (Berlin: Kornfeld, 1897), 9, 24.

59. For a discussion of the significance of this terminological choice in Moll's own terms, see Moll, *Untersuchungen über die Libido sexualis,* 10.

2

Translation as Transposition

Leopold von Sacher-Masoch, Darwinian Thought,
and the Concept of Love in German Sexual Modernity

BIRGIT LANG

This chapter takes a fresh look at the relationship between science and literature in the production of modern sexuality by examining the role of translation in the work of the Austrian writer Leopold von Sacher-Masoch (1836–1895), who, via his novellas, popularized Darwinism in the German-speaking world. It focuses on the changes and modifications that occurred when Sacher-Masoch translated Darwinian concepts into literary fiction in a collection of six novellas titled *Love*, which was published in the 1870s. While critics tend to focus specifically on how Sacher-Masoch's work inspired the coinage of the term "masochism," one of the key modern pathologies of sex, I argue that Sacher-Masoch had a much broader influence on the shaping of German sexual modernity. Writing two decades before the rise of sexology and psychoanalysis, he turned to Darwinism to develop a new framework for investigating love and sex. In what follows, I read Sacher-Masoch's fiction for the insights it provides into how Darwinism influenced his thinking, and how the literary works in turn popularized Darwin's ideas in the German-speaking world. I suggest that Sacher-Masoch's translations of Darwin's work are best understood as "transpositions": rearrangements of the scientific ideas into a new literary language of "love." By tracing how Sacher-Masoch adapted Darwinian theories to problematize gender relations and portray the sexual desires and behaviors that subsequently came to be known as masochism and homosexuality, and by further considering how translation between languages is itself portrayed in the novellas, the chapter demonstrates how science and literature, Darwinism and

Sacher-Masoch's fictions, together contributed to the modern articulations of love, sex, and desire in German.

Translation as Transposition

Within the history of sexuality, the translational turn of recent years has opened up new avenues of scholarship that aim to expand the transnational scope of the field and unveil the competing "regimes of translation" at play in different cultural and intellectual contexts.[1] The quest for a more global understanding of sexual modernity has made such an investigation particularly pertinent.[2] The challenge of acknowledging the significance of translation for the history of sexuality has so far been met most decidedly by historians of British sexology, who turn to translation to examine the cultural specificities of sexological concepts.[3] Historians of German sexology, in contrast, have mostly focused on the role played by translations between languages in the development of modern scientific discourses about sex in German. These distinct critical trajectories reflect national particularities in the development of modern sexuality. Unlike in Britain, where literary culture played an overt role in the shaping of modern sexual discourses—Heike Bauer has recently highlighted "the distinct literary dimension of English sexology"— German sex research was overtly scientific in approach and outlook.[4]

Scholars of modern German sexuality discourses have shown that the interests of translators left a demonstrable impact on the development of sexology and science in Germany. For instance, Sander Gliboff, in his landmark study of the dissemination of Darwinism in Germany, has shown that the translation strategies used by Heinrich Georg Bronn (1800–1862), Germany's most prominent paleontologist and the first translator of Darwin's work into German, purposefully tried to embed Darwin's ideas into German scientific debates of the time. Gliboff demonstrates how Bronn's translation on the one hand aimed to find a common ground with Darwin, while on the other hand the explanation of Darwin's theory in the already established scientific language of transcendental morphology impaired such a goal, since it is commonly perceived as contradicting Darwin.[5] Given that Bronn reformulated Darwin's theories with the latter's knowledge and consent to make it fit his own ideas as well as German scientific debates, at the time, the question arises—as Scott L. Montgomery pertinently asks in *Science in Translation*—"what [else] happens to knowledge when it is given a wholly new voice and context?"[6]

This expands the existing scholarship by showing that literary representations of "love" played an important role in the transmission of Darwinian ideas in German. It draws on the work of translation theorists and historians Susan Bassnett and André Lefevere, whose "Horace model" draws attention to the significance of the translator. According to the "Horace model," which takes its name from the Roman poet famous for adapting Greek sources, the translator functions as a reliable cultural mediator who fashions his translation in accordance with the perceived expectation of his readers.[7] This role of the translator has also been described in terms of "directional equivalence," a concept that not only acknowledges that "two translations of the same text will never be the same" but also pays attention to the role of the translator in the transmission of a text into another language.[8] My own reading of Sacher-Masoch's debts to Darwin further suggests that literary translations, which do not render a specific source text but play with the ideas it contains, can be understood more specifically as a form of "transposition." French narratologist Gérard Genette has defined transposition as a "serious transformation" and "without a doubt the most important of all hypertextual practices."[9] He argues that transpositions can be purely formal or deliberately thematic, and that the transformation of meaning is manifestly part of the purpose of transposition.[10] In this chapter, I read Sacher-Masoch's fictional rendering of Darwinian ideas as transpositions and argue that his novellas can be a read as "transpositions" of some of the key ideas contained in Darwin's *On the Origin of Species*. I demonstrate that the writer successfully and deliberately translated the concern with evolutionary theory into a new discourse about "love" that would influence the conception of sexuality in the German-speaking world.

A close reading of Sacher-Masoch's construction of "love" shows that the novelists aimed to familiarize the wider German reading public with *his* interpretation of Darwinian ideas. Sacher-Masoch became the first literary champion of Darwinism in Germany, and his self-modeling after foremost German poet-naturalist Johann Wolfgang von Goethe (1749–1832) allowed him to embrace scientific discourse—and its translational paradigm of "directional equivalence"—with open arms. Yet Sacher-Masoch's rendition of Darwinian ideas also went several steps further than Bronn's, formulating these with a view not only to a specifically German scientific audience but to a broad literary audience. Sacher-Masoch furthermore preempted some of the insights formulated by Darwin in *The Descent of Man* (1871), which appeared a year after the publication of *Love*. *Love* was not a scientific translation in the conventional sense, then, and it was also more than a literary adaptation, that is, a reconfiguration of genre or medium. Rather, Sacher-Masoch used Darwin's theories as an intellectual framework, on the basis of which he developed six original literary case studies that illustrated and discussed Darwin's ideas using aesthetic means. In what follows, then, I will explore different aspects of this process, concluding with an analysis of Sacher-Masoch's self-conscious discussion of his translational practice in *Marzella*, the final novella of *Love*, which underlines the importance of

transposition for his work and can be seen as the author's attempt to problematize his conflation of literary and scientific discourses for the German
public by aesthetic means.

Darwinism and the Making of *Love*

Translation between languages was part of Sacher-Masoch's life from the
outset. Born in Lviv in Austrian Galicia, where his father was chief of the
local police force, he was in many ways a typical upper-middle-class subject
of the Habsburg Empire, liberal in his political leanings and adept at several
languages. His mother tongue was Ukrainian, and, like many children of his
social standing, he was taught French by his nanny.[11] In 1848, when Sacher-
Masoch was twelve years old, the family moved to Prague, where he also
learned German. Six years later the family moved to the city of Graz, where
Sacher-Masoch attended university and subsequently pursued his academic
career as a historian. Similarly, according to his autobiography, Sacher-
Masoch's interest in nature and science began in childhood, partly fueled
by his father, who was an avid collector of "beetles, butterflies, plants, miner-
als and fossils."[12] Darwinism was a wider public discourse at the time when
Sacher-Masoch came of age. Among the broader reading public as well as in
the narrower sphere of science, the impact of Darwin's new evolution-based
explanation of life on Earth, and the accompanying shift from a religious
to a historical epistemological framework, was profound.[13] In the German-
speaking world, political liberalism was thwarted in 1848, and the debate
about Darwinism became an ersatz, a means for the middle classes to express their beliefs through science rather than religion.[14] Not without reason
did Darwin in a letter from March 1868 describe his support in Germany as
"my chief ground for hoping that our views will ultimately prevail."[15]

That Darwinism shaped Sacher-Masoch's own writing is not difficult to
see in his novels. In the late 1860s, when he was a lecturer in history at the
University of Graz, he embarked on what would become the largest literary
project of his career. Titled *The Legacy of Cain* (*Das Vermächtnis Kains*),
this multivolume work was intended to circle around six key themes: love,
property, the state, war, work, and death. Sacher-Masoch completed only the
first two of these collections of novellas, and, spurred by the wide literary
success of the first volume of *Love* (1870), he resigned from his university
position in order to follow his literary calling.[16] *Love* can be read as a transposition of Darwinian thought into literary case studies, in that it used key
Darwinian ideas and illustrated them in the six novellas provided. It furthermore explored a topic that Darwin had identified as ground-breaking
but had not yet engaged with in full: the role of love for the development
of humankind. Darwin did not explore this idea until *The Descent of Man*

(1871). However, he had already conceded in the conclusion to the first edition of *On the Origin of Species* in 1859 the effects of evolutionary theory
on human history: "psychology will be based on a new foundation, that of
necessary acquirement of each mental power and capacity by gradation.
Light will be thrown on the origin of man and his history."[17] This passage,
omitted in Bronn's translation into German, can be described as motto-like
for Sacher-Masoch's *The Legacy of Cain* in general and *Love* in particular,
although it remains unclear if Sacher-Masoch references Darwin's original
text or if he refers to Bronn's translation of the latter. The key Darwinian
concepts explored in *On the Origin of Species*—the struggle for existence,
that is, the drive to survive and reproduce; the laws of variation, that is,
the innate variety of individuals within a given species; and the powers of
natural selection, that is, the process by which well-adapted life forms tend
to survive and reproduce in greater numbers than others of their kind—
function as the leitmotifs of *Love*.

Critical analyses of Sacher-Masoch's Darwinian leanings have mainly
centered on the literary Prologue to *The Legacy of Cain*, which was printed
as front matter of *Love*. Werner Michler and Peter Sprengel, for instance,
in their different readings of the Prologue, have both pointed out that the
text employs key Darwinian phrases—such as "the struggle for existence"
(German: *Kampf ums Dasein*)—arguing that this language makes Sacher-
Masoch's engagement with Darwinian ideas appear somewhat superficial
and unsophisticated.[18] A more productive way to analyze the Prologue,
however, is through asking to what end the author Sacher-Masoch used the
main character of the wanderer—a member of a Russian-Orthodox sect—to
present key issues and questions to his readership.

The reader first encounters the ascetic wanderer through the eyes of the
homodiegetic narrator—henceforth referred to as Leopold—while hunting
in the Galician woods. After Leopold has ordered his gamekeeper to shoot
an eagle, the wanderer steps in and accuses the narrator of having murdered
his feathered brother as the biblical Cain murdered Abel. The wanderer thus
equates animal and human existence, a worldview that permeates his ensuing dialogue with Leopold. The wanderer argues that men are neither innately good nor do they possess a natural sense of morality.[19] Society for him
becomes the arena for the struggle of existence and is deemed to contradict
human nature. His answer consists of a complete retreat from the world. As
for the struggle of existence, the wanderer explains how nature forces human
beings to reproduce and is the single reason for passion between the sexes:

> Who was not wooed by fad to believe that the satisfaction of the
> superhuman longing in us, the possession of the beloved wife would
> not bring nameless bliss, and who has not at last dolefully laughed

at his imaginary joys? For us, it is the abashing insight that nature instills us with such longing, only to make us her blind and willing tool, as she does not ask us. She only wants to procreate our species.[20]

This worldview presents human beings without agency and as mere subjects of nature, which rules their desires and passions. The struggle for existence clearly functions as a leitmotif in this passage and becomes the underlying reason for the inevitable battle of the sexes, since the wanderer considers society's attempt to steady the relationship between the sexes through marriage to be futile.[21] The fact that Sacher-Masoch references *On the Origin of Species* in this context indicates that unlike Darwin he was particularly concerned with questions of "passion" and desire. However, to conflate his position with that of the wanderer, as previous scholarship has done, seems futile. Rather the Prologue raises the very questions that Sacher-Masoch answers in the six ensuing novellas.

The novellas in *Love* develop Sacher-Masoch's concerns with the topic, as they portray five instances (or variations) of problematic cases of love followed by the resolution in the final novella. The first three novellas are devoted to the question of procreation, marriage, and its impact on gender relations: *Don Juan of Kolomea* sets forth the detrimental impacts of children on married life, including the protagonist's resultant womanizing; this situation results in both partners being trapped in a loveless marriage. *The Capitulation* in turn illustrates the price a woman pays for being upwardly mobile and marrying for money rather than love, while her "true love" accepts what he perceives to be "the nature of women"—their capacity to place the financial security of their children over their feelings for men. The third story, titled *Moonlit Night*, further addresses the estrangement between married estate owners. Here the exclusion of women from the sphere of male work—men's struggle for existence—expresses itself in the ensuing alienation between the married couple, and in female infidelity.

While the first three novels in the series thus critique existing gender conventions partly by adapting Darwinian ideas about "struggle" and "improvement," the following novels illustrate Sacher-Masoch's queer engagement with ideas about "variation." The novellas *Venus in Furs* and *The Love of Plato*, which portray a gradual escalation in problematic gender relations, represent articulations of "masochism" and "homosexuality" *avant la lettre*. These texts indicate Sacher-Masoch's unique transposition of Darwinian ideas onto sexual desire, even as they also indicate how literature would in turn inspire the coinage of new sexological vocabularies.

Venus in Furs, arguably the best known of Sacher-Masoch's works, deals with the confusion of Severin, a psychologically domineering and physically intimidating man who explains his misogynistic behavior by suggesting that it originates in his own suffering of "enslavement" at the hand of his first lover. In 1890, sexologist and psychiatrist Richard von Krafft-Ebing (1840–1902) identified "masochism" as one of the key sexual pathologies of modernity, which he named after Sacher-Masoch in his work *Neuere Forschungen zur Psychopathia Sexualis*. In this context *Venus in Furs* was singled out and appropriated into sexological and psychoanalytic discourse at the turn of the nineteenth century, its author soon labeled a "masochist." Such discursive accretions around Sacher-Masoch and his literary output continue to deter today's readers from a broader appreciation of the author's ideas about love and sexuality.[22] For Sacher-Masoch, Severin represented a specific variation of male sexuality that eroticized the hierarchical aspect of the struggle between the sexes: a man who feared women/nature and was sexually dominated by his first partner and later sexually dominated a female partner.

The less well-known novella *The Love of Plato* in contrast explores the failed marriage of Count Henryk, an advocate of "platonic love," a story told to the narrator by Count Henryk's mother. According to a later reference in another work by Sacher-Masoch, *The Love of Plato* represents a fictionalization of the first marriage of Count St——, who, on first meeting his wife, told her that he "would be quite capable of falling head over heels in love if she only was a man."[23] The content of *The Love of Plato* unfolds correspondingly. The "misogynist" Henryk is psychologically but not physically attracted to Nadeschda Princess Baragress.[24] Once she—unbeknownst to him—masquerades as her "brother" Anatol, his attraction becomes forceful, and he falls in love for the first time in his life. Henryk first finds Anatol "beautiful, but his soul is even more beautiful," and later—ironically at the point when he begins to fall out of love in a platonic sense—physically attractive; "to say so directly—seductive."[25] Once the princess reveals her true physical nature, Henryk rejects her, only to marry her six years later after they meet again by chance. They divorce shortly afterward. At the close of the novella his mother reports that Henryk now resides in Hungary with his friend Schuster, where they live in adjoining living quarters, at one with nature and their scientific studies.[26]

The Love of Plato is part of the emerging discourses about male same-sex love and desire. Six years before its publication, the Hanoverian lawyer Karl Heinrich Ulrichs (1825–1895) published the first volume of his *Forschungen über das Räthsel der mannmännlichen Liebe* (Studies in the riddle of manmanly love). Ulrichs demanded the decriminalization of same-sex acts at the Deutsche Juristentag, a German legal association, in 1867. Two years later, in 1869, Austrian writer Karl Maria Kertbeny (1824–1882) published an anonymous pamphlet also concerning the decriminalization of same-sex relations. In this pamphlet, he coined the term "homosexual," describing it as one of five classifications of sexual types. *The Love of Plato* contributes to this growing body of literature on love between men. Loosely engaging with the Darwinian concept of "variation," Sacher-Masoch here transposes the evolutionary theory onto a more specific and affirmative discussion about love and desire between men. In the novella Henryk's mother, Countess Tarnow, describes her son as different from other men and as a purehearted idealist. Such idealists, she explains, sometimes hide their gentleness out of fear of being compromised "as if it was a crime."[27]

Sacher-Masoch's novellas were unique in the German literature of the time for the wide-ranging, nuanced, and unprejudiced representation of a wide range of gender relations and sexual proclivities. Together, the series of texts represents Sacher-Masoch's engagement with Darwin's understanding of "variation," that is, his concern with the different manifestations of certain traits within a species. For Darwin variation was a natural phenomenon and explained the existence of distinct species. It was shaped by two forces: chance and natural selection, the latter defined by the struggle for existence, which leads to adaptation.[28] In contrast, Sacher-Masoch transposed the Darwinian ideas into a literary context to consider specifically the different manifestations of what he called "love" and its manifestations in contemporary society. The fact that he presented it in the form of literary case studies meant the highly successful work gained a broad appeal among the German (and French) reading public, with editions of Love published in 1870, 1871, and 1878—and the work was considered paramount in Sacher-Masoch's literary oeuvre.[29]

Furthermore, the deliberations of the Prologue preempt debates that took place in Germany in the decade after the publication of Love. The wanderer anticipates the position of conservative thinkers like Friedrich von Hellwald (1842–1892), an ardent social and racial Darwinian popular among the German bourgeoisie and the author of Cultural History in Its Natural Development until Current Times (Kulturgeschichte in ihrer natürlichen Entwicklung bis zur Gegenwart, 1875), who argued that the struggle for existence ruled over moral considerations in natural as well as in human history.[30] Sacher-Masoch resisted this move to a more conservative interpretation of Darwin's theories in the 1880s, publishing, for instance, in 1883 a book review of Hellwald's cultural history, which was highly critical of Hellwald's ideas. The review was published in Auf der Höhe (1881–1885), an internationally oriented German journal founded and edited by Sacher-Masoch. The review asks: "how can we separate cultural history from the history of arts and science, without being at risk of giving an inadequate, shallow and superficial account of the historical development of humanity?"[31] Sacher-Masoch's own Love, which predates Hellwald's work, partly offers an answer to this question as it makes the case for the necessity of fusing the histories of arts and science when trying to understand love. The

Prologue introduces the character of the wanderer to explore Darwinian ideas and the questions they raise for humanity. It portrays humanity as a species endowed with reason, morality, and a sense of aesthetics. Via this wide-ranging focus on what we might call science and culture, evolution and aesthetics, Sacher-Masoch transformed Darwinian scientific concepts into a literary investigation of the shape, meanings, and (im)possibilities of love.

Translation and Social Transformation: Modern Matrimony in *Marzella*

While Sacher-Masoch's "perverse" novellas most clearly indicate how his work speaks to, and to some extent anticipates, sexological studies, his study of matrimony, *Marzella*, offers arguably the most useful insights into Sacher-Masoch's debts to Darwin and how he transformed the scientific ideas into a provocative sexual politics. *Marzella*, the sixth and final novella in the collection, not only reveals the "true" answers to the questions raised in the Prologue of *Love* but also contains the key to understanding the philosophy behind Sacher-Masoch's transposition of Darwin and the effects he hoped his fiction would have on the reader.

Marzella provides an idealistic solution to the modern problems of gender and sexuality outlined in the preceding novellas. The main character, Alexander, and his wife, Marzella, are represented as the role models for Sacher-Masoch's vision of gender equality, namely "the happiness of moral matrimony," as Sacher-Masoch described it in a rare surviving letter to his publisher, Carl Cotta.[32] This state worth aspiring to involves both partners overcoming their "natural status": Alexander actively involves Marzella in the management of their feudal estate—the male struggle for existence—while she refrains from putting her children above him and instead remains a passionate companion throughout their marriage. This new morality represents Sacher-Masoch's answer to the nihilism of the ascetic wanderer. Moreover, it denotes a practical answer to the challenges posed by Darwin's observations on (human) nature: the novel suggests that economic equality and an emphasis on loving relationships would alleviate the often harsh and cruel realities of the "struggle for existence."

Translation plays a pivotal role in this novella, since it becomes the tool through which the aristocratic Alexander, the widely traveled and well-educated main character of the novella, educates Marzella and by which he asks her to consider his marriage proposal. After his return to Galicia, Alexander seems frustrated with the corruption of educated women who—for lack of an alternative—focus their intellectual pursuit on gossip, or "at best on theatre." Rather than marrying within his social class, Alexander prefers his mésalliance with the daughter of his Ruthenian wet nurse. He and Marzella are physically attracted to one other and have similar interests; they also share similar values. As part of his courtship Alexander does something peculiar: he translates Goethe's most famous work, *Faust*—the "greatest poem ever written," as Alexander attests himself—into Ukrainian prose, to make it accessible to his future wife.[33] Alexander's friend Leopold mockingly asks about the motivation behind this translation from the German verse of the original to "Ukrainian and prose . . . are you thinking of having it printed?"[34] Shortly afterward, Leopold comments, half surprised and half contemptuous: "Do you find her [Marzella] to be educable?"[35] For Marzella, the matter of class inequalities becomes obvious through her identificatory reading of Alexander's Ukrainian *Faust*. Like Leopold, Marzella has preconceived notions of class difference, and for her, a relationship with Alexander seems inconceivable. She reacts strongly to Alexander's version of *Faust* and assumes that Alexander envisions her in the role of Gretchen. In an earnest and passionate reply to Alexander, she points out: "I do not know if you are such a Faust, but I know that I am not a Gretchen to admire this Faust and throw herself away for him."[36] Furthermore, she finds that Faust mistreats Gretchen and suggests that rather than seducing her, he should have educated her. The translated Faust serves to render conscious Marzella's underlying crisis.

Accordingly, this passage in the novella is followed by Alexander's explanation of modern matrimony to his friend Leopold. "The sexual drive," Alexander argues using a rather Darwinian language (or, if I express myself more delicately, love), remains the pivotal element, the seed of the relationship between man and woman, but only a seed from which—with advancing evolution of the intellectual nature—the need for a higher unity in attitudes and interests develops. And this alone can be the foundation of modern matrimony.[37]

Marzella does not realize that her interpretation of *Faust* is anticipated by Alexander, who, through the translation, educates her to be his wife. In return, she will selflessly teach him the ways of nature. While Marzella initially refuses Alexander's marriage proposal, she eventually faces her love for him, but only after she has saved his life; he is bitten by a snake that he thinks harmless, while she comprehends the gravity of the situation and sucks the poison from the bite, risking her own life.

The references to the translation of *Faust* suggest that Sacher-Masoch's own understanding of translation may be based on that of Goethe. In an essay from 1819 Goethe differentiates three translational models. "The first," he argues, "acquaints us with the foreign country on our own terms." For such a (culturally infused) translation, "prose in and of itself serves as the best introduction."[38] He continues by saying that "much would have been gained, for instance, if the *Nibelungen* had been set in good, solid prose at the outset, and labeled as popular literature." Next he differentiates between the *parodistic* translation (parodistic not in intent, but in its limitations), which translates what seems of interest to the translator, and an *interlinear* translation that "attempts to identify itself with the original."[39] That Sacher-Masoch seems to have followed the first of these three translational modes is unusual. Ideas about translation at the time were influenced by the German theorist Friedrich Schleiermacher (1768–1834), who referenced only the latter two of Goethe's modes of translation in his influential essay *On the Different Methods of Translation* (1813) and favored an interlinear—or as he called it, "foreignizing"—over a domesticating approach. Sacher-Masoch's turn to translation as a way of acquainting Marzella with Alexander's "new country" on her own terms here reinforces Sacher-Masoch's concern with greater sexual equality.

The translation of *Faust* is only the beginning of Alexander's continuing education of his partner and reveals Alexander to be a patient pedagogue. After their marriage, he teaches Marzella languages through the so-called nature method, his overall teaching methodology based on vividness involving the senses.[40] He focuses on her strengths, that is, her unaffectedness, and her deeply emotional character and gradually tutors her to an appropriate level of knowledge. After a year, she reads *Faust* in the original, as well as Goethe's *Werther*, Shakespeare's *Macbeth*, and Cervantes's *Don Quixote*, as well as the Russian classics and the works of Ovid.[41] Alexander thus raises Marzella from her class background and from the constraints usually associated with her sex by enabling her to read literature in different languages. He simultaneously provides himself with a loyal partner, and—as he discusses with his friend Leopold—with "new blood" in his aristocratic "pedigree."[42] While *Marzella* thus refers to Darwinian ideas about reproduction, Sacher-Masoch clearly privileges language and literature, aesthetics and culture, over a narrowly defined biology of humankind.

While Alexander's *Faust* represents a cultural and linguistic translation, Sacher-Masoch's *Love* can be understood better as a transposition of Darwinian ideas by which he sought to educate his readers. As Sacher-Masoch points out in the Prologue, such a transposition embeds scientific thinking into a literary aesthetics and in so doing fosters readers' consciousness of their feelings.[43] For Sacher-Masoch, education remained the means to appeal to and shape the morality and the intellect of men and women alike. Where Alexander's successful education of his bride-to-be through reading is based on the translation of literature between languages, the *Love* novellas together constitute an idealistic literary transposition of the Darwinian struggle for existence. For Sacher-Masoch, the role of literature is to "communicate knowledge and truths . . . by coining the dead gold barrels of scientific knowledge for the masses."[44] If we read *Love* as an example of such an attempt at popularizing Darwinism for a wider audience, readers find themselves in the role of Marzella. Sacher-Masoch transposes the new concepts of Darwinism into a language his middle-class readers were adept in interpreting: that of literature. From this perspective, the overarching goal of *Love* appears to be a concern with educating readers on matters of Darwinism—and love, desire, and the limits of social conventions more broadly. Whereas later sexological works were concerned with mapping bodies and classifying desires, Sacher-Masoch's *Love* provides an imaginative account of love and gender relations that brings into question the sexed and gendered norms that define contemporary lives.

Conclusion: Sacher-Masoch, Love, and Modern Sexuality

Sacher-Masoch's novellas show, then, that literary explorations were crucial to the emergence of a modern discourse of "love" in German, a discourse that would come to be assimilated and reinterpreted in the works of scientific sexologists whose ideas about sexual pathology are generally associated with the "birth" of modern sexuality. Similar to the ways in which Sacher-Masoch transformed Darwin's ideas, so his works would be reinterpreted and his literary ambitions did not come to fruition as he had planned. For a while his transposition of Darwin was the first to explore a new brand of discourse of "love," which equated literary and scientific sources and challenged conventional literary modes of representation, but the reception of his work soon focused on what became understood as the "perverse" representations of "masochism" and—surprisingly less controversial—"homosexuality" in *Venus in Furs* and *The Love of Plato*. *Marzella* was sidelined. At the very point, then, when the new Darwinian paradigm took hold in Germany and Austria—a paradigm that Sacher-Masoch helped to popularize— readers reinterpreted his idealized notions of Darwin's human variety from a decisively modern perspective: as the expression of individualized sexual identities (including that of the author) and not as the author's concerted pedagogical efforts to help resolve the modern crisis between the sexes.

What is gained from paying attention to Sacher-Masoch's translations—including the representation of translation in the novellas as well as the ways in which he transposed Darwinian evolutionary theory into literary form—is a better understanding of how modern ideas about sexuality developed in the nexus between science and literature. *Love* undoubtedly contributed to more psychologized understandings of sexuality, articulated insights that would come to underpin the formation of sexual identity categories, and makes a distinct contribution to the modern history of sexuality. Unlike much later literature, Sacher-Masoch's literary interest in the depiction of human "passions and follies" was not informed by the narrative of degeneration that structured late nineteenth-century sexology and psychiatry. Instead, Sacher-Masoch's representation of "love" was shaped by the Darwinian notion of variation. The insight that human beings are innately different in their sexual proclivities and preferences was reinforced by the notion that variety was a natural occurrence and included different expressions of passion and different forms of what in the twentieth century came to be described as sexual identities. The other key difference between Sacher-Masoch and later sexologists was his understanding of sexuality as always relational; that is, directed at a love object with the eventual goal of forming a union—an understanding psychoanalysis shared decades later. This relational constellation is represented in its most idealized, albeit not prescriptive, solution through his idea of moral matrimony to existing problems between the sexes; Sacher-Masoch's characters Henryk and Schuster in *The Love of Plato* also form an example of a happy union. This constitutes a thus far unacknowledged representation of homosexuality in nineteenth-century literature.[45]

To reflect on the uses of translation in Sacher-Masoch's work, then, not only provides new insights into the production of sexual ideas but also draws attention to the question of language in general and the fact that literature— as Sacher-Masoch stressed on several occasions—is capable of "explor[ing] new truths itself."[46] If self-reflexivity "is a crucial part of what links participants in a common practice or discipline we can call history of science," as Carla Nappi has recently argued, then *Love* might also be considered a work of science.[47] After all, Sacher-Masoch's work did not only popularize a particular view of Darwinian ideas that proved evocative and ambiguous for generations to come, but he also reflected on the ways in which such a transposition between science and culture, evolution and aesthetics could be communicated.

NOTES

This research was funded by an Australian Research Council Discovery Project Grant for "Making the Case: The Case Study Genre in Sexology, Psychoanalysis and Literature," with Joy Damousi and Katie Sutton, 2010–2014.

1. Naoki Sakai, "How Do We Count a Language? Translation and Discontinuity," *Translation Studies* 2, no. 1 (2009): 75. For example, see Stella Sandford, "Thinking Sex Politically: Rethinking 'Sex' in Plato's *Republic*," *South Atlantic Quarterly* 104, no. 4 (2005): 613–630.

2. For the European debates about sex and sexological exchanges, see Franz X. Eder, Lesley A. Hall, and Gert Hekma, eds., *Sexual Cultures in Europe: National Histories* (Manchester, UK: Manchester University Press, 1999), and *Sexual Cultures in Europe: Themes in Sexuality* (Manchester, UK: Manchester University Press, 1999); Harry

Oosterhuis, "Sexual Modernity in the Works of Richard von Krafft-Ebing and Albert Moll," *Medical History* 56, no. 2 (2012): 133–155; Anna Katharina Schaffner, *Modernism and Perversion: Sexual Deviance in Sexology and Literature, 1850–1930* (Basingstoke, UK: Palgrave Macmillan, 2012).

3. See, for example, Heike Bauer, "'Not a Translation but a Mutilation': The Limits of Translation and the Discipline of Sexology," *Yale Journal of Criticism* 16, no. 2 (2003): 381–405; Heike Bauer, *English Literary Sexology: Translations of Inversion, 1860–1930* (Basingstoke, UK: Palgrave Macmillan, 2009); Sean Brady, ed., *John Addington Symonds (1840–1893) and Homosexuality: A Critical Edition of Sources* (Basingstoke, UK: Palgrave Macmillan, 2012); Chiara Beccalossi, *Female Sexual Inversion: Same-Sex Desires in Italian and British Sexology, c. 1870–1920* (New York: Palgrave Macmillan, 2012).

4. Bauer, *English Literary Sexology*, 15.

5. Sander Gliboff, *H. G. Bronn, Ernst Haeckel, and the Origins of German Darwinism: A Study in Translation and Transformation* (Cambridge, MA: MIT Press, 2008), 7.

6. Scott L. Montgomery, *Science in Translation: Movements of Knowledge through Cultures and Time* (Chicago: University of Chicago Press, 2000), 253.

7. Susan Bassnett and André Lefevere, eds., *Constructing Cultures: Essays on Literary Translation* (Clevedon, UK: Multilingual Matters, 1998), 3. "Natural equivalence," on the other hand, dominates popular notions of translation. Such translations aspired to have "the same value as (some aspect of) its corresponding source text." While this does not imply word-for-word accuracy, natural equivalence makes possible a comparative study of source and target texts that reveal cultural differences in the construction of sex. See Anthony Pym, *Exploring Translation Theories* (London: Routledge, 2012), 7–8.

8. Pym, *Exploring Translation Theories*, 25.

9. Gérard Genette, *Palimpsests: Literature in the Second Degree*, trans. Channa Newman and Claude Doubinsky (Lincoln: University of Nebraska Press, 1998), 212.

10. Ibid., 214.

11. Leopold von Sacher-Masoch, "Eine Autobiographie," *Deutsche Monatsblätter: Centralorgan für das literarische Leben der Gegenwart* 2, no. 3 (1879): 260.

12. Ibid.

13. Cf. Gliboff, *Bronn*; Alfred Kelly, *The Descent of Darwin: The Popularization of Darwinism in Germany, 1860–1914* (Chapel Hill: University of North Carolina Press, 1981); Richard Weikart, *From Darwin to Hitler: Evolutionary Ethics, Eugenics, and Racism in Germany* (New York: Palgrave Macmillan, 2004); Richard Weikart, *Socialist Darwinism: Evolution in German Socialist Thought from Marx to Bernstein* (San Francisco: International Scholars, 1998); Paul J. Weindling, "Dissecting German Social Darwinism: Historicizing the Biology of the Organic State," *Science in Context* 2 (1998): 619–637.

14. Kelly, *Descent of Darwin*, 5; Werner Michler, *Darwinismus und Literatur: Naturwissenschaftliche und literarische Intelligenz in Österreich, 1859–1914* (Vienna: Böhlau, 1999), 12.

15. Cited in Diane B. Paul, "Darwin, Social Darwinism and Eugenics," in *The Cambridge Companion to Darwin*, ed. Jonathan Hodge and Gregory Radick (Cambridge: Cambridge University Press, 2003), 219.

16. Celebrated in the 1870s, he later struggled to make a living—as did other authors at the time—and was involved in a range of short-lived attempts to found new journals.

Secondary literature usually ascribes the perceived decline in the quality of his novellas to financial pressures, as well as the resulting "writing frenzy." For example, see Lisbeth Exner, *Leopold von Sacher-Masoch* (Reinbek, Germany: Rowohlt, 2003), 7.

17. Charles Darwin, *On the Origin of Species by Means of Natural Selection or the Preservation of Favoured Races in the Struggle for Life* (London: Murray, 1859), 488.

18. Michler, *Darwinismus und Literatur*, 108–164; Peter Sprengel, *Darwin in der Poesie: Spuren der Evolutionslehre in der deutschsprachigen Literatur des 19. und 20. Jahrhunderts* (Würzburg, Germany: Königshausen und Neumann, 1998), 55–59.

19. Leopold von Sacher-Masoch, "Der Wanderer. Prolog," *Das Vermächtniß Kains. Novellen. Erster Theil: Die Liebe*, 2 vols. (Bern: Frobeen, 1877), 12–13.

20. Ibid., 15. The German original reads: "Wer war nicht in dem Wahne befangen, die Befriedigung dieser übermenschlichen Sehnsucht, die ihn erfüllt, der Besitz des geliebten Weibes müsse ihm vollkommenes Genügen, namenlose Seligkeit bringen, und wer hat nicht zuletzt trübselig über seine eingebildeten Freuden gelacht? Es ist eine beschämende Erkenntniß für uns, daß die Natur diese Sehnsucht in uns gelegt, nur um uns zu ihrem blinden, willigen Werkzeug zu machen, denn was fragt sie um uns? Sie will unser Geschlecht fortpflanzen!" All translations by the author.

21. Ibid., 16–17. The first volume of *Die Liebe* contains the prologue "Der Wanderer" followed by the first three novellas of the novella cycle under the section title "Die Liebe. First Volume." The pagination between the prologue and the novellas is not continuous, presumably because "Der Wanderer" represents the prologue for the six novella cycles that Sacher-Masoch envisaged, not only for the first novella two-volume cycle *Die Liebe*.

22. For a detailed analysis of the reinterpretation of Sacher-Masoch's oeuvre, see Birgit Lang, "The Shifting Case of Masochism: Leopold von Sacher-Masoch's *Venus in Furs*," in *Making the Case: The Case Study Genre in Sexology, Psychoanalysis and Literature*, by Birgit Lang, Joy Damousi, and Alison Lewis (Manchester, UK: Manchester University Press, forthcoming).

23. Leopold von Sacher-Masoch, *Die Messalinen Wiens: Geschichten aus der guten Gesellschaft* (Leipzig: Ernst Julius Günther, 1873), 139.

24. Sacher-Masoch, *Die Liebe*, 1:57.

25. Ibid., 2:71, 107.

26. Ibid., 2:119.

27. Ibid., 1:8.

28. Gliboff, *Bronn*, 101, 104. As distinct from the term "struggle for life," Sacher-Masoch did not comment overtly on matters of adaptation in his work. Nonetheless, both chance and elements of chance play a crucial role in *Love*. For instance, the frame tale of the six novellas of *Love* sees the narrator travel to the country of his youth, where chance defines the encounters with those human subjects whose stories the reader will be told. In the first novella, *Don Juan von Kolomea*, Leopold is stopped by the Polish peasant guard and is forced to spend the night in a public house where he meets the main character of the first novella. Similarly, at the beginning of the second novella, the narrator is almost lost in a snowstorm, only to meet a well-known local character who is nicknamed "Capitulant," the German term for voluntary re-enlistees in the army—and the main character of this novella (Sacher-Masoch, *Die Liebe*, 1:175). The fact that chance also constitutes a key element in the novella genre more broadly only underlines Sacher-Masoch's approach.

29. Exner, *Leopold von Sacher-Masoch*, 85.

30. Weikart, *From Darwin to Hitler*, 169.

31. Jenny Marr, "Darwinismus und Culturhistorik," *Auf der Höhe: Internationale Revue* 2, no. 8 (1883): 463. The journal was edited by Leopold von Sacher-Masoch. The German original reads: "Wie kann man die 'Culturgeschichte' von der 'Geschichte der Künste und Wissenschaften trennen,' ohne sich der Gefahr auszusetzen, eine mangelhafte, flache und oberflächliche Auffassung von der historischen Entwicklung der Menschheit zu geben?"

32. Sacher-Masoch to Carl Cotta, March 7, 1870, Deutsches Literaturarchiv Marbach.

33. Sacher-Masoch, *Die Liebe*, 2:426.

34. Ibid., 2:414.

35. Ibid., 2:415.

36. Ibid., 2:433.

37. Ibid., 2:438.

38. "Goethe: Translations," in *Theories of Translation: An Anthology of Essays from Dryden to Derrida*, ed. Rainer Schulte and John Biguenet (Chicago: University of Chicago Press, 1992), 60.

39. Ibid., 63.

40. Sacher-Masoch, *Die Liebe*, 2:473.

41. Ibid., 2:474.

42. Ibid., 2:419.

43. Sacher-Masoch, "Der Wanderer," 32.

44. Ibid.

45. Klaus Müller, *Aber in meinem Herzen sprach eine Stimme so laut: Homosexuelle Autobiographien und medizinische Pathographien im neunzehnten Jahrhundert* (Berlin: Rosa Winkel, 1991).

46. Sacher-Masoch, "Der Wanderer," 32.

47. Carla Nappi, "The Global and Beyond: Adventures in the Local Historiographies of Science," *Isis* 104, no. 1 (2013): 109.

3

Representing the "Third Sex"

*Cultural Translations of the Sexological Encounter
in Early Twentieth-Century Germany*

KATIE SUTTON

S exual science and sex reform movements each attracted considerable attention in early twentieth-century Germany. The year 1919 saw the world's first establishment of an Institute for Sexual Science under the leadership of doctor and homosexual rights campaigner Magnus Hirschfeld in Berlin, while the end of the war ushered in a range of reform activities, with feminists, socialists, and doctors campaigning on issues ranging from abortion reform to maternal protection and the decriminalization of homosexuality.[1] The findings of sexual science and the efforts of reformers resonated with particular force among the increasingly vocal metropolitan sexual publics that Hirschfeld in 1904 had collectively designated "Berlin's third sex."[2] Partly in response to Germany's draconian Paragraph 175 that criminalized male homosexual acts, and facilitated by the liberalization of the public sphere in the Weimar era, networks of self-identified "homosexuals" and, by the mid-1920s, "transvestites" were increasingly organizing into official associations, producing periodicals and campaigning in the interests of sex-gender minorities.[3]

This chapter focuses on the cultural mediation, or "translation," of encounters between the sexological profession and the individuals collectively and variously designated by that profession as "sexual intermediaries," "inverts," or members of a "third sex" in fin de siècle and interwar Germany. Specifically, it investigates how sexological classifications, medical case histories, and clinical encounters were negotiated in different textual and filmic genres, and what was at stake in these representations for nonscientific audiences. This line of inquiry is partly prompted by recent "rereadings" of Michel Foucault's account of the historical production of sexuality in ways that complicate earlier "top-down" interpretations of disciplinary discourses and the doctor-patient relationship. Critics such as Scott Spector, Edward R. Dickinson, and Richard F. Wetzell, among others, acknowledge the "more complex and contradictory" aspects of Foucault's model, and in particular, his emphasis on "sexual subjects and emancipation."[4] The chapter extends these debates, turning to issues of translation to map some of the textual and disciplinary intersections between the rapidly professionalizing discipline of modern sexology and the products of early twentieth-century German culture. A translation perspective, which focuses on what Doris Bachmann-Medick refers to as "contact zones," highlights the processes of negotiation, appropriation, and resistance involved in transferring knowledge across disciplines and genres. Unlike the "smoother" category of interdisciplinarity, translation attends explicitly to "the differences, tensions and antagonisms between disciplines or schools of thought."[5] In what follows, I argue that a "translation" focus helps to illuminate the shifts in authorship and audience that take place in the transition from sexological texts and case studies produced for a medical-forensic readership, to cultural representations produced by or for individuals who claimed "third sex" identifications, whether as "homosexuals," "inverts" or "transvestites." At the same time, it foregrounds the agency of the "translator"—a role assumed in the following examples by the author, filmmaker, or magazine column writer.

I first explore representations of sexual science in two novels about female homosexuality from the first decades of the twentieth century: Aimée Duc's *Sind es Frauen? Roman über das dritte Geschlecht* (Are they women? Novel about the third sex, 1901), and Anna Elisabet Weirauch's *Der Skorpion* (The scorpion, 1919, 1921, 1931). I then investigate the 1919 film *Anders als die Andern* (*Different from the Others*, directed by Richard Oswald), which confronts the problem of male homosexual blackmail as a result of Paragraph 175. Finally, I examine magazine columns produced for a self-identified "transvestite" readership during the Weimar Republic era. Each example reflects a different aspect of the conceptual shift from older sexological theories of inversion, which had viewed same-sex desire and cross-gendered characteristics as two aspects of a single condition, to newer categories of homosexuality and transvestism—although they also demonstrate that, as scholars have shown, this was by no means a clean transition, particularly in relation to female inversion.[6] Together, they illustrate how cultural representations of "third sex" individuals from this period do not simply posit sexual science as a pathologizing, hierarchical force, although neither are they uncritical of the theories and practices of sexologists. Rather, these cultural translations of sexological knowledge, whether literary, cinematic, or journalistic, employ science as a resource in actively redefining categories of sexual citizenship and in highlighting the liberating potential of the sexologist and his discipline.

Ambivalent Encounters: Resisting Pathologies in Novels of Female Homosexuality

Historians of sexuality have demonstrated the mutually constitutive relationship between sexology and its "subjects" in late nineteenth- and early twentieth-century sexual modernity—what Harry Oosterhuis describes as a reliance on the "voices of perverts" in the sexological construction of new classificatory regimes of the "normal" and the "pathological."[7] Scholars have also highlighted the pivotal role played by literary texts and authors prior to the establishment of a coherent patient base for sexual science. In his pioneering catalog of sexual pathologies, *Psychopathia Sexualis* (first edition 1886), for example, psychiatrist Richard von Krafft-Ebing used the writings of Leopold von Sacher-Masoch as a case study for naming and illustrating the newly coined "perversion" of masochism. Such "translations" from literary into medico-forensic discourse occurred in both directions, with literature also examining sexological themes.[8]

Fictional negotiations of medico-forensic categories of "inversion" and "homosexuality" began to appear in German from the 1870s, following the publication of lawyer Karl Heinrich Ulrichs's groundbreaking theoretical studies on "Urnings." As Klaus Müller has shown, this early male "invert" literature represented a distinct shift from the autobiographical mode of third-sex self-representation dominant in the early decades of the nineteenth century, and tended to prioritize emancipatory over aesthetic aspirations. In contrast, the early twentieth century saw an increase in "high culture" literary negotiations of inversion and homosexuality, including Robert Musil's *Die Verwirrungen des Zöglings Törleß* (*The Confusions of Young Törless*, 1906), Thomas Mann's *Tod in Venedig* (*Death in Venice*, 1912), and the homoerotic aesthetic poetry of Stefan George.[9]

The fin de siècle also saw some of the first literary negotiations of female sex-gender inversion. Among these was the short 1901 novel *Sind es Frauen?* by Duc, a pseudonym of author Minna Wettstein-Adelt.[10] This novel has lately enjoyed somewhat of a scholarly renaissance; one recent critic describes it as an example of "explicitly lesbian popular fiction, written for a niche market."[11] In *Sind es Frauen?*, the translation of sexological theories of female inversion into literary form highlights various shifts of motive and readership, as scientific discussions are adapted to suit the needs, self-image, and political goals of its self-identified "third sex" characters.

Sind es Frauen? falls broadly into the realm of "trivial" literature on the basis of its central romantic plot, although it supplements this narrative with a detailed treatment of political themes relating to the situation of the "third" as well as the "second" sex, including extensive dialogue on female emancipation.[12] The ensemble cast consists of a pan-European and multi-lingual group of emancipated and largely same-sex-attracted female university students, who at the beginning of the novel are living and studying in Geneva, at a time when women had only restricted access to the German universities. They explicitly refer to themselves as members of a "third sex," and even at one point as "belonging to the ranks of the "Krafft-Ebing types" (SeF: 54), suggesting a presumption by Wettstein-Adelt that her readers would be familiar with that psychiatrist's best-selling textbook, despite its target audience of medical and legal professionals. The characters also physically embody a number of the characteristics ascribed to the "masculinized" female invert at this period by sexologists such as Krafft-Ebing (who had distinguished between two major categories, the "masculine women," whose condition was defined as congenital and possibly degenerate, and feminine "pseudohomosexuals," whose condition was acquired), and Havelock Ellis, who in 1897 had contrasted the "masculine" female invert's "brusque, energetic movements" and "masculine straightforwardness" with those "feminine" women whose homosexuality "is only slightly marked."[13] Likewise, Wettstein-Adelt's characters display a range of "masculine" features in their dress and habits, with main protagonist Minotschka Fernandoff a key example: sporting an "energetic" gait, she wears stiff white collars with broad cuffs and gentlemen's ties and straw hats, and she carries what one scholar describes as a decidedly phallic silver cane (SeF: 5–6).[14]

Yet *Sind es Frauen?* also confounds sexological attempts to distinguish between the "congenital," masculine female invert and the more feminine, "pseudohomosexual" woman—scholars note that the novel's ostensibly "masculine" characters also display a range of traditionally "feminine" traits and aesthetic elements.[15] Fernandoff, for example, is described as both "strong and well-built" and possessing a "curvaceous" body; her combination of "boyishness" and "youthfulness" lend a "unique character" to her "unconscious feminine coquettishness" (SeF: 5). Wettstein-Adelt's refusal to allow her characters to straightforwardly embody sexological types can be interpreted as one of the ways in which she actively occupied the role of "translator," reworking sexological knowledge in order to better reflect "third sex" priorities and subjectivities.

In a theoretically innovative analysis of this novel, Claudia Breger interprets the resulting depiction of female inversion in terms of "incoherence" and "feminine masculinity." With parallels to Laura Doan's arguments concerning the "topsy-turvydom" of sex-gender identity categories in early twentieth-century Britain, Breger argues that rather than trying to locate "homosexual" or "transgender" identifications in texts of this period, "we need to look more closely at the ways in which incoherent identifications are staged and used in different texts and contexts for a variety of political agendas."[16] She concludes that Wettstein-Adelt's novel offers "a more radical supplement" to Krafft-Ebing's hegemonic theorizing of female inversion.[17] It does so in part, I suggest, by "translating" sexological theory in a way that is broadly affirmative, but also selective.

The critical impetus of this translation process is most explicit at those points in the narrative where the characters actively resist pathologizing labels such as "diseased," while at the same time—somewhat paradoxically—critiquing the perceived scientific neglect of the "third sex." Fernandoff, for example, challenges her medical friends to write a dissertation scientifically proving the "existence of a third sex," while in the same conversation dismissing as "derogatory" or "dishonorable" (*unwürdig*) the "clauses . . . according to which we are classified by psychiatrists" (SeF: 17). In the heated discussions that make up much of this novel, these characters insist on the value of their own particular brand of humanity and critique the political threat that can accompany scientific categorizations. Thus Fernandoff's lover, the Polish countess Marta Kinzey, declares,

> We do not stand up for ourselves enough, we don't assert our own theses, we don't allow ourselves to be freely recognized as human beings who are neither woman nor man. At all times we must be our own advocates, we must stand our ground again and again, and not let ourselves be forced back into the position of diseased . . . , rather, we must show that we are representatives of a hybrid form, of a species of human being that has a right to acknowledgement. . . . (SeF: 20)[18]

This passage, with its overtones of Hirschfeld's theory of "sexual intermediaries," creatively appropriates medical ideas around sexual and gendered "hybridity" (*Mischung*).[19] Kinzey's critical perspective is reinforced later in the same conversation, when Russian doctor Tatjana Kassberg blames the majority of women's nervous illnesses on the "false" and "brutal" sex lives forced on them within marriage, describing such aberrations as "diseased" (SeF: 23, 25). Wettstein-Adelt thus redirects the pathologizing labels of psychiatry away from the third sex and toward the many "average" women caught in unhappy relationships.

Yet there is more to this literary translation of sexological discourses than a rejection of pathologizing labels. By drawing attention to notions of social and legal "recognition" or "acknowledgement" (*Berücksichtigung*), Countess Kinzey's outburst also suggests an emerging discourse of identity politics quite specific to the German-speaking world at this period. Four years earlier, in 1897, Hirschfeld had cofounded the Wissenschaftlich-humanitäres Komitee (Scientific Humanitarian Committee) as an instrument through which to organize politically against the criminalization of male homosexuality, followed in 1899 by the establishment of the scientific journal *Jahrbuch für sexuelle Zwischenstufen* (Yearbook of sexual intermediaries), dedicated to the study of inversion and related themes. As Spector observes, "the emergence of homosexual self-consciousness and political activism was a largely German-language affair."[20] Although female inversion and homosexuality were not criminalized under the German criminal code, the speeches of Wettstein-Adelt's characters, as Marti Lybeck observes, "closely resembled the campaign rhetoric of the homosexual rights movement of the time," not least in their characterizations of inverted individuals as "highly cultured" and intelligent.[21] *Sind es Frauen?* points to the politically empowering potential of sexological knowledge by showing characters who rely on new forms of scientific categorization in order to define themselves as members of a "third sex," and who deliberately distinguish themselves from "average" individuals in order to articulate a political agenda based on notions of recognition and rights.

At the same time, both the "original" scientific text and its cultural "translation" reflect the multiple and sometimes conflicting registers between which each author was moving. Krafft-Ebing did not, as Breger and Oosterhuis emphasize, set out to pathologize or demonize the third sex; on the contrary, he was considered by contemporaries to be a liberal who approached inversion from a medical rather than a moral standpoint. Nonetheless, his study is overlaid by discourses that appear to contradict this progressive agenda, such as his consideration of degeneration as a factor in inversion, which he only fully rejected toward the end of his career. This connection between inversion and degeneration is likewise present in *Sind es Frauen?* in details such as Fernandoff's weak foot, even though it is also counteracted, as Breger shows, by an emphasis on her keen cycling habit.[22] Translation theorist Dilek Dizdar writes that "the possibility of perversion, with the implication that the promise might not be kept, is a condition of translation," clarifying that this "promise" refers to the translator's dual responsibility "both to the text she/he reads and to the reader who asks for his/her mediation."[23] In her role as translator, Wettstein-Adelt on the one hand draws on the kind of contradictory yet progressive scientific theories of female inversion with which emancipated, highly educated women such as her characters would have been familiar, using dialogue to provide additional explanation as required: "'But with regard to Krafft-Ebing! Isn't he the one who stands up for the perverse people?' . . . 'Certainly, it is he, the writer of the work "Psychopathia sexualis,"'" upon which most lay readers pounce in

greed and lust" (SeF: 54).[24] At the same time, her translation "perverts" those
same sexological texts in order to better speak to particular political invest-
ments: the emancipation demands of the contemporary feminist movement,
and an emerging minority rights discourse associated with the "third sex."

In contrast to the dialogue-heavy *Sind es Frauen?*, Anna Elisabet
Weirauch's interwar novel *Der Skorpion*, published in three volumes between 1919 and 1931, offers a more embodied translation of sexology into
culture. Weirauch's melodramatic novel enjoyed considerable popularity
among Weimar-era female homosexuals, as reflected in its conspicuous
coverage in subcultural magazines such as *Die Freundin*.[25] In bildungsro-
man fashion, it traces the emotional, sexual, and spiritual development of its
main protagonist Mette, including her troubled childhood, her adventures in
the metropolitan homosexual subculture, and her eventual decision to settle
down in the countryside. Encounters with sexual science are depicted in two
scenes in particular: Mette's unwilling treatment by a doctor, and a scene in
which Mette discovers and reads a collection of sexological texts.

The first of these scenes reveals a clear skepticism concerning the medical profession's treatment of homosexuality. A teenage Mette, whom her
family suspects of being led astray by her older governess, Olga, and who
consequently treat her as "diseased" and "infectious," is forced to meet with
a psychiatrist. This male representative of medical science, simply labeled
"the Professor," has been instructed to inspect her for "physical abnormali-
ties" (S1: 139). Although not identified as a sexologist, the questions that the
"Professor" poses concerning Mette's smoking and stealing habits reveal his
familiarity with contemporary theories of female inversion linking same-
sex desires to criminal tendencies and "masculine" behaviors. Ellis, for example, had suggested that "a considerable proportion of . . . cases in which
inversion has led to crimes of violence, or otherwise acquired medico-legal
importance, has been among women."[26] The novel's critique of such pathologizing approaches is implicit as the "Professor" attempts to intervene in
Mette's budding relationship with Olga and redirect her toward a "normal"
life path. It is again apparent later in the narrative, when Mette sarcastically
informs her cousin that there is no "danger of infection" (*Ansteckungsgefahr*)
with the particular kind of "disease" (*Krankheit*) from which she suffers (S1:
142–143).

This ambivalence toward sexological categorizations also characterizes
Mette's discovery of a series of medical works in her father's office. Mette
is repulsed by the "strange and uncanny stories" of murder, orgies, cross-
dressing, and "unnatural sexual acts" that she finds here, and refuses to consciously identify with them: "She became physically ill just from touching
the books" (S1: 207).[27] Weirauch's novel thus not only criticizes sexological
attempts to treat inversion—through the scene with the Professor—it also

challenges science's ability to define "third sex" individuals in ways that align with their own self-image. While Mette's discovery of these texts sparks a recognition of her own same-sex desires, and a curiosity about urban sexual subcultures that she subsequently pursues, the physical repulsion that accompanies this discovery "perverts" the translation of sexology into literature, opening up a critical space for the depiction of a range of third sex subjectivities.

These two texts demonstrate, then, how literary representations of female inversion translated sexological theories for third sex audiences in ways that were both explicit (citing prominent sexologists, depicting physical encounters between "inverts" and medical practitioners) and implicit (assigning to "third sex" characters a range of gendered characteristics, same-sex desires, and features such as "nervous weakness"). At the same time, their selective and critical approach toward sexological knowledge highlights the agency of the translator-author. Wettstein-Adelt and Weirauch, as Doan writes of later British writers such as Radclyffe Hall, show themselves to be "supremely capable of negotiating sexological material intelligently, rejecting the irrelevant and embracing what seemed germane."[28] Their translations of science into literature are characterized by important shifts in motive and audience—even though, as Breger cautions, it would be incorrect to argue for any categorical difference between these fields that guarantees the subversive status of literature. On the contrary, it is their shared reliance on narrative form—specifically, the genre of the medical case study—that enables the construction of knowledge about inversion within each of these discursive registers, as well as in the intertextual dialogue between them: "if Krafft-Ebing's book presents a theoretical account supplemented by unruly case stories, Duc's novel presents a particular fictional case story supplemented by intradiegetic theory."[29]

In sexological texts, individual "inverts" feature as the subjects of case studies, their life stories selected and framed by the sexologist. Sexologists "translated" these patient histories for their medico-forensic audience via theoretical contextualization, with a view to furthering disciplinary knowledge. Yet studies have shown that these patient histories frequently exceeded sexologists' attempts to contain them within clear taxonomical boundaries. As a result, sexological texts were actively shaped not just by sexologists themselves, but also by a range of nonmedical and nonprofessional informants and readers, including many who identified as "inverts" or "third sex."[30] In contrast, literary texts such as Wettstein-Adelt's and Weirauch's foreground the particular needs of a nonmedical readership of self-identified "inverts," translating sexological knowledges accordingly. Although the resulting works encompass sometimes ambivalent, even paradoxical, approaches to questions of gender, sexuality, degeneration, and the role of sexologists, I suggest that these contradictions are best interpreted not as examples of flawed rhetoric, but as symptomatic of categories and identities in flux. An "invert" or "third sex" identity at this historical moment meant different things to different people, whether in regard to gendered appearances, sexual behaviors, or political views, and had not (yet) been overtaken by any straightforward categories of the "homosexual" or "transvestite." Despite such contradictions, scientific categorizations play a central role in these early twentieth-century literary texts. By drawing on sexological assessments of a "third" or "intermediary" sex, these authors provided their characters—and readers—with a language through which to begin articulating a discourse of sexual citizenship.

Blurring Fact and Fiction: The Sexologist as Himself in *Anders als die Andern*

A more self-reflexive example of the translation of sexology into culture, and the role of the sexologist in particular, can be found in the 1919 silent film *Anders als die Andern*, which appeared in the same year as the first volume of Weirauch's trilogy. Written and directed by up-and-coming filmmaker Richard Oswald, this "social hygiene" film was produced in close cooperation with Hirschfeld, who appears in a number of scenes as himself, and who acted as co-writer and "scientific advisor." In contrast to the novels examined earlier, with their orientation toward "third sex" readers, *Anders als die Andern* can be characterized as an educational narrative film (*Aufklärungsfilm*) intended for a mainstream audience, featuring a star-studded cast that included expressionist heartthrob Conrad Veidt and actress and cabaret dancer Anita Berber. As with previous *Aufklärungsfilme* on topics such as syphilis, abortion, and alcoholism, the filmmakers hoped to appeal to a broad cross-section of the German population; in this case, they sought to change public opinion on Paragraph 175, which left many homosexual men vulnerable to extortion. The final product was a box office hit until it was banned shortly after its release, with screenings permitted only for medical and scientific audiences, and was instrumental in prompting the reintroduction of film censorship shortly after the founding of the Weimar Republic.[31]

Anders als die Andern tells the tale of talented homosexual violinist Paul Körner (Conrad Veidt), who begins an erotic relationship with one of his male students, Kurt Sivers (Fritz Schulz). Unbeknownst to the pair, they have been recognized as a homosexual couple by blackmailer Franz Bollek (Reinhold Schünzel), who extorts money from Körner in exchange for not denouncing him to the authorities. An unhappy ending sees both Körner and his blackmailer brought before court and sentenced, leading firstly to Körner's social and career demise, followed soon afterward by his death by suicide. A distraught Kurt, who has been estranged from Körner, vows to follow him to his death but is convinced by Hirschfeld to instead take up the fight for justice and legal reform.

In at least four separate scenes (the film exists only as reconstructed fragments), sexological theories are self-referentially translated into the fictional text via the persona of Hirschfeld. In the first, Hirschfeld appears as the medical expert to whom Körner sends his parents so that they might be enlightened about his homosexual disposition; in the second, a flashback, we see Körner as a younger man visiting a sympathetic Hirschfeld in order to seek clarification about his own apparently abnormal desires. In the third and most extensive appearance, Körner attends a lecture by Hirschfeld on his theory of intermediary sexual forms (*sexuelle Zwischenstufen*), where he is accompanied by a female admirer—Kurt's sister, Else Sivers (Anita Berber), whom he wishes to gently inform about his condition. Reconstructed intertitles and still images indicate that Hirschfeld later appears at Körner's trial as an expert witness for the defense. Finally, Hirschfeld appears at Körner's funeral, where he encourages Kurt to use science to fight against prejudice, echoing the motto of Hirschfeld's own recently established institute, Justice through Science (Durch Wissenschaft zur Gerechtigkeit).[32]

These translations of sexology into the framework of a narrative film deliberately blur the boundaries of genre, fact, and fiction to political effect. In each of these scenes, Hirschfeld uses his screen time to emphasize his view— familiar to contemporaries from the *Jahrbuch für sexuelle Zwischenstufen* or his 1914 study *Die Homosexualität des Mannes und des Weibes* (The homosexuality of man and woman) as well as his more popular 1901 pamphlet "Was soll das Volk vom dritten Geschlecht wissen?" (What should the people know about the third sex?)—that homosexuality is a natural and even "noble" variation of human sexuality, and that the problems surrounding it lie in society's prejudices rather than the homosexual himself.[33] He thus advises Körner's parents that homosexuality is

> neither a vice nor a crime, not even a disease, but rather a variant, one of those borderline cases that are so common in nature. Your son does not suffer from his condition, but rather from the false appraisal of that condition; it is [from] the legal and social condemnation of his sensibility.[34]

Although this nonpathologizing statement is somewhat tempered by the opening credits, which link homosexuality to "congenital weakness" (*erblicher Belastung*) and a "flawed predisposition" (*fehlerhafter Veranlagung*), each of these statements aligns with Hirschfeld's theory of homosexuality as an inborn condition deserving of legal recognition.[35]

Through the identificatory powers of narrative, viewers are encouraged to sympathize with Körner's plight and become outraged at his mistreatment by society and the legal system. Fiction, as Jason Tougaw argues, is easier to identify with than the medical case history; at the same time, its very realism enables readers to appropriate stories sympathetically.[36] Yet *Anders als die Andern* also reaches beyond the boundaries of fiction through these references to Hirschfeld's real-life scientific authority. By appearing as himself, Hirschfeld was following in the footsteps of other prominent figures such as Ernst Haeckel and Margaret Sanger, who had featured as herself in the 1917 film *Birth Control*.[37] At the same time, he was drawing on his own prominence in the field of sex reform, including as an active participant in the establishment of marriage counseling centers, and as a popular public lecturer on topics such as contraceptive techniques. These activities formed part of a heightened public discourse around questions of sex and sexual "anomalies" in the interwar period, reinforced in the pages of high-circulation national newspapers such as the *Berliner Illustrirte Zeitung*, which took voyeuristic delight in reports of female impersonators or cross-dressing army colonels and showed a sustained interest in the latest developments in fields such as hormone research.

Through this self-referential emphasis on his own medical and scientific expertise, Hirschfeld in a sense makes *himself* into a case, in the interests of furthering his political agenda.[38] He does not, however, go so far as to "out" himself as homosexual at any point in the narrative—while Hirschfeld's "abnormal" sexuality was, together with his Jewishness, frequently alluded to in right-wing caricatures in publications such as *Der Stürmer*, and although his homosexual tendencies were known to many of his colleagues and acquaintances, and can also be assumed on the basis of his long and active history of homosexual rights campaigning, it did not form part of his official public profile.[39] Instead, Hirschfeld focuses in this film, as in his writings more broadly, on how the authoritative discourses of science might be used to further the cause of social justice for sexual minorities. Accordingly— in a rhetorical move that parallels the references to Krafft-Ebing in *Sind es Frauen?*—Hirschfeld uses his fictionalized lecture to draw attention to that sexological pioneer, showing to his audience "the image of one of the first German campaigners against this grave miscarriage of justice, Professor of Psychiatry Richard Freiherr von Krafft-Ebing."[40]

The genre of the medical case study facilitates this translation of Hirschfeld's political agenda into the film's narrative structure on several levels. First, during his lecture Hirschfeld draws on real patient histories and photographs from his clinical practice and publications. These include images of a "masculine woman as a house painter," "virile women" in suits and men's hats, and two photographs of a "man with feminine feelings in men's and women's clothing." These are accompanied by the following explanation (on intertitles):

> Between all opposites there are transitions, and so, too, between the sexes. Thus apart from man and woman there are also men with the physical and psychological characteristics of a woman, and women with all kinds of masculine characteristics.[41]

Hirschfeld's photographic material, well suited to the visually oriented genre of silent film, underlines his medical authority while also overlaying the fictional suffering of the film's characters with the power of authentic human experience. This productive blurring of fact and fiction gains further impetus when we learn of Hirschfeld's court appearance in defense of Körner, an inclusion that references Hirschfeld's participation as an expert witness in numerous real-life legal cases featuring homosexual or transvestite defendants.[42]

The film does not simply cite medical cases, however; it also takes on some of the typical functions of the case study genre. The case, as Lauren Berlant observes, "organizes singularities into exemplary, intelligible patterns."[43] The story of Körner's tragic life is not told for its own sake but gains power from its representative function: this individual tale of blackmail and persecution comes to stand for the miserable plight of "the" homosexual in early twentieth-century Germany. This is highlighted at several points in the narrative: the first occurs when Körner reads in the morning paper about a number of allegedly unexplained suicides, which he soon realizes are a result of homosexual persecution—a scene that also foreshadows the nature of his own tragic death. The second example consists of two separate scenes featuring a parade of historical figures including Pyotr Ilyich Tchaikovsky, Leonardo da Vinci, Oscar Wilde, Friedrich II of Prussia, and Ludwig II of Bavaria, the Sword of Damocles engraved with the sign of Paragraph 175 hanging over their heads. These scenes not only align Körner's fate with that of cultural elites throughout European history now designated by science as "homosexual," but also emphasize the weight of historical persecution of homosexual "others." Finally, Körner's representative role—now as victim—is highlighted in the closing titles, when Hirschfeld urges Kurt not to follow Körner to the grave but instead to fight for "rights and honor" on behalf of "the many thousands who came before us, who walk with us, and who will come after us."[44] The case study genre thus serves in *Anders als die Andern* as a vehicle for translating sexology's message into the cultural realm.

Together with the self-referential inclusion of real medical case histories from Hirschfeld's practice, Körner's story gives a human face to the problems facing Germany's homosexuals at the beginning of the Weimar era. Unlike the novels examined earlier, this example of sexology's translation into culture focuses almost entirely on the emancipatory potential of sexual science. Even as it employs a contemporary scientific discourse on homosexuality that continues to be overlaid with notions of hereditary weakness, it does so with the concerted agenda of highlighting the interventionary power of the sexologist and of science.

The Agency of the Translator:
Sexology in 1920s Transvestite Magazines

The third and final example examined here centers on short fiction published in the new transvestite magazine columns of the Weimar era. Like novels of female "inversion" or films about "homosexual" blackmail, the existence of these columns was a product of the dialogue between sexual science and culture, and in particular, of the increasing sexological distinction, particularly from the 1910s, between categories of the "invert," the "homosexual," and the "transvestite." Following the publication of works such as Hirschfeld's *Die Transvestiten* (Transvestites) in 1910 or Ellis's studies of "sexo-aesthetic inversion" and "Eonism" from 1913 onward,[45] networks of individuals were beginning to adopt the label "transvestite" and use it as a basis of community organization and publishing activities, particularly in Berlin. By the mid-1920s, columns with titles such as "Der Transvestit" (The transvestite) and "Die Welt der Transvestiten" (Transvestite's world) had begun to appear in publications otherwise targeting a female homosexual audience, alongside at least one exclusively transvestite magazine, *Das 3. Geschlecht* (The third sex).[46] Like the texts examined earlier, these columns—which primarily addressed male-to-female transvestites—draw explicitly on sexological findings to articulate an identity politics agenda grounded in science.

Sexology features in these columns in a number of guises. Regular feature articles provided explanations of, and critical commentary on, the latest medical research relating to sex-gender "intermediaries," pitched toward interested and informed lay readers.[47] Sexological theories and encounters were also thematized in letters to the editor and the autobiographical confessional literature that dominated these columns: contributors reported, for example, on their experiences—frequently positive—of seeking medical advice about their cross-gendered identifications, or of voluntarily participating in medical research. Such reports suggest a level of patient agency that supports Oosterhuis's account of the sexological encounter as both eye-opening and comforting, offering individuals a chance to speak about hidden desires and reflect upon social constraints.[48] Short fiction contributions to these columns likewise tended to highlight sexology's emancipatory potential, suggesting the potential of medical interventions to foster a sense of transvestite well-being in the face of society's prejudices. One story by Hale Fürstenberg, published in 1930, takes the form of a fictionalized letter signed with the masculine name "Rudi." The narrator, a male-to-female transvestite in a long-term relationship with a man, recalls the years of mockery and misunderstanding he endured at the hands of his family and provincial hometown, until a sympathetic friend encouraged him to move to the city and visit a doctor about his condition. Echoing the scenes in *Anders als die Andern* in which Hirschfeld contacts Körner's family, Rudi's doctor writes to and meets with his patient's parents in order to explain Rudi's condition from a scientific perspective. This intervention forms a turning point in familial relations, as the parents begin to acknowledge how happy Rudi is with his boyfriend, and accept "his" wish to live as a woman. As a result, Rudi reports that he now feels himself to be a "truly reborn human being" (*wahrhaft neugeborener Mensch*).[49]

In other short stories, the transvestite media itself features in self-reflexive fashion as a stand-in for sexological expertise, with protagonists finding reassurance in such publications that they are neither perverse nor alone in their cross-gendered identifications. A tale by female-to-male contributor Hansi—a regular participant in subcultural debates around female masculinity at this period—tells of a male-to-female transvestite who goes by the name of Mieze. In this tale, published just weeks before the National Socialist seizure of power caused a rapid shutdown of third sex publishing avenues, we learn that Mieze had always had the urge, but never the opportunity, to wear women's clothing. As a result of this repressed desire, she had become mentally ill and even contemplated suicide. One day while she was trying on a hat in a store, however, a kindly stranger encouraged Mieze to buy the said hat, accompanying her recommendation with the understanding words: "Surely you are a transvestite" (*Sie sind doch sicher Transvestit*). The stranger gives Mieze, who had never previously heard this term, a copy of *Die Freundin* (Girlfriend)—the same publication in which the story was published. Reading that magazine's transvestite column proves a revelation, as Mieze discovers that she has thousands of transvestite "sisters": her fate, she now realizes, need not be death or madness.[50]

Such utopian narratives demonstrate the power of fiction to supply readers with strategies for negotiating non-normative sex-gender identifications. Like the "third sex" texts discussed earlier, these stories draw attention to the agency of the translator-authors, who adapted sexological findings and encounters in order to address the specific needs and desires of an emerging transvestite public.

Conclusion

So what exactly does the concept of "translation" add to our understanding of the uptake of sexological knowledges by minority sexual publics in the Weimar era, and how might a focus on this term open up productive new approaches to the history of sexuality?[51] This chapter has shown that the cultural translations of sexology examined reflect dynamic processes of transformation and negotiation oriented toward the political and identificatory priorities of the "third sex." Whereas in the texts of sexual science the voice of the sexologist provided the dominant narrative of "inverted" subjectivities, organizing patient case histories into neat taxonomies (even though that categorical neatness was often exceeded by the content of the case histories themselves), these fictional texts—whether novels of female "inversion," a film about male "homosexuality," or short stories describing "transvestite" experience—resituate sexological discourse as narrative element and cultural reference point. Although they draw on the authority of sexual science where this offers a defense of the homosexual or transvestite condition, they also challenge aspects of disciplinary knowledge that threaten to pathologize or undermine third sex subjectivity. Most importantly, these cultural translations draw on sexology as a resource in articulating new forms of sexual citizenship, appealing to the rationality and "enlightened" categories of science to promote social and political change.

This chapter thus highlights how translation might be productively applied in ways that go beyond understandings of "intertextuality" or "interdisciplinarity." Among the key advantages of a translation perspective for such an analysis are that it foregrounds the agency of the translator-author, and the "perversions" of the original text that the translator-author must undertake in order to address, in suitable lay terms, the identificatory needs and political priorities of his or her audience. Reflecting on a "translational turn" in the humanities, Bachmann-Medick emphasizes that a translation perspective can shed light on "disciplinary links and overlaps," and on how these affect individuals' understanding of concepts—for as Gillian Beer argues, "when concepts enter different genres they do not remain intact."[52] The medical case history represents an example of such an "overlap" in the translation from science to culture—as the primary form of early sexological evidence, it served as a central vehicle between these very different discursive registers. As sexologists shifted from notions of "inversion" to increasingly distinct categories of the "homosexual" and the "transvestite," cultural "translations" of sexual science—its theories, practitioners, and case histories—provided a means for subcultural authors and audiences to negotiate this shift and begin formulating identity-based discourses of sexual citizenship.

NOTES

Acknowledgments: This publication was supported under the Australian Research Council's Discovery Projects funding scheme (Making the Case: The Case Study Genre in Sexology, Psychoanalysis and Literature, 2010–2014). Thanks to Heike Bauer, Birgit Lang, and the readers at Temple University Press for their comments on earlier drafts of this chapter.

1. Atina Grossmann, *Reforming Sex: The German Movement for Birth Control and Abortion Reform, 1920–1950* (Oxford: Oxford University Press, 1995); Cornelie Usborne, *The Politics of the Body in Weimar Germany: Women's Reproductive Rights and Duties* (Basingstoke, UK: Macmillan, 1992).

2. Magnus Hirschfeld, *Berlins Drittes Geschlecht* (Berlin: Rosa Winkel, 1991 [1904]).

3. See Robert Beachy, "The German Invention of Homosexuality," *Journal of Modern History* 82, no. 4 (2010): 801–838; Michael Bollé, ed., *Eldorado: Homosexuelle Frauen und Männer in Berlin 1850–1950: Geschichte, Alltag und Kultur* (Berlin: Rosa Winkel, 1984); Andreas Sternweiler and Hans Gerhard Hannesen, eds., *Goodbye to Berlin? 100 Jahre Schwulenbewegung* (Berlin: Rosa Winkel, 1997).

4. Scott Spector, "Introduction: After *The History of Sexuality*? Periodicities, Subjectivities, Ethics," in *After* The History of Sexuality: *German Genealogies with and beyond Foucault*, ed. Scott Spector, Helmut Puff, and Dagmar Herzog, Spektrum: Publications of the German Studies Association (New York: Berghahn, 2012), 6; Edward R. Dickinson and Richard F. Wetzell, "The Historiography of Sexuality in Modern Germany," *German History* 23, no. 3 (2005): 291–305.

5. *Translation Studies* 2, no. 1 (2009), particularly Doris Bachmann-Medick in "Introduction: The Translational Turn," 12. See also Susan Bassnett's foundational "The Translation Turn in Cultural Studies," in *Constructing Cultures: Essays on Literary Translation*, ed. Susan Bassnett and André Lefevere (Clevedon, UK: Multilingual Matters, 1998), 123–140.

6. George Chauncey Jr., "From Sexual Inversion to Homosexuality: The Changing Medical Conceptualization of Female 'Deviance,'" in *Passion and Power: Sexuality in History*, ed. Kathy Peiss, Christina Simmons, and Robert A. Padgug (Philadelphia: Temple University Press, 1989); Michel Foucault, *The History of Sexuality*, vol. 1, *The Will to Knowledge* (London: Penguin, 1998).

7. Harry Oosterhuis, "Sexual Modernity in the Works of Richard von Krafft-Ebing and Albert Moll," *Medical History* 56, no. 2 (2012): 133–155; Harry Oosterhuis, *Stepchildren of Nature: Krafft-Ebing, Psychiatry, and the Making of Sexual Identity* (Chicago: University of Chicago Press, 2000). See also Heike Bauer, *English Literary Sexology: Translations of Inversion, 1860–1930* (Basingstoke, UK: Palgrave Macmillan, 2009); Laura Doan, *Fashioning Sapphism: The Origins of a Modern English Lesbian Culture* (New York: Columbia University Press, 2001), 126–163; Merl Storr, "Transformations: Subjects, Categories and Cures in Krafft-Ebing's Sexology," in *Sexology in Culture: Labelling Bodies and Desires*, ed. Lucy Bland and Laura Doan (Cambridge: Polity, 1998), 11–26.

8. See Anna Katharina Schaffner, *Modernism and Perversion: Sexual Deviance in Sexology and Literature, 1850–1930* (Basingstoke, UK: Palgrave Macmillan, 2012); Birgit Lang, "The Shifting Case of Masochism: Leopold von Sacher-Masoch's *Venus in Furs*," in *Making the Case: The Case Study Genre in Sexology, Psychoanalysis and Literature*, by Birgit Lang, Joy Damousi, and Alison Lewis (Manchester, UK: Manchester University Press, forthcoming).

9. Klaus Müller, *Aber in meinem Herzen sprach eine Stimme so laut: Homosexuelle Autobiographien und medizinische Pathographien im neunzehnten Jahrhundert* (Berlin: Rosa Winkel, 1991), 55–110, 269ff.

10. Aimée Duc, *Sind es Frauen? Roman über das dritte Geschlecht* (Berlin: Eckstein, 1901). Page references to this novel will be included in parentheses in the main text (SeF).

11. Catherine Bailey Gluckman, "Constructing Queer Female Identities in Late Realist German Fiction," *German Life and Letters* 65, no. 3 (2012): 318; see also 327–331.

12. Claudia Breger, "Feminine Masculinities: Scientific and Literary Representations of 'Female Inversion' at the Turn of the Twentieth Century," *Journal of the History of Sexuality* 14, no. 1–2 (2005): 84–85.

13. Richard von Krafft-Ebing, *Psychopathia Sexualis: Mit besonderer Berücksichtigung der konträren Sexualempfindung: Eine medizinisch-gerichtliche Studie für Ärzte und Juristen*, 15th ed. [first edition 1886] (Stuttgart: Enke, 1918), 281–286; Havelock Ellis, *Sexual Inversion: A Critical Edition*, ed. Ivan Crozier (Basingstoke, UK: Palgrave Macmillan, 2007 [1897]), 175, 166.

14. Biddy Martin, *Femininity Played Straight: The Significance of Being Lesbian* (New York: Routledge, 1996), 56.

15. Breger, "Feminine Masculinities," 76–107; Martin, *Femininity*, 54–70.

16. Breger, "Feminine Masculinities," 94; Laura Doan, *Disturbing Practices: History, Sexuality, and Women's Experience of Modern War* (Chicago: University of Chicago Press, 2013).

17. Breger, "Feminine Masculinities," 93.

18. "Wir treten nicht genug für uns ein, wir verfechten nicht unsere Thesen, wir geben uns nicht frei zu erkennen als Menschen, die weder Weib noch Mann sind. Wir müssen zu jeder Zeit eintreten für unser Selbst, wir müssen uns immer und immer wieder behaupten, und nicht zurückdrängen lassen als Kranke . . . , sondern wir müssen zeigen, dass wir Vertreter einer Mischung, eine Menschenspezies sind, die ein Recht auf Berücksichtigung hat. . . ."

19. Breger, "Feminine Masculinities," 93–102.

20. Spector, "Introduction," 3.

21. Marti M. Lybeck, "Gender, Sexuality, and Belonging: Female Homosexuality in Germany 1890–1933" (Ph.D. diss., University of Michigan, 2007), 74.

22. Breger, "Feminine Masculinities," 95–96; on Krafft-Ebing, degeneration, and inversion, see Oosterhuis, *Stepchildren of Nature*, 52ff., 65ff., 100ff., 158ff.

23. Dilek Dizdar, "Translational Transitions: 'Translation Proper' and Translation Studies in the Humanities," *Translation Studies* 2, no. 1 (2009): 98.

24. "'Aber apropos: Krafft-Ebing! Ist das nicht der, der für die perversen Menschen eintritt?' / 'Gewiss,' sagte Minotschka, 'das ist derselbe, der Verfasser des Werkes "Psychopathia sexualis," auf das die meisten Laien und Unberufenen sich in Gier und Lüsternheit stürzen!'"

25. On the novel's popularity, see Claudia Schoppmann, *"Der Skorpion": Frauenliebe in der Weimarer Republik* (Hamburg: Libertäre Assoziation, 1985), 10. References to this novel, all of which are to the first volume, are included in parentheses in the main text (S1).

26. Ellis, *Sexual Inversion*, 160–161n4.

27. Nancy Nenno, "*Bildung* and Desire: Anna Elisabet Weirauch's *Der Skorpion*," in *Queering the Canon*, ed. Christoph Lorey and John Plews (Columbia, SC: Camden House, 1998), 207–221.

28. Doan, *Fashioning Sapphism*, 137; Bauer, *English Literary Sexology*, 113–142.

29. Breger, "Feminine Masculinities," 86.

30. See Breger, "Feminine Masculinities," 85–86; Ivan Crozier, "Havelock Ellis, Eonism and the Patient's Discourse; or, Writing a Book about Sex," *History of Psychiatry* 11 (2000): 125–133.

31. The film had its official premiere on May 31, 1919, in Berlin and was banned on October 16, 1920. See James Steakley, "Film und Zensur in der Weimarer Republik," in *Anders als die Andern: Ein Film und seine Geschichte* (Hamburg: Männerschwarm, 2007), 31–123; Richard Dyer, "Less and More than Women and Men: Lesbian and Gay Cinema in Weimar Germany," *New German Critique*, no. 51 (1990): 5–31; Alice Kuzniar, *The Queer German Cinema* (Stanford, CA: Stanford University Press, 2000), 27–30.

32. Steakley, *Anders*, 47.

33. Magnus Hirschfeld, *Die Homosexualität des Mannes und des Weibes*, 2nd ed. (Berlin: Louis Marcus, 1920 [1914]); Magnus Hirschfeld, *Was soll das Volk vom dritten Geschlecht wissen?* [pamphlet] (Leipzig: Spohr, 1901). On Hirschfeld's scientific and political activities, see, for example, Andreas Seeck, ed., *Durch Wissenschaft zur Gerechtigkeit? Textsammlung zur kritischen Rezeption des Schaffens von Magnus Hirschfeld* (Berlin: LIT, 2003); Manfred Herzer, *Magnus Hirschfeld: Leben und Werk eines jüdischen, schwulen und sozialistischen Sexologen* (Hamburg: MännerschwarmSkript, 2001); Elke-Vera Kotowski and Julius H. Schoeps, eds., *Der Sexualreformer Magnus Hirschfeld: Ein Leben im Spannungsfeld von Wissenschaft, Politik und Gesellschaft* (Berlin: Be.bra Wissenschaft, 2004); Chandak Sengoopta, "Glandular Politics: Experimental Biology, Clinical Medicine, and Homosexual Emancipation in Fin-de-Siècle Central Europe," *Isis* 89 (1998): 445–473.

34. "weder ein Laster noch ein Verbrechen, ja nicht einmal eine Krankheit, sondern eine Variante, einer der Grenzfälle, wie sie in der Natur zahlreich sind. Ihr Sohn leidet nicht unter seinem Zustand, sondern unter dessen falscher Beurteilung; es ist die gesetzliche und gesellschaftliche Aechtung seiner Empfindungen und ihrer meist verkannten Betätigung."

35. Steakley points to the possible influence of Soviet translators on such statements, as the current intertitles were largely reconstructed from a Ukrainian version: *Anders*, 13.

36. Jason Daniel Tougaw, *Strange Cases: The Medical Case History and the British Novel* (New York: Routledge, 2006), 14.

37. Steakley, *Anders*, 36–37.

38. Johanna Gehmacher analyzes how feminist activist Käthe Schirmacher made herself into a "case" in the context of a specific political agenda in her article "A Case of 'Token Identity': Radical Activism before World War I and the Public Image of

Käthe Schirmacher (1865–1930)," in *Cases and the Dissemination of Knowledge*, ed. Joy Damousi, Birgit Lang, and Katie Sutton (New York: Routledge, 2015), 66–81.

39. See Herzer, *Magnus Hirschfeld*; Charlotte Wolff, *Magnus Hirschfeld: A Portrait of a Pioneer in Sexology* (London: Quartet, 1986).

40. "das Bild eines der ersten deutschen Vorkämpfer gegen diesen schwerwiegenden Justizirrtum, des Professors der Psychiatrie Richard Freiherr von Krafft-Ebing."

41. "Zwischen allen Gegensätzen gibt es Übergänge, so auch zwischen den Geschlechtern. Daher gibt es außer Mann und Weib auch Männer mit körperlichen und seelischen Eigenschaften einer Frau und Frauen mit allerlei männlichen Eigenschaften."

42. Hirschfeld's role as forensic expert was also thematized in Alfred Döblin's later novella (based on a real murder court case involving two women in a sexual relationship), *Die beiden Freundinnen und ihr Giftmord* (Düsseldorf: Artemis und Winkler, 2001 [1924]). At the same time, the filmmakers attempted to gloss over this potential jarring of fact and fiction: a cast list in a brochure accompanying the film refers to Hirschfeld only as "a doctor" (*ein Arzt*): Steakley, *Anders*, 10–11.

43. Lauren Berlant, "On the Case," *Critical Inquiry* 33, no. 4 (2007): 670.

44. "so gilt es hier, vielen Tausenden vor uns, mit uns und nach uns Recht und Ehre wiederzugeben."

45. Havelock Ellis, *Eonism and Other Supplementary Studies*, vol. 7, *Studies in the Psychology of Sex* (Philadelphia: Davis, 1919); Havelock Ellis, "Sexo-Aesthetic Inversion," *Alienist and Neurologist* 34 (May and August 1913): 156–167, 249–279; Magnus Hirschfeld, *Die Transvestiten: Eine Untersuchung über den erotischen Verkleidungstrieb* (Berlin: Pulvermacher, 1910).

46. On these columns, see Rainer Herrn, *Schnittmuster des Geschlechts: Transvestitismus und Transsexualität in der frühen Sexualwissenschaft* (Gießen, Germany: Psychosozial-Verlag, 2005), 142ff.; Katie Sutton, "'We Too Deserve a Place in the Sun': The Politics of Transvestite Identity in Weimar Germany," *German Studies Review* 35, no. 2 (2012): 335–354.

47. The authors of these articles were sometimes sexologists themselves, including two article series by entomologist and anthropologist Ferdinand Karsch-Haack, published in *Die Freundin* ("Historische Männinen," 1927) and *Garçonne* ("Junggesellin und Junggeselle," 1930–1931), respectively.

48. Oosterhuis, *Stepchildren of Nature*, 10–12 and passim.

49. Hale Fürstenberg, "Der gute Weg," *Die Freundin*, no. 30 (July 23, 1930).

50. Hansi, "Mieze," in "Die Welt der Transvestiten," *Die Freundin*, no. 1 (January 4, 1933).

51. As Bachmann-Medick warns, "In individual cases we must ask very carefully what insights are really gained, what empirical research is furthered by working with the category of translation, and whether we might not merely be witnessing the start of a new metaphor's triumphal march": "Translational Turn," 14. Similarly, Dizdar suggests that a "translational turn" can only be effective if it maintains "translation proper" as its reference: "Translational Transitions," 90.

52. Bachmann-Medick, "Translational Turn," 12, citing Gillian Beer, *Open Fields: Science in Cultural Encounter* (Oxford: Oxford University Press, 1999), 186.

4

Data of Desire

Translating (Homo)Sexology in Republican China

HOWARD CHIANG

Carnal Transformations

The translation into Japanese in 1705 of the erotic novel *The Carnal Prayer Mat* (肉蒲團) is a well-known example of the rich cross-cultural currents between Qing China (1644–1911) and Tokugawa Japan (1603–1867). Written in 1657, only thirteen years after the northern Manchus took over Beijing, the novel is generally attributed to the playwright Li Yu (李漁, 1611–1680) even though his name did not appear on the cover of the book.[1] The novel is replete with graphic descriptions of the sexual pursuit of the protagonist, Wei Yangsheng (未央生). As the front page of the Japanese translation indicates (Figure 4.1), the book was considered by many in the early modern period as "the most promiscuous story in the world." Given its explicit content, the book still cannot be sold to minors in Taiwan and continues to be banned in the People's Republic of China. An examination of the representations of intimacy and desire in the text provides a useful introduction to the historical context and the main concerns of this chapter: the translation of homosexuality as a sexological concept in early twentieth-century China.

The Carnal Prayer Mat can be situated in the genre of literary pornography similar to the way in which other erotic novels have been perceived in and out of China's past. The late-Ming *The Plum in the Golden Vase* (金瓶梅), for instance, which appeared only a few decades before *The Carnal Prayer Mat*, is perhaps the best example of this kind of literature. What these

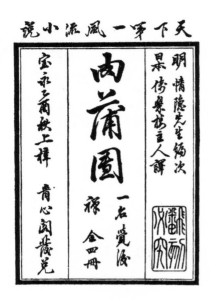

Figure 4.1: Front cover of the Japanese translation of *The Carnal Prayer Mat* (1705)

seventeenth-century erotic novels capture, some observers have argued, is the hedonistic and amoral urban behaviors associated with the growing consumer culture in the waning decades of the Ming.[2] Feminist historians and other literary scholars, too, point to the loosening of gender boundaries and sexual mores of the time, as reflected in the blossoming of women's cultural creativity and alternative arrangements of love and intimacy, especially in the south.[3] But the most striking thing about these novels is the considerable degree of popular interest they continue to attract in contemporary Chinese culture. The plots of *The Carnal Prayer Mat* and *The Plum in the Golden Vase* have been adapted time and again in the production of new computer games and films, including, most recently, *3-D Sex and Zen: Extreme Ecstasy*, a three-dimensional cinematic adaptation of *The Carnal Prayer Mat* released in 2011.[4]

If one focuses on the book itself, certain episodes of *The Carnal Prayer Mat* appear surprisingly queer. Granted, as many critics have pointed out, the story brings a sense of closure to Wei Yangsheng's erotic adventure, reinstating a normative sense of Confucian discipline through eventual punishment. Having mistreated all the women with whom he had sexual relationships, including his wife, Wei eventually castrates himself and becomes a Buddhist monk to atone for his sins. However, as Angela Zito has suggested, it might be more compelling to foreground Li Yu's narrative method and the protagonist's constant subversion of Confucian orthodoxy: "Li Yu presents [the choices of male characters] as the ineluctable outcome of their karmic fates, using against the patriarchal norm, even queering, a

Buddhism that, in complex ways, shored up patriarchal familial arrangements in this time."[5]

Indeed, the homoerotic contents of the novel are as explicit as the heterosexual ones. After leaving his wife, Wei meets a stranger who would eventually become his buddy, Sai Kunlun (賽崑崙). Spending a night together, naked, Wei insists that Sai share stories of his past sexual encounters with women. Sai accepts the request, and his stories fulfill Wei's desires:

> At this point, it is as if the voice of a promiscuous woman comes from right next to Wei, causing his body to tremble. He suddenly ejaculates a dose of semen that he has kept to himself for too long. Unless he is asked otherwise, it is unquestionable what has just happened.[6]

Similar to the kind of male–male intimacy that Eve Sedgwick uncovers in English literature, Wei's homosocial desire for Sai becomes intelligible by being routed through an implicit triangular relation involving women.[7] And before he acquires a hugely expanding dog's penis through surgery, Wei makes love to his sixteen-year-old boy servant one last time.[8]

Neither the implicitly homoerotic nor the explicitly homosexual scene appears in any of the twentieth-century adaptations of the story. Despite their prominence and wide circulation in contemporary popular culture, the modern versions of *The Carnal Prayer Mat* and *The Plum in the Golden Vase* in film and other media are notorious for being consistently marketed as commodities fulfilling the heteronormative desires of men. If one treats these "texts" as immediate historical evidence of sexuality across time, one might be inclined to conclude that homoeroticism "disappeared" in the twentieth century. Or, more specifically, the juxtaposition between the seventeenth-century novels (with their frank and open homoerotic depictions) and their modern, more conservative variations seems to imply a neat discrepancy between the *presence* of same-sex sexuality before its twentieth-century *absence*. It is perhaps more accurate to conclude that the afterlife and proliferation of these pornographic texts in the contemporary period rely on an indirect censorship of their homoerotic content. This censorship exemplifies what Sedgwick has called an "epistemological privilege of unknowing," a successful concealment of certain ways of thinking within the broader structures of knowledge.[9] In Sedgwick's words, "many of the major modes of thought and knowledge in twentieth-century Western culture as a whole are structured—indeed, fractured—by a chronic, now endemic crisis of homo/heterosexual definition, indicatively male, dating from the end of the nineteenth century."[10]

Similarly, we can interpret the evolving cultural representations of such novels as *The Carnal Prayer Mat* and *The Plum in the Golden Vase* through

the lens of this "endemic crisis of homo/heterosexual definition." By highlighting the rise of sexology in the 1920s as a pivotal turning point in the
history of sexuality in China, this chapter offers an alternative explanation
for the disappearance of homoerotic representations in their modern adaptations. After all, what the trajectory of this historical evolution reveals
is not so much the coincidental "disappearance" of homosexuality, *but its
very emergence.* With the removal of their homoerotic contents, Ming-Qing
erotic texts have essentially become heterosexualized in today's mass culture. The heteronormalization of *The Carnal Prayer Mat*, therefore, points
to something more fundamental to the conceptual transformation of sex
in the twentieth century: the emergence of its scientific designation as the
subject of desire.

Translating (Homo)Sexology

From the late Qing period on, biologists and other life science writers translated the epistemological authority of natural science through the production
of anatomical, morphological, and chromosomal images of sexual difference. These images affirm a certain kind of distance from the viewer, making
it possible to decipher truth's relation to nature through their means of vi-
sual objectivation.[11] However, a different kind of relationship between truth
and nature and a different type of distance between the subject and object of
knowledge emerged in the 1920s. By that point, biological sex had become a
commonsense in the popular imagination. With that commonsense, some
iconoclastic intellectuals began to contend that the hidden nature of erotic
preference could also be discovered and known. Sex, they argued, was no
longer something only to be seen, but it was something to be desired as well.
They participated in a new concerted effort, though not without friction,
to emulate European sexological sciences. Their translation and appropriation of Western sexological texts, concepts, methodologies, and styles of reasoning provided a crucial historical condition under which, and the means
through which, sexuality emerged as an object of empirical knowledge. The
disciplinary formation of Chinese sexology in the Republican period, therefore, added a new element of carnality to the scientific meaning of sex.

　　In the aftermath of the New Culture Movement (1915–1919), an en-
tire generation of cultural critics promoted sex education and sexological
studies in an unprecedented, systematic fashion. Among the famous May
Fourth iconoclastic intellectuals, some not only translated texts and adopted
methodological rigor from European sexology but also developed their own
theories of human sexual behavior and desire. They frequently engaged in
heated debates over the meaning, principles, and boundaries of a science
of sexuality. In the 1920s and 1930s, they greeted high-profile European

sexologists, including Magnus Hirschfeld and Margaret Sanger, in major cities such as Beijing and Shanghai. Questions of competence, credentials, expertise, and authority preoccupied those of the early twentieth-century urban intelligentsia who spoke seriously about sex in public. By 1935, disparate efforts and conversations converged in the founding of such monthly periodicals as *Sex Science* (性科學). For the first time in China, sexuality was accorded a primacy of scientific "truthfulness."[12]

In my previous work, I have explored the intellectual journey of two pivotal figures in this rich tradition of Republican Chinese sexology: Zhang Jingsheng (張競生) and Pan Guangdan (潘光旦).[13] Here, I would like to use their oeuvres as the historical background from which to offer more in-depth remarks on the historiographical significance of sexological translation. First and foremost, their writings on homosexuality provide an important resource for extending and revising the limited scholarly literature on the history of Chinese sexology. In his earlier study of the medico-scientific constructions of sex, Frank Dikötter argues that early twentieth-century Chinese modernizing elites did not fully grasp or reproduce European concepts of sexual "perversions," including homosexuality.[14] Similarly, Joanna McMillan asserts that while "sexological studies of perversions were widespread in European medial circles, the literature in Republican China remained almost entirely silent on these enquiries."[15] More recently, in response to Dikötter's thesis, other scholars such as Tze-lan D. Sang and Wenqing Kang have exposed the ways in which selected May Fourth intellectuals—through various debates in the urban press—actually contributed to the increasing awareness of foreign categorizations of human sexuality in early twentieth-century Chinese mass culture.[16]

Nonetheless, taken together these studies tend to depict Republican Chinese sexology as a unified field that treated homosexuality merely as a social, rather than a personal, problem.[17] According to Kang, for example,

> Whereas in the West, sexological knowledge pathologized homosexuality as socially deviant, thus reducing it to an individual psychological problem, in China sexology as a form of modern knowledge was used more to diagnose social and national problems . . . As Chinese writers and thinkers introduced Western sexology to China, male same-sex relations were stigmatized more as a disruptive social deviance than a personal medical condition.[18]

Sang's analysis, too, seems to support the claim that no effect similar to the European "individualization" of homosexuality took place in Republican China. In the context of the May Fourth era, Sang observes, "*tongxing ai* ['same-sex love'] is primarily signified as a modality of love or an intersubjective rapport rather than as a category of personhood, that is, an identity."[19]

On the contrary, a more critical attention to issues of knowledge translation shows that this interpretation is an oversimplification. The view that homosexuality was only a social problem was not consistently shared by such pivotal sexologists as Zhang Jingsheng and Pan Guangdan. In the process of establishing sexuality as an appropriate object of scientific inquiry, they held different opinions on the etiology, prevention, and significance of same-sex love. They even disagreed on the fundamental principles of sexological research. Given the multiple perspectives competing at the time, it is perhaps more compelling to suggest that homosexuality appeared to Chinese experts and popular audiences to be as much a personal problem as it was a social one—an explicit issue of personhood, subjectivity, and identity. Open communications between "sexperts," their readers, and other "sexperts" further enriched this incitement of a discourse that found truth in sex. To borrow Michel Foucault's insight on the incitement to speak about sex in modern bourgeois society, "Whether in the form of a subtle confession in confidence or an authoritarian interrogation, sex—be it refined or rustic—had to be put into words."[20] Sexology in Republican China was indeed a new system of knowledge in which, literally, new subjects were made.[21]

Ultimately, participants of this new discourse established for China what Foucault has called *scientia sexualis*, which first distinguished itself in nineteenth-century Europe: a new regime of truth that relocated the discursive technology of the sexual self from the theological sphere of pastoral confession to the secular discourse of science and medicine.[22] From the 1920s through the 1940s, the conceptual space for articulating a Western-derived homosexual identity emerged in China precisely from the new regime of truth circumscribed by the arrival of European sexology. Moreover, whereas Dennis Altman, Lisa Rofel, and Judith Farquhar have respectively claimed that "gay identity" and *scientia sexualis* first appeared on the China scene only by the post-socialist era, my historicization suggests that both have deeper roots that can be traced to an earlier epistemic turning point—in the Republican period.[23]

Readers with some familiarity with the history of sexuality in China would perhaps turn to the rich history of male homoeroticism in traditional China, a topic of in-depth scholarly discussion, as a potential counterpoint to my argument.[24] This history, however, is not static but dynamic: over the years, the social significance of same-sex relations in premodern China evolved according to the relevant historical factors. As Matthew Sommer's work on Chinese legal history has shown, sodomy appeared as a formal legislation in China only by the late imperial period. During the eighteenth-century Yongzheng reign (1723–1735), male same-sex practice was for the first time directly "assimilated" to heterosexual practice under the rubric of "illicit sex." This Qing innovation, according to Sommer, fundamentally reoriented the organizing principle for the regulation of sexuality in China: a universal order of "appropriate" gender roles and attributes was granted some foundational value over the previous status-oriented paradigm, in which different status groups were expected to hold unique standards of familial and sexual morality.[25] But whether someone who engaged in same-sex behavior was criminalized due to his disruption of a social order organized around status or gender performance, the world of imperial China never viewed the experience of homosexuality as a separate problem.[26] The question was never homosexuality per se, but whether one's sexual behavior would potentially reverse the dominant script of social order. If we want to *isolate* the problem of homosexuality in China, we must jump to the first half of the twentieth century to find it.

The relationship between forms of experience and systems of knowledge thus occupies a central role in this historical problem, if only because what we have come to call "sexuality" is a relatively recent product of a system of medico-scientific knowledge that has its own unique style of reasoning and argumentation.[27] In the European context, Arnold Davidson has identified the emergence of sexuality from the new conceptual space conditioned by the nineteenth-century shift from an anatomical to a psychiatric style of medical reasoning.[28] The historical specificity and uniqueness of sexual concepts cannot be overstated, especially since our modern formulation of homosexuality, as the classicist David Halperin reminds us, does not anchor on a notion of object-choice, orientation, or behavior alone but "seems to depend on the unstable conjunction of all three."[29]

Indeed, if we consider homosexuality not as a strictly "modern" category but as a by-product of a contested historical process that yielded specific cultural associations with the traditional, the modern, and the authentic, we can begin to take the growing global hegemony of Western conceptions of health and diseases seriously without necessitating a full-blown self- or re-Orientalization. By that I mean an intentional project that continually defers an "alternative modernity" and essentializes non-Westernness (including Chineseness) by assuming that the genealogical status of that derivative copy of an "original" Western modernity is somehow always already hermeneutically sealed from the historical apparatus of Westernization.[30] Now that studies in the history of sexuality in non-Western regions have begun to mature,[31] historians should be even more (not less) cautious of any effort to view the broader historical processes of epistemic homogenization as having any lesser bearing than forms of local (or "Oriental") resistance.[32] The idea that "local" configurations of gender and sexuality cannot be overridden by modern Western taxonomies of sexual identity is by now a standard interpretation of both the historical record and cultural archive of non-Western same-sex desires. But a variant of this interpretation has already generated controversial repercussions in the field of Middle Eastern sexuality studies. Consider Joseph Massad's infamous claim that all social significations of homosexuality, including internal gay rights activism, reflect the growing penetration of Western cultural imperialism: "The categories of gay and lesbian are not universal at all and can only be universalized by the epistemic, ethical, and political violence unleashed on the rest of the world by the very international human rights advocates whose aim is to defend the very people their intervention is creating."[33] It bears striking similarity, however ironically and uncomfortably, to Lisa Rofel's adamant critique of a "globalized gay identity."[34] Whether the target of critique is global gay or global sex, post-Orientalist critical thinking should not deter the historian's interest in the condition of the translatability of such concepts as homosexuality especially since they were frequently invoked by historical actors themselves.

The Threshold of Scientificity

To redress the analytical conundrums concerning the relationship between transnationalism and sexuality from a strong historicist viewpoint, what we are concerned with, then, is not a social history of homosexuals in China "from below," but an *epistemological history* in the Foucauldian sense that "is situated at the threshold of scientificity."[35] In other words, what is at stake here is "how a concept [like homosexuality]—still overlaid with [earlier] metaphors or imaginary contents—was purified, and accorded the status and function of a scientific concept. To discover how a region of experience [such as same-sex intimacy] that has already been mapped, already partially articulated, but is still overlaid with immediate practical uses or values related to those uses, was constituted as a scientific domain."[36] In Republican China, what constituted the socio-cultural foundations for the establishment of sexology was the creation of a public of truth, in which the authority of truth could be contested, translated across culture, and reinforced through new organizational efforts.

In the context of Zhang Jingsheng's sexology, whether it is the dualism between literary representations of love versus scientific truthfulness of sex, or the juxtaposition between Daoist cultivational ideas in Chinese medicine versus the bio-psychological language of Western biomedicine, two registers of truth production on which sexological claims operated always proceeded in a reciprocal fashion: one concerning explicit claims about the object of scientific knowledge (human sexuality) and another concerning implicit claims about cultural markers of traditionality, authenticity, and modernity (modes of narrating sex, theoretical foundations of medicine, etc.). But Zhang's project quickly turned into the antithesis of science and modernity in the eyes of his contemporaries, including Pan Guangdan and Zhou Jianren (Lu Xun's youngest brother). Moving beyond the limitations of his work, they aimed to establish an independent discipline with greater resemblance to European sexology. By the mid-1930s, disparate efforts in making sexuality a legitimate subject of scientific discussion and mass education culminated in such projects of disciplinary consolidation as the founding of *Sex Science*. Similar to its Western counterparts such as the *Journal of Sexual Science* in Germany and *Sexology* in the United States, *Sex Science* functioned as a textual archive reinforcing the specialized authority of sexology across culture. The founding and circulation of this journal—alongside other periodicals famous for their introduction of foreign ideas about feminism, mental hygiene, gender relations, individualism, and other cosmopolitan concepts, such as *New Women, New Culture, Ladies Journal, Sex Magazine*, and *West Wind*—thus marked an important episode in the intellectual translation and disciplinary consolidation of *scienta sexualis* in Republican China.[37] These unprecedented achievements gave rise to a radical reorganization of the meaning of same-sex desire in Chinese culture around a new psychiatric style of reasoning.

In the politically volatile context of Republican China, the introduction of Western sexology often reframed same-sex desire as an indication of national backwardness. In *Sexological Science*, after documenting the prevalence of homosexual practice in different Western societies, the author Zhang Mingyun concluded that "the main social cause for the existence of homosexuality is upper-class sexual decadence and the sexual thirst of the lower-class people."[38] And this, according to Zhang, should help shed light on "the relationship between homosexuality and nationality."[39] "For the purpose of social improvement," according to another concerned writer, "the increasing prevention of homosexuality is now a pressing task."[40] Pan Guangdan expressed a similar nationalistic hostility toward the boy actors of traditional Peking opera: since they often participated in sexual relationships with their male literati patrons, Pan described them as "abnormal" and detrimental to social morality. He explained that their lower social status prevented them from participating in the civil examination system, implying that a modernizing nation in the twentieth century certainly has no place for them.[41] The physician Wang Yang, known for his expertise in human sexuality and reproduction, went so far to identify homosexuality as "a kind of disease that eliminates a nation and its races."[42]

If we take the insights of Lydia Liu and others concerning cultural translation seriously, the transmission of *scientia sexualis* to China ultimately characterizes a *productive* historical moment.[43] When Republican Chinese sexologists viewed the *dan* actors and other cultural expressions of homoeroticism as signs of national backwardness,[44] they in essence domesticated the Western psychiatric style of reasoning and turned it into a new *nationalistic style of argumentation* about same-sex desire. In addition to staging certain elements of the Peking opera field as being out of time and place, epistemic modernity occasioned an entrenched nationalistic platform, on which other aspects of this cultural entertainment also functioned as a powerful symbol of quintessential Chinese tradition and authenticity. Rendered as a prototypical exemplar of the modern homosexual, the twentieth-century *dan* actor became a historic figure signifying a hybrid embodiment of the traditionality and what Prasenjit Duara aptly calls "the regime of authenticity" of Chinese culture.[45]

It is therefore possible to contrast this new nationalistic style of argumentation with the *culturalistic* style of argumentation that underpinned the comprehensibility of same-sex desire in the late imperial period.[46] For this purpose, we can turn to the late Ming essayist and social commentator, Zhang Dai (張岱), who reflects on his friend Qi Zhixiang's fondness for a young man named Abao in his *Tao'an mengyi* (Dream reminiscence of Tao'an). Tao'an is Zhang's pen name, and this collection of miscellaneous notes serves as a good window onto the literati lifestyle circa the Ming-Qing transition, since Zhang is often considered to embody the bona fide literati taste of the time. An example from the late Ming is also most apt because the period is infamous for marking the peak of a flourishing "male love" (男色, *nanse*) homoerotic culture in late imperial China. The title of this passage is "The Obsession of Qi Zhixiang," and because it places seventeenth-century male same-sex love in the context of multiple desires, it is worth quoting in full:

If someone does not have an obsession (*pi*), they cannot make a good companion for they have no deep passions; if a person does not show some flaw, they also cannot make a good companion since they have no genuine spirit. My friend Qi Zhixiang has obsessions with calligraphy and painting, football, drums and cymbals, ghost plays, and opera. In 1642, when I arrived in the southern capital, Zhixiang brought Abao out to show me. I remarked, "This is a divine and sweet voiced bird from [the paradise of] the western regions, how did he fall into your hands?" Abao's beauty was as fresh as a pure maiden's. He still had no care for decorum, was haughty, and kept others at a distance. The feeling was just like eating an olive, at first bitter and a little rough, but the charm is in the aftertaste. Like wine and tobacco, the first mouthful is a little repulsive, producing a state of tipsy lightness; yet once the initial disgust passes the flavor soon fills your mind. Zhixiang was a master of music and prosody, fastidious in his composition of melodies and lyrics, and personally instructing [his boy-actors] phrase by phrase. Those of Abao's ilk were able to realize what he had in mind. In the year of 1645, the southern capital fell, and Zhixiang fled from the city to his hometown. En route they ran across some bandits. Face to face with death, his own life would have been expendable, but not his treasure, Abao. In the year of 1646, he followed the imperial guards to camp at Taizhou. A lawless rabble plundered the camp, and Zhixiang lost all his valuables. Abao charmed his master by singing on the road. After they returned, within half a month, Qi again took a journey with Abao. Leaving his wife and children was for Zhixiang as easy as removing a shoe, but a young brat was as dear to him as his own life. This sums up his obsession.[47]

This passage also sums up what a man's interest in young males meant in the seventeenth century remarkably well: it was perceived as just one of the many different types of "obsessions" that a male literatus could have—a symbol of his refinement. For Zhang, a man's taste in male lovers was as important as his "obsessions" in other arenas of life, without which this person "cannot make a good companion." Despite all the hardship, the romantic ties between Qi and Abao still survived, and perhaps even surpassed Qi's relationship with his wife and children.

To assess the epistemological transformation of same-sex desire in Chinese culture from an indigenous historical perspective, then, we can begin to reconstruct some of the polarized concepts that constitute two opposed styles of argumentation. We are presented, for instance, with the polarities between literati taste and sick perversion, refined obsession and pathological behavior, cultural superiority and psychological abnormality, markers of elite status and signs of national backwardness. The first of each of these pairs of concepts partially makes up the culturalistic style of argumentation about same-sex desire, while the second of each of these pairs helps to constitute the nationalistic style of argumentation. These polarities therefore characterize two distinct intellectual modes of representation, two conceptual spaces, two different kinds of deep epistemological structure. In mediating the translation of the foreign category of homosexuality, Chinese sexological knowledge had not only pushed the concept of same-sex desire over the threshold of scientificity, but also left a distinct legacy in catalyzing an internal shift in the indigenous conceptual paradigm of same-sex relations.

Historicism Uncontested

In light of the prevailing criticisms of Foucauldian genealogy, many historians of sexuality have refrained from advancing a claim about the occasioning of an epistemological break in the Republican era by showing that earlier concepts associated with male same-sex sexual practice (e.g., *nanse* or *pi*) jostled alongside and informed the new sexology discourse.[48] However, it has been my intention to show that the congruency between earlier and later understandings of same-sex practice *is itself* a cultural phenomenon unique to the Republican period and not before. Wenqing Kang, for example, has argued that preexisting Chinese ideas about male favorites and *pi* "laid the ground for acceptance of the modern Western definition of homo/heterosexuality during [the Republican] period in China." His first explanation is that "both the Chinese concept *pi* (obsession) and Western sexology tended to understand same-sex relations as pathological." He then relies on Eve Sedgwick's model of the overlapping "universalizing discourse of acts and minoritizing discourse of persons" to suggest that indigenous Chinese understandings shared a comparable internal contradiction in the conceptualization of male same-sex desire. In his words, "The concept *pi* which Ming literati used to characterize men who enjoyed sex with other men, on the one hand implied that men who had this kind of passion were a special type of people, and on the other hand, presumed that the obsession could happen to anyone."[49]

My interpretation of Zhang Dai's passage on *pi* suggests that isolating both a pathological meaning and this internal conceptual contradiction of *pi* represents an anachronistic effort that reads homosexuality into earlier modes of thought. Zhang's remark precisely reveals the multiplicity of the meaning and cultural significance of *pi* that cannot be comprehended through a single definition of pathology or an independent lens of same-sex relations decontextualized from other types of refined human desire. Kang therefore seems to forget that the very semblance between what he calls "the internal contradictions within the Chinese indigenous understanding of male same-sex relations" and "those within the Western modern homosexual/heterosexual definition" was made possible and meaningful only in contemporaneity with the emergence of the concept of homosexuality in China.[50] In this regard, the following statement confuses his interpretation of historical sources with the very colonial landscape it claims to exceed: "When Western modern sexology was introduced to China in the first half of the twentieth century, the Chinese understanding of male same-sex relations as *pi* (obsession) was very much alive, as evidenced in the writings of the time. It was precisely because of the similarity between the two sets of understandings that Western modern sexology could gain footing in China."[51] The claim is confusing because the similarity Kang points to would not have made much sense in a context without the epistemological salience of the very concept of homosexuality itself, that is, before the twentieth century. Treating the discursive nature of discourse seriously requires us to pay closer attention to how old words take on a new meaning (and life) in a different historical context, rather than imposing later familiar notions onto earlier concepts.[52] A distinct problem with Kang's reading remains the way he turns a blind eye to the *hierarchical nature* of the invocation of *pi* in literati discourses. It might be useful to rephrase this problem by borrowing David Halperin's remark: "Of course, evidence of conscious erotic preferences does exist in abundance, but it tends to be found in the context of discourses linked to the senior partners in hierarchical relations of pederasty or sodomy. It therefore points not to the existence of gay sexuality per se but to one particular discourse and set of practices constituting one aspect of gay sexuality as we currently define it."[53]

Despite how Pan Guangdan's condemnation of the homosexuality of boy actors (and, by implication, their patrons) was informed by the long-standing and still-continuing practices of male prostitution, his condemnation was made possible—and comprehensible—only by the arrival of a psychiatric style of reasoning that construed same-sex relations in negative terms. In their study of nineteenth-century "flower guides" (*huapu*), Wu Cuncun and Mark Stevenson have probed the many social taboos surrounding this literary genre that extolled the beauty of boy actors, including "rules about money and taste and passion and lust, and also rules about the representation of social competition." They conclude that "none of these were concerned with fears of same-sex desire or of stigma through connection to the world of Beijing's homoerotic nightlife."[54] The scientific reasoning of desire that gained rapid momentum in the 1920s, on the other hand, ushered in a new era of the social stigmatization of male same-sex relations. Pan and other sexologists isolated homosexuality as a conceptual blueprint for individual psychology *independent of* hierarchical indexes of power relations, social status, class subjectivity, and so on, but it was a concept that, unlike heterosexuality, carried a pathological connotation and linked to notable cultural signifiers of traditionality contributing to, according to these elites, China's growing national deficiency. It was in this context that homosexuality came to set itself apart from gender transgression as two distinct nodes of conceptualization in modern Chinese culture.

The twelve cases of male homosexuality and the one case of female homosexuality that Pan enumerated in his annotated translation of *Psychology of Sex* should be understood less as historical evidence of homosexual experience in the Ming and Qing dynasties than as a reflection of how the epistemological reorientations brought about by a new psychiatric style of reasoning culminated to generate the condition of their comprehensibility. Here is where I part company with Giovanni Vitiello, who interprets Pan's effort "as if to provide a Chinese perspective on an experience inadequately represented in the Western book. These negotiation attempts remind us that the transformation of sexual culture in twentieth-century China cannot be read simply as the replacement of one model with another."[55] Two major assumptions are embedded in Vitiello's statement: first, that the internal coherence of a unified structure of homoerotic sentiment had *always already existed* in China before the Western concept of homosexuality, and second, the congruency between the former and the latter structures of knowledge was inevitable and unproblematic.

I would not suggest that the heart of the matter concerns the question of whether the contested process of translation is itself fraught with the possibility of "losing" or "adding" new dimensions of knowledge (because of course it is). But what escapes Vitiello's reading is the way in which the internal coherency of an indigenous structure of knowledge on which the foreign model of homosexuality could be easily mapped and the condition of possibility of this mapping *were both themselves* historically contingent on—even historically produced by—the very process whereby "homosexuality" was translated into Chinese in the early twentieth century. Likewise, when Pan and other sexologists used examples from ancient Greece to render the modern category of homosexuality intelligible, the result was a similar moment of epistemic alignment in the establishment of *scientia sexualis* in China. Their debates on "true" or "fake," "inborn" or "acquired," "natural" or "curable," homosexuality in the pages of *Sex Science* already takes for granted the new psychiatric style of reasoning and so treats sexuality and its attendant disorders, such as homosexuality, as if they were naturally given and carrying broader implications for the modern nation. Simply put, the epistemic continuity forged by Chinese sexologists between the foreign concept of homosexuality and earlier examples of homoeroticism do not undermine the kind of Foucauldian epistemological rupture that I have been suggesting but actually exemplify it. Before the rupture, according to the normative definition of desire in male spectatorship and connoisseurship, the possibility of having the same (homo)sexuality as either the *dan* actor or the male favorite would have appalled the literati gentleman.

If we ever wonder how to make sense of the prevalence of same-sex sexual practice in China before the rise of an East Asian *scientia sexualis*, as so vividly captured in *The Carnal Prayer Mat*, we only need to remind ourselves that as little as a century ago, the very notion of (homo)sexuality did not fall within the possible parameters of Chinese thinking.

NOTES

1. For a discussion of the authorship of the book, see Nathan K. Mao and Liu Ts'un-Yan, *Li Yü* (Boston: Twayne, 1977), 90–95.

2. Timothy Brook, *The Confusions of Pleasure: Commerce and Culture in Ming China* (Berkeley: University of California Press, 1999).

3. Dorothy Ko, *Teachers of the Inner Chamber: Women and Culture in Seventeenth-Century China* (Stanford, CA: Stanford University Press, 1995); Sophie Volpp, "The Discourse on Male Marriage: Li Yu's 'A Male Mencius's Mother,'" *positions: east asia cultures critique* 2 (1994): 113–132; Sophie Volpp, "Classifying Lust: The Seventeenth-Century Vogue for Male Love," *Harvard Journal of Asiatic Studies* 61 (2001): 77–117; Giovanni Vitiello, *The Libertine's Friend: Homosexuality and Masculinity in Late Imperial China* (Chicago: University of Chicago Press, 2011).

4. The first Chinese 3-D pornographic film came out in early 2011 and is based on *The Carnal Prayer Mat*. See Stephen Shiu, Stephen Shiu Jr., and Mark Wu, *3-D Sex and Zen: Extreme Ecstasy*, dir. Christopher Suen (Hong Kong: One Dollar Production, 2011). For an earlier version, see Lee Ying Kit, *Sex and Zen*, dir. Michael Mak (Hong Kong: Golden Harvest, 1991).

5. Angela Zito, "Queering Filiality, Raising the Dead," *Journal of the History of Sexuality* 10, no. 2 (2001): 201.

6. Li Yü, *Rouputuang miben* (肉普團密本) [The carnal prayer mat] (Taipei: Guojia Chubanshe, 2011), 45. All translations are mine.

7. Eve Kosofsky Sedgwick, *Between Men: English Literature and Male Homosocial Desire* (New York: Columbia University Press, 1985), 201–202.

8. Li, *Rouputuang*, 71–73.

9. Eve Kosofsky Sedgwick, *Epistemology of the Closet* (Berkeley: University of California Press, 1990), 5.

10. Ibid., 1.

11. See Howard Chiang, "The Conceptual Contours of Sex in the Chinese Life Sciences: Zhu Xi (1899–1962), Hermaphroditism, and the Biological Discourse of *Ci* and *Xiong*, 1920–1950," *East Asian Science, Technology and Society: An International Journal* 2, no. 3 (2008): 401–430.

12. See the notion of truthfulness used by Bernard Williams in *Truth and Truthfulness: An Essay in Genealogy* (Princeton, NJ: Princeton University Press, 2002). I take a cue from Ian Hacking and use "truth" in this chapter as a formal (as opposed to a strictly realist) concept. Ian Hacking, *Scientific Reason* (Taipei: National Taiwan University Press, 2008), 1–48.

13. Howard Chiang, "Epistemic Modernity and the Emergence of Homosexuality in China," *Gender and History* 22, no. 3 (2010): 629–657.

14. Frank Dikötter, *Sex, Culture, and Modernity in China: Medical Science and the Construction of Sexual Identities in the Early Republican Period* (Honolulu: University of Hawai'i Press, 1995), 143–145.

15. Joanna McMillan, *Sex, Science and Morality in China* (New York: Routledge, 2006), 90.

16. See Tze-lan D. Sang, *The Emerging Lesbian: Female Same-Sex Desire in Modern China* (Chicago: University of Chicago Press, 2003); Wenqing Kang, *Obsession: Male Same-Sex Relations in China, 1900–1950* (Hong Kong: Hong Kong University Press, 2009).

17. Dikötter, *Sex, Culture, and Modernity*, 140–141; Chou Wah-shan, *Tongzhi: Politics of Same-Sex Eroticism in Chinese Societies* (New York: Haworth, 2000), 50; Sang, *Emerging Lesbian*, 7, 118; Kang, *Obsession*, 42–43.

18. Kang, *Obsession*, 42–43. Some Western sexologists (and eugenicists) were concerned that the homosexual type was both a sign of racial/national degeneracy and a

threat to the health of the nation. Although the remainder of this chapter will focus on revising Kang's point with respect to China, it is equally important to acknowledge the limitation of his point with respect to the West as well.

19. Sang, *Emerging Lesbian*, 118.

20. Michel Foucault, *The History of Sexuality*, vol. 1: *An Introduction*, trans. Robert Hurley (London: Penguin, 1990), 32.

21. Ian Hacking, "Making Up People," in *Reconstructing Individualism: Autonomy, Individuality, and the Self in Western Thought*, ed. Thomas Heller, Morton Sosna, and David Wellbery (Stanford, CA: Stanford University Press, 1986), 222–236.

22. Foucault, *History of Sexuality*.

23. Dennis Altman, *Global Sex* (Chicago: University of Chicago Press, 2001), 86–105; Lisa Rofel, *Desiring China: Experiments in Neoliberalism, Sexuality, and Public Culture* (Durham, NC: Duke University Press, 2007), 85–110; Judith Farquhar, *Appetites: Food and Sex in Post-Socialist China* (Durham, NC: Duke University Press, 2002), 211–242. See also Loretta Wing Wah Ho, *Gay and Lesbian Subculture in Urban China* (London: Routledge, 2010); Travis Kong, *Chinese Male Homosexualities: Memba, Tongzhi, and Golden Boy* (London: Routledge, 2010); McMillan, *Sex, Science and Morality in China*; James Farrer, *Opening Up: Youth Sex Culture and Market Reform in Shanghai* (Chicago: University of Chicago Press, 2002). On the argument for an emphasis shift in modern Chinese historiography to the Republican era, see Frank Dikötter, *The Age of Openness: China before Mao* (Berkeley: University of California Press, 2008); Howard Chiang, "Liberating Sex, Knowing Desire: *Scientia Sexualis* and Epistemic Turning Points in the History of Sexuality," *History of the Human Sciences* 23, no. 5 (2010): 42–69.

24. Robert Hans van Gulik, *Sexual Life in Ancient China* (Leiden, Netherlands: Brill, 1974); Xiaomingxiong (小明雄) [Samshasha], *Zhongguo tongxing'ai shilu* (中國同性愛史錄) [The history of homosexual love in China] (Hong Kong: Fenhong Sanjiao Chubanshe, 1984); Bret Hinsch, *Passions of the Cut Sleeve: The Male Homosexual Tradition in China* (Berkeley: University of California Press, 1990). For a lucid analysis of Xiaomingxiong's study in its proper historical context, see Helen Leung, "Archiving Queer Feelings in Hong Kong," *Inter-Asia Cultural Studies* 8 (2007): 559–571.

25. Matthew Sommer, *Sex, Law, and Society in Late Imperial China* (Stanford, CA: Stanford University Press, 2000). For earlier works on the legal construction of sodomy in China, see Marinus J. Meijer, "Homosexual Offences in Ch'ing Law," *T'oung Pao* 71 (1985): 109–133; Vivian W. Ng, "Ideology and Sexuality: Rape Laws in Qing China," *Journal of Asian Studies* 46 (1987): 57–70; Vivian Ng, "Homosexuality and State in Late Imperial China," in *Hidden from History: Reclaiming the Gay and Lesbian Past*, ed. Martin B. Duberman, Martha Vicinus, and George Chauncey Jr. (New York: New American Library, 1989), 76–89.

26. For an explanation of why homosexuality was not criminalized in the Republican period, see Wenqing Kang, "Male Same-Sex Relations in Modern China: Language, Medical Representation, and Law, 1900–1949," *positions: east asia cultures critique* 18, no. 2 (2010): 489–510.

27. On the epistemological applicability of "style," see Howard Chiang, "Rethinking 'Style' for Historians and Philosophers of Science: Converging Lessons from Sexuality, Translation, and East Asian Studies," *Studies in History and Philosophy of Biological and Biomedical Sciences* 40 (2009): 109–118.

28. Arnold I. Davidson, *The Emergence of Sexuality: Historical Epistemology and the Formation of Concepts* (Cambridge, MA: Harvard University Press, 2001), 36.

29. David M. Halperin, *How to Do the History of Homosexuality* (Chicago: University of Chicago Press, 2002), 131. On the historicism of homosexuality, see also David M. Halperin, *One Hundred Years of Homosexuality and Other Essays on Greek Love* (New York: Routledge, 1990); on heterosexuality, see Jonathan Ned Katz, *The Invention of Heterosexuality* (Chicago: University of Chicago Press, 2007 [1995]).

30. For recent reflections on the problem of Chinese self- or re-Orientalization, see Ien Ang, *On Not Speaking Chinese: Living between Asia and the West* (New York: Routledge, 2001); Chu Yiu-Wai, "The Importance of Being Chinese: Orientalism Reconfigured in the Age of Global Modernity," *boundary 2* 35 (2008): 183–206. For a similar argument on how certain formulations within queer studies could be complicit with homophobic reticent poetics by positing culturally essential "Chinese" non-homophobic subjects and situations, see Liu Jen-peng and Ding Naifei, "Reticent Poetics, Queer Politics," *Inter-Asia Cultural Studies* 6, no. 1 (2005): 30–55.

31. See, for example, Khaled El-Rouayheb, *Before Homosexuality in the Arab-Islamic World, 1500–1800* (Chicago: University of Chicago Press, 2005); Afsaneh Najmabadi, *Women with Mustaches and Men without Beards: Gender and Sexual Anxieties of Iranian Modernity* (Berkeley: University of California Press, 2005); Dror Ze'evi, *Producing Desire: Changing Sexual Discourse in the Ottoman Middle East, 1500–1900* (Berkeley: University of California Press, 2006); Kathryn Babayan and Afsaneh Najmabadi, eds., *Islamicate Sexualities: Translations across Temporal Geographies of Desire* (Cambridge, MA: Harvard University Press, 2008); Keith McMahon, *Polygamy and Sublime Passion: Sexuality in China on the Verge of Modernity* (Honolulu: University of Hawai'i Press, 2009); Afsaneh Najmabadi, *Professing Selves: Transsexuality and Same-Sex Desire in Contemporary Iran* (Durham, NC: Duke University Press, 2013).

32. See Dennis Altman, "Rupture or Continuity? The Internationalization of Gay Identities," *Social Text* 14 (1996): 77–94; Dennis Altman, "Global Gaze / Global Gays," *GLQ: A Journal of Lesbian and Gay Studies* 3 (1997): 417–436; Peter Drucker, "Introduction: Remapping Sexualities," in *Different Rainbows*, ed. Peter Drucker (London: Gay Men's Press, 2000), 9–42; Linda Garber, "Where in the World Are the Lesbians?" *Journal of the History of Sexuality* 14 (2005): 28–50; Afsaneh Najmabadi, "Beyond the Americas: Are Gender and Sexuality Useful Categories of Analysis?" *Journal of Women's History* 18 (2006): 11–21; Evelyn Blackwood, "Transnational Discourses and Circuits of Queer Knowledge in Indonesia," *GLQ: A Journal of Lesbian and Gay Studies* 14 (2008): 481–507; Peter A. Jackson, "Capitalism and Global Queering: National Markets, Parallels among Sexual Cultures, and Multiple Queer Modernities," *GLQ: A Journal of Lesbian and Gay Studies* 15 (2009): 357–395; Howard Chiang, "(De)Provincializing China: Queer Historicism and Sinophone Postcolonial Critique," in *Queer Sinophone Cultures*, ed. Howard Chiang and Ari Larissa Heinrich (London: Routledge, 2013), 19–51.

33. Joseph Massad, *Desiring Arabs* (Chicago: University of Chicago Press, 2007), 41.

34. Joseph Massad, "Re-Orienting Desire: The Gay International and the Arab World," *Public Culture* 14, no. 2 (2002): 361–385; Massad, *Desiring Arabs*; Rofel, *Desiring China*. The target of Rofel's critique is Altman, *Global Sex*. Note how strikingly similar are the titles of Massad's and Rofel's books.

35. See Howard Chiang, ed., "Queer Transnationalism in China," topical cluster, *English Language Notes* 49, no. 1 (2011): 109–144. See also Chiang and Heinrich, *Queer Sinophone Cultures.*

36. Michel Foucault, *The Archeology of Knowledge and the Discourse on Language*, trans. A. M. Sheridan Smith (New York: Pantheon, 1972 [1969]), 190.

37. See Wen-Ji Wang, "*West Wind Monthly* and the Popular Mental Hygiene Discourse in Republican China," *Taiwanese Journal for Studies of Science, Technology and Medicine* 13 (2011): 15–88 (in Chinese); Geoffrey Blowers and Shelley Wang Xuelai, "Gone with the *West Wind*: The Emergence and Disappearance of Psychotherapeutic Culture in China, 1936–68," in *Psychiatry and Chinese History*, ed. Howard Chiang (London: Pickering and Chatto, 2014), 143–160.

38. Zhang Mingyun (張敏筠), *Xing kexue* (性科學) [Sexological science] (Shanghai: Shidai Shuju, 1950), 78.

39. Zhang, *Xing kexue*, 75.

40. Yang Youtian (楊憂天), "Tongxing'ai de wenti" (同性愛的問題) [The problem of same-sex love], *Beixin* (北新) 3, no. 2 (1929): 436.

41. Pan Guangdan (潘光旦), trans., *Xing xinlixue* (性心理學) [Psychology of sex] (Shanghai: Commercial Press, 1946), reprinted in *Pan Guangdan wenji* (潘光旦文集) [Collected works of Pan Guangdan], 14 vols. (Beijing: Peking University Press, 1994), 12: 708–709. See also Pan Guangdan (潘光旦), *Zhongguo lingren xieyuan zhi yanjiu* (中國伶人血緣之研究) [Research on the pedigrees of Chinese actors] (Shanghai: Commercial Press, 1941), reprinted in *Pan Guangdan wenji* (潘光旦文集) [Collected works of Pan Guangdan], 14 vols. (Beijing: Peking University Press, 1994), 2:255–258.

42. Wang Yang (汪洋), *Fufu xingweisheng* (夫婦性衛生) [The sexual hygiene of married couples] (Shanghai: Zhongyang Shudian, 1935), 49, 53.

43. Lydia H. Liu, *Translingual Practice: Literature, National Cutlure, and Translated Modernity—China, 1900–1937* (Stanford, CA: Stanford University Press, 1995). See also the essays collected in Liu Kang and Xiaobing Tang, eds., *Politics, Ideology, and Literary Discourse in Modern China: Theoretical Interventions and Culture Critique* (Durham, NC: Duke University Press, 1993); Lydia H. Liu, ed., *Tokens of Exchange: The Problem of Translation in Global Circulations* (Durham, NC: Duke University Press, 1999).

44. On the association of male homosexual practice with national backwardness in the Republican period, see also Kang, *Obsession*, 115–144; Cuncun Wu and Mark Stevenson, "Male Love Lost: The Fate of Male Same-Sex Prostitution in Beijing in the Late Nineteenth and Early Twentieth Centuries," in *Embodied Modernities: Corporeality, Representation, and Chinese Cultures*, ed. Fran Martin and Ari Larissa Heinrich (Honolulu: University of Hawai'i Press, 2006), 42–59.

45. Prasenjit Duara, "The Regime of Authenticity: Timelessness, Gender, and National History in Modern China," *History and Theory* 37 (1998): 287–308. On the complicated historical layering of the *dan* figure, see John Zou, "Cross-Dressed Nation: Mei Lanfang and the Clothing of Modern Chinese Men," in Martin and Heinrich, *Embodied Modernities*, 79–97; Joshua Goldstein, *Drama Kings: Players and Publics in the Re-creation of Peking Opera, 1870–1937* (Berkeley: University of California Press, 2007).

46. For the transformation from "culturalism" to "nationalism" in the Chinese political sphere, see Joseph R. Levenson, *Confucian China and Its Modern Fate: A Trilogy* (Berkeley: University of California Press, 1965).

47. Zhang Dai (張岱), *Tao'an mengyi* (陶庵夢憶) [Dream reminiscences of Tao'an] (Shanghai: Shanghai Shudian, 1982), 35–36, as translated [with my own modifications] and cited in Cuncun Wu, *Homoerotic Sensibilities in Late Imperial China* (London: Routledge Curzon, 2004), 42–43.

48. Criticisms of Foucault have been voiced most prominently in lesbian historiography. See Terry Castle, *The Apparitional Lesbian: Female Homosexuality and Modern Culture* (New York: Columbia University Press, 1993); Bernadette J. Brooten, *Love between Women: Early Christian Responses to Female Homoeroticism* (Chicago: University of Chicago Press, 1996); Judith M. Bennett, "Confronting Continuity," *Journal of Women's History* 9, no. 3 (1997): 73–94; Judith M. Bennett, "'Lesbian-Like' and the Social History of Lesbianism," *Journal of the History of Sexuality* 9 (2000): 1–24; Louis Fradenberg and Carla Freccero, eds., *Premodern Sexualities* (London: Routledge, 1996); Carolyn Dinshaw, *Getting Medieval: Sexualities and Communities, Pre- and Postmodern* (Durham, NC: Duke University Press, 1999); Martha Vicinus, *Intimate Friends: Women Who Loved Women, 1778–1928* (Chicago: University of Chicago Press, 2004). For an excellent defense of the social constructionist approach to lesbian history, see Valerie Traub, "The Present Future of Lesbian Historiography," in *A Companion to Lesbian, Gay, Bisexual, Transgender, and Queer Studies*, ed. George E. Haggerty and Molly McGarry (Malden, MA: Blackwell, 2007), 124–145; Valerie Traub, "The New Unhistoricism in Queer Studies," *PMLA* 128, no. 1 (2013): 21–38. For criticisms of the Foucauldian genealogical method raised in the historiography of Chinese sexuality, see Kang, "Male Same-Sex Relations"; Vitiello, *Libertine's Friend*, 13–14, 200–201.

49. Kang, *Obsession*, 21. For Sedgwick's original formulation, see Sedgwick, *Epistemology of the Closet.*

50. Kang, "Male Same-Sex Relations," 490.

51. Ibid., 492.

52. My disagreement with Kang can be viewed as partially reflective of an earlier debate between Sedgwick and Halperin, with whom my analysis sides, on the genealogy of homosexuality in Western culture. See Halperin, *How to Do the History of Homosexuality.* For a defense of an essentialist approach to the history of sexuality, see John Boswell, "Revolutions, Universals, and Sexual Categories," in *Hidden from History: Reclaiming the Gay and Lesbian Past*, ed. Martin B. Duberman, Martha Vicinus, and George Chauncey Jr. (New York: Meridian, 1989), 17–36. For critiques of Boswell's tendency to elide historicism, see David Halperin, "Sex before Sexuality: Pederasty, Politics, and Power in Classical Athens," in Duberman, Vicinus, and Chauncey, *Hidden from History*, 37–53; Robert Padgug, "Sexual Matters: Rethinking Sexuality in History," in Duberman, Vicinus, and Chauncey, *Hidden from History*, 54–64.

53. David Halperin, "How to Do the History of Male Homosexuality," *GLQ: A Journal of Lesbian and Gay Studies* 6, no. 1 (2000): 98–99.

54. Cuncun Wu and Mark Stevenson, "Speaking of Flowers: Theatre, Public Culture, and Homoerotic Writing in Nineteenth-Century Beijing," *Asian Theatre Journal* 27, no. 1 (2010): 121. Wu and Stevenson diverge from Andrea Goldman, who discusses *huapu* authors' "awareness of the stigma that was associated with the sex trade in boy actors." Andrea Goldman, "Actors and Aficionados in Qing Dynasty Texts of Theatrical Connoisseurship," *Harvard Journal of Asiatic Studies* 68, no. 1 (2008): 5.

55. Vitiello, *Libertine's Friend*, 201.

II

Formations

How did national and transnational concerns shape the emergence of sexology in different parts of the modern world? Historians of sexuality have shown that one of the defining features in the emergence of modern sexuality around the globe is that debates about sex, desire, and the body are typically linked to issues of national politics: that the regulation of sexuality tends to play a central role in the institution of the medical, scientific and legal apparatuses that make up the modern state. Furthermore, national debates about sexual rights, ranging from campaigns for the decriminalization of same-sex acts to women's right to vote, have played an important role in the way states have justified their attacks, both real and rhetorical, on the sovereignty of other nations and cultures. At the same time, however, scholarship on the emergence of sexology in central Europe and North America has indicated that many sexologists pursued social reform aims that often directly challenged the narrow conventions of the time and that brought them into dialogue with colleagues from around the world, both individually and via international congresses and organizations such as the World League for Sexual Reform. Yet while this scholarship and the recent explosion of publications on the national histories of sexuality in Asia has considerably expanded understanding of what we might call the "national histories of sexology" and some of the key people that linked them, we still need more detailed insights into how transnational frameworks and nationally contingent debates shaped the global emergence of a sexual science at the turn of the last century. The chapters in this part begin to address this gap. They examine the emergence of distinct "national sexologies" in England, Russia, Egypt and Palestine, and China, focusing on translations between languages, disciplines, and regions to gain a better understanding of how sexual science in these areas emerged from the intersections between transnational, cross-national, and national contingencies.

Part II opens with a chapter by Kate Fisher and Jana Funke that revisits the substantial body of scholarship on the formation of a modern sexual science in Britain. Fisher and Funke analyze the role of translations across time, disciplines, and national contexts in the shaping of British sex research. They pay particular attention to the dissonances between British and German writings on sex, arguing that here we find new evidence of the cultural framework that shaped British sexual science as well as an indication of how generational squabbles complicate existing narratives about the importance of continental sexology for the development of a sexual science in Britain. If continental sexology formed a point of departure for British sexual scientists, Brian Baer's analysis of the translations of central European sexological and psychological writings into Russia in turn tracks the changes that occurred when "Western" ideas moved into Russian contexts. Baer pays attention to both conceptual and disciplinary modifications and the role of translators in this process, arguing that these translations reveal the marginal status of Russia in turn-of-the-century European scientific and literary culture even as they also indicate how a distinctly Russian take on same-sex sexuality shaped the emergence of sexology and sexual politics in the country.

The final two chapters in this part—Liat Kozma's study of sexology in Egypt and Palestine and Leon Rocha's examination of Chinese sex research—both explicitly engage with the (trans)national politics of sexological discipline formation. Kozma explores how two men who were trained at Hirschfeld's Institute of Sexual Science in Berlin returned to their respective homes in Egypt and Palestine to set up sexological practices. By comparing the distinct ways in which they went about this business and how their efforts, in different ways, both challenged and were subsumed into wider debates about national modernity and unity in Egypt and Palestine, Kozma shows that sexuality and nationhood in this part of the Middle East share an interlinked history. In contrast, the final chapter in this part, Rocha's analysis of the emergence of sex research in China, demonstrates that national and cross-national influences shaped two distinct sexological traditions in the country. His examination of two competing "Chinese sexologies" picks up on the debates about the relationship between indigenous and imported knowledges in the country discussed by Howard Chiang, but here the emphasis lies on the emblematic role played by Chinese sexology in constructing differences between East and West. Rocha reveals that the transmission of a (mis)reading of sexual debates in China influenced the problematic distinction drawn by Foucault between "occidental" and "oriental" sexual traditions, a distinction that has considerably influenced the Anglo-American historiography of sexuality.

Read together, the chapters in this part, as well as those by Chiang and Suzuki, strengthen the argument that sexology is not a "Western" invention that was transmitted around the world. Instead these chapters show that sexology is a global phenomenon whose transnational dimensions indicate the complex ways in which modern sexuality was produced culturally as well as socially, scientifically, and politically. What emerges, then, when we compare the formations of modern sex research in a wide range of geographical contexts is new evidence that indicates that the scientific and cultural attention lavished on bodies and desires forms a crucial part of the sociopolitical and intellectual transformations wrought by modernity. The examinations of sexual science in the countries and regions represented here deliberately expand and decenter the critical focus on a "Western" emergence of sexology. They demonstrate that culturally contingent national sexologies also have transnational and global dimensions that trouble assumptions about the central role played by Europe in the intellectual shaping of modernity.

5

British Sexual Science beyond the Medical

Cross-Disciplinary, Cross-Historical,
and Cross-Cultural Translations

KATE FISHER AND JANA FUNKE

In 1907, Havelock Ellis, who was beginning to establish himself as the most eminent sexual scientist in Britain, wrote a review of his German colleague Iwan Bloch's *Das Sexualleben unserer Zeit* (The sexual life of our time) in the *British Journal of Psychiatry*.[1] Ellis championed Bloch as the author of works in which "history and medicine meet" and praised his cross-disciplinary approach that made this and other books "weighty, learned, comprehensive, even brilliant."[2] For Ellis, it was the translation between different disciplinary approaches (in this case, the medical and the historical) that made Bloch's work so important. Ellis argued that Bloch's writings were required reading even for those "who have given most study of the subjects here discussed" and he called for the book to be "translated into English."[3] This review of a German text by a British author indicates not only that sexual science emerged as a result of transnational dialogue and processes of translation across cultural and linguistic boundaries; it also highlights the centrality of cross-disciplinary translation to the project of sexual science and demonstrates, in particular, that sexual scientists like Ellis and Bloch sought to draw on cross-cultural and cross-historical forms of knowledge alongside medical approaches. This chapter explores these processes of translation between cultures, disciplines, and national boundaries and, in so doing, reconfigures what writing scientifically about sexuality meant at the turn of the twentieth century.

Uses of Translation and the Development
of Sexual Science

Western sexual science, emerging from the mid-nineteenth century onward, has often been understood as a new form of medical knowledge that served to identify, classify, and pathologize a range of sexual behaviors.[4] In this account, sexual science is viewed as a narrow medical field, tied specifically to psychiatry. It is seen as a project that progressed by reinforcing its scientific credentials and that affirmed its authority by relying on a specific methodology, namely, the patient case study.[5] Ivan Crozier, for instance, maintains that sexual science needs to be understood as distinct from other nonmedical debates about sexuality and emphasizes the need to "keep one's attention within the field."[6] According to this view, the development of sexual science saw the self-conscious construction of a field of knowledge that differentiated itself from other nonmedical views of sexuality, including feminist, social purist, or reformist approaches, and was populated exclusively by medical professionals.

Arguing that sexual scientists themselves viewed processes of cross-disciplinary translation as integral to the development of sexual science, this chapter questions a narrow understanding of sexual science as a clearly defined and exclusively medical field. In making this point, we draw on and contribute to important scholarship, particularly from the fields of cultural history and literary studies, which has shown that the rise of sexual science cannot be understood in scientific isolation; sexual science was part of broader intellectual debates about sexuality and sex reform and needs to be situated in a wider political and cultural context.[7] More specifically, we add to recent debates about the disciplinary shaping of sexual science.[8] Howard Chiang, for example, has called attention to the fact that sexual science became a more "multi-layered discourse" at the turn of the twentieth century and proposes to think of these developments in terms of "scientification" rather than medicalization.[9] However, even the term "scientification" is arguably too narrow to capture the more radical cross-disciplinary exchange that was at the heart of sexual science in this particular historical moment. Chris Waters goes a step further in suggesting that the "new intellectual type, the 'sexologist,'" which had emerged by the early 1900s, drew knowledge from a broad range of disciplines, including "anthropology, biology, history, psychiatry and the medical sciences."[10]

This chapter goes further still: it charts the rise of a second generation of European sexual scientists who explicitly and self-consciously turned away from narrow medical understandings of sexuality and called for cross-disciplinary exchange and collaboration. As sexual science developed and sought to demonstrate its scientific authority, various voices from a range of disciplinary perspectives were called upon to create a lively debate about what "science" meant and what methodologies could serve to develop a thorough and balanced understanding of sexuality. In this context, medically trained authors did not simply draw on nonmedical writings about sexuality, such as those produced by anthropologists, historians, or literary writers; rather, the project of sexual science was fundamentally shaped by a diverse network of contributors who worked together to construct a new scientific approach to the study of sexuality. Moreover, the expansive vision of sexual science these writers developed was not just a matter of different debates about sexuality intersecting or coinciding; it was the product of a particular critique of narrowly medical approaches to understandings of sexuality. The case study and related clinical methodologies were perceived as inadequate, as psychiatric cases provided a limited and distorted view of human sexuality. Alternative forms of expertise and cross-disciplinary contributions were thus seen as essential to a fully comprehensive and scientific understanding of sexuality. In this sense, it was precisely a process of translation—here understood as the negotiation of the medical and the nonmedical—that made sexual science "scientific" and provided the basis of its particular intellectual authority.

To develop these ideas, the following discussion maps cross-disciplinary processes of translation and cross-national exchange with a particular focus on the emergence of British sexual science and its relation to Germany. As the present volume and the past scholarship of its editor, Heike Bauer, demonstrate, translation offers a useful means to capture the complex processes of thinking and working across disciplinary, cultural, national, and linguistic boundaries that shaped sexual science.[11] We argue that many British and German sexual scientists at the end of the nineteenth and beginning of the twentieth century were dissatisfied with the narrowly medical approach of their predecessors. As a result, they began to look beyond the medical sphere and turned toward a broader range of evidence and field of disciplines, including, in particular, history and anthropology, to develop a more expansive understanding of sexual behaviors and practices across different historical periods and cultural spaces. We thus identify a second generation of sexual scientists, who self-consciously and explicitly broadened the disciplinary scope of sexual science. Recovering this crucial moment of intentional disciplinary expansion in the history of sexual science has far-reaching implications for our understanding of the emergence of sexual science as a project that went beyond the medical in its remit. In what follows, then, we show that recognizing the ways in which sexual science positioned itself as a broad field of knowledge, open to a range of methodologies and forms of evidence, including history and anthropology, radically shifts our understanding of the contours and protocols of the discipline.

We are interested in asking why second-generation sexual scientists sought cross-disciplinary expansion beyond the medical in the first place. What did other forms of evidence drawn from nonmedical disciplines like history or anthropology and the cross-cultural and cross-historical comparisons they facilitated offer sexual scientists? Moreover, to what extent can the inclusion of historical-anthropological evidence be understood as part of a cross-national network of exchange that connects the projects of sexual science in Britain, Germany, and beyond?

So far, the fact that some sexual scientists began to attack the pathologizing emphasis of their predecessors at the turn of the twentieth century has been correctly understood as part of their liberalizing and reformist agenda. Sexual scientists who were keen to challenge the criminalization of homosexuality, for instance, criticized their predecessors for exploring sexual behavior in terms of deviance, degeneration, and morbidity.[12] This emphasis on the political and reformist outlook underpinning the project of sexual science has informed, in particular, accounts of the rise of German and to an even greater degree British sexual science. Key texts such as John Addington Symonds and Havelock Ellis's *Sexual Inversion* (1896/1897) have been interpreted in this vein, as a form of reverse discourse that used the medical rhetoric of sexual science to challenge pathological understandings of homosexuality, change social and medical attitudes, and open up the possibility of legal reform.[13] Such interpretations also draw on biographical understandings of key figures in sexual science whose work is seen to reflect their own homosexual desires, or their own personal sympathies for and friendships with people who experienced such desires. These readings are inspired further by the fact that some of the most influential figures writing about sexuality in Britain (with the exception of Havelock Ellis, who had a basic medical degree but did not practice as a doctor for a sustained period of time), such as Symonds or Edward Carpenter, were not medically or scientifically trained.

Missing from this account is an understanding of the intellectual reasons behind the increasing dissatisfaction with purely medical and pathological understandings sexuality presented by first-generation sexual science. It is important to recognize that second-generation sexual scientists sought to move beyond pathological readings of sexuality not only because of a politically informed homosexual agenda or a desire to reclaim homosexuality as "non-pathological." Instead, the rejection of a narrow medical approach was part of a broader shift within sexual science toward the exploration of sexual variation and sexual difference. Here, cross-cultural and cross-historical translation played a crucial role: drawing on historical and anthropological accounts allowed sexual scientists to encounter diverse sexual customs and sexual behaviors. Often, it was precisely the difficulties of translating—the untranslatability—of such evidence into the modern Western world that made it useful in demonstrating the wide variety of sexuality. What the disciplinary expansion of sexual science served to illustrate was the diversity of sexual behaviors and types across cultures and historical periods. For second-generation sexual scientists, the aim was not simply to "rehabilitate" forms of sexual behavior that had previously been seen as pathological, but to offer a broader and more expansive view of human sexuality that could only be achieved by drawing on a range of disciplines, including history and anthropology.

Cross-national exchange also becomes important here, as British sexual science was not isolated in being less "medical" or less "scientific" in its turn to history, anthropology, and other nonmedical disciplines. In other words, the fact that British sexual science was interested in such nonmedical forms of knowledge was not simply a result of the fact that there were so few medical practitioners populating the field of sexual science in this particular country. Quite the contrary, the cross-disciplinary turn, for instance, toward history and anthropology, needs to be understood in terms of cross-national exchange itself—it is part of a broader epistemic shift that can also be traced in Germany. British sexual science, then, was not exceptional in its more "cultural" or "historical" focus but rather needs to be written into the broader history of a second generation of sexual science that explicitly sought cross-disciplinary expansion and was interested in cross-cultural and cross-historical comparison and knowledge formation.[14] Processes of translation across national and linguistic as well as disciplinary borders were thus at the heart of the project of sexual science as it developed at the turn of the twentieth century.

"The Medical View Is One-Sided": Expanding the Disciplinary Focus of Sexual Science

From the 1890s, a second generation of sexual scientists began to view the work of their predecessors as prejudiced and reductive because of its predominantly medical framing.[15] This second generation argued that in looking only at individuals encountered in the psychiatric clinic or prison, sexual scientists in the past had limited their investigations to cases with sexual problems and pathologies. When sexual science developed in Britain, it emerged directly from this criticism of first-generation sexual science on the continent. Early on, then, British sexual science in particular was characterized by an attempt to broaden the scope of its investigations beyond medical methods, techniques, and forms of evidence in a bid to work against narrowly medical views of sexuality.

Indeed, this challenge was at the heart of Symonds's criticism of European sexual science as articulated in *A Problem in Modern Ethics* (1891), his correspondence with Ellis, and their co-authored book *Sexual Inversion*. Symonds dissected in much detail the problems he identified in the publications of earlier continental sexual scientists and through his critique entered into cross-national dialogue with such writers. For instance, he singled out the work of Russian physician Benjamin Tarnowsky as flawed in precisely these terms:

> The author is a Russian, whose practice in St. Petersburg has brought him into close professional relations with the male prostitutes and habitual paederasts of that capital. He is able therefore to speak with authority, on the ground of a quite exceptional knowledge of the moral and physical disturbances connected with sodomy. I cannot but think that the very peculiarities of his experience have led him to form incomplete theories. He is too familiar with venal pathics, paedicators, and effeminates who prostitute their bodies in the grossest way, to be able to appreciate the subtler bearings of the problem.[16]

For Symonds, Tarnowsky and other members of the first generation of sexual science, including Richard von Krafft-Ebing, could only view homosexuality as pathological, because their observations were limited to the study of unhealthy individuals.

Edward Carpenter, whose writings on sexuality differed from works such as *Sexual Inversion* in that they were more overtly poetic and philosophical in tone, articulated a similar critique:

> it must never be forgotten that the medico-scientific enquirer is bound on the whole to meet with those cases that are of a morbid character, rather than with those that are healthy in their manifestation, since indeed it is the former that he lays himself out for. . . . As Krafft-Ebing says in his own preface, "It is the sad privilege of Medicine, and especially of Psychiatry, to look always on the reverse side of life, on the weakness and wretchedness of man."[17]

Thus, second-generation sexual scientists maintained that their predecessors had developed a flawed understanding of sexuality; they had failed to explore sexual variation and difference beyond the pathological and had not attempted to interrogate the overlap between healthy and pathological forms of sexual behavior.

It was the argument that medical methodologies provided too limited a perspective that drove a reshaping of the framing of sexual science and the disciplinary basis of its authority. To correct such narrow medical and pathological understandings of sexual behavior, it was deemed necessary to engage with a broader and more diverse range of evidence and research methodologies. While the case study was not abandoned as an important form of evidence, the disciplinary scope of sexual science was broadened and involvement from practitioners who were not medical doctors was explicitly invited. To be sure, medical expertise remained central to affirm scientific authority and scholarly legitimacy, but sexual scientists nevertheless increasingly saw their project as one that involved working and thinking across different disciplines and translating various forms of evidence into the framework of sexual science.

In the first years of the twentieth century, German dermatologist Iwan Bloch was particularly forthright in calling for an engagement with nonmedical knowledge to expand and enrich sexual science and to provide a well-rounded and balanced understanding of sexuality:

> I am compelled to point out that his [Krafft-Ebing's] purely medical view of sexual aberrations is one-sided, and to insist that it must be amplified and rectified by anthropological and ethnological researches.[18]

Although conceding that "the purely medical consideration of sexual life" would always "constitute the nucleus of sexual science," Bloch maintained that it would not do "full justice to the many-sided relationships between the sexual and all the other provinces of human life."[19] Instead, he encouraged his colleagues to "leave the hospital and the medical consulting-room . . . [and to] observe the sexual activity of the genus homo in its manifold phenomena."[20] He called for an understanding of sexual science (Sexualwissenschaft) as an all-encompassing union of various sciences; sexual science was no longer the domain of medical doctors alone; it also needed to comprise ethnographers and anthropologists, literary writers and poets, historians and classicists, philosophers and psychologists:

> this particular branch of inquiry must be treated in its proper subordination as a part of the general "science of mankind," which is constituted by a union of all other sciences—of general biology, anthropology and ethnology, philosophy and psychology, the history of literature, and the entire history of civilization.[21]

Bloch thus promoted a view of sexual science not just as cross-disciplinary, but as potentially interdisciplinary: sexual science was reconceptualized as a field of knowledge that comprised and combined a range of medical and nonmedical disciplinary approaches.

Thus, as sexual science developed from the 1890s in Britain and in the early twentieth century in Germany, there was an increasing emphasis on incorporating a wide range of different intellectual and disciplinary perspectives. In the British context, Crozier has charted a national nineteenth-century medical tradition of psychiatric writings about homosexuality, which he argues framed British contributions to sexology, alongside their translations of and responses to continental works of sexual science.[22] In addition to these earlier medical writings, however, it is also crucial to pay attention to equally significant traditions of writing about sexuality that had emerged in the fields of anthropology and history, for example, and that shaped British sexual science from the very start.[23]

In 1893, for instance, Ellis, sketched out a plan for a new international journal titled *Man: A Journal of Psychology and Anthropology*, which explicitly sought to advance science by bringing together a variety of disciplines. The aim of the journal, according to Ellis, was as follows:

> To deal with psychology and anthropology in the widest sense—including also Sociology, Ethnography, Demography, Hypnotism, the study of genius, and, of course, criminal anthropology, with those branches of medical research which border on anthropology and psychology and are of general interest. . . . It would not be a journal for specialists in any one branch but would bring together the groups of specialists interested in man, on a common ground, and would especially seek the "cross-fertilisation" of anthropology and psychology, which in the future is bound to be very productive.[24]

Ellis here reveals his early commitment to a scientific method that was based on the "cross-fertilisation" of different disciplinary fields. His focus on the relation between psychology and anthropology (as well as a host of other disciplines) is particularly significant with regard to the emergence of sexual science in Britain, which developed under the label of "sex psychology." Indeed, Ellis would continue to draw on a range of disciplinary approaches and various forms of evidence throughout his life, as is evident in the seven volumes of his *Studies in the Psychology of Sex* (1896/1897–1928), in which he persistently draws on historical and anthropological evidence. Ellis was thus keen to create a cross-disciplinary dialogue to expand the scope of psychology and anthropology. Indeed, the interesting metaphor of "cross-fertilisation" suggests that he envisioned a process of disciplinary translation that was two-directional, resulting in a richer and fuller understanding of all involved disciplines.

"A Union of All Sciences": Toward a Cross-Disciplinary Sexual Science

Recognizing the centrality of cross-disciplinary translation is thus crucial to understand the particular shape taken by sexual science, especially in Britain and Germany. Given that sexual science was not defined by the adoption of clinical methodologies and that sexual scientists explicitly sought to move beyond the medical by engaging in cross-disciplinary dialogue, we need to rethink radically our understanding of the contours of sexual science and ask new questions about what it meant to take part in sexual science and who was deemed a qualified or authoritative voice in this context. Over the course of the early twentieth century, different organs, societies, and professional bodies emerged that gave institutional shape to the Western project of sexual science, but the increasing professionalization of sexual science did not result in the consolidation of a particular approach or the championing of a specific set of methodologies. In fact, societies like the BSSSP (British Society for the Study of Sex Psychology, founded in 1914) or the World League for Sexual Reform (officially founded in 1928) or publications like Magnus Hirschfeld's *Jahrbuch für sexuelle Zwischenstufen* (Yearbook of sexual intermediates, 1899–1923) were open to members or contributors who did not have formal medical credentials. The *Jahrbuch*, for instance, included articles from a wide range of disciplines, including literary and classical scholarship, history, and ethnography. Such organs and institutions also facilitated a lively exchange of knowledge across national and linguistic boundaries and contributed to the fact that sexual science was increasingly characterized by cross-disciplinary and cross-national dialogue. Sexual science, then, was an explicitly multidisciplinary and multilingual project.

In particular, attention to translations between and across disciplines shows that many key figures of sexual science (especially in Britain) did not emerge from medical circles. While there was an earlier nineteenth-century British tradition of writing about homosexuality, and Ellis himself was a trained doctor, from the end of the nineteenth century onward, key contributions to debates about sexuality, sexual pathology, sexual taxonomies, and sex reform came from figures outside or at least not actively involved in the medical profession.[25] Their important roles indicate the openness of sexual science to cross-disciplinary contributions and the conception of sexual science as requiring a comprehensive approach to knowledge that required input from a variety of perspectives and areas of expertise.

Edward Carpenter provides an excellent example of this cross-disciplinary nature of sexual science. Scholars have struggled to understand Carpenter's place in the history of sexual science: he was not medically trained; he had a degree in mathematics, worked for a short time as a curate for the Church of England, and became a socialist activist and sex reformer.[26] Carpenter's work as homosexual reformer is well known, but he was also keen to depathologize sexual relations more broadly and was, for instance, involved in debates about marriage reform, thus moving beyond the narrow focus on same-sex desire.[27] Some historians and literary scholars argue that Carpenter was not seen as an "acceptable" voice within sexual science. Anna Katharina Schaffner, for example, maintains that Carpenter belongs "properly to the literary field" and that he only drew upon "biological and sexological conception" in a bid to "strengthen the credentials" of his position.[28] Crozier, too, argues that Carpenter cannot be viewed as a sexual scientist, claiming that his work was not taken seriously by his contemporaries, pointing in particular to the reviews of Carpenter's work in the *British Medical Journal*.[29] However, such reviews reveal not so much a particular objection to Carpenter's credentials as a sexual scientist; they are more concerned with the question of whether the topic of homosexuality was significant enough to warrant consideration in a prestigious medical journal. In other words, the review attacked the study of homosexuality in general, not Carpenter's authority in particular. Moreover, other reviews placed Carpenter's work firmly within the emerging field of sexual science. The *Medical Times*, when discussing Carpenter's *Intermediate Sex* in a review titled "Carpenter on the Sexes" (1909), for instance, compared it with the "careful" work of Hirschfeld in Germany and urged British readers to follow Carpenter in treating the subject as seriously as it was treated on the continent.[30]

Unlike Ellis and Symonds in *Sexual Inversion*, Carpenter did not often deliberately employ the language of science to explain his approach to sexual questions. Yet he absorbed, analyzed, and directly engaged with the work of continental sexual scientists in the production of his own synthesis of such writings. He also sought to have his work read within medical circles, and asked Ellis, for example, to send notices of his publication of *The Intermediate Sex* to medical and scientific journals in 1909. Moreover, he corresponded with many of the key thinkers in sexual science, including Albert Moll, Bloch, and Hirschfeld.[31] It is clear that Carpenter saw his work as scientific in important ways and that he was keen to contribute to European debate about sexual questions under the general and broad umbrella of sexual science. In particular, like Symonds and Ellis, Carpenter wanted to challenge continental first-generation sexual science, work against the pathological views of sexuality it promoted, and criticize its narrow approach to scientific inquiry. In *Intermediate Types among Primitive Folk* (1914), he presented the pathologization of homosexuality as unscientific, arguing that to "insist" on the evils of such desires "would not be the method either of common-sense, or of science."[32] The properly scientific approach was to "inquire first . . .

what place it [homosexuality] may possibly have occupied in social life and what (if any) were its healthy rather than its unhealthy manifestations."[33]

What made Carpenter's work "scientific," and what made it a key contribution to the emerging science of sex, was that sexual science was itself refigured at the turn of the twentieth century as a cross-disciplinary field that did not erect exclusionary credentials around its practice. A number of sexual scientists wrote about sexuality from a psychiatric standpoint, but it is far from clear that there was any concerted effort from outside or within to limit scientific discussion of sexuality to a narrowly defined group of medically trained men. The display of medical credentials played a key role in asserting the legitimacy of sexual knowledge, but it did not do so exclusively or by marginalizing nonmedical forms of knowledge. Rather, sexual scientific authority was derived from the attempt to understand sexuality in its entirety from all disciplinary perspectives and by drawing on a wide range of expertise. Sexual science as a project, then, was shaped by a variety of individuals from across disciplines, who consciously and strategically sought to bring together different areas of knowledge, including various branches of medicine, psychology, anthropology, history, literature, and the classics.

Carpenter, for instance, contributed an article on the relation between homosexuality and prophetism and the significance of what he called "sexual intermediates" in early historical and cultural periods to Hirschfeld's *Jahrbuch* in 1911.[34] He was also invited (along with Ellis) to present a paper at the First International Congress for Sexual Research in 1914, which was canceled after the outbreak of World War I.[35] Importantly, the congress was organized by the International Society for Sexual Research (Internationale Gesellschaft für Sexualforschung) and Carpenter received an invitation from the society's vice president, Albert Moll.[36] The fact that Moll invited Carpenter might seem surprising, given that Moll is generally viewed as a proponent of a more narrowly medical approach to sexual science. His rejection of Hirschfeld's political and reformist stance, in particular, indicates an increasing split between a clearly defined medico-scientific strand of German sexual science and a methodologically more open-ended and overtly political branch.[37] Still, in 1914, Carpenter's international standing within sexual science was sufficiently established to warrant a personal invitation from Moll despite his lack of medical credentials.

Moreover, Moll, who wrote to Carpenter in English to invite him to contribute a paper on any topic he chose, explicitly spelled out the broad and cross-disciplinary focus of sexual science:

> Herewith we take the liberty of inviting you to our *First International Congress for Sexual Research* which will take place in Berlin on Oct 31st, Nov 1st and Nov 2nd 1914. It will embrace the total sphere

of scientific sexual research, and will probably be divided into a
biological-medical section, a sociological section (including history
of civilisation and ethnology), a legal section (including criminal-
anthropology and psychology) and a philosophical, psychological,
educational section.[38]

Moll's vision of a congress reflecting "the total sphere of scientific sexual research" echoes Bloch's ambitious broadening of the scope of sexual
science. The different sections proposed by Moll show that disciplinary
boundaries were not obsolete; the "biological-medical sphere," for instance, was set apart from other approaches to the study of sexuality. It
is also worth noting that Carpenter responded to Moll (in German), suggesting a paper on the importance of homosexuality in cultural history
("Die Bedeutung der Homosexualität in der Kulturgeschichte"). Moll replied asking if Carpenter could be persuaded to change the title to "Die
Homosexualität in der Kulturgeschichte," thus dropping the term "importance" (Bedeutung). He explained: "We want to stay clear of value
judgments in the Society, at least officially. In practice this is not always
possible" (Wir wollen uns wenigstens offiziell in der Gesellschaft von
Werturteilen fernhalten. Praktisch ist dies nicht immer möglich).[39] While
the suggested change of title indicates Moll's wish to *appear* objective and
unbiased, there is no doubt that the historical-anthropological perspective
Carpenter had to offer was considered valuable within the framework of
sexual science. Moreover, the complex perceptions of disciplinary boundaries that allowed for various disciplinary "crossings" is reflected in the
printed program of the congress: Ellis's and Moll's papers are listed under "cultural history and sociology" (despite the fact that both speakers
had a medical background), whereas Carpenter's paper, which approaches
the topic of homosexuality from a comparative cross-cultural and cross-
historical perspective, appears in the "biological-medical" section.[40]

This not only indicates the increasing openness of sexual science in
general but also shows the strong affinities and cross-lingual dialogue between sexual science in England and Germany, where a second generation
of sexual scientists consciously sought to renegotiate the boundaries, aims,
and purposes of sexual science. The position of Moll within the evolving cross-disciplinary and cross-national project of sexual science war-
rants further investigation; however, it is clear that even a sexual scientist
like Moll—well known for his more rigid biological-medical understanding of sexual science—recognized the value of cross-cultural and cross-
historical approaches to the scientific study of sexuality. The focus on
cross-disciplinary translation thus draws attention to the conscious shaping and reshaping of sexual science over the course of the late nineteenth

and early twentieth century and also allows for a reconsideration of the place of nonmedically trained figures within the project of sexual science.

Cross-Cultural and Cross-Historical Translation and the Writing of *Sexual Inversion*

Such questions about cross-disciplinary dialogue, scientific expertise, and the significance of cross-cultural and cross-historical approaches to the scientific study of sexuality are particularly important in understanding the intellectual collaboration between Ellis and Symonds, whose coauthored *Sexual Inversion* is often seen as a foundational document in the history of British sexual science. It is crucial to recognize that the impetus behind this text did not come from Ellis but from Symonds, who did not have formal medical or scientific training and who began corresponding with Ellis after reading his literary analysis of the work of Walt Whitman in *The New Spirit* (1890). As has often been noted, Symonds was reform-minded and personally invested in the project of legitimating homosexual relations in Britain. In this sense, it is likely that he sought to collaborate with Ellis to gain access to medical credentials and scientific authority. Yet Symonds did not simply rely on Ellis's scientific expertise for strategic reasons but approached the collaboration from a position of considerable scientific expertise. Despite his lack of formal medical or scientific training, Symonds's correspondence with Ellis (conducted from 1890 until his death in 1893) together with his detailed critical engagement with continental sexual science in *A Problem in Modern Ethics* make it clear that he was at that time far more knowledgeable about scientific discussions of sexuality than Ellis. It was Symonds, for instance, who encouraged Ellis to read Moll and who proposed to write a "scientific" book about sexual inversion in England.[41] Thus, Ellis and Symonds discussed and debated the work of continental sexual scientists on equal terms, with Ellis asking Symonds for his opinion on the scientific literature just as frequently as Symonds sought clarification of Ellis's views.

Moreover, the making of *Sexual Inversion* demonstrates forcefully the open-ended disciplinary boundaries of sexual science. The collaboration between Ellis and Symonds has often been misconstrued as indicating a split between historical or cultural understandings of sexuality (supposedly proposed by Symonds) and an allegedly more rigid scientific approach (purportedly adopted by Ellis).[42] Such flawed understandings of the intellectual exchange between Ellis and Symonds are representative of broader misunderstandings of the project of sexual science at this particular historical moment. To be sure, the question of how to use historical and anthropological evidence in the context of sexual science raised questions concerning the translation of different kinds of knowledge and methodologies across disciplinary boundaries. However, these difficulties did not result in an abandonment of cross-cultural and cross-historical approaches; quite to the contrary, sexual science in Britain was informed and shaped by the challenges of cross-disciplinary translation from the start.

Ellis and Symonds's negotiation of historical evidence about male same-sex desire in the ancient Greek world illustrates this point. Symonds, whose earlier work—in particular *A Problem in Greek Ethics*—was part of the homosocial culture of Victorian Hellenism, believed that the history of ancient Greece provided an important corrective to pathological readings of homosexuality presented in first-generation sexual science.[43] He explained to Ellis that "the so-called scientific 'psychiatrists' are ludicrously in error, by diagnosing as necessarily morbid what was the leading emotion of the best and noblest men in Hellas."[44] Scholarship to date has maintained that Ellis was sympathetic toward Symonds's desire to use the Greek past to demonstrate that homosexual desires could be healthy but ultimately rejected his collaborator's historical approach. This view has been supported by the fact that Symonds's stand-alone chapter on ancient Greece, published as part of the main text in the first German edition of *Sexual Inversion* in 1896, was delegated to the appendix in the first English edition in 1897, and then excised entirely in subsequent editions of the text, which were prepared by Ellis after Symonds's death. It was been argued that the reason Ellis deleted the chapter on ancient Greece was that it did not fit the model of congenital or inborn inversion promoted in *Sexual Inversion*. In Joseph Bristow's view, Symonds's history could not be reconciled with Ellis's heredity.[45]

While the history of ancient Greece did pose a challenge to a congenital model of homosexuality, this must not, however, be misconstrued as indicative of a strict division between history and science. For a start, Symonds and Ellis were both aware of the political advantages of presenting inversion as inborn or hereditary.[46] Moreover, and more importantly for the purposes of this chapter, their correspondence also demonstrates that both collaborators were eager to expand the scope of sexual science by taking into account historical evidence. The main question Ellis and Symonds confronted was one of cross-historical translation: how could ancient Greek models of same-sex desire inform a discussion of sexual inversion in the modern world? Here, both Ellis and Symonds agreed that it was important to acknowledge the *difference* between ancient Greece and the modern world: between a classical past that appeared to accept and even encourage same-sex relations between males, and a contemporary European world that largely criminalized and stigmatized such behaviors.[47] In this more hostile modern world, it made more sense to understand homosexual desires as congenital or hereditary rather than viewing them as the product of social influences or acculturation.

Crucially, however, this acknowledgment of the difference between forms of desire in the ancient and modern worlds did not result in the rejection of history altogether. Quite to the contrary, ancient Greece continued to be relevant for Ellis and Symonds and to have a place in all editions of *Sexual Inversion* and in the project of sexual science more generally. What turned out to be valuable about ancient Greece was precisely the fact that it could not easily be translated into a model that presented homosexuality as inborn; it was the "untranslatability" of ancient Greek same-sex desires, the fact that such desires could not be subsumed under a congenital explanation of sexual inversion, that made historical evidence valuable and intriguing.[48] The reason for this is that Ellis and Symonds, like other sexual scientists at the time, aspired to move beyond narrow medical understandings of sexuality and to grasp sexuality in its cross-cultural and cross-historical variation. Ancient Greece served this purpose, first, by demonstrating that individuals who experienced same-sex desire were not necessarily pathological, and, second, by showing that homosexual desires could be acquired rather than congenital.

The fact that ancient Greece continued to have a place within British sexual science is indicated by the fact that all three editions of *Sexual Inversion*, including the much-revised third edition of 1915, continued to discuss the ancient world, especially in the first chapter. Here, ancient Greece no longer stood alone as a special place or unique historical moment in which healthy same-sex desires flourished. Greece did not only offer a strategy to legitimate same-sex desires and authorize calls for sexual reform, as has often been assumed.[49] Rather, ancient Greece was integrated into the broader project of second-generation sexual science and used alongside a wide range of historical and anthropological evidence to demonstrate sexual diversity through cross-historical and cross-cultural comparison. It is easy to assume that Symonds would have rejected this use of ancient Greece as part of a wider discussion of cultures and historical periods, holding on to a celebratory vision of the Greek past that was characteristic of Victorian Hellenism.[50] Importantly, however, *A Problem in Modern Ethics* suggests that Symonds, like Ellis, was interested in charting the variety of homosexual desires, which, he emphasized, could be found "everywhere and in all periods of history."[51] Moreover, it illustrates that Symonds himself (in this later work) moved toward a historical-anthropological framework in which ancient Greece (and other historical periods) were considered alongside anthropological evidence from different cultures around the world. Ellis and Symonds thus both insisted that the scientific study of homosexuality necessitated an engagement with a wide range of historical and anthropological evidence; they both affirmed the centrality of cross-cultural and cross-historical translation within the project of sexual science.

Conclusion

This chapter has offered a new reading of the emergence of British sexual science and its dialogue with German debates about the scientific study of sexuality. It has demonstrated that cross-disciplinary dialogue in general—and the embrace of cross-cultural and cross-historical perspectives on sexuality in particular—were at the heart of second-generation sexual science. The failure of many scholars to appreciate fully this disciplinary diversity of sexual science is, in part, attributable to a misunderstanding and, indeed, a mistranslation of early twentieth-century languages of science and knowledge. The call for a scientific approach to the study of sexuality did not automatically imply a focus on the natural sciences. Bloch's original German usage of Sexualwissenschaft, for instance, did not imply a distinction between the natural sciences (Naturwissenschaften) and human or social sciences (Geisteswissenschaften). Quite the contrary, this chapter has demonstrated that Bloch and his contemporaries in Britain and Germany considered various forms of knowledge as essential in the construction of a fully comprehensive scientific understanding of sexuality. Sexual scientists at the turn of the twentieth century, then, used a wide range of research methodologies and forms of evidence drawn from across the natural sciences, human sciences, and social sciences.[52] They actively and consciously engaged in processes of cross-disciplinary translation to move beyond narrow medical approaches and to work toward a more comprehensive, balanced, and, in this sense, "scientific" study of sexuality.

NOTES

Note: The authors are jointly and equally responsible for the text and accompanying research.

1. We have decided to use the term "sexual science" rather than the more familiar "sexology" to capture the more open-ended and broader field of knowledge we are beginning to map in this chapter. The shift in terminology aims to indicate the diversification of research methodologies and forms of evidence within sexual science at the turn of the twentieth century.

2. Havelock Ellis, "*Das Sexualleben unserer Zeit* by Dr. Iwan Bloch," *British Journal of Psychiatry* 53 (1907): 637.

3. Ibid., 639.

4. In *The History of Sexuality,* vol. 1, *The Will to Knowledge* (New York: Vintage, 1979), Foucault has influentially identified the pathologizing and medicalizing imperative through which sexuality was constituted as a scientific subject of knowledge. This text has shaped the history of sexuality and forms the base assumptions behind many accounts of the emergence of sexual science. For a good overview of the rise of sexual science, see Chris Waters, "Sexology," in *Palgrave Advances in the Modern History of*

Sexuality, ed. Harry G. Cocks and Matt Houlbrook (Basingstoke, UK: Palgrave, 2005), 41–63.

5. For a discussion of the scientific authority of the case study, see Ivan Crozier, "Pillow Talk: Credibility, Trust and the Sexological Case History," *History of Science* 46, no. 4 (2008): 375–404. See also Harry Oosterhuis, *Stepchildren of Nature: Krafft-Ebing, Psychiatry, and the Making of Sexual Identity* (Chicago: University of Chicago Press, 2000).

6. Ivan Crozier, "Nineteenth-Century British Psychiatric Writing about Homo-sexuality before Havelock Ellis: The Missing Story," *Journal of the History of Medicine and Allied Sciences* 63, no. 1 (2008): 66n.

7. See Lucy Bland and Laura Doan, eds., *Sexology in Culture: Labelling Bodies and Desires* (Cambridge: Polity, 1998). For more on sexual science and feminism, see Lesley Hall, "Hauling Down the Double Standard: Feminism, Social Purity and Sexual Science in Late Nineteenth-Century Britain," *Gender and History* 16 (2004): 36–56.

8. For more on the relation between literature and sexual science, see Heike Bauer, *English Literary Sexology: Translations of Inversion, 1860–1930* (Basingstoke, UK: Palgrave Macmillan, 2009); Vernon A. Rosario, *The Erotic Imagination: French Histories of Perversity* (Oxford: Oxford University Press, 1997); Anna Katharina Schaffner, *Modernism and Perversion: Sexual Deviance in Sexology and Literature, 1850–1930* (Basingstoke, UK: Palgrave Macmillan, 2012).

9. Howard Chiang, "Liberating Sex, Knowing Desire: *Scientia Sexualis* and Epistemic Turning Points in the History of Sexuality," *History of the Human Sciences* 23, no. 5 (2010): 46–47. See also Howard Chiang, "Double Alterity and the Global Historiography of Sexuality: China, Europe, and the Emergence of Sexuality as a Global Possibility," *e-pisteme* 2, no. 1 (2009): 33–52.

10. Waters, "Sexology," 42.

11. See Bauer, *English Literary Sexology*.

12. Following Harry Oosterhuis, "Sexual Modernity in the Works of Richard von Krafft-Ebing and Albert Moll," *Medical History* 56, no. 2 (2012): 133–155, we need to be careful not to overlook the fact that even first-generation sexual scientists such as Richard von Krafft-Ebing and Albert Moll had already begun to blur the boundaries between the pathological and the healthy and to suggest that there might be a greater overlap between pathological and nonpathological forms of sexual behavior. For a simi-lar argument concerning Italian sexual science, see Chiara Beccalossi, "Madness and Sexual Psychopathies as the Magnifying Glass of the Normal: Italian Psychiatry and Sexuality, c. 1880–1910," *Social History of Medicine* 27, no. 2 (2014): 303–325. However, it is still crucial to recognize the rise of a second generation of sexual scientists that perceived their predecessors' work as reductive and thus defined themselves against this first generation.

13. See Ivan Crozier, "Introduction: Havelock Ellis, John Addington Symonds and the Construction of Sexual Inversion," in *Sexual Inversion: A Critical Edition*, ed. Ivan Crozier (Basingstoke, UK: Palgrave Macmillan, 2007), 1–86.

14. For more on how non-Western sexualities were incorporated into the project of Western sexual science, see the work of postcolonial historians of sexuality such as Rudi Bleys, *The Geography of Perversion: Male-to-Male Sexual Behaviour outside the West and the Ethnographic Imagination, 1750–1918* (New York: New York University

Press, 1995); Irvin C. Schick, *The Erotic Margin: Sexuality and Spatiality in Alteritist Discourse* (London: Verso, 1999). Importantly, it was the new outlook within second-generation sexual science that demanded a global approach to the study of sexuality; it was through the deployment of historical and anthropological materials in particular that sexual scientists sought to map variation on a global scale. See Kate Fisher and Jana Funke, "'Let Us Leave the Hospital [. . .]; Let Us Go on a Journey around the World': Sexual Science and the Global Search for Variation and Difference," in *Towards a Global History of Sexual Science, 1880–1950*, ed. Veronika Fuechtner, Douglas E. Haynes, and Ryan Jones (forthcoming).

15. The understanding of European sexual science as a narrowly medical discipline that drew on nineteenth-century psychiatric traditions, viewed the clinical consulting room as the central locus of its evidential work, and was disseminated primarily through networks of medically trained professionals is perhaps sustainable for the mid- to late nineteenth century. Even here, however, more research needs to be done on role of non-medical perspectives, such as those of jurist Karl Heinrich Ulrichs, in the first generation of sexual science. For more on Ulrichs, see Sebastian Matzner, "From Uranians to Homosexuals: Philhellenism, Greek Homoeroticism and Gay Emancipation in Germany 1835–1915," *Classical Receptions Journal* 2, no. 1 (2010): 60–91. Moreover, some medical doctors of the first generation, such as Paul Moreau and Albert Moll, did draw on anthropology or history, although this engagement with nonmedical evidence was perceived as flawed by the following generation, as Symonds's critical engagement with continental sexual science shows.

16. John Addington Symonds, *A Problem in Modern Ethics Being an Inquiry in the Phenomenon of Sexual Inversion* (London: privately printed, 1896), 39.

17. Edward Carpenter, *The Intermediate Sex: A Study of Some Transitional Types of Men and Women* (London: Allen and Unwin, 1921), 63–64.

18. Iwan Bloch, *The Sexual Life of Our Time in Its Relations to Modern Civilization* (London: Rebman, 1908), 455–456.

19. Ibid., ix.

20. Ibid., 455–456.

21. Ibid., ix.

22. Crozier, "Nineteenth-Century British Psychiatric Writing."

23. Influential writers in these nonmedical fields include, for instance, Richard Burton, James George Frazer, and William Lecky.

24. Ellis cited in Phyllis Grosskurth, *Havelock Ellis: A Biography* (New York: Knopf, 1980), 152.

25. In "Pillow Talk," Crozier points out that one of the reasons why Ellis became a doctor was so that he could contribute to debates about sex. However, this does more to reveal the cross-disciplinary status of Ellis than it does to demonstrate that being a doctor was a necessary condition of being a sexual scientist.

26. Carpenter first met Ellis at the Fellowship of the New Life in the early 1880s. He made Symonds's acquaintance because of their shared interest in Whitman, and Symonds asked to meet Carpenter in 1890.

27. Sheila Rowbotham, *Edward Carpenter: A Life of Liberty and Love* (London: Verso, 2008), 188.

28. Schaffner, *Modernism and Perversion*, 103.

29. The *British Medical Journal*'s opposition to sexual science was regularly articulated throughout the 1900s. See Matt Cook, *London and the Culture of Homosexuality, 1885–1914* (Cambridge: Cambridge University Press, 2003), 76–77. Cook maintains that it was the cross-disciplinary nature of sexual science in Britain, and the ways in which its practitioners were also sex reformers, radical thinkers, socialist agitators, utopia visionaries, bohemian figures, free love advocates, and so on, that prevented sexual science attaining the kind of dispassionate scientific authority it obtained on the continent.

30. "Carpenter on the Sexes," *Medical Times*, February 27, 1909, clipping in Sheffield Archives, CC Box 6-23b.

31. Carpenter, like Symonds, was aware of not being a doctor and sought Ellis's advice because of the latter's medical credentials. This did not, however, prevent Carpenter from viewing his work as part of scientific debates and from asserting his place in medical publications.

32. Edward Carpenter, *Intermediate Types among Primitive Folks: A Study in Social Evolution* (New York: Kennerly, 1921), 10.

33. Ibid.

34. The article was Edward Carpenter, "Über Beziehungen zwischen Homosexualität und Prophetentum und die Bedeutung der sexuellen Zwischenstufen in frühen Kulturepochen" [On the relations between homosexuality and prophetism and the importance of sexual intermediates in early cultural periods], *Vierteljahresberichte des wissenschaftlich-humanitären Komitees* 2, no. 3–4 (1911): 289–316, 386–396.

35. Carpenter's paper, which draws heavily on historical and anthropological data, survives in draft form (Sheffield Archives MS 186).

36. Such processes of transnational exchange between England and Germany in the 1910s and 1920s have not yet been explored in sufficient detail and are of particular interest in relation to the disciplinary broadening out of the project of sexual science taking place at the turn of the twentieth century in both countries. So far, Robert A. Nye, "The History of Sexuality in Context: National Sexological Traditions," *Science in Context* 4, no. 2 (1991): 387–406, has highlighted the need to understand the changing cosmopolitanism of sexual science. See also Nicholas Matte, "International Sexual Reform and Sexology in Europe, 1897–1933," *Canadian Bulletin of Medical History* 22, no. 2 (2005): 253–270.

37. See, for instance, Ralf Dose, *Magnus Hirschfeld: The Origins of the Gay Liberation Movement* (New York: Monthly Review Press, 2014).

38. Moll to Carpenter, May 1914, Sheffield Archives, CC MSS 271-145.

39. Moll to Carpenter, July 6, 1914, Sheffield Archives, CC MSS 271-148. Authors' own translation.

40. Sheffield Archives, MS 271-146.

41. Chiang, "Double Alterity," 40, mistakenly argues that "Ellis integrated the literary and historical information about homosexuality that Symonds and Carpenter had provided with his own medical and psychological insights." The correspondence between Ellis and Symonds and the latter's independent publications indicate, however, that this process was much more equal and reciprocal. Symonds also drew Ellis and Carpenter's attention to the work of Ulrichs, who made extensive use of classical and historical material, as Matzner, "From Uranians to Homosexuals," shows.

42. The collaboration between Ellis and Symonds is presented in largely antagonistic terms in Joseph Bristow, "Symonds' History, Ellis' Heredity: Sexual Inversion,"

in *Sexology in Culture: Labelling Bodies and Desires*, ed. Lucy Bland and Laura Doan (Cambridge: Polity, 1998), 79–99; Crozier, "Introduction"; Wayne Koestenbaum, *Double Talk: The Erotics of Male Literary Collaboration* (New York: Routledge, 1989).

43. See Linda Dowling, *Hellenism and Homosexuality in Victorian Oxford* (Ithaca, NY: Cornell University Press, 1994).

44. Symonds to Ellis, June 20, 1892, in *John Addington Symonds (1840–1893) and Homosexuality: A Critical Edition of Sources*, ed. Sean Brady (Basingstoke, UK: Palgrave Macmillan, 2012), 221.

45. Bristow, "Symonds' History."

46. For more on Ellis and Symonds's strategic reception of Greece, see Jana Funke, "'We Cannot Be Greek Now': Age Difference, Corruption of Youth and the Making of Sexual Inversion," *English Studies* 94, no. 2 (2013): 139–153.

47. See Ellis to Symonds (July 1, 1892) and Symonds's reply (July 7, 1892) in Brady, *John Addington Symonds*, 222–225.

48. Bauer, *English Literary Sexology*, 45, demonstrates that Hirschfeld "was also aware that the meanings of certain culturally-specific acts and practices are untranslatable." For more on Hirschfeld's interest in cross-cultural comparison as a means to grasp sexual variation and diversity, see Mark Johnson, "Transgression and the Making of 'Western' Sexual Sciences," in *Transgressive Sex: Subversion and Control in Erotic Encounters*, ed. Hastings Donnan and Fiona Magowan (New York: Berghahn, 2009), 167–189; Jana Funke, "Navigating the Past: Sexuality, Race and the Uses of the Primitive in Magnus Hirschfeld's World Journey of a Sexologist," in *Sex, Knowledge and Receptions of the Past*, ed. Kate Fisher and Rebecca Langlands (Oxford: Oxford University Press, forthcoming).

49. On the relation between ancient Greece and sexual reform, see Robert Aldrich, *The Seduction of the Mediterranean: Writing, Art, and Homosexual Fantasy* (London: Routledge, 1993); Matzner, "From Uranians to Homosexuals."

50. See Dowling, *Hellenism and Homosexuality*.

51. Symonds, *Problem in Modern Ethics*, 1.

52. See Roger Smith, *The Fontana History of the Human Sciences* (London: Fontana, 1997).

6

Translating Sexology in Late-Tsarist and Early-Soviet Russia

Politics, Literature, and the Science of Sex

BRIAN JAMES BAER

Translation plays a central role in the movement of theories across languages and cultures. If, as Edward Said has argued, "the movement of ideas and theories from one place to another is both a fact of life and a usefully enabling condition of intellectual activity," then it is important "to specify the kinds of movement that are possible, in order to ask whether by virtue of having moved from one place and time to another an idea or a theory gains or loses in strength, and whether a theory in one historical period and national culture becomes altogether different for another period or situation."[1] This chapter takes Said's observations as its prompt to examine the "gains" and "losses" that occurred when the ideas of Western European sexology and psychology, which emerged during the heyday of scientific positivism and Western colonialism, "traveled" to a rapidly modernizing and politically turbulent Russia. It explores the transformations that occurred when the competing conceptualizations of homosexuality developed by Western sex researchers were translated into Russian contexts. While the focus of the investigation lies on the early twentieth century, the chapter also speaks to current debates about homosexuality in the country. The introduction in 2013 of a law banning "homosexual propaganda" in Russia indicates that the history of homosexuality in the country remains distinct from that of many other European nations. Critics have attributed this difference to the decades-long Soviet silence on the subject of homosexuality and on sexual matters in general. However, this chapter will demonstrate that a uniquely Russian engagement with homosexuality can be traced back to the period before the October Revolution, when the works of Western sexology were being translated for the first time into Russian. It shows that the sudden lifting of censorship restrictions following the 1905 revolution played a decisive role in shaping Russian reception of Western writings on sex and sexology, creating a kind of false synchrony in which works of sexology from different schools and time periods were presented in Russian translation at the same time, "without any logic or chronology," making them, one could argue, even more vulnerable to pressures from the reception environment as they had already been decontextualized.[2]

In what follows, I will examine the Russian environment that shaped the reception of Western sexological ideas. In particular, I pay attention to what Said has called "the set of conditions—call them conditions of acceptance, or, as an inevitable part of acceptance, resistances—which then confronts the transplanted theory or idea, making possible its introduction or toleration, however alien it might appear to be."[3] I argue that three distinct cultural features defined Russia at the fin de siècle and shaped how Russians received the key texts of Western sexology. The first of these concerns Russia's sexual culture. The virtual absence of a Russian erotic literary tradition, which may have prepared readers in the country—as it did in England, France, and Germany—for the "discoveries" of sexology, made especially fraught public discussions regarding sex and sexuality that were precipitated by, among other things, the translation of sexological works. This helps to explain the distinctly spiritual tones of Russia's sexual discourse of the time, character- ized by a tendency to present sexuality in metaphorical, if not metaphysical, terms. The second aspect concerns Russia's political culture, specifically the political orientation of Russia's medical professionals who served as the pri- mary translators of Western research in the fields of sexology and psycho- analysis. Russian doctors were, for a number of historical reasons, overtly engaged in the public and political life of the nation and so preferred to look for the source of psychological illnesses, or neuroses, not in the Freudian libido but in the social and political conditions of late-tsarist Russia. Finally, the third defining aspect of the Russian reception environment was the ex- alted role played by literature in the intellectual life of the nation. A host of factors ranging from a general Russian suspicion of Western rationalism to censorship practices made literature into an especially important site for generating new "knowledge" about sex and sexuality. The exalted status of literature in Russian culture may help to explain one of the major contribu- tions made by Russians to the evolution of psychoanalysis: the application of psychoanalytic approaches to the study of literary works. In fact, among the signatories on a petition to allow the creation of the first Soviet psycho- analytic society were a professor of literature, two professors of art history, and a belle-lettrist, something that distinguished the Russian psychoanalytic community from its Western European counterparts, which were composed almost exclusively of medically trained professionals.

While I will treat Russia's sexual, political, and literary cultures separately for the sake of clarity, I recognize, of course, that sex, politics, and literature in the modern world are thoroughly intertwined, and were, perhaps, especially so in early twentieth-century Russia, where, as Laura Engelstein put it, the question of sex "was deeply embedded in social and political concerns."[4]

Translation Studies and the Science of Sex

Critical debates within the field of translation studies can be applied to research in the history of sexuality and in turn benefit from the insights gained from the historiography of sexology. Gideon Toury's statement that translations should be considered "facts of the target culture" marks a general reorientation of research in the field of translation studies toward the reception of translated texts.[5] Moving beyond the positivist conceptualization of translation as a more or less faithful "reflection" of a stable and unified source text, scholars today understand source text meaning not as given but rather as constructed in the act of interpretation, which is necessarily and unavoidably shaped by the desires and needs of the reception environment. As Michael Cronin puts it, "Translation does not exist in a vacuum, of course. It is part of an interpretive community."[6] This focus on reception has expanded beyond consideration of individual translators and their translations to include the sociopolitical context, or habitus, of the translators, as well as the various cultural "agents"—such as editors, publishers, scholars, critics, and readers—who, as members of a common interpretive community, are instrumental in (re)constructing meaning in translated texts.

Applying such a constructivist approach to the study of sexology in the late nineteenth and early twentieth century can expand debates within translation studies. It sets up a productive tension between two opposing models of translation, which George Steiner refers to as "universalist" and "monadic."[7] The "universalist" model asserts the existence of translinguistic and transcultural phenomena, such as deep linguistic structures common to all languages à la Chomsky or the enlightenment notion of a universal Reason, which makes everything ultimately translatable. The monadic model, on the other hand, posits that each language is the unique product of a specific culture and even terrain so that what is articulated in one language can never be fully translated into another.[8] Monadic studies of the cultural transfer of scientific works, therefore, unavoidably challenge, along with the premise of universal translatability, pretensions to universal knowledge that have for centuries characterized scientific claims in the West. As products of the nineteenth-century European positivist culture of science, many of the foundation texts of the modern field of sexology are characterized by such a universalist view, a belief in the ultimate translatability of scientific knowledge, with the human body posited as an irrefutable and universal given. Rereading these texts through a postpositivist or monadic lens, however, necessarily undermines or deconstructs the universalist pretensions of these works, thereby pluralizing sexology.

Understanding of the power differential that shapes the transfer of ideas across languages and cultures has been deepened by postpositivist and postcolonial theories of translation. By challenging the traditional linguistics-based models of translation that assume transfer between two unified, autonomous, and essentially equal language systems, postcolonial studies of translation have demonstrated that translation is almost always an "unequal exchange," which, in the words of Pascale Casanova, takes place between "dominating" and "dominated" languages.[9] Translation into a dominating language consecrates authors and works from dominated cultures, while translation into a dominated language contributes to the accumulation of cultural capital in the dominated language, necessary for it to compete in the world literary market. And so, to put it in Casanova's terms, while the translations of Freud into English had the effect of consecrating the Viennese author, lending him an international reputation, the translation of the works of Freud and other Western sexologists into Russian was more an act of accumulation of cultural capital on the part of the Russians, for the Russian language at that time did not have the power to consecrate. This is obvious when one compares the far greater percentage of translated works in the Russian journal *Psikhaterapiia* (Psychotherapy) as compared to Freud's journal *Jahrbuch für psychoanalytische und psychopathologische Forschungen* (Yearbook for psychoanalytical and psychopathological research), which was founded at roughly the same time.

Furthermore, while Russian was not spoken widely in, for example, Germany or Austria, many members of the medical establishment and the psychoanalytical community in Russia could read and speak German. As Irina Mason puts it, "At this time German was in vogue: most representatives of the intelligentsia knew this language well."[10] The bilingual nature of the Russian medical community was reflected in the fact that when Alexander Luria founded the Kazan Psychoanalytic Association in 1922, he had stationery printed with the association's name in both Russian and German.[11] This bilingualism also ensured the rapid translation of German sexological texts into Russian. For example, when the Russian psychoanalyst Moshe Wulff (1878–1971), who would become president of the Russian Psychoanalytic Society after the revolution, lost his position at the Berlin-Lankwitz sanatorium, he returned to Russia, where he supported himself largely through his work as a translator of Western psychoanalytic texts, mostly the works of Freud. Of course, their bilingualism also gave these Russians the opportunity to train in the European centers of sexology and psychoanalysis—Zurich, Berlin, and Vienna—and to publish their own research directly in German. In fact, Sabina Spielrein's 1907 paper "The Psychological Content of a Case of Schizophrenia," written in German under the supervision of Jung, was the first research paper by a Russian author to be published in Freud's journal.

The opposite, however, was not true. None of the leading German sex researchers was fluent in Russian, although Freud had many relatives in Odessa, and Alfred Adler was married to a Russian Jew from St. Petersburg who traveled regularly to Russia. In other words, while the number of bilinguals in Russia allowed Russians to participate in the evolution of psychoanalysis in a number of ways, it was mostly as students and patients, reflecting the unequal exchange between dominating and dominated cultures.[12] This may help to explain why none of the works of Russia's sexologists rose to a "meta-discursive" level, that is, they were not read widely outside Russia, something members of the Moscow psychoanalytic group acknowledged in a 1922 report to the scientific-pedagogical section of the State Scientific Soviet: "until now [psychoanalysis abroad] has known little of Russian clinicians and researchers who work in this field."[13] For Freud and other sexologists of his time, Russians were an intriguing object of analysis rather than a source of new ideas and knowledge.[14] Alexander Etkind notes that from his letters it appears that Freud believed Russians to be "closer to the Unconscious than Western people."[15] In this way, Western sexologists reproduced an imaginative geography first created by Western Enlightenment thinkers who situated Russia on the developmental periphery of a civilized Europe.[16] This view was to some extent transported back into Russia in the translations of Western sexology, but these translations also helped to build a distinctly Russian sexual discourse. Framing the history of the Russian science of sex in terms of the critical debates addressed by translation studies thus helps to draw out the unequal cultural exchange that shaped sexual debates in the country.

The Russian Translations of Modern Sex Research

The translation of key Western texts in the emerging fields of sexology and psychoanalysis experienced a boom in early twentieth-century Russia, peaking first in the period following the 1905 revolution and ending with the outbreak of World War I. As Dan Healey remarks, "the brief interlude of quasi-constitutional rule and Duma (parliamentary) politics (1905–1917) was marked by fresh discussions conducted by liberals and socialists on the problems of regulating sexuality."[17] These discussions were in large part initiated and fueled by Russian translations of the latest works in the field of sexology and psychoanalysis. As Magnus Ljunggren notes, "Nowhere outside the centers of German-speaking Europe in Vienna and Zurich did psychoanalysis emerge so early and so fully as in Russia."[18] Indeed, Russian translations of Freud appeared almost twenty years before the French and Italian translations.[19] The second boom occurred during the early years of the Soviet regime. This period aligns roughly with the New Economic Policy, or NEP (1921–1928), which introduced limited capitalism and relatively lax censorship. During this period, the boom in translations was state-sponsored. The end of this second period aligns with Stalin's consolidation of power and the consequent centralization of Soviet culture in the late 1920s and early 1930s.

However, Russians had shown an interest in sexology well before 1905. For example, a Russian contribution to the emerging field of sexology was made as early as 1843 by the Russian doctor Heinrich Kaan (1816–1893), who was, among other things, the personal physician to Tsar Nicholas I. In his book *Psychopathia Sexualis*, Kaan offered a typology of sexual pathologies, which he referred to as "sexual mental diseases," that would be greatly expanded and refined by the German sexologist Richard von Krafft-Ebing in his now classic work of the same title. Kaan's work reflected the Enlightenment project of redefining sexual "perversions" by translating the religious discourse of sin into a scientific discourse of disease.[20] Kaan's book, which was published in Leipzig, was written in Latin at a time when Latin was the lingua franca of the European scientific community, underscoring the universalist pretensions of Western positivist science. The Latin language of Kaan's work meant that it was one of the few Russian works on the topic of sexuality that was available to a non-Russian-speaking audience for quite some time. Furthermore, the fact that Kaan opens his work with epigraphs from three European authors—the first in Latin from Persius's third Satire ("Quem te Deus esse jussit et humana / qua parte locates in re, Disce"), another in English from Alexander Pope's "Essay on Man" ("The proper study of mankind is man"), and the third in French from Voltaire ("Que suis-je, où suis-je, et d'où suis-je tiré?")—further underscores the universalist claims of the new science of sex.[21] When Krafft-Ebing published a work of the same title some forty years after Kaan, these linguistic conventions had changed. Krafft-Ebing's *Psychopathia Sexualis* was written mostly in German, with only some selected passages in Latin. Such selective use of Latin had become at that time a norm and was meant, ostensibly, to discourage lay readers and to disguise overtly sexual content while at the same time making that content available to an educated lay audience of men interested in representations of same-sex desire.

Like Kaan's monograph, Western works translated into Russian before 1905 focused on the medical and legal regulation of sexual behavior
by pathologizing "abnormal" behaviors—that is, nonreproductive heterosexual relations. Krafft-Ebing's *Psychopathia Sexualis* was translated into
Russian in 1887 and had a strong effect on Russian thinking of the time.[22]
Homosexuality became a topic of public discussion in the context of ongoing
reforms to the Russian legal system, which lasted from the late 1880s until
the partial adoption of a new code in 1903, considered "a model of current
European jurisprudence."[23] Vladimir Dmitrievich Nabokov, father of the
writer Vladimir Nabokov, who would become world famous for his sexually
provocative novel *Lolita*, was a strong proponent of decriminalizing homosexuality as part of a broader effort to construct a legally protected private
sphere. He discussed his legal position in two publications, one in Russian
and the other in German, which appeared in 1902 and 1903, respectively.
Nabokov's effort to decriminalize homosexuality, however, failed, and the
ban on consensual sodomy remained in the new code, although there is
evidence to suggest that it was not rigorously enforced, especially when the
case involved a member of the elite.

Other sexological texts intended for jurists were also translated before
1905, notably Lombroso and Ferrero's *La femme criminelle et la prostituée*
(*The Criminal Woman and the Prostitute*; trans. 1898), and Martineau's
La prostitution clandestine (*Clandestine Prostitution*; trans. 1885, 1887),
which promoted the negative association of female sexuality with crime
and prostitution. The first Russian translation of a work by Sigmund Freud,
On the Interpretation of Dreams, appeared in 1904. Most of these pre-1905
translations were intended for specialized audiences—namely, doctors and
lawyers—and were concerned with classifying and pathologizing "abnormal" sexual behaviors and desires. This orientation was also reflected in
original Russian writings of the period, such as P. Ia. Rozenbakh's "On the
Causes of Sexual Perversion" (1897), F. E. Rybakov's "On Perverse Sexual
Feelings" (1989), and S. A. Sukhanov's "On the Causes of Sexual Perversions"
(1900). It is perhaps no coincidence, then, that Magnus Hirschfeld's monumental study of homosexuality, *Die Homosexualität des Mannes und des
Weibes* (1914), which presented an alternative to the pathologization of homosexuality, was never translated into Russian.[24]

While important works on sexology were thus translated into Russian
before 1905, they cannot be compared in terms of number and variety to
the texts published after the loosening of censorship restrictions in 1905.
Alexandre Mikhalevitch refers to the period from 1904 to 1914 as "the silver
age of Russian psychoanalysis."[25] Alberto Angelini singles out 1908 as the
"crucial year" in the reception of psychoanalysis in Russia as it marked the

founding of Russia's first and only journal dedicated to psychoanalysis, titled *Psikhoterapiia* (Psychotherapy), which was an important venue for the dissemination of Western theories and research.[26] Incidentally, the first issue of this journal appeared six months before Freud's own journal.[27] "Things became so lively," Ljunggren notes, "that at one point [1912] two different translations of Freud's study of Leonardo da Vinci came out simultaneously in Moscow and St. Petersburg."[28]

During that period, translations far outnumbered original Russian writings. Between 1905 and 1915, Russian translations of psychoanalytic texts totaled forty-three, as compared with thirty-three original Russian works on the subject.[29] The overwhelming majority of the translations were of works by Freud, followed by Alfred Adler. The translation of psychoanalytic texts reached its peak in the two years preceding the outbreak of World War I, with seventeen in 1912 and fourteen in 1913. Other notable Russian translations during this period include Edward Carpenter's *Intermediate Sex* (*Promezhutochnyi pol*, 1916) and Iwan Bloch's *Das Sexualleben unsere Zeit in seinen Beziehungen zur modernen Kultur* (trans. 1910 and 1911). A Russian translation of Magnus Hirschfeld's *Berlins drittes Geschlecht* (1904) appeared in 1908 (Tret'ii pol Berlina: Dokumenty bol'shogo stolichnogo goroda), and a translation of Albert Moll's *Untersuchung über die Libido sexualis* in 1910.[30] The Russian translation of Havelock Ellis's *Sexual Inversion* (1897) is not dated but is likely to have come out after 1905. A retranslation of Krafft-Ebing's *Psychopathia Sexualis* was published in 1909, as well as several editions of Oscar Weininger's *Sex and Character*. Erik Naiman estimates that the print run of Weininger's book in Russian translation totaled no less than 39,000 between 1908 and 1912, not including published excerpts from the translations and paraphrases that appeared in the popular press.[31] The number of works treating homosexuality suggests an implicit association between the political and social turmoil of this period and concerns over sexual "perversion," an association that would assume new life during the chaotic transition that followed the fall of the Soviet Union.

This interest in homosexuality was also reflected in works originally penned by Russian authors and journalists. In fact, literary works played an important role in popularizing issues of sex and sexuality. Russia's first "gay" novel, *Wings*, by Mikhail Kuzmin, was published in 1906, and the novel *Thirty-three Abominations*, a tragic tale of lesbian attraction by Lidiia Zinov'eva-Annibal, in 1907. 1907 also saw the publication of the first Russian book-length "study" of homosexuality by the writer and philosopher Vasilii Rozanov, titled *People of the Moonlight*, followed in 1908 by the book *People of the Intermediate Sex*, written by an unknown author under the pseudonym P. V. Ushakovskii, as well as V. P. Ruadze's sensationalist *To Court! Homosexual Petersburg*. The conservative journalist G. S. Novopolin condemned the explosion of public debate on sex and sexuality with his book *The Pornographic Element in Russian Literature* (1909). Only Kuzmin's novel, however, could be considered "nonpathologizing." The other works promoted a variety of negative associations of nonnormative (homo)sexuality: with tragedy (Zinov'eva-Annibal), crime (Ruadze), promiscuity (Novopolin), and social decay (Rozanov). As would occur in post-Soviet Russia, the homosexual in the final decade of the tsarist era became a metonym, or symptom, as well as a metaphor for the turbulent process of modernization that Russian society was experiencing between 1905 and 1917.

World War I, the Bolshevik Revolution, and the subsequent civil war not only stopped the translation of sexological texts but required medically trained doctors to turn their attention away from psychological issues to treat physical injuries. Following the civil war in the early 1920s, during the period of relative freedom inaugurated by Lenin's New Economic Policy, another boom in the publication of works dedicated to psychoanalysis and sexology appeared. The Moscow Institute for Psychoanalysis, founded in 1922 by the Russian psychologists Mosche Wulff (also spelled Woolf) and Ivan Ermakov, had an ambitious publishing agenda. As Martin Miller writes, "The intention was to publish all of Freud's most influential works in Russian translation, followed by volumes with the important papers of Jung, Sandor Ferenczi, Melanie Klein, and other leading European psychoanalysts."[32] The State Publishing House later agreed to sponsor a book series titled *The Psychoanalytic and Psychological Library*. Fifteen of the projected twenty-three volumes were published in the course of the 1920s, with Wulff serving as the primary translator and Ermakov as general editor. Despite the large number of translations that were published in this period, we see a significant shift in the ratio of published translations to original works (thirty-nine versus seventy-one).[33] Original works in Russian now far outnumber translations, suggesting the rapid growth of psychoanalysis in early Soviet Russia, although, as mentioned earlier, few of those works were translated out of Russian.

While the existence of translations may tell us something about domestic interest in a foreign author or text, numbers alone cannot fully explain the reception of these works. For example, the fact that many Russian psychologists studied under the founders of Western psychology—"Charcot, Kraepelin, Valentin Magnan, Paul Flechsig, and Theodor Meynert in the late nineteenth century, and with Bernheim, Dubois, Freud, and Carl Jung in the early twentieth"—should not imply that these Russians simply adopted the views of their Western teachers.[34] As Irina Sirotkina notes: "Those who visited European celebrities often informed their compatriots about what they had learned in reports that resembled travelers' stories. The authors, like travelers to distant countries, wrote about Western 'discoveries' in psychiatry as something exotic that should be adjusted to Russian conditions before being adopted."[35] I will examine the nature of those adjustments in the following three sections.

Sexual Cultures

While the existence of biological sex may be considered a "universal" phenomenon, "the social forms of sexuality vary from culture to culture."[36] Several features distinguish the sexual culture of modern Russia from that of its Western European counterparts. Igor Kon, one of post-Soviet Russia's leading sexologists, has noted the sharp dichotomy between body and soul, which rendered romantic love and carnality largely incompatible. A secular literary and artistic culture developed late in Russia, following Peter I's policy of forced Westernization in the late seventeenth and early eighteenth centuries—Russian artists were forbidden to paint nudes until the late eighteenth century!—leaving its writers and artists to look to Western models for an erotic vocabulary. But censorship in Russia continued to be, for most of its history, "strict and all-embracing," thwarting the emergence of an erotic culture.[37] Alexei Lalo goes so far as to argue that "nineteenth-century and modern Russian literature and culture are characterized by an almost complete absence of vocabulary for dealing with erotic life within social contexts."[38] The effect of this was that attempts to introduce a vocabulary to talk about sex and sexuality were often considered examples of unwanted influence from the West. As Kon comments, "Erotica was considered not only corrupt but also alien, having nothing to do with the Russian national heritage."[39] And so, while some Russians embraced sexology as providing Russians at last with a way to talk about sex that was neither moralizing, on the one hand, nor pornographic, on the other, others felt that a science of sex was utterly incompatible with Russian culture mores, and made no distinction between erotica and pornography.[40]

Russia's sexual culture, therefore, presented a special challenge to those who were intent on disseminating the latest scientific research on sex and sexuality from the West. It certainly helps to explain the ambivalence Russian doctors and lay people felt about the centrality of sex in Freudian approaches to psychoanalysis. Russian psychiatrists saw Freud's great contribution to the field to be his method, which they saw as an important alternative to hypnosis, and largely rejected his views on human sexuality. As Ljunggren notes, "Various objections to Freud's sexual dogma had been raised as early as 1909."[41] Alexandre Mikhalevitch elaborates: "Because [Russian psychoanalysts] found it very difficult to admit that an infantile sexuality and a sexual etiology of neuroses could exist, the editorial boards of these publications [*Psikhoterapiia* and the Psychotherapeutic Library] largely favored the writings of Adler, Stekel, Jung and Dubois."[42] In fact, even Nikolai Osipov, who had trained under Jung but was a great champion of the psychoanalytic method, "believed that psychoanalysis unnecessarily stressed sex."[43] Osipov recounted how his mentor, Dr. Vladimir Serbskii, pronounced Freud's name in two syllables—*Fre-ud*—placing the stress on the second syllable. "In ancient usage," Sorotkina explains, "the Russian word *ud* meant the male or female sexual organ; in Serbskii's time one could still find it in medical books."[44] Rather than embracing Freud's "pansexualism," that is, his concept of "polymorphous perversity"—according to which everyone feels same-sex desire to some degree and at certain stages of development—Osipov defended Freud *against* the charge in a lecture titled "O 'Panseksualizme' Freida" (The "pansexualism" of Freud), which he delivered at the First Congress of the Russian Union of Psychiatrists and Neuropathologists in 1911.[45] Osipov in this way sought to contain the anti-normative implications of Freud's concept and to downplay the role of the libido in an individual's identity. All of this supports Lalo's claim that for a variety of cultural and historical reasons, Russia lacked a viable erotic culture that could provide a public language with which to speak of sex and sexuality, one that was neither moralizing nor obscene, and that validated (individual) sexual pleasure.

Political Contexts

The increasingly polarized political climate in early twentieth-century Russia played a major role in shaping the reception of key sexological texts, leading researchers and cultural figures to seek solutions to sexual pathologies not ahistorically in a patient's childhood—the eternal family romance—but in contemporary social conditions, in particular, political repression. As Laura Engelstein has shown in her magisterial study of Russia in the late nineteenth and early twentieth century, *The Keys to Happiness: Sex and Society in Fin-de-Siècle Russia*, there was little willingness by anyone anywhere along the political spectrum to champion the liberal bourgeois cause of sexual pleasure and personal happiness. While conservatives saw the current obsession with sex as a deleterious effect of left-wing politics, "for the populist and social democratic critics 'erotic individualism' and pornography were the products of dissolute bourgeois culture."[46] The focus of Freudian psychoanalysis on personal sexual satisfaction was seen by Russians across the political spectrum as egotistical and individualistic, especially when viewed against the political backdrop of the time. It should be noted here that the right to sexual pleasure never played a significant role in the Russian woman's movement, as it did in Western feminism. In fact, Western feminists found common cause with LGBT activists in the 1960s and 1970s in promoting nonreproductive sexual pleasure as central to individual happiness and fulfillment. This was not the case in Russia.

For a variety of historical reasons, Russian physicians and psychoanalysts were more distinctly progressive and engaged than their Western European counterparts. It is not surprising then that Vladimir Voloshinov would attribute Freud's ahistorical approach to psychic dynamics to his bourgeois class affiliation. "Freud's notion of the 'sexual,'" Voloshinkov writes, "is at the extreme pole of this fashionable biologism," which Voloshinov sees as a central motif in "contemporary bourgeois philosophy."[47] Within the sharply class-divided society of pre-Soviet Russia, most Russian doctors came from the ranks of the *raznochintsy*, who fell somewhere between the nobility and the peasantry. They were the sons of merchants, clergy, and freed peasants, who tended to be among the most politically progressive—and radical—groups in Russian society. Moreover, the fact that many Russian physicians were state servants also helped to politicize the profession. As Irina Sirotkina comments: "The growing radicalization of the medical profession placed it in the vanguard of the opposition movement."[48] Sirotkina goes on to note, "Psychiatrists were as much involved in politics as was the [Russian] medical profession in general."[49] Their oppositional politics predisposed many Russian psychiatrists to look for the causes of mental disease not in a patient's sexual past but in the social and political oppression of the autocratic Russian state.[50] This predisposition only intensified following the 1905 Revolution. As Ljunggren remarks, "The rapid spread of psychoanalysis in Russia should probably be viewed against the background of the abortive 1905 Revolution and the psychical and moral crises that the rising wave of tsarist repression triggered among the intelligentsia."[51]

The close ties between sexuality and politics in Russia are reinforced by the fact that the Russian adjective *repressirovannyi* refers not to sexual repression but to political persecution. The politicization of sex in Russia, or rather, Russians' resistance to Freud's depoliticization of sex, helps to explain the popularity of the famous Austrian psychologist Alfred Adler, one of the founders of psychoanalysis, with Freud. Married to a Russian Jewish socialist who was herself a friend of Trotsky, Adler would become the second most translated Western psychiatrist in Russia of that period, after Freud. To borrow Ljunggren's words, many Russian psychiatrists "found that Adler's theories, giving less emphasis to the instincts and more to the role of social factors in illness, complemented Freud in essential respects,"[52] and so, as Mikhalevitch notes, "accorded well with the progressive engagement of the young Russian psychiatrists."[53]

The challenge of "accommodating", what leftists saw as the bourgeois individualism of Freud's sex-focused theories with the needs of society would become increasingly acute in the Soviet period. The Bolshevik Aron Zalkind, for example, saw sexual desire as a waste of energy that could be put to use "in healthier 'collectivist activities' which would benefit the working class and the party."[54] But the most comprehensive political critique of Freudian psychoanalysis was put forward by Voloshinov in his 1927 monograph *Freudianism: A Critical Sketch*. James V. Wertsch summarizes Voloshinov's position in the following way: "From the outset he criticizes Freud for grounding his theory in universal, ahistorical constants, namely, sex and age."[55]

Political censorship played a significant role in shaping the reception of sexological texts both before and after the 1905 revolution. The sudden loosening of censorship restrictions in 1905, for example, led to the simultaneous translation of works from various times and schools, producing what could be referred to as a false synchrony. Natalia Avtonomovna commented on this phenomenon in late Soviet Russia, which witnessed the "second coming" of Freud, after a hiatus of over fifty years: "Freud's second arrival on Russian cultural soil . . . corresponded with the opening of all previously closed floodgates, when Western culture of the past half century rained down on the Russian reader *without any logic or chronology*."[56] The effect of such sudden lifting of censorship restrictions is to confuse the course of development of concepts and theories, producing in turn Russian works that are conceptual hybrids, marked by what Dan Healey refers to as "bricolage." Commenting on Ushakovskii's 1908 work *People of the Intermediate Sex*, Healey notes the wide variety of competing and often conflicting conceptualizations of homosexuality, taken from a wide variety of sources, ranging from scientific studies to journalism to literary and autobiographical works.[57]

This discursive bricolage can also be observed, to some degree, in Russia's leading scientific journal of psychiatry, *Psikhoterapiia* (Psychotherapy). Rather than serving as the mouthpiece of a single school, the journal published Freud's work right alongside articles by his critics and detractors, such as Dubois and, later, Adler.[58] Unlike Western journals, which tended to champion one school of thought, the Russian journal presented competing theoretical points of view, even the most sharply opposed, side by side, refusing, in a sense, to take sides, which may be one of the reasons that a Russian psychoanalytic school never emerged.[59]

Literary Contexts

The important role of literature in the Russian reception environment may be responsible for Russians' perhaps greatest contribution to the evolving field of psychoanalysis: the application of psychoanalytic approaches to the study of literary works. In fact, the first Russian psychological investigation of a literary work, V. F. Chizh's *Dostoevskii kak psikhopatalog* (Dostoevsky as a psychopathologist), appeared in 1885, only four years after the author's death. Chizh, a practicing psychoanalyst followed up with the study "Bolezn' N. V. Gogolia" (The illness of N. V. Gogol, 1903), which appeared nine years before Albert Adler's student Otto Kaus would publish his own Adlerian study of the Russian writer.[60] In 1911, Tatiana Rozenthal published a paper titled "The Dangerous Age of Karen Michaelis in Light of Psychoanalysis," which Martin Miller describes as "a pioneering exploration of the relationship between psychoanalysis and literature."[61] Although this work was published in Russian, she was studying at the time at the Vienna Psychoanalytic Society and continued to visit the society after completing her degree, which gave her an opportunity to present her work on Michaelis.[62] Rozenthal's Freudian study of Dostoevsky's work, published in 1919 under the title "Suffering and the Creative Work of Dostoevsky: A Psychological Study," appeared eight years before Freud's own study of the Russian author, and four year's before Jolan Neufeld's study, *Dostoevsky: A Psychological Note* (1923), done under Freud's supervision. Interestingly, while Neufeld's work appeared in a Russian translation in 1925, Freud's book on the author, *Dostoevsky and Patricide* (1928), was never translated in the Soviet Union; the first Russian translation of that work was published only in 1968 by an émigré press in London.

Acknowledging the role of literature in shaping the reception of works on sexology and psychoanalysis may help us to make sense of the unprecedented popularity in Russia of Otto Weininger's quasi-scientific treatise *Sex and Character*. The book's strange admixture of scientific modernity with cultural pessimism, of extreme misogyny and strong anti-Semitism, despite the fact that Weininger was himself Jewish, spoke directly to Russians during a time marked by both revolutionary foment and fears of social decadence. I discuss it as part of the Russian literary context because the phenomenal success of Weininger's book in Russia was more of a reflection of fin de siècle Russia's fascination with Nietzsche rather than a reflection of the book's scientific merits.[63] If, as Bernd Magnus, Stanley Steward, and Jean-Pierre Mileur claim, Nietzsche's writing blurs the boundary between philosophy and literature, then we might say that Weininger's writing blurs the boundary between science and literature.[64] It is no coincidence that Russian writer and journalist Vasilli Rozanov clearly patterned Russia's first book-length study of homosexuality, *People of the Moonlight* (1907), on Weininger, not Freud.

Weininger's suicide at age twenty-three just before the publication of the first German edition of the book underscored its apocalyptic undertones.

Akim Volynskii noted in his preface to the first Russian edition of *Sex and Character* that "under the influence of Weininger's ideas and, it seems, of the captivating example of his own tragic death, three [Russian] young ladies committed suicide"[65]—a uniquely "literary" response first observed among readers of Goethe's *Sorrows of Werther*, who committed suicide as a sign of their total identification with Werther's hero, a phenomenon that has come to be known as the Werther effect. Moreover, Weininger's notion of an inherent bisexuality—every human body, Weininger claimed, contained both masculine and feminine cells—aligned well with the philosophical discussions of gender difference among the Russian poets and writers known as the Symbolists who saw sex in terms of gendered binaries, with androgyny representing the ideal union of male and female traits and the resolution of all antinomies.[66]

Moreover, Weininger's identity as a "conscientious student," as he was described in the preface to the sixth German edition, also played an important role in the work's reception in Russia, where the meaning of "student" was overdetermined in the late nineteenth and early twentieth centuries. As the semiotician Juri Lotman points out, in Russia at that time, "*being a student* was not at all synonymous with study at a university or institute." It had come to mean a revolutionary intellectual.[67] This is significant in that it connected the young Viennese author with his first Russian translator— both were students in the Russian sense of the term. (*Sex and Character* was Weininger's doctoral dissertation.) The Russian translator, Vladimir Likhtenshtadt, translated *Sex and Character* while imprisoned in the Schlusselberg Fortress in St. Petersburg for his participation in 1906, at age twenty-three, in the failed assassination attempt on Russian prime minister Petr Stolypin—twenty-five people died in the attempt, but Stolypin survived.

Both Weininger's suicide—he shot himself in the heart in the very room where Beethoven had died—and the translator's incarceration appealed to the Russian ideal of *zhiznetvorchestvo*, or "life creation," which posited a seamless connection between an artist's life and creative work as the ultimate mark of authenticity.[68] As Evgenii Bershtein comments:

> The suicide of Weininger—the young "genius" from Vienna—was interpreted in Russia as a metaphysical act. It signaled Weininger's success in realizing a tragic and radical life scenario, reflecting the Nietzschean "philosophy of life," which was of such fundamental importance for modernism. The circumstances of the translation of Weininger's book into Russian once again demonstrated how the Nietzschean search for the tragic combined in Russia with extreme political gestures.[69]

The decadent interpretation Weininger gave to the sex drive, associating it with a general cultural decline or degeneration, clearly spoke to the preoccupations of Russians in the interrevolutionary period—in particular to the Nietzschean strain in contemporary Russian culture—more directly than what Russians saw as Freud's "bourgeois" take on sex.

Conclusion

The peculiar amalgam of politics, literature and science that characterized Russian culture between 1905 and 1917 was in some ways epitomized by the medical doctor Vikenty Veresaev (1867–1945), a Marxist and prolific writer whose professional knowledge of Latin and Greek allowed him to engage in translations of classical literary works. He would publish in 1915 what are generally considered to be the canonical Russian translations of the Greek poet Sappho. A proponent of engaged literature, Veresaev rejected the idea that Sappho could have been a lesbian, arguing in the preface that she was the headmistress of a school for noble girls and that the sentiment expressed in the poems was that of a devoted mentor and, therefore, devoid of any sexual content. The association of Sappho with that "disgusting, unnatural love (merzostnaia, protivoestestvennaia liubov'), which still today carries the name 'Sapphic' or, based on her birthplace, 'lesbian'" is, Veresaev insists, "entirely made up (vydumki)."[70] To prove his point in the absence of detailed biographical sources, Veresaev projects contemporary homophobia onto ancient Greece, "If the Hellenes understood Sappho's songs the way later readers understood them, it would be impossible to explain the profound respect that surrounded her name in Heliad."[71] And later: "However, all these circumstances do not give us the right to conclude that Sappho's relations with her students had that specific character, which is today associated with the name of Sappho. Her disposition was too *pure* and *elevated*."[72] For Veresaev, Sappho's lesbianism proves untranslatable—indeed, unspeakable, as his reliance on euphemism suggests.[73]

And so, while the enormous number of translations into Russian of the foundation texts of the modern field of sexology would appear to suggest a welcoming environment, close analysis of the reception of sexology in late-tsarist and early-Soviet Russia reveals a pronounced resistance to some key concepts, in particular, the central role played by the libido in the diagnosis of neurosis and the value of (individual) sexual pleasure, which stand at the heart of the Western construction of the modern subject. As Tatiana Zarubina argues, "There is an incompatibility in the representations of the Subject in Russia and the West, which opens a discussion of the history and intercultural transference of ideas and the reasons for rejecting this or that scientific theory imported into Russia from the West."[74] What we see emerging from the Russian engagement with the Western science of sexology is a distinctly Russian sexual discourse that continues to shape in some important ways Russians' views on sex and sexuality today.

NOTES

1. Edward Said, "Traveling Theory," in *The Edward Said Reader*, ed. Moustafa Bayoumi and Andrew Rubin (New York: Vintage, 2000), 196.

2. Natalia Avtonomovna, "Freid v Evrope i Rossii: Paradoksy 'vtorogo prishstviia'" [Freud in Europe and Russia: Paradoxes of the "Second Coming"], *Voprosy Filosofii* 9 (2000): 16.

3. Said, "Traveling Theory," 196.

4. Laura Engelstein, *The Keys to Happiness: Sex and the Search for Modernity in Fin-de-Siècle Russia* (Ithaca, NY: Cornell University Press, 1992), 2.

5. Gideon Toury, *Descriptive Translation Studies and Beyond* (Amsterdam: Benjamins, 1995), 29.

6. Michael Cronin, "The Cracked Looking Glass of Servants: Translation and Minority Languages in a Global Age," in *Critical Readings in Translation Studies*, ed. Mona Baker (New York: Routledge, 2010), 258, 247–262.

7. George Steiner, *After Babel: Aspects of Language and Translation*, 3rd ed. (Oxford: Oxford University Press, 1998), 18.

8. For more on the "translatability" of sexological texts, see Heike Bauer, "'Not a Translation but a Mutilation': The Limits of Translation and the Discipline of Sexology," *Yale Journal of Criticism* 16, no. 2 (2003): 381–405.

9. Pascale Casanova, "Consecration and Accumulation of Cultural Capital: Translation as Unequal Exchange," in Baker, *Critical Readings in Translation Studies*, 285–303.

10. Irina Mason, "Comment dit-on 'psychanalyse' en russe?" [How do you say "psychoanalysis" in Russian?] *Revue Internationale d'Histoire de la Psychanalyse* 4 (1991): 407. Unless otherwise indicated, all translations from French and Russian are mine.

11. Martin Miller, *Freud and the Bolsheviks: Psychoanalysis in Imperial Russia and the Soviet Union* (New Haven, CT: Yale University Press, 1998), 58.

12. See Alexander Etkind, *Eros of the Impossible: The History of Psychoanalysis in Russia* (Boulder, CO: Westview, 1997); James L. Rice, *Freud's Russia: National Identity in the Evolution of Psychoanalysis* (New Brunswick, NJ: Transaction, 1993).

13. Miller, *Freud and the Bolsheviks*, 63.

14. For example, one of Freud's most famous case studies, "The Wolfman," was of a Russian (Sergei Pankeev). At roughly the same time, Freud was treating the Russian political leftist Ivan Il'in. Freud also published a monograph psychoanalyzing the life and works of the Russian novelist Fyodor Dostoevsky, titled *Dostoevsky and Patricide*. Carl Jung also published an important case study of a Russian patient, Sabina Spielrein, and Iwan Bloch included as a special appendix in his monumental *Sexual Life of Our Time in Its Relations to Modern Civilization* (1908) the confessions of a Russian anarchist who suffered from sado-masochistic tendencies. Krafft-Ebing published the autobiography of a Russian pedophile, the manuscript of which had supposedly been left in his mailbox, under the title *Confession sexuelle d'un anonyme russe* [The sexual confession of an anonymous Russian].

15. Alexander Etkind, "Russia (until 1989)," in *Psychoanalysis International: A Guide to Psychoanalysis throughout the World*, ed. Peter Kutter, vol. 2 (Stuttgart: Frommann-Holzboog, 1995), 334.

16. For more on the construction of Russia and Eastern Europe as Europe's internal other, see Larry Wolff, *Inventing Eastern Europe: The Map of Civilization on the Mind of the Enlightenment* (Stanford, CA: Stanford University Press, 1994).

17. Dan Healey, *Homosexual Desire in Revolutionary Russia: The Regulation of Sexual and Gender Dissent* (Chicago: University of Chicago Press, 2001), 101.

18. Magnus Ljunggren, "The Psychoanalytic Breakthrough in Russia on the Eve of the First World War," in *Russian Literature and Psychoanalysis*, ed. Daniel Rancour-Laferriere (Amsterdam: Benjamins, 1989), 173.

19. Tatiana Zarubina, "La psychanalyse en Russie dans les années 1920 et la notion de Sujet" [Psychoanalysis in Russia in the 1920s and the concept of the Subject], *Cahiers de l'ILSL* 24 (2008): 271.

20. As Erwin Haeberle notes, "The sexual manifestations of [his patients'] sickness were carefully listed and, as a rule, ascribed to degeneration." Erwin J. Haeberle, Introduction, *The Birth of Sexology: A Brief History in Documents*, available at http://www.kinseyinstitute.org/resources/sexology.html.

21. "What sort of a man did God wish you to be, / Playing what sort of role? . . . / Don't skew off, hear!" This English translation of the lines from Persius's Third Satire is by William Harris and is available at http://community.middlebury.edu/~harris/Translations/Persius.html.

22. For the reception and influence of Krafft-Ebbing's work in Russia, see Evgenii Bershtein, "'Psychopathia sexualis' v Rossii nachala veka: Politika i zhenr" [*Psychopathia sexualis* in Russia at the beginning of the century: Politics and genre], in *Eros and Pornography in Russian Culture*, ed. Marcus C. Levitt and Andrei L. Toporkov (Moscow: Ladomir, 1999), 414–441.

23. Healey, *Homosexual Desire in Revolutionary Russia*, 108.

24. Ibid., 299n17.

25. Alexandre Mikhalevitch, "L'âge d'argent de la psychanalyse russe: Les premières traductions des oeuvres de Freud en russie prérévolutionnaire (1904–1914)," *Revue Internationale d'Histoire de la Psychanalyse*, no. 4 (1991): 399.

26. Alberto Angelini, "History of the Unconscious in Soviet Russia: From Its Origins to the Fall of the Soviet Union," *International Journal of Psychoanalysis* 89 (2008): 369.

27. Ljunggren, "Psychoanalytic Breakthrough," 174.

28. Ibid.

29. V. M. Leibin, "Bibliography," in *Zigmund Freid, Psikhanaliz i russkaia mysl'* [Sigmund Freud, psychoanalysis and Russian thought], ed. V. M. Leibin (Moscow: Respublika, 1994), 373–378.

30. Engelstein, *Keys to Happiness*, 134n.

31. Eric Naiman, *Sex in Public: The Incarnation of Early Soviet Ideology* (Princeton, NJ: Princeton University Press, 1997), 39n.

32. Miller, *Freud and the Bolsheviks*, 60.

33. These statistics are taken from the bibliography in Leibin's *Zigmund Freid, Psikhanaliz i russkaia mysl'*, 373–378.

34. Irina Sirotkina, *Diagnosing Literary Genius: A Cultural History of Psychiatry in Russia, 1880–1930* (Baltimore: Johns Hopkins University Press, 2002), 103.

35. Ibid.

36. Franz X. Eder, Lesley A. Hall, and Gert Hekma, "Introduction," in their *Sexual Cultures in Europe: National Histories* (Manchester, UK: Manchester University Press, 1999), 1.

37. Igor Kon, "Sexuality and Politics in Russia, 1700–2000," in Eder, Hall, and Hekma, *Sexual Cultures in Europe*, 203.

38. Alexei Lalo, *Libertinage in Russian Culture and Literature: A Bio-History of Sexualities at the Threshold of Modernity* (Leiden, Netherlands: Brill, 2011), 1.

39. Kon, "Sexuality and Politics in Russia," 203.

40. See the essay "O pornografii" [On pornography] by Vladislav Khodosevich on the distinction between eroticism and pornography, which appeared in the émigré newspaper *Vozrozhdenie* on February 11, 1932.

41. Ljunggren, "Psychoanalytic Breakthrough," 175.

42. Mikhalevitch, "Âge d'argent de la psychanalyse russe," 405.

43. Sirotkina, *Diagnosing Literary Genius*, 106.

44. Ibid.

45. Ibid.

46. Kon, "Sexuality and Politics in Russia," 206.

47. V. N. Voloshinov, *Freudianism: A Critical Sketch*, trans. I. R. Titunik (Bloomington: Indiana University Press, 1976), 14.

48. Sirotkina, *Diagnosing Literary Genius*, 36.

49. Ibid.

50. Ibid., 41.

51. Ljunggren, "Psychoanalytic Breakthrough," 175.

52. Ibid.

53. Mikhalevitch, "Âge d'argent de la psychanalyse russe," 404.

54. Miller, *Freud and the Bolsheviks*, 95–96.

55. James V. Wertsch, "Foreword," in Voloshinov, *Freudianism*, viii.

56. Natalia Avtonomovna, "Freid v Evrope i Rossii," 16.

57. Healey, *Homosexual Desire in Revolutionary Russia*, 103–104.

58. Mikhalevitch, "Âge d'argent de la psychanalyse russe," 400.

59. Zarubina, "Psychanalyse en Russie dans les années 1920," 270.

60. Ljunggren, "Psychoanalytic Breakthrough," 175.

61. Miller, *Freud and the Bolsheviks*, 41. For more on the relationship between literature and psychoanalysis in Russia, see Sirotkina, *Diagnosing Literary Genius*.

62. Miller, *Freud and the Bolsheviks*, 41.

63. For more on the significance of Nietzsche in fin de siècle Russian culture, see Bernice Glatzer Rosenthal, *Nietzsche in Russia* (Princeton, NJ: Princeton University Press, 1986).

64. Bernd Magnus, Stanley Steward, and Jean-Pierre Mileur, *Nietzsche's Case: Philosophy as/and Literature* (London: Routledge, 2014).

65. Quoted in Evgenii Bershtein, "Tragediia pola: Dve zametki of russkom veiningerianstve" [The tragedy of sex: Two notes on Russian Weiningerism], *NLO* 65 (2004), online.

66. Ibid. For more on the metaphysical dimension of gender and sex in Russian Silver Age culture, see Olga Matich, *Erotic Utopia: The Decadent Imagination in Russia's Fin-de-Siècle* (Madison: University of Wisconsin Press, 2007).

67. Iurii Lotman, *Nepredskazuemye mekhanizmy kul' tury* [The unpredictable workings of culture] (Tallinn, Estonia: University of Tallinn Press, 2010), 97–98.

68. During his incarceration Likhtenshtadt also translated Baudelaire's *Les Paradis artificiels* [Artificial paradises] and Max Stirner's 1844 *Der Einzige und sein Eigentum*, translated into English as *The Ego and Its Own*.

69. Bershtein, "Tragediia pola."

70. V. V. Veresaev, "Safo," in *Safo: Lira, lira sviashchennaia* [Sappho: Lyre, sacred lyre] (Moscow: Letopis' M, 2000), 5.

71. Ibid., 11.

72. Ibid., 13.

73. Incidentally, Veresaev's translations of Sappho and the 1915 preface continue to be republished in Russia today, without commentary and without the date of original publication.

74. Zarubina, "Psychanalyse en Russie dans les années 1920," 268.

7

Translating Sexology, Writing the Nation

Sexual Discourse and Practice in Hebrew
and Arabic in the 1930s

LIAT KOZMA

This chapter explores the translations of sexology into Hebrew and Arabic during the 1920s and 1930s. It turns to translation to trace how ideas traveled from Europe, and especially German sexology, to the Middle East, before exploring how the new sexological knowledge was transmitted into popular culture and received by some of the women and men who turned to sexual advice columns to better understand their bodies and desires. While sexology is commonly understood as a scientific project that supports modern European nation formation, I argue that sexological debates also played a significant role in the shaping of ideas about both the individual body and the national body in Palestine and Egypt.

The chapter begins with a discussion of the medico-scientific context in Palestine and Egypt in the 1920s, before examining the writings of two medical doctors—Avraham Matmon in Palestine and Faraj Fakhri in Egypt—who were key figures in the scientific debates about sexuality in their respective societies. Both men authored books and articles on sexology, both studied—ten years apart—in Magnus Hirschfeld's Institute for Sexual Science in Berlin, and both were self-professed sexologists. Their work not only demonstrates the contribution of sexology to the nation-building efforts in Egypt and Palestine, but it also indicates what was acceptable to say about sex in Tel Aviv and in Cairo during the 1920s and 1930s. The remaining part of the chapter explores in more detail the dissemination and reception of sexology in these two cities—and beyond—by examining the sexual advice columns that were published in health journals. These columns provide further insights into the gendered reception of sexology in Egypt and Palestine, as they include the voices of women and men who turned to the scientific knowledge on sexuality, for instance to better control their desires or to lead more fulfilling marital lives. By examining the scientific and popular translations of sexology in this way, the chapter aims to gain a better understanding of the social history of sexuality in Egypt and Palestine. It reveals that both Jews and Arabs, in parallel trajectories, translated the new scientific ideas about sex into pedagogical practices that aimed to support national health and strength by transforming individual lives, adapting "European" sexology to form distinct discourses about sex, society, and the nation.

The Translation of Knowledge:
Sexology in Hebrew and Arabic

In comparable yet distinct ways, Jews and Arabs (as well as other colonized peoples) were constructed as the "others" of modern medicine whose norm was the (male) white body. Sander Gilman has shown how central anti-Semitism was to the European medical understanding of sexuality, where deviance, neurosis, and lack of self-control became markers of Jewish masculinity.[1] Edward Said in turn has famously highlighted the significance of sensuality and uncontrollable sexuality in Orientalist constructions of the Muslim.[2] Historians of colonial medicine have further demonstrated how those assumptions were translated into medical theorizing and practices, for example in North Africa.[3] Building on this research, I add consideration of the translations of sexology into Hebrew and Arabic to show how Jewish and Arab medical doctors alike engaged with the European ideas about sex. I suggest that their translations of the European knowledge both refuted racist assumptions but also internalized them, as they urged a reform of the Jewish or Arab (male) body.

Modern debates about sexuality had first emerged in these communities in the later nineteenth century. Medical doctors educated mainly in Cairo and Beirut started publishing monographs on sex around the 1880s. Their writings were premised on the assumption that rationality could now answer questions that had previously been relegated to superstition and religion. These authors deliberated such controversial issues as the permissibility of masturbation, the intensity of the female orgasm, and the regulation of prostitution. The Yishuv (Jewish community in Palestine) in turn witnessed its own renaissance of sexual medical literature. Medical doctors who immigrated to Palestine from both Germany and Russia formed the core of its nascent medical profession and were also the ones who opened and operated sexual consultation centers in Tel Aviv.[4]

In the 1920s, Egyptian medical practitioners started reclaiming their professional status and identity against the domination of foreign doctors and demanded recognition in the local and international spheres. Unlike other colonial contexts, Egyptian modern medical education and practice had been well established prior to the British occupation. The professional struggles of the 1920s may thus be seen as a "re-Egyptianization" of the profession: establishing a medical association with its own bulletin, conducting scientific research, specializing in certain medical fields, and by the late 1920s, enhancing their professional status through legislation.[5] The re-Egyptianization of education, practice, and research in the medical profession, as well as others, was seen as a national goal. Medical research conducted by local doctors on "Egyptian problems" (such as bilharzia, a parasitic infection endemic to the Nile valley, and parasitology in general) was seen as a sign of indigenous competence and intellectual success, further buttressing the legitimacy of the Egyptian medical profession.[6]

Palestine did not have its own medical school until the establishment of the State of Israel. Jewish medical doctors were educated mostly in Europe, and to a lesser extent, in Cairo and Beirut's medical schools. European schools were opened to Jewish students only in the late nineteenth century, and in spite of quota limitations, they came to be overrepresented in the medical profession, particularly in Central and Eastern Europe. From 1933, however, when Nazi persecution specifically targeted Jewish doctors, many of them lost their public jobs and left Germany in large numbers, often resettling in Palestine, but some of them also made their way to Egypt.[7]

Jews had been immigrating to Egypt for decades, and the Egyptian Jewish community grew from seven thousand in the late nineteenth century to about seventy thousand by the 1930s, about 10 percent of them European Jews. However, despite the fact that Jews were generally well received in Egypt, and the general condemnation of their prosecution in Germany in the local press, the Egyptian government and the Egyptian Medical Association opposed the immigration of Jewish doctors, who constituted unwelcome competition so shortly after securing a monopoly over the profession.[8] While some Jewish physicians did manage to restart their careers in Cairo (including Hirschfeld's colleague at the Berlin Institute, Ludwig Levy-Lenz), the official position of the Egyptian Medical Association was to pressure their government to curtail the immigration of Jewish doctors. This meant that while the Egyptian medical community readily absorbed the sexological knowledge produced in Central Europe, it largely refused to accept the Jewish medical doctors who left Berlin from 1933 onward. Thus while the ideas of Jewish sexologists such as Hirschfeld were widely read and debated in Egypt, the people behind them were seen as a threat to the Egyptian medical profession and as such not welcomed.

The situation in Palestine was almost the exact opposite. Here Jewish immigrant doctors were part of the national project from the outset. Not necessarily Zionist, they fled to Palestine from a homeland that had rejected them, to become part of the growing Yishuv. This led to an oversupply of doctors. Some of them found employment among Palestine's Arabs, while others remained unemployed or underemployed. In contrast to Egypt, the ideas were welcomed but not the people; Jewish doctors were more than welcome as individuals in Palestine, but their radical ideas were rejected. While sexological knowledge thus played a more affirmative role in modern Egyptian nation-building, it was deemed as too threatening in Palestine, especially for the emerging vision of Zionist masculinity and pro-natalism.[9]

Matmon and Fakhri: Norms and Innovation

The careers of two medical doctors—one based in Palestine, the other in Egypt—illustrate the different issues at stake in establishing sexology in these two countries. Avraham Matmon and Faraj Fakhri both returned from Berlin to the Middle East after studying sexology in Berlin, with the purpose of bringing the knowledge they had acquired to their respective societies: Fakhri returned to Cairo in 1921 and Matmon to Tel Aviv eleven years later. Matmon founded the Institute of Sexual Science in Tel Aviv, where he offered weekly lectures and consultation hours. In 1932–1935, he also edited a monthly health journal that included a sexual advice column. A book he authored on sexual life was published in eight editions from the late 1930s onward; in 1933 he also published a booklet on eugenics.[10] Fakhri in turn authored several monographs on female sexuality, prostitution, venereal diseases, and sexual deviance. Upon returning from Berlin he gave public talks on sexology at the American University in Cairo, and these were published in the Egyptian Medical Association's journal. Unlike Matmon, he did not edit his own journal, but he did contribute regularly to the popular Cairo monthly *al-Riyada al-Badaniyya* (literally, bodily culture; henceforth, *RB*), which also featured an advice column. His plan to establish a sexual science institute in Cairo never materialized.[11] While the particulars of their careers may differ, their contributions to the development of sexology in Egypt and Palestine via sexual advice columns, journals, and clinical practice clearly followed what both men had learned in Berlin.

The writings and the career paths of Matmon and Fakhri reflect the large variety and scope of contemporary sexology in the Middle East. Reflecting a general medical skepticism toward sexology, both doctors were marginal figures in their respective scientific communities. Fakhri's lectures were not welcome outside the American University, and in his books he complained about being misunderstood, in spite of his potential contribution to

Egyptian public life. In 1931 he was charged (and subsequently acquitted) for a lecture he had held on the need to reform the personal status law.[12] Of Matmon's institute we know very little outside the accounts he gives in his own journal, which is one indication of its relative marginality. Another indication is Matmon's regular letters to the Tel Aviv Municipality, asking for a tax reduction because of the deteriorating state of one of its rooms, which he evidently could not afford to renovate.[13]

While both Matmon and Fakhri saw sexology as a pedagogical project, the aims and conclusions of their work differed in many respects. To Matmon, sexual science should serve the formation of a normative family and a better nation, composed of fit individuals and lasting marital unions. Assisting the heterosexual couple and preventing marital problems were central to his project. Furthermore, his fields of interest included eugenics, which he considered key to promoting the Jewish race. Fakhri, on the other hand, saw science as a new arbiter on social and moral questions, which had the potential of destabilizing, rather than reaffirming, existing social norms. On many issues, though not all, he maintained that what used to be seen as the truth could now be put into question. The difference between the two doctors reflects tensions within the German sexual reform movement and the challenges it was facing. It may also be related to the timing of their studies. Fakhri arrived in Berlin shortly after Hirschfeld's institute had been founded in 1919, at the height of a brief moment of freedom in the Weimar Republic. Matmon, in contrast, left Berlin around the same time as Hirschfeld, at a time of increasing Nazi agitation. The Nazis would shut the institute down in May 1933.

Matmon had a keen interest in communicating sexological ideas to a wider public. He held a series of lectures on anatomy, physiology, hygiene, sexual development, and pathology, attended by dozens of men and women. Both of his books were based on lectures held in his Tel Aviv institute and were later published in his journal. Furthermore, he offered two weekly consultation hours for men, and a colleague of his offered weekly consultation hours for women. The institute also issued health certificates for couples intending to get married.[14] Every couple, he believed, should consult a doctor before marriage, to make sure they did not harbor an ailment that could be passed on to the spouse and to future offspring. Importantly, his definition of ailments also included social ills such as prostitution, alcoholism, and homosexuality.[15] Matmon reminded his readers that such consultation could prevent the birth of individuals who would burden their families and the public. "Protect your future and the future of the nation!" was his motto.[16] Matmon saw eugenics as a progressive idea, promising to eliminate so-called undesirable elements from the nation. He preached against what he saw as ignorance that threatened the reproductive couple, the basic unit of the nation: "Any disorder leads, even unwittingly, to a deep fracture in family life, one that will never heal, and only deepens as long as the disorder lasts. How many families were destroyed, and how many divorces could have been prevented had people known that they had to seek advice on sexual matters at the right time."[17]

Fakhri's main agenda was different, but like Matmon he was interested in developing sexology in his own country. His lectures at the American University dealt with questions he would later develop in his books, such as the male and female orgasm, sadism, premature ejaculation, and the physiology of erection. Fakhri concludes a March 1925 article by stating that he would like to establish a sexology school in Egypt, "as a service to our profession and our patients."[18] Fakhri clearly situates his own writing as more advanced than that of earlier generations, particularly among the Arabs, whose writing on sexuality "we now might find embarrassing."[19] In a 1923 lecture to the Egyptian Medical Association, later published in their journal, Fakhri reproached his hosts for censoring its title: "The Physiology of Reproduction" instead of "The Physiology of Orgasm": "Your association, may God forgive it . . . succumbed to the usual embarrassment when one speaks of anything directly or indirectly related to reproduction."[20] For this reason, he continued, the science of sexology remained buried under the feet of reactionary forces for centuries. Elsewhere in the civilized world, and particularly in Germany, he insisted, reproduction was a serious science, with its own research, associations, and journals, studied without the slightest embarrassment, but with courage and zeal aiming to unveil its mysteries.[21] Here Fakhri presented his project as an effort to promote free speech in a field dominated by silence and euphemism. To him, talking about sex was not only medically important; it also distinguished the civilized from the less civilized nations.

In contrast to Matmon, Fakhri wrote extensively about non-normative sexual practices and marginalized individuals and practices. In Paris, he visited brothels specializing in sadomasochistic services. He knew little about the prevalence of such practices in Egypt, he explained, but maintained that these would correlate with "the spread of modern civilization," for better or worse.[22] In line with conventional ideas about active masculinity and passive femininity, he argued that sadism was more "natural" for men and masochism for women. Yet he also pointed out that these "natural" dispositions were subject to social influence. For instance, he argued that sadism could erupt as a result of "a sudden transition of the ignorant to a great fortune or a much higher social position," such as from a servant to the master's wife.[23] Given Fakhri's concern with societal influences on sexual behavior, his discussion about homosexuality stands out for its assertion that homosexuality is a universal phenomenon and that it constitutes a "defect" or an "illness" rather than a "crime," which is why consensual homosexual acts should not be criminalized.[24] These ideas are clearly influenced by Hirschfeld. However, Fakhri adapts Hirschfeld's views by contextualizing them in relation to homosexuality in Arab and Islamic society. Arguing that homosexuality has existed throughout history, including Pharaonic and Islamic times, he points out that texts ranging from the medieval poetry of Abu Nawwas and Ibn al-Farid to Arabic belles lettres (*adab*) and the *Arabian Nights* are all evidence of the historic existence of homosexuality and the availability of knowledge about it to every Arabic reader. Like Hirschfeld, then, Fakhri claims that homosexuality is present in all cultures, but in contrast to Hirschfeld, who looks across cultures to stake his claims, Fakhri turns to evidence from his own cultural—and national—context.

In summary, then, the sexologies of Matmon and Fakhri indicate a shared commitment to advancing sexual knowledge, which they nevertheless interpreted very differently. To Fakhri, sexology meant studying the wide range of human sexuality, and breaking taboos was a sign of progress as science enabled him to diagnose the pitfalls of Egypt's encounter with modernity. To Matmon, it meant specifically improving the welfare and sexual lives of married couples, as basic units of the nation. Their respective foci on non-normative sexualities versus marriage may help to explain their distinct reception in their own countries: while Fakhri in many ways remained a lone voice in the Egyptian scientific and reform communities, Matmon's concern with heterosexuality fit in well with the project of nation-building in Palestine.

Gendered Nation-Building and the Emergence of Sexual Advice Columns

While historians of sexology and sexual knowledge tend to focus on producers and translators of such knowledge—medical doctors and to lesser extent, novelists and public intellectuals—I am concerned also with how the sexological ideas were received by "lay" women and men. Advice columns published in both Arabic and Hebrew newspapers in the early 1930s offer insights into the way sexology entered popular discourse and how debates about "sex" and nation were gendered. This line of investigation follows Paul Ryan's work on Irish advice columns, which has examined how Irish men (and to lesser extent, women) learned from such popular columns new ways to communicate their problems and pains and readjust their sexual and emotional lives to the cultural transformations of the middle decades of the twentieth century. In a culture in which sexual ignorance was seen as a norm, or even a virtue, advice columns were legitimate venues for sexual questions.[25] Taking Ryan's work as a model, I situate the advice columns within the historical contexts that produced them—the migration of medical knowledge in the 1930s; the Egyptian and Zionist national projects; and finally, the medical profession and the transformation it underwent, in both locales, in the interwar period. I argue that these advice columns not only reflect historical change and the specific cultural circumstance of Egypt and Palestine, but they also allow glimpses at the ways in which the "expert" sexological knowledges became popularized.

In Palestine, Matmon published a journal titled *HaBr'iut* between 1932 and 1935, which featured original and translated medical articles, as well as Matmon's own lectures. Around the same time, in 1928, three Egyptians—Muhammad Fa'iq al-Jawahiri and his two brothers, Mukhtar and Ra'uf—opened a physical education center in Cairo. *RB* began appearing the following year and remained in publication until the early 1950s.[26] The journal's editor, Muhammad al-Jawahiri, claimed that his mission was to educate the public about "sex, love, and physical beauty." Both *HaBr'iut* and *RB* featured an advice column, which ended up being dedicated mostly to sexual questions. Both journals advocated sexual education for youth and condemned their ignorance and especially the role played by laypersons in educating youth about sexuality. Both promised their readers an individualized answer if they enclosed a stamped envelope to their letters.

RB has been analyzed in depth by Wilson Jacob in his influential work on masculinity in early twentieth-century Egypt. Arguing that the journal self-consciously mimicked the terms, loci, and visions of the European social order, Jacob demonstrates how readers, particularly men, wrote to *RB* and expressed their gratitude after it had helped them return to the straight and narrow, for example, to stop frequenting prostitutes. Wilson sees *RB* as an artifact of colonial modernity: a style of performing gender that emerged in other parts of the world as well since the second half of the nineteenth century. Since these new discourses were presented specifically in terms of national modernity, they constantly confronted the Egyptian premodern self and contributed to the formation of bourgeois subject. In the process, *RB* normalized heterosexuality as a key to Egyptian modernity, criticizing "deviation" as the result of a lack of masculine self-control, namely excessive sexual energy, directed either at oneself or at prostitutes.[27]

Similarly, *HaBr'iut* can be situated within the context of the emergence of modern nationhood, here specifically in relation to Zionist constructions of masculinity. Sex and the body were part of the Zionist project, which both rejected and adopted contemporary scientific ideas, but related notions about respectability and manliness also became a vital part of many other nineteenth-century national movements. Whereas in contemporary European medical discourses the Jewish male was constructed as effeminate and degenerate, the "other" of modern masculinity, Jewish thinkers sought to counteract this stereotype by creating a new "muscle Jew" devoted to physical exercise and self-restraint, a Jew who would liberate diasporic Jews not only from tradition but also from the confines of the diasporic body. Immigration to Palestine and renewed connection to the land were to free the Jewish body from the degenerating effects of diasporic urban life.[28]

The emerging advice columns thus indicate some of the gendered assumptions that underpinned ideas about sex and the national body in both Egypt and Palestine, and they also make clear the complex processes by which sexual discourses in these countries adopted and adapted colonial ideas and negative cultural stereotypes.

Supporting Marriage

Providing marital sexual advice became increasingly important to European sexology in the early twentieth century. It was central to the work of Hirschfeld's Berlin Institute, and marriage columns also flourished from the mid-1930s onward in Britain, a country where the work of Marie Stopes would become hugely influential for transmission of sexual knowledge and in shaping attitudes toward sex and marriage.[29] Similarly, marital sex played a crucial role in sexual advice columns in Egypt and Palestine.

The ideal of marriage began to change for the emerging Egyptian middle class in the early decades of the twentieth century. More couples (and particularly men) were choosing their marital partners and could get to know each other before marriage. The average age of marriage was rising, and the bourgeois press advocated love-based companionate monogamous marriage over the previous norm of arranged marriage, as well as over the relatively rare but religiously sanctioned polygamy. At the same time, the national press lamented a perceived marriage crisis, which was emblematic of a national one. Egyptian nationalists used images of homes, marriages, and domestic relations to demonstrate their preparedness for self-rule. The Egyptian elites linked monogamy with modernity, in response to the colonial emphasis on polygamy and domestic practices as indicative of Egypt's degraded national culture. In this context, debates over women's status in Egyptian society revolved around their education, seclusion, and veiling. Educated women could make better wives and thus secure more stable marital unions and also nurture better national subjects. Nevertheless, the ideal bride remained a sexually ignorant virgin, while no such requirement was made of men.[30]

The Zionist case was somewhat different but nevertheless also concerned with the transformation of women's role within their families and communities. Young men and women emigrated to Palestine from highly patriarchal, gender-segregated, traditional Jewish societies, in which women were supposed to enjoy no break between their role as daughters and their roles as wives and mothers; they immigrated to a new national project in which they were supposed to participate in the labor force and in nation-building. Immigration thus freed them from the confines of communal control but also deprived them of the support networks traditional Jewish communities could offer. Furthermore, in spite of the Yishuv's purported egalitarian vision, women continued to perform the bulk of housework and childrearing in addition to their integration into the workforce. As in other national projects, their role as mothers took precedence, and choosing to refrain from motherhood was considered a betrayal of both their biological essence and their national role. At the same time, motherhood and housework were medicalized, in the sense that they were no longer seen as natural but rather as requiring expert guidance—and this was offered in both the national press and in childcare clinics across Palestine.[31]

Both *RB* and Matmon's *HaBr'iut* emphasized men's responsibility for their wives' sexual pleasure and rebuked men who failed in this regard. One A. Sami from Cairo wrote to *RB* complaining that his sexual relations with his wife of seven years were no longer satisfactory. The editors' reply laid the responsibility strictly on the husband's shoulders and recognized women's sexual subjectivity. It was his sexual incompetence, weakness of nervous system, and selfishness that probably accounted for his marital problems: "You care only for your own pleasure, without concerning yourself with hers."[32] Matmon similarly reprimanded a man for being oblivious to his wife's sexual experience with him. He advised L.S. of Petakh Tikva about his wife's "frigidity" and explained that it could be ascribed to an internal resistance to the act, which might stem from either fear of sex or fear of pregnancy. "Now, after she agrees, after persistent seduction, or because she felt she must obey her husband's demands, she sees it as rape on her husband's part. Her reaction is thus indifference and incompliance to sexual life she does not fancy."[33]

In a long article, Mukhtar al-Jawahiri explains that men should be better informed on the nuptial night. Brides, he explained, are normally virgins, undress for the first time in the presence of a stranger, have no idea what to expect, and often find their first sexual experience traumatic, painful, and degrading. Men, in contrast, often do have former sexual experience, normally with prostitutes, and thus treat their bride like one. This why for al-Jawahiri premarital education is important, because it would teach men that women also have sexual desires, and this knowledge would help prevent marital problems, which currently begin with this first sexual encounter. While women's own experiences were not heard in such discussions, but rather dubbed by experts such as al-Jawahiri, women's sexual pleasure was nevertheless now taken into account.[34]

Contraception and abortion were part of the new marriage discourses. In contrast to Matmon and Fakhri, who were inspired by Central European sexology, Jawahiri, *RB*'s chief editor, was clearly inspired by Stopes. He published translations of her articles about contraception and female sexual pleasure, and some of the journal's original articles also touched these topics. Responding to criticism, moreover, *RB*'s editors explained that they did not, by any means, encourage premarital sex or childlessness. Instead, they encouraged an ideal average of three or four children per family to afford a better quality of life for all family members. They argued that contraception was legitimate for newlyweds who needed an adjustment period, or in cases of inherent defects in the family of one of the spouses or in their older children.[35] Not every form of contraception was recommended, however. A certain H. Kasim was told, for example, that coitus interruptus was not an effective contraceptive, but it was harmful to the nervous system, particularly of the wife, who would not be sexually satisfied as a result of the practice.[36] It should be noted that *RB*'s attitude toward abortion was not as positive, as it restricted permissible abortions to life-threatening situations. To one A.Z. Sh. from Khartoum the editors replied that abortion was absolutely illegal, unless performed by a medical doctor and only if absolutely necessary to save the woman's life. Abortions performed by midwives were dangerous and might cause sterility or even death. Midwives had neither training nor sterile equipment and thus could cause potentially fatal internal bleeding.[37] A man who considered aborting a fetus conceived before he and his wife realized they were inflicted by syphilis was reprimanded and strongly advised not to do so.[38]

Rather similarly, Matmon's responses to questions on contraception and nonreproductive sex were both medical and moral. He noted the effectiveness of certain contraceptives but at the same time warned his readers that marital abstinence could be harmful to the nervous system and that marital happiness, eventually, lay in reproduction. He advised readers to refrain from coitus interruptus because of its adverse effects on the female nervous system[39] and claimed that mutual manual stimulation was but a form of masturbation and as such should also be avoided.[40] Condoms were preferable to other forms of contraception, but not as license for nonmarital or even commercial sex.[41] Even within marriage, however, "the culmination of happiness can be reached if all contraceptives are abandoned with the purpose of having children."[42] Matmon was rather ambivalent about abortions. To one Lina S. he wrote that abortion in the fifth month of pregnancy could be dangerous to the woman. This was followed, however, by nonmedical advice to use rabbinical or civil courts to force the child's father to marry her, at least until birth, after which she was advised to divorce him, since this was not the kind of man one would want to spend her life with. "There is no shame here," he concluded, "since motherhood is an honor to a woman, not disgrace." It was not her who should be ashamed, but rather the man and his like "who become abundant in our country, to our great dismay, who tarnish women's name and honor."[43] To one Rachel Naiman, he wrote that he did not consider abortion a socialist question but a medical one. Permitting abortion would liberate neither the worker nor the proletariat. Abortion should be overseen by a committee of medical doctors who would take both medical and socioeconomic factors into account.[44]

The fact that medical doctors in Cairo and Tel Aviv were asked similar questions and reached similar conclusions indicates a generational shift in attitudes toward sex. The marital ideal was changing in both places, to a companionate marriage in the Egyptian case and to an egalitarian one in the case of the Yishuv. Women's role in society was also changing, as their education and integration in public life increased including via the opening of new roles as wage earners. In this context the marital bed, as much as the baby's crib and housework in general, were undergoing medicalization—and men and women were told that they needed expert advice to engage in lasting and fulfilling marital life. As young couples were readjusting to new marital realities—more couples were choosing their marital partners and marrying later in life, and control of the family and community was less strict than in their parents' time—they appreciated the advice columns for offering insights into a reality their parents could not comprehend.

Self-Control, Masturbation, and the (National) Economy of Sperm

If the Arabic and Hebrew advice columns thus encouraged both men and women to commit to lasting marital unions, then the related discourses about health and self-discipline nevertheless tended to focus specifically on male sexuality. The most common questions in *HaBr'iut* concerned masturbation and the related issues of morning erections, spontaneous ejaculation, and nocturnal emission. This pattern was consistent with late-turn-of-the-century European advice columns, which shifted from outright condemnation of masturbation to presenting it as a habit to be overcome, as evidence of manliness and self-restraint.[45] For instance, Matmon advised one reader to urinate upon waking up and reassured him that the phenomenon he described was normal and would be resolved upon marriage.[46] To another reader, Matmon advised physical exercise, bathing in the sea twice a day, taking a shower before bedtime, and covering himself with a light blanket at night.[47] He advised a reader who appeared obsessed with sexual thoughts to concentrate on his work and prescribed Émile Coué's method of autosuggestion. To another reader concerned with masturbation, he explained that although his habit was not harmful in itself, it should be avoided, for reasons of courtesy and decorum, because of its negative mental impact, and since "in a few years you will no longer be able to conceal it from society." This habit should be combated soon, "as long as you are young and full of life," since later he would not have the power to prevent it from occupying "a significant place in your life and your being."[48]

In a similar vein, one article in *RB* argued that masturbation was harmful to the nervous system because it caused excessive agitation and could result in degeneration of the nervous system and subsequently insanity. In response, a certain M.N. from Cairo wrote to the journal and cited a medical doctor and a mufti, both of whom claimed that masturbation was permissible especially for single men and was preferable to nonmarital sex. The editors replied that the opinions cited were minority views, and that complete abstinence, rather than masturbation, was the solution for single men.[49] This indicates the conflicting kinds of authorities men turned to for advice, even as it suggests that on the topic of masturbation *RB* was more conservative than some other parts of the medical profession and religion. *RB* seemed to draw a somewhat curious distinction between masturbation—on which they frowned[50]—and sexual dreams, which they thought permissible. To one Amil S. from Alexandria, *RB* replied that nocturnal emissions were nothing to worry about and no impediment to marriage, but that they were natural for men leading a healthy life and avoiding "unnatural" sexual relations.[51] In other words, then, *RB* treated sexual dreams and acts differently.

But this disciplining of individual bodies was not merely the concern of a "civilizing" elite of medical doctors. In both Cairo and Tel Aviv, men wrote to the press in order to find out how to control their urges and secretions. The privileged status of medicine in regimenting individual and national life was clearly internalized by these individuals. Indeed, echoing the European medical discourse that marked both the Jew and the Arab as lacking in self-restraint, emerging medical advice columns in Palestine and Egypt urged young men to practice self-restraint and better control their bodies. The debates about marriage suggest, then, that the sexual advice columns were not entirely radical in the advice they gave, as they maintain some older anti-sex attitudes even as they also helped to educate people about sex and free them from some negative sexual norms.

(Un)Speakable Homosexuality

While homosexuality was a central concern of European sexology, it featured only rarely in the Hebrew and Arabic advice columns. When homosexuality was mentioned, the advice given tended to be negative, arguing that homosexual attraction should be either ignored or overcome. Nevertheless, the very existence of a homosexual discourse in these journals is significant because homosexuality generally was rarely mentioned in contemporary Arabic and Hebrew writing, and female homosexuality was an even rarer topic to enter public discourse. Against this negative representation, Fakhri's writings acknowledged, legitimized, and historicized male homosexuality—even as his discussion of female homosexuality was much more implicit. For instance, on one occasion a girl wrote to *RB* explaining that she was in love with a female school friend of hers. "I studied in a foreign school," she explains,

> and . . . she studied there with me. We slept together, studied together, we shared our study room. . . . I could not bear being apart from her. She still visits me every day. She recently told me that she is distressed because her family had her engaged to a man. I cried, and she cried with me. I realize I love her, and the jealousy, that thought of her getting married, is nearly killing me. I read about sexual problems, and I don't think that this is a perverse desire. I am very distressed and need advice.[52]

RB's response to the letter was discouraging. Yet its very publication publicized the existence of love and desire between women, which otherwise tended to remain unspoken in public.

HaBr'iut does not contain similar testimonies by women. A reply by Matmon to Ita B. nevertheless indicates that female same-sex sexuality played a role: "Your case is very interesting, though not very rare at all," he writes, diagnosing her "sexual complex" as a probable internal secretion problem. The "proof," he explains, is that "alongside your 'disgust' with sexual relations with a man, you also long to be a mother. You might be suffering from a homosexual problem, which requires rectification." He advises her to contact a sexologist, since "based on experience, such phenomena can be set to rights." Curiously, this discussion also anticipates much later debates about lesbian parenting. She asks him about the possibility of artificial insemination, to which he replies that the success rate of such a procedure is merely 1 percent.[53]

In both cases, then, a woman's desire for another woman is presented as something to be abandoned or even corrected. However, it is significant that both cases testify to the existence of female same-sex desire even if they try to suppress or pathologize it. Ryan argues that in the Irish case, publishing letters by homosexual readers gave voice to men and women whose lives were understood only in language of pathologies; their readers thus learned that they were not alone.[54] While such evidence in both the Arabic and Hebrew cases is scarce, it nevertheless suggests that the advice columns gave voice and public presence to homosexual desires, making it part of the national discourses about sex that circulated at the time.

Conclusion: National Sexologies

By tracing how European scientific sexology was translated and incorporated into local professional communities in both Cairo and Tel Aviv, this chapter has shown that sexual discourse was used to serve the national cause in both Egypt and Palestine. Both the Egyptian and the Zionist sexual advice projects were designed to resolve the perceived crisis of the family. Emerging medical discourses in both national contexts furthermore told men their bodies were deficient because they did not know how to control themselves—thus responding to and adopting European medical discourses, which portrayed the Jewish or Arab body as lacking self-control and thus unworthy of integration or national independence. At the same time, these columns also sought to instruct men how to be better husbands, better attuned to the sexual needs of their wives. As the Jewish traditional family was dislocated with the immigration to Palestine, and as monogamous marriage were advocated in both societies as the hallmark of national modernity, men were to be taught how to cope with the new woman—now a companion, or a partner to the national project.

Comparing Fakhri and Matmon makes the Egyptian sexology project seem more liberal than the Zionist one. However, close attention to their sexological translations and the public debates about sex at the time reveals that both Hebrew and Arabic sexual discourses operated within and against a scientific discourse that saw Jewish *and* Arab sexuality as perverse and was designed to correct and discipline Jewish and Arab bodies to strengthen the nation. While Matmon and Fakhri promoted rather different sexologies— the Jewish doctor totally ignored the more radical, destabilizing aspects of German sexology, while his Egyptian contemporary made them his main concern—the sexual advice columns show that sexology in both Tel Aviv and Cairo was part of a strictly normalizing discourse about sex and gender. Attention to the specific translations of European sexology indicates that certain negative aspects were adopted—such as the assumption that medical knowledge could engineer individual and national lives—while other, more progressive aspects, such as the strong support of many European sexologists for homosexuality, were left out. These transformations mark the specific contours that define how European sexological discourses were adapted to open up new discursive spaces in both Egypt and Palestine, where they shaped new national discourses about sex, gender, and the body.

NOTES

I would like to thank the participants in the *Sexology in Translation* workshop for their useful feedback, which contributed to the final version of this paper. I am particularly grateful to Iris Rachamimov, Roii Ball, José Bruner, and Sean Brady for their comparative insights and for helping me develop and nuance my argument, and to Lucie Ryzova for referring me to *al-Riyada al-Badaniyya*. This research was enabled by the Israeli Science Foundation (grant 304/11), which I acknowledge with gratitude.

1. Sander L. Gilman, *Differences and Pathology: Stereotypes of Sexuality, Race and Madness* (Ithaca, NY: Cornell University Press, 1985), 169–190; Sander L. Gilman, *The Jew's Body* (London: Routledge, 1991).

2. Edward Said, *Orientalism* (London: Penguin, 1978), 182–190. See Nina Salouâ Studer, "'Pregnant with Madness': Muslim Women in French Psychiatric Writing about Colonial North Africa," *Maghreb Review* 35 (2010): 439–452; Wilson Chacko Jacob, "Overcoming 'Simply Being': Straight Sex, Masculinity and Physical Culture in Modern Egypt," *Gender and History* 22 (2010): 658–676; Isabel Jiménez-Lucena, "Gender and Coloniality: The 'Moroccan Woman' and the 'Spanish Woman' in Spain's Sanitary Policies in Morocco," *Historia, Ciencias, Saude Manguinhos* 13 (2006): 33–54.

3. See Patricia M. E. Lorcin, *Imperial Identities: Stereotyping, Prejudice and Race in Colonial Algeria* (London: Tauris, 1995); Richard C. Keller, *Colonial Madness: Psychiatry in French North Africa* (Chicago: University of Chicago Press, 2007).

4. Liat Kozma, "Sexology in the Yishuv: The Rise and Decline of Sexual Consultation in Tel Aviv, 1930–39," *International Journal of Middle East Studies* 42, no. 2 (2010): 231–249; Liat Kozma, "'We, the Sexologists . . .': Arabic Medical Writing on Sexuality, 1879–1943," *Journal of the History of Sexuality* 22, no. 3 (2013): 426–445.

5. Amira El Azhary Sonbol, *The Creation of the Medical Profession in Egypt* (Syracuse, NY: Syracuse University Press, 1991), 106–132.

6. Sylvia Chiffoleau, *Médecines et médecins en Egypte: Construction d'une identité professionnelle et projet médical* (Paris: Harmattan, 1997), 59–80.

7. David Preston, "The German Jews in Secular Education, University Teaching, and Science: A Preliminary Inquiry," *Jewish Social Studies* 38 (1976): 99–116; Geoffrey Cocks and Fritz Stern, "Partners and Pariahs: Jews and Medicine in Modern German Society," *Leo Baeck Institute Yearbook* 36 (1991): 191–205; Harriet Pass Freidenreich, "Jewish Women Physicians in Central Europe in the Early Twentieth Century," *Contemporary Jewry* 17 (1996): 79–105.

8. Doron Niederland, "The Emigration of Jewish Academics and Professionals from Germany in the First Years of Nazi Rule," *Leo Baeck Institute Yearbook* 33 (1988): 298; on Jewish immigration to Egypt, see Gudrun Krämer, *The Jews in Modern Egypt, 1914–1952* (London: Tauris, 1989), 8–12, and on the Jewish German doctors, 136. On anti-Nazism in Egypt, see Israel Gershoni and James Jankowski, *Confronting Fascism in Egypt: Dictatorship versus Democracy in the 1930s* (Stanford, CA: Stanford University Press, 2009).

9. Doron Niederland, "Hashpa'at HaRof'im Ha'Olim MiGermaniya 'al Hitpatkhut HaRefu'a BeEretz Israel (1933–1948)" [The impact of German immigrant doctors on the development of medicine in the Land of Israel (1933–1948)], *Katedra* (1983): 119–120.

10. Avraham Matmon, *Hayey HaMin shel HaAdam* [Human sex life] (Tel Aviv: Hamakhon le-Higyena U-Madei Hamin, 1939); Avraham Matmon, *Hashbakhat HaGeza*

shel HaMin HaEnoshi VeErka LeAmenu [Eugenics and its value to our nation] (Tel Aviv: Hamakhon le-Higyena U-Madei HaMin, 1933). On Matmon, see David Tidhar, "Dr. Avraham Matmon," *Encylopedia Le-Halutzei Ha-Yeshuv U-Bonav* (Tel Aviv: Sifriyat Rishonim, 1971), 3713.

11. Faraj Fakhri, *Al-Mar'a wa-Falsafat al-Tanassuliyyat* [The woman and the philosophy of sexuality] (Cairo: Al-Matba'a al-'Asriyya, 1924), 23.

12. Wilson Chacko Jacob, *Working Out Egypt: Effendi Masculinity and Subject Formation in Colonial Modernity, 1870–1940* (Durham, NC: Duke University Press, 2011), 167–168; Faraj Fakhri, *Al-Du'f al-Tanassuli 'inda al-Dhukur wa-l-Anath, Anwa'uhu wa-Turuq al-Wikaya Minhu wa-'Ilajihi* [Sexual weakness in men and women, its types, preventive measures and treatment] (Cairo: Al-Matba'a al-'Asriyya, n.d.), 3; Faraj Fakhri, *Kitab al-Amrad al-Tanassuliyya wa-'Ilajiha wa-Turuq al-Wikaya minha* [The book of venereal diseases, their treatment and prevention measures], 2nd ed. (Cairo: Al-Matba'a al-'Asriyya, 1931), 5–11; Faraj Fakhri, *Al-Mar'a wa-Falasafat al-Tanassuliyyat*, 6–7, 12–14, 20–24.

13. Tel Aviv Municipality Archives, 9 Hertzel Street file.

14. "MiYediot HaMakhon LeHigyena UMadei HaMin BeTel Aviv" [Some news from the Institute for Hygiene and Sexual Sciences in Tel Aviv], *HaBr'iut* 1, no. 4 (1932): 8.

15. John M. Efron, *Defenders of the Race: Jewish Doctors and Race Science in Fin-de-Siècle Europe* (New Haven, CT: Yale University Press, 1994); Dafna Hirsch, "Zionist Eugenics, Mixed Marriage, and the Creation of a 'New Jewish Type,'" *Journal of the Royal Anthropological Institute* 15 (2009): 592–609; Sachlav Stoler-Liss, "Kakh Agadel Tinok Tzioni: Havnayat HaTinok VeHaEm HaEretz Yisraelim BeEmtzaut Sifrei Hadrakha LaHorim" ["This is how I shall raise a Zionist baby": The construction of the baby and the mother in instruction manuals for parents], *Iyunim BiTkumat Yisrael* 13 (2003): 277–285.

16. Q&A, *HaBr'iut* 1, no. 2–3 (1932): 8.

17. A., "Al Tahanat ha-Hitya'atsut be-She'elot Haye ha-Min ve-ha-Nisu'in she-al Yad ha-Makhon le-Higyenah u-Made ha-Min be-Tel Aviv" [On the consultation station for sexual and marital life at the Institute for Hygiene and Sexual Sciences in Tel Aviv], *HaBr'iut* 1, no. 1 (September 1, 1932).

18. Faraj Fakhri, "Lidhdhat al-Jima' al-Kubra" [Orgasm], *Al-Majalla al-Tibiyya al-Misriyya* 8, no. 3 (1923): 203.

19. Fakhri, *Al-Du'f al-Tanassuli*, 39.

20. Fakhri, "Fisyulujiyat al-Tanassul (Liddhat al-Jima' al-Kubra)" [The physiology of sex (orgasm)], *Al-Majalla al-Tibiyya al-Misriyya* 8, no. 6 (1923): 521–523.

21. Ibid.

22. Ibid., 95–123.

23. Ibid., 104.

24. Ibid., 134–174.

25. Paul Ryan, *Asking Angela Macnamara: An Intimate History of Irish Lives* (Dublin: Irish Academic Press, 2011).

26. Jacob, *Working Out Egypt*, 163.

27. Ibid., 156–185.

28. George L. Mosse, *Nationalism and Sexuality: Respectability and Abnormal Sexuality in Modern Europe* (New York: Fertig, 1985), 10, 33; George L. Mosse, *The*

Image of Man: The Creation of Modern Masculinity (New York: Oxford University Press, 1996), 63–68, 151–153; Moshe Zimmermann, "Muscle Jews versus Nervous Jews," in *Emancipation through Muscles: Jews and Sports in Europe,* ed. Michael Brenner and Gideon Reuveni (Lincoln: University of Nebraska Press, 2006), 13–26; Michael Gluzman, *HaGuf HaTziyoni: Le'umiyut, Migdar UMiniyut BaSafrut HaIvrit HaKhadasha* [The Zionist body: Nationalism, gender and sexuality in modern Hebrew literature] (Tel Aviv: HaKibutz HaMeukhad, 2007); Gilman, *Differences and Pathology,* 150–162.

29. Adrian Bingham, "Newspaper Problem Pages and British Sexual Culture since 1918," *Media History* 18 (2012): 51–63; Atina Grossmann, *Reforming Sex: The German Movement for Birth Control and Abortion Reform, 1920–1950* (Oxford: Oxford University Press, 1995), 14–16, 28–29; Evelyn Faulkner, "'Powerless to Prevent Him': Attitudes of Married Working-Class Women in the 1920s and the Rise of Sexual Power," *Local Population Studies* 49 (1992): 51–61; Lesley A. Hall, "'Somehow Very Distasteful': Doctors, Men and Sexual Problems between the Wars," *Journal of Contemporary History* 20 (1985): 553–574; Lesley A. Hall, "Impotent Ghosts from No Man's Land, Flappers' Boyfriends, or Crypto-Patriarchs? Men, Sex and Social Change in 1920s Britain," *Social History* 21 (1996): 54–70.

30. Hanan Kholoussy, "Monitoring and Medicalising Male Sexuality in Semi-Colonial Egypt," *Gender and History* 22 (November 2010): 677–691; Hanan Kholoussy, *For Better, for Worse: The Marriage Crisis That Made Modern Egypt, 1898–1936* (Stanford, CA: Stanford University Press, 2010), 2–4, 39–40, 49–67, 99–105; Lisa Pollard, *Nurturing the Nation: The Family Politics of Modernizing, Colonizing and Liberating Egypt, 1805–1923* (Berkeley: University of California Press, 2005), 2–6; Lisa Pollard, "From Husbands and Housewives to Suckers and Whores: Marital-Political Anxieties in the 'House of Egypt,' 1919–48," *Gender and History* 21 (2009): 647–669; Omnia El Shakry, "Barren Land and Fecund Bodies: The Emergence of Population Discourse in Interwar Egypt," *International Journal of Middle East Studies* 37 (2005): 360–361; Mona Russell, *Creating the New Egyptian Woman: Consumerism, Education, and National Identity, 1863–1922* (London: Palgrave Macmillan, 2004), 80–84, 136–137; Beth Baron, "Making and Breaking Marital Bonds in Modern Egypt," in *Women in Middle Eastern History: Shifting Boundaries in Sex and Gender,* ed. Beth Baron and Nikki R. Kedie (New Haven, CT: Yale University Press, 1991), 275–291.

31. Bat Sheva Margalit Stern, "Beyn Hok Hateva Le-Din HaTnu'a: Imahut VeAl Imahut BaHevra HaTzionit BeEretz Israel (1920–1945)" [The "law of nature" versus the "dictate of the movement": Motherhood and non-motherhood in the Yishuv (1920–1945)], in *Migdar BeYisrael: Mehkarim Hadashim al Migdar BaYeshuv Ubamedina* [Gender in Israel: New studies on gender in the Yishuv and state], ed. Margalit Shilo and Gideon Katz (Beer Sheva: Ben Gurion University Press, 2011), 176, 187–193; Dafna Hirsch, "HaMedicalizatzia shel HaImahut: Yakhasim Etniyim Ve-Hinukh Imahot Mizrahiyot le-Tipul Higyeni BaTinok BeTkufat HaMandat" [The medicalization of motherhood, ethnic relations and the education of Jewish Mizrahi mothers in Mandate Palestine], in Shilo and Katz, *Migdar BeYisrael,* 106–110; Deborah S. Bernstein, "Introduction," in *Pioneers and Homemakers: Jewish Women in Pre-State Israel,* ed. Deborah S. Bernstein (Albany: State University of New York Press, 1992), 2–4; Sylvie Foigel-Bijaoui, "From Revolution to Motherhood: The Case of Women in the Kibbutz, 1910–1928," in Bernstein, *Pioneers and Homemakers,* 213–222; Deborah S. Bernstein,

"Human Being or Housewife: The Status of Women in the Jewish Working Class Family in Palestine in the 1920s and 1930s," in Bernstein, *Pioneers and Homemakers*, 235–241.

32. "Istisharat Sihiyya" [Health advice], *RB* 8, no. 162 (1936): 330.

33. Q&A, *HaBr'iut* 1, no. 23 (August 20, 1933), 195. Robin Kent notes a similar rebuke in 1930s Britain in his *Aunt Agony Advises: Problem Pages through the Ages* (London: Allen, 1979), 90.

34. Mukhtar al-Jawahiri, "Al-Zawj al-Jahil" [The ignorant husband], *RB* 12, no. 365 (1940): 112–114.

35. M.F.J., "Hawl Tahdid al-Nasl Aydan" [More about contraception], *RB* 3, no. 10 (1931): 1160–1163; Muhammad al-Jawahiri, "Hal Nahnu Ibahiyyin" [Are we permissive?], *RB* 12, no. 405 (1940): 844–847; "Dr. Mahmud Isma'il, "Kayfa Nasughu al-Ijhad" [How would we allow abortion], *RB* 10, no. 291 (1938): 927–934; Mukhtar al-Jawahiri, "Akhtar Tahdid al-Nasl fi Sanawat al-Zawaj al-Ula" [The dangers of contraception in the first years of marriage], *RB* 12, no. 361 (1940).

36. "Istisharat Sihiyya" [Health advice], *RB* 11, no. 325 (May 1939): 489–491.

37. "Istisharat Sihiyya" [Health advice], *RB* 10, no. 279 (June 1938): 587; see also an article about abortions, Dr. Mustafa al-Qalali, "Al-Ijhad" [Abortion], *RB* 11, no. 338 (August 1939).

38. "As'ila wa-Ajwiba," *RB* 10, no. 304 (1938): 1133–1137.

39. Q&A, *HaBr'iut* 1, no. 16 (May 5, 1933): 135; Q&A, *HaBr'iut* 1, no. 15, (April 1933), 127.

40. Q&A, *HaBr'iut* 1, no. 6 (October 27, 1932): 52.

41. Q&A, *HaBr'iut* 2, no. 4 (December 15, 1933): 38.

42. Q&A, *HaBr'iut* 1, no. 22 (July 18, 1933): 186.

43. Q&A, *HaBr'iut* 2, no. 8 (June 17, 1934): 74.

44. Q&A, *HaBr'iut* 3, no. 3 (November 21, 1934): 32.

45. Kent, *Aunt Agony Advises*, 153; Thomas Laqueur, *Solitary Sex: A Cultural History of Masturbation* (New York: Zone Books, 2003), 248–347.

46. Q&A, *HaBr'iut* 1, no. 18 (June 1, 1933): 151.

47. Q&A, *HaBr'iut* 1, no. 2–3 (September 1, 1932): 8.

48. Q&A, *HaBr'iut* 1, no. 5 (October 1, 1932): 42.

49. "Al-'Ada al-Sirriyya" [The secret habit], *RB* 3, no. 3 (March 1931): 290–292; "Al-'Ada al-Sirriyya Aidan" [More on the secret habit], *RB* 3, no. 3 (March 1931): 300–301.

50. "Istisharat Sihiyya" [Health advice], *RB* 11, no. 325 (May 1939): 489–491.

51. *RB* 7 no. 139 (November 1935): 1269–1271.

52. "Madha ta'malu fi Hadhihi al-Hala" [What would you do in such a situation], *RB* 8, no. 158 (February 1936): 210–212.

53. Q&A, *HaBr'iut* 3, no. 6 (January 27, 1934): 48.

54. Ryan, *Asking Angela Macnamara*, 165.

8

Translation and Two "Chinese Sexologies"

Double Plum *and* Sex Histories

LEON ANTONIO ROCHA

B etween June 1926 and November 1927, two figures featured prominently in almost every issue of *The Crystal* (*Jingbao*), one of the most
popular tabloids, or "mosquito newspapers" (*xiaobao*), in Republican
Shanghai:[1] the "Pock-Faced" (*mazi*) scholar Ye Dehui (1864–1927), and the
"Bullshit Professor" (*hushuo boshi*) Zhang Jingsheng (1888–1970). Both
men were relentlessly lampooned for their sexological research (*xingxue*).
Ye Dehui was portrayed as a "perverted," feudalist, and villainous character, who finally got his comeuppance when he was executed in 1927. Zhang
Jingsheng, on the other hand, was depicted as the university professor cor-
rupted by Western philosophy, sprouting fashionable nonsense on the health
benefits of vaginal fluids. The two men were painted by *The Crystal*'s writers
as "signs of the times": "monsters" who in a period of chaos and upheaval
would multiply and spread obscene and confusing ideas among the general
populace.

This chapter examines the role of translation in the work of Ye Dehui and
Zhang Jingsheng to show that they constructed two very different "Chinese
sexologies" in the early twentieth century. Specifically, I analyze Ye Dehui's
famous *Shadow of the Double Plum Tree Anthology* (1903–1917) and Zhang
Jingsheng's equally notorious *Sex Histories* (1926), two projects—one from
a self-fashioned vanguard of Confucianism disturbed and dismayed by the
collapse of the Qing Empire, the other from a French-trained public intellectual and self-appointed agent of modernity—that despite their differences
shared the same aim: to produce a new nation inhabited by a stronger and

more intelligent Chinese race, more able to defend itself against foreign powers.[2]

By turning attention to how Ye and Zhang developed their ideas in and through the translation of existing texts, I show that these two men drew on radically different cultural traditions and sources of authority: while Ye's sexology was indebted to Han Dynasty religious and medical texts, which he reconstructed from Japanese collections, Zhang turned to the Western philosophy of Jean-Jacques Rousseau and the sexology of Havelock Ellis and Marie Stopes. Exploring their biographical background, I argue that Ye Dehui attempted to embargo the translation and movement of Western knowledge into China by establishing an "indigenous," supposedly superior precedence, while Zhang Jingsheng made the case that thinkers such as Rousseau, Ellis, and Stopes urgently needed to be imported into Chinese culture. I will trace the critical afterlives of their work in China and the West, showing that Ye Dehui's *Anthology* became an essential document for Western Sinologists whose scholarship was then appropriated by Michel Foucault in *History of Sexuality, Vol. 1*, while Zhang's *Sex Histories* was republished in Taiwan in 2005 and in China in 2014 and hailed as an inspiration for the emancipation of sexual subjectivities. By comparing how translation shaped these two works and their reception, then, this chapter tracks the movement of ideas about sexuality and reproduction in Republican China and beyond. It shows that modern ideas about sexuality in China as well as the way in which Chinese sexology is understood in the West is shaped by complex cultural appropriations and politics.

Ye Dehui, Defender of Confucianism

Ye Dehui was born in 1864 in Changsha, Hunan Province, to one of the wealthiest and most prominent families in the region.[3] A powerful member of the Southern Chinese elite, who controlled major agricultural and commercial enterprises in his native Changsha, he had strong ties with scholar-officials in the Jiangnan region, allying himself with the conservative faction of late-Qing literati. Following his success at the palace examination in 1892, he enjoyed a short-lived career as a secretary at the Ministry of Personnel and Civil Appointments. After he resigned from his post in Beijing and returned to his native Changsha, Ye became thoroughly enmeshed in the network of conservative Hunanese elites and developed a close alliance with the classicist Wang Xianqian (1842–1918). Wang and Ye amassed considerable fortune through controlling the rice and salt trades;[4] in turn Ye's commercial activities financed an exceptional collection of rare books and manuscripts—one of the largest in China at the turn of the century, with an estimated 200,000 to 300,000 *juan*.[5]

In the late 1890s, Ye Dehui and a collective of conservative scholar-officials launched a campaign of attacks on the late-Qing reformers Kang Youwei (1858–1927) and Liang Qichao (1873–1929). Some of Ye's fiercest polemic, which also clearly articulated his political and intellectual orientations, could be found in the volume *Collected Essays on Defending Confucianism* (1898).[6] To cut short a heated and protracted debate, Kang Youwei wrote two incendiary critiques of the Confucian canon: *An Exposé of the Forged Classics* (1891) and *Confucius as a Reformer* (1892–1898).[7] Here he claimed to have discovered a classical and thoroughly "indigenous" legitimation for political reform, which would involve the adoption of parliamentary democracy and constitutional monarchy. In response, Ye Dehui and his allies staunchly defended their version of Confucianism. For them, the only legitimate ethical principles, social configurations, and political institutions were those prescribed by the classical texts. While acknowledging that there were some useful ideas and technologies from the West, which China could adopt in a highly selective fashion, Ye Dehui insisted on the absolute superiority of Chinese culture. Any reform, let alone "Westernization," had to be resisted.[8]

As Ye's worldview was resolutely anti-reform, anti-foreign, and Sinocentric, he believed that although China was engulfed in political turmoil, this was not because Chinese values were fundamentally faulty, but because the people deviated from Chinese traditions. He argued that everything that was important and useful had already been said millennia ago by Confucian sages and thus, for Ye, people who admired Western things were superficial fools. The only valid solution to present problems was to return to the Chinese classics. This outlook animated Ye's intellectual projects: he regarded himself as the last of the champions and vanguards of Chinese knowledge and as a disseminator of truths that would remedy the state of ignorance and impropriety.

Given this agenda, it is unsurprising that Ye Dehui devoted himself to Chinese philology, specifically "elementary studies" (*xiaoxue*), which combined phonetics, semantics, etymology, and the analysis of Chinese characters.[9] The aim of this enterprise was to determine the correct pronunciation, appearance, and meaning of words; this would in turn guarantee the accurate transmission of knowledge. Ye's "elementary studies" went hand in hand with his bibliographic projects (*mulu banbenxue*), which were concerned with the authentication and rectification of classical texts, as well as the production of standard, canonical editions. Although Ye's philological research is largely forgotten, his bibliographical writings, such as *Plain Talks on the Forest of Books* (*Shulin qinghua*, 1911) and *The Bookman's Decalogue* (*Chuangshu shiyue*, 1911), remain crucial to historians of the Chinese book. They furthermore indicate the importance of Chinese culture for Ye's sexological ventures.[10] According to him the correct use of language was the prerequisite to the accurate transmission of the ancient sages' messages that were urgently needed in a degenerating China, and the medium that carried those messages had to be verified, preserved, and recirculated. When Ye Dehui encountered European and American texts on reproduction and sexual hygiene, his response followed his general intellectual and political trajectory: he reconstructed and published several classical texts, arguing that they contained a "Chinese sexology" that was antecedent and superior to Western science.

Zhang's "Competition for Survival"

In contrast to Ye Dehui's Sinocentrism, the outlook of "Professor Bullshit" Zhang Jingsheng was cosmopolitan and resolutely anti-tradition.[11] Born in Raoping, Guangdong, in 1888, Zhang attended the Whampoa Military Primary School, where he studied French and acquired proficiency in translation. He also studied at Beijing's Imperial Capital University, and during those formative years Zhang encountered many new scientific theories and philosophies from the West. He developed an impressible enthusiasm for Social Darwinism and changed his name from Zhang Jiangliu (flowing river) to Zhang Jingsheng, literally "competition for survival."

Zhang Jingsheng's interest in sexology was inspired by Carl Heinrich Stratz's *Die Rassenschönheit des Weibes* (1901).[12] This book featured approximately four hundred photographs of nude women and young girls from around the world. Stratz argued that ideal bodily ratios were to be found among the Germanic race, and that the more highly developed a race, the greater the secondary sexual differences between men and women would be. The "inferior races" tended to be more "androgynous"; male Asian bodies were apparently not so distinguishable from female Asian bodies.[13] Absorbing Stratz's scientific racism, Zhang suggested that the "pathological" and "stunted" Chinese body needed urgent eugenic intervention. In 1912 he traveled to France as part of an elite corps of young men sponsored by the Nationalist Party to study abroad, "to seek modernity in China's name."[14] He obtained a *diplôme d'études* in 1916 from the University of Paris and was awarded a *diplôme de docteur* by the University of Lyon for his thesis on Rousseau's pedagogical theory.[15] Rousseau was Zhang Jingsheng's hero; he later produced the first Chinese translations of Rousseau's *Confessions* and *Reveries of a Solitary Walker*.[16] In 1920 Zhang returned to China and was appointed professor of philosophy at Peking University. He belonged to the group of fresh, energetic, and internationally focused scholars with qualifications from foreign institutions. When Margaret Sanger visited Beijing in 1922 and delivered a series of rapturously received lectures on birth control,

Zhang Jingsheng acted as one of her hosts and translators.[17] During his ten-
ure at Peking University, Zhang earned a reputation as an innovative if occasionally eccentric thinker who held radical viewpoints on romantic love,
the future of marriage, female sexuality, and eugenics.[18]

Zhang Jingsheng's intellectual output can be situated squarely in the context of the May Fourth New Culture Movement.[19] The May Fourth movement,
usually said to have begun in the mid-1910s, marked the upsurge of Chinese
nationalism, coupled with a relentless attack from many iconoclastic intellectuals on "Confucianism" and traditional culture. The highlight of May
Fourth was a mass demonstration in Tian'anmen Square on May 4, 1919. The
protesters, chiefly intellectuals and university students, voiced their dissatisfaction with the "humiliation" of China at the hands of the foreign, colonial
powers. Typical of the May Fourth generation, Zhang aimed to find put the
best possible "cure" for China's weaknesses. He took part in a frantic drive
to translate and appropriate all kinds of knowledges and discourses from
the West and from Japan.[20] Intellectuals established new journals and study
societies, delivered lectures, worked as editorial staff for publishing houses,
or set up their own bookstores, all in an attempt to "awaken" the Chinese
masses. They built up what Leo Ou-fan Lee called a "business of enlightenment," which promoted a high-minded politics and was concerned with
simple ideas and big causes.[21] Political activity no longer needed to be chan-
neled through state institutions. Instead, purposeful research, diligent reading, critical self-reflection, diary writing, group debating, submitting letters
to editors, experimentation with alternative ways of thinking and living—
all of these activities could lead to a bottom-up revolution of the heart.

These currents came together in Zhang's *Sex Histories* project. He argued
that traditional morality had painstakingly repressed sexuality and denied
man's very nature. What was most urgently needed, to create a "New China"
inhabited by a "New People," was the fullest affirmation and emancipation
of the sexual instinct. As befitting a disciple of Rousseau, Zhang suggested
that this could be achieved, first and foremost, via the narrativization of
the sexual self through autobiographical writing. *Sex Histories*, released in
May 1926, contained seven confessions that Zhang solicited from the public, plus his sexological commentaries written in the vein of British sexologist Havelock Ellis's *Studies in the Psychology of Sex* (1897–1928, 6 volumes).
Sex Histories turned out to be one of the most sensational and controversial
books of Republican China.

Saving Confucianism: *Double Plum Tree Anthology*

In the early 1900s, the conservative, anti-Western scholar Ye Dehui became
deeply invested in recovering sexual knowledge and techniques from early

China. This culminated in the publication of the *Shadow of the Double Plum Tree Anthology* (*Shuangmei jing'an congshu*, 1903–1917). The 1917 edition contained eighteen texts, which could be classified under four headings: (i) early Chinese treatises discussing sexual techniques or medicine (six items); (ii) songs and lyrics, or "best of" quotations from various operas and dramas (three items); (iii) "Who's Who" lists (*dianjiang lu*) (three items); and (iv) "Green Bowers and Pear Gardens" (*qinglou liyuan*) literature (six items). Categories (ii) and (iii) do not deal with sexuality and reproduction; Ye's motives for including them in the *Anthology* remain unclear. The texts under category (iv) were gossipy accounts on life in so-called "green bowers and pear gardens," basically adult entertainment complexes from brothels to opera troupes.[22] They suggest that Ye Dehui wanted to exhibit the sophisticated erotic cultures from the past, alongside six early Chinese writings on sex (category (i)).[23] For instance, *The Formulae of the Plain Girl* (*Sunü fang*) recorded numerous recipes for dealing with illnesses that arose from overindulgence in sex or from having intercourse at the incorrect times of the day or month.[24] *The Heaven and Earth, Yin and Yang Songs of Great Satisfaction in Sex* (*Tiandi yinyang jiaohuan dale fu*) was a manuscript from the Dunhuang Caves. This work was not so much an instruction manual but a paean to good sex between husband and wife (or concubines), which would lead to familial harmony and spiritual fulfillment.[25]

Other texts—*The Classic of the Plain Girl* (*Sunü jing*), *Secrets of the Jade Chamber* (*Yufang mijue*), *Essentials of the Jade Chamber* (*Yufang zhiyao*), and *Master Dongxuan* (*Dongxuan zi*)—were Ye Dehui's reconstructions of treatises on Daoist "bedchamber techniques" for the cultivation of health (*fangzhong yangsheng*), specifically those concerning the achievement of longevity via heterosexual intercourse. One practice was the so-called *coitus reservatus*, which involved the male adept's absorption of female (*yin*) essence through intercourse with numerous maidens. At the same time, the male practitioner would attempt to prevent ejaculation and to "return the semen to the brain" (*huanjing bunao*), so that the spirit could be nourished and longevity achieved.[26] Although Ye Dehui thought these four texts came from the Sui and Tang Dynasties, *The Classic of the Plain Girl* can probably be dated to as early as the Western Han (206 B.C.E.–9 C.E.). *Essentials of the Jade Chamber* was indeed a Sui-Tang work but was in fact a compilation of numerous earlier bedchamber texts. Ye found fragments of these four treatises in chapter 28 ("Inside the Bedchamber," *fangnei*) of *The Core Prescriptions of Medicine* (*Ishinpo*, 984). *Ishinpo* was the oldest surviving medical work from Japan, edited by Tamba Yasuyori (912–995), and was itself a compilation containing excerpts from various Chinese texts. The circulation of *Ishinpo* requires more research, and it is difficult to ascertain how Ye Dehui acquired the text.[27] I argue that Ye encountered only chapter 28 of *Ishinpo* and not the full work, as physicians in China did not appear to be aware of the text's existence throughout the nineteenth and early twentieth century. If, in 1903, Ye really did possess a complete copy of *Ishinpo*, it would be surprising that he elected not to publish the text in its entirety.

The following passage from Ye Dehui's preface for *The Classic of the Plain Girl* indicates the complex role issues of translation played in the reconstruction of the text:

> Today, Western scholars in hygiene from afar, investigate and speculate on the subtle and hidden causes behind sexual relations, and their works are translated into new books such as *Genitalia* [*Shengzhi qi*], *New Theories on Sexual Intercourse* [*Nannü jiaohe xinlun*], and *The Hygiene of Marriage* [*Hunyin weisheng xue*]. The ignorant people treat them as treasures, not knowing that the descendants of China's sacred emperors and ancient sages had already discussed this learning four thousand years ago. For instance, *The Records of Confucius Closing Off the House* [*Kongzi bifang ji*] is mentioned in the apocryphal texts . . . Or take the ancient methods of foetal education [*taijiao*] recorded in the *Abundant Dew on the Spring and Autumn Annals* [*Chunqiu fanlu*] and *Records of the Ritual Matters by Dai Senior* [*Da Dai liji*]. These were invariably about the rectification of the parents' characters [*duan xingqing*], the multiplication of descendants and the continuation of the family's progeny [*guang si xu*], to maximise the function of orderly cultivation [*weiyu*]. The spirit of this sexology [*xingxue*], how could those pedantic Confucian scholars possibly be able to see its essence?[28]

This passage illustrates the importance of translation for the development of Ye Dehui's work. This includes translations of past knowledges, making numerous references to Chinese texts.[29] While the *Abundant Dew on the Spring and Autumn Annals* and *Records of the Ritual Matters by Dai Senior* did contain discussions on reproduction, the texts that Ye Dehui compiled for the *Shadow of the Double Plum Tree Anthology* actually had nothing to do with reproduction. Instead *The Classic of the Plain Girl*, *Essential Secrets of the Jade Chamber*, and other texts focused on the cultivation of health via sexual techniques. Sexual pleasure was important only insofar as it helped promote longevity, and the production of quality offspring was completely irrelevant. Ye was thus misreading the Daoist texts that he reconstructed from the *Ishinpo*; contrary to what he suggests, they were not "proto-eugenics" in contents.

Furthermore, the passage shows that translation from other languages played an important role in Ye Dehui's work. He mentions a number of foreign texts—*Genitalia, New Theories on Sexual Intercourse,* and *The Hygiene of Marriage.* Scholars have overlooked these book titles hitherto, thus foreclosing the opportunity to connect Ye Dehui's project to the global travels of texts on reproduction and sexuality. However, *New Theories on Sexual Intercourse* is a reference to the Chinese translation of a Japanese, heavily abridged rendering of a curious American work, written by Orson Squire Fowler (1809–1887): *Creative and Sexual Science: or Manhood, Womanhood, and Their Mutual Interrelations* (1875).[30] Fowler's book is best described as a bricolage of advice on courtship, intercourse, childbirth, race, and selection, infused with a spiritual and phrenological language. Part VI of the book, titled "Generation" and covering the anatomy of male and female genitalia, was rendered into Japanese in 1878 by Hasizume Kanichi (1820–1884) and published as *Danjo kogo shin ron.*[31] The Japanese rendering was then translated into Chinese by Youyazi (a pseudonym) around the 1880s.[32] While Fowler was a medical faddist in America, now more likely to be remembered for his popularization of the octagonal houses found on the East Coast of the United States,[33] his manual on reproduction enjoyed a fascinating life cycle in late nineteenth- and early twentieth-century East Asia, where it became a "must-read" exemplar of Western reproductive science.[34] This text and the reference to it in Ye's preface shows, then, the importance of global transmissions to the formation of modern sexual discourse.

The second non-Chinese item mentioned by Ye Dehui, *The Hygiene of Marriage,* is most likely a reference to the Japanese text *Danjo seishoku kenzenho* (1900) by Matsumoto Yasuko (dates unknown), sometime president of the Central Nursing Guild of Tokyo and an accredited midwife.[35] This was translated into Chinese by Youminzi (a pseudonym) and published in Yokohama in 1902 by "F. Kingsell," the English name of Chinese publisher Feng Jingru (?–1913).[36] The third item in Ye Dehui's passage is *Genitalia,* which pointed toward the Chinese translation of *Tsuzoku seishoku ron* (1878), itself a heavily abridged Japanese rendering by physician Hasegawa Tai (1842–1912) of the chapters on gynecology from Henry Hartshorne's (1823–1897) *A Conspectus of the Medical Sciences: Comprising Manuals of Anatomy, Physiology, Chemistry, Medicine, Surgery and Obstetrics, for the Use of Students* (1874).[37]

Not coincidentally, these three works were listed in *Bibliography of Japanese Books (Riben shumu zhi,* 1898), compiled by Ye Dehui's archenemy Kang Youwei. Kang expressed admiration for these texts and suggested that the scientific principles within these Western works actually developed out of the ancient Chinese medical manual *The Yellow Emperor Inner Canon (Huangdi neijing)*![38] While both Kang and Ye mobilized two variations of the so-called "Chinese Origin of Western Learning" (*Xixue zhongyuan*) argument, their aims were completely divergent.[39] Kang wanted to facilitate the transmission of Western science by claiming that it developed from Chinese learning—and therefore was entirely compatible with Chinese culture. Kang kept the door ajar for East–West syncretism. Ye, on the other hand, sought to dismiss Western sexology by arguing that Chinese inquiries into human sexuality predated Western science by centuries if not millennia. Ye Dehui was not so much constructing a "counterdiscourse" to Western sexology, that is, a Chinese sexology radically different from the West. In fact, Ye insisted that both Western and Chinese inquiries in sex *pointed in the same direction.* The texts in *Shadow of the Double Plum Tree Anthology* were invaluable for Ye Dehui because he wanted to combat the influx of Western knowledge by putting back into public circulation a proper canon of "Chinese sexology."

Vaginal Fluidology: *Sex Histories*

In contrast to Ye Dehui's "Chinese sexology," Zhang Jingsheng's project was overtly influenced by European sexology. In *Sex Histories* (1926), Zhang states that not only was his project inspired by Rousseau's *Confessions*, but he wanted to emulate "the great English maestro [Havelock] Ellis and his six-volume work on the psychology of sex."[40] Zhang admired Ellis's inclusion of many sex histories in his commentaries on various sexual behaviors and "perversions." Ellis's case histories, particularly of homosexual men, had a chief polemical objective: to naturalize and legitimize "deviant" behaviors by demonstrating that homosexuals were not insane, criminal, or diseased, but were a different "species" and were often "normal," "functional" members of society. Zhang Jingsheng, on the other hand, prescribed a heteronormative "correct path of sex" (*xing de zhenggui*) and a "hygienic cure" (*weisheng jiuzhi*)—a kind of "eugenic sex" that, if followed exactly, could lead to stronger health, better offspring, and by extension a prosperous Chinese nation.

Zhang's theorization of the "correct path of sex" revolved around the "Third Kind of Water" (*disanzhong shui*), first discussed in *Sex Histories*.[41] Marie Stopes's famous work *Married Love* (1918) is key to understanding the "Third Kind of Water." Zhang praised very highly chapter 5, titled "Mutual Adjustment," of Stopes's *Married Love*, in which she suggested that "the internal absorption of secretions from the sex-organs plays so large a part in determining the health and character of remote parts of the body; it is extremely likely that the highly stimulating secretions which accompany man's semen can and do penetrate and affect the woman's whole organism."[42] The absorption of fluids took place "through the large tract of internal epithelium with which they come into contact."[43] In Stopes's account, the perfect sexual act was penile-vaginal penetration, which culminated in mutual and simultaneous orgasm. After the climax, the couple ought to continue to lie in a "coital embrace" or "locking position" such that husband and wife could both absorb all the highly beneficial sexual secretions. According to Stopes, this "Law of Union," if universally practiced, would truly revolutionize society by making all marriages harmonious. Both men and women would find genuine fulfillment: husbands would no longer seek out prostitutes, and wives would not have to worry about neurosis that could arise from chronic sexual dissatisfaction.[44] Stopes even recommended that women who were temporarily separated from their husbands and wished to remain chaste, or women whose husbands failed to provide sexual satisfaction, take daily capsules containing glandular, prostatic extracts.[45]

Zhang Jingsheng developed Stopes's discussions on sexual fluids to suggest that a woman's genitals could secrete three kinds of fluids: from the labia, the clitoris, and the Bartholin's glands, which were located near the vaginal opening and secreted mucus to provide lubrication for penetration. Zhang argued that a woman had to release all three kinds of fluids via extensive foreplay and intercourse. All sexual secretions ought to be absorbed for their health-promoting effects—a woman had to absorb a man's semen, and a man had to absorb the precious "Third Kind of Water." It was a husband's duty to train up his stamina so he could penetrate his wife for at least twenty to thirty minutes, and discipline himself to delay ejaculation so that it could coincide exactly with the female orgasm.

Zhang Jingsheng's "vaginal fluidology," however, went beyond Stopes's ideas as it argued that sexual fluids and the perfect union led to better offspring. According to Zhang, a woman's "Third Kind of Water" was alkaline and could facilitate the sperm's journey toward the uterus. The spasm experienced during the female orgasm hastened the ovum's descent through the Fallopian tube, and the "electrical energy" from the "Third Kind of Water" would also "enliven" the ovum. Zhang thought that a child conceived at the moment when the parents achieved simultaneous orgasm, with the egg and sperm surrounded by the "Third Kind of Water," would be physically stronger and more intelligent. In one move, Zhang reconciled the individual pursuit of sexual pleasure with the collective responsibility of nation-building. Making love became scientized through Zhang's "fluidology," and a couple's eugenic duty became something that was seemingly compatible with sensuality and satisfaction. The feebleness of the Chinese race was reduced to the fact that Chinese couples were ignorant of the "Third Kind of Water," and the offspring produced through "bad sex" could not compete with Westerners.[46]

This idea, as bizarre and "pseudoscientific" as it might sound, was not exclusive to Zhang Jingsheng. Historian Michael Gordon discovered that the first reference to the eugenic function of synchronized orgasm was in George Washington Savory's *Marriage: Its Science and Ethics, or Love's Consummation* (1900).[47] Angus McLaren showed that some medical practitioners, from the sixteenth to nineteenth century, promoted the idea that the female orgasm either was necessary for fertilization or would lead to "better" conception.[48] McLaren also argued that a large number of marriage manuals in late nineteenth- and early twentieth-century Europe and America also linked successful reproduction with simultaneous orgasm.[49] Zhang's "Third Kind of Water" can be situated, then, in the context of this global genealogy and traffic of sexological ideas.

Zhang Jingsheng's contemporaries were not kind to his theory of the "Third Kind of Water." His most fierce critics included the science popularizer and journalist Zhou Jianren (1888–1984), as well as the sociologist and eugenicist Pan Guangdan (1899–1967).[50] Zhou and Pan both argued that Zhang Jingsheng's "Third Kind of Water" was a rehash of "Daoist," superstitious junk—"bullshit," to put it bluntly. One could indeed discern the similarities between the theory of the "Third Kind of Water" and the discourse of Daoist sexual cultivation for health and longevity contained in the texts reconstructed by Ye Dehui for the *Shadow of the Double Plum Tree Anthology*. So-called *coitus reservatus* was one of the practices associated with Daoist self-cultivation, involving the absorption of female sexual fluids and the retention of semen, achieved via the constriction of the anus at the point of male orgasm. As the "female essence" was absorbed by the male practitioner, the "male essence" was believed to "return to the brain" to rejuvenate the spirit. The difference between *coitus reservatus* and "Third Kind of Water" was that Zhang Jingsheng insisted on the mutual, profitable transaction of genital fluids between men and women. Moreover, Zhang Jingsheng claimed that his ideas were based solidly on cutting-edge Western sexology: the substance of Stopes's *Married Love* combined with the methodology of Ellis's *Studies in the Psychology of Sex*. There is a remarkable double irony in this scenario. In the Western science, which Zhang represented, his opponents saw the remnants and ghosts of China's "degenerate" past, which they were desperately trying to exorcise. In contrast, many early twentieth-century Western intellectuals were looking to the "Orient" to find an Eastern Other in order to rejuvenate themselves.

While Zhang's sexology was influenced by British sexology, Chinese ideas also flowed—sometimes via multiple detours—in the other direction. Havelock Ellis had this to say about Chinese civilization after reading *The Book of Rites* (*Liji*), one of the five classics in the Confucian canon:

> How delighted I was to learn that in China life was regulated by music and ceremony . . . [China] was the highest point of urban civilisation to which man has ever attained, characterised by "courtesy," "fair dealing," an imperial exercise of justice, and hospitals in every city and no beggars . . . ever to be seen . . . [The Chinese were] devoid

of those conservative instincts by which we are guided in Europe . . . simple, childlike, yet profound attitude towards life.[51]

The imagined end point of Ellis's sexual revolution appears similar to the vision of Chinese society as prescribed by *The Book of Rites*. Yet for the May Fourth generation of Chinese intellectuals, *The Book of Rites* was an obstacle to China's modernization that had to be eradicated—and the end point of a sexual revolution for men like Zhang Jingsheng was that China would finally be *just like* the West. This was a chiasmatic situation: Zhang Jingsheng's *Sex Histories* was a "Chinese sexology" constructed out of Western sources of authority to transform the nation by intervening with the most intimate parts of people's lives. Zhang Jingsheng's critics, however, thought he was reviving "pseudoscientific" nonsense when China desperately needed positivist, materialist, empirical science. Meanwhile, the one sexologist, Havelock Ellis, held in such high esteem by May Fourth intellectuals for his fearless investigations into human sexuality, was looking to early China in which people apparently had some enlightened, privileged connection to nature, in contrast to the conservatism, prudery, and repression in post-Victorian England.

The Afterlives of Two "Chinese Sexologies"

Although it is difficult to assess what kind of impact *Shadow of the Double Plum Tree Anthology* had in Ye's lifetime, it enjoyed an intriguing afterlife. Ye's *Anthology* became an important source for a number of mid-twentieth-century European Sinologists who studied the history of religion, medicine, bodily practices, and sexuality in China. One of them was the eminent Sinologist Joseph Needham (1900–1995), inaugurator of the monumental *Science and Civilisation in China* project. Needham constructed his arguments by using Ye's *Anthology*. He insisted that there was an ancient Chinese culture of eroticism that was far more liberated than Western Judeo-Christian sexuality. For Needham, Ye Dehui's "bedchamber texts" offered proof that the Chinese were preoccupied with the enhancement of intensity and pleasure, as opposed to the regulation of reproduction and gender. Needham thought that there was a "pure milk of Daoist Gospel," which could be extracted and distilled for the consumption by alienated men and women in present times.[52] Embedded within that "Daoist Gospel" was the hope of constructing a new, universal sexual ethics free from "the bondage of conventional ideas," from "those Gnostic and Manichean heresies which attributed all evil to matter, and took all sex as sin." The way to achieve that, Needham argued, was to fuse Daoist "naturalism" and sensual intensification that he apparently witnessed in Ye Dehui's textual reconstructions, with the ideas of "great visionaries like William Blake, D. H. Lawrence, Edward Carpenter, and Havelock Ellis."[53] Needham appropriated Ye Dehui thus for the production of scholarly "truths" about China as well as for his own vision of a sexual revolution.

Again, this was a misunderstanding of Daoist self-cultivation "bedchamber texts": while Ye misread the texts he reconstructed as a Chinese equivalent to Western eugenics and reproductive hygiene, Needham misread Ye Dehui's anthology as an antidote to Judeo-Christian sexuality, a Chinese *ars erotica* that was about seeking pleasure purely for the sake of pleasure. As I have discussed elsewhere, Needham's ideology found its way into Michel Foucault's *History of Sexuality, Vol. 1*, coming to underpin Foucault's distinction between Western *scientia sexualis* and Eastern *ars erotica*.[54] Even though Foucault subsequently disowned this problematic dichotomy in the 1980s, and even though "governmentality" and "biopolitics" proved to be more fruitful categories of historical analysis compared to *scientia sexualis*, Foucault nevertheless remained utterly convinced that China had an *ars erotica*, a configuration of pleasure and desire that was diametrically opposite to the West.

Retracing Foucault's sources of authority on China, I discovered that he relied exclusively on the work of Dutch Sinologist Robert van Gulik (1910–1967), specifically *Sexual Life in Ancient China* (originally published in English in 1961, French translation in 1971).[55] Van Gulik's work was enthusiastically received by the 1968 generation of Parisian intellectuals. However, van Gulik initially had a negative view of certain elements of Chinese sexual culture, until Needham vehemently criticized him. Needham believed that Chinese sexuality was wholesome and healthy *tout court*, and so van Gulik corrected himself when he penned *Sexual Life in Ancient China*. The two Sinologists therefore ended up promoting a romantic vision of Chinese eroticism, which Foucault assimilated in *History of Sexuality*. Paying attention to the migration of ideas in this way thus reveals a convoluted genealogy that reaches from Ye Dehui, via Joseph Needham and Robert van Gulik, all the way to Michel Foucault. In other words, an early twentieth-century anthology, produced by a Sinocentric scholar in an attempt to stem the invasion of Western reproductive science, is thus connected to one of the foundational works in Western gender and sexuality studies.

Zhang Jingsheng's *Sex Histories* has a no less significant afterlife. In May 2005, a scandal erupted in Taiwan, which received several days of press and television coverage. Dala Books, a Taipei-based publisher specializing in erotica and popular works on sexuality, reprinted *Sex Histories*—the first time that the text was published in its entirety in eighty years. As part of its advertising campaign, Dala placed an announcement in Taiwanese newspapers inviting the general public to submit stories of their sexual development and erotic life, imitating Zhang Jingsheng's call for confessional narratives. A panel of three Taiwanese intellectuals decided the winners of the competition: Shu Yu-shen, a sexologist trained at the Institute for Advanced Study of Human Sexuality in San Francisco; poet Yang Che; and novelist India Ch'en Ying-shu. The winner received approximately two thousand U.S. dollars. Dala's representative explained in a television interview her desire to produce "a record of the sex lives of the Chinese people," emphasizing that she was not calling for submissions of "obscene sexual stories." The submissions ought to be "pleasant and enjoyable to read," and controversial topics such as incest and bestiality would be acceptable provided that the authors did not "exaggerate" or "include anything sickening."[56]

Shortly after the announcement of the competition, Dala Books was publicly denounced by a Catholic priest. Father Wu Chung-yüan said that sex ought to be "private" and therefore it ought not be openly discussed. Father Wu also worried that if the submissions, which were to be printed in a collection entitled *Sex Histories 2006* (*Xingshi 2006*), contained "sexual perversions," then the general public would be "misled" and "deviant behavior" would be legitimized. Chun Hsiu-hsien, director of the Department of Publication Affairs in Taiwan, subsequently held a press conference, "reminding the publishers" that the distribution of obscene publications was punishable by a maximum jail sentence of two years. The story was reported widely, and anti-censorship activists in turn criticized the government, lamenting that the Taiwanese state's repressive attitudes toward sexual publications "had not advanced at all in the past eighty years," when Zhang Jingsheng's *Sex Histories* was first published in Shanghai.[57] In September 2005, the winners of the competition were announced, and both *Sex Histories 1926* and *Sex Histories 2006* were published without incident.

The incident offers a glimpse at the appropriation of Zhang's *Sex Histories* in the early twenty-first century. Zhang is presented as a genius, a pioneer, a revolutionary prophet; his *Sex Histories* is described as the earliest "sexological report" of the Chinese people that apparently "predated Alfred Kinsey's *Sexual Behaviour in the Human Male* by 22 years." Dala's promotional materials further emphasized that Kinsey was born in 1894, six years after Zhang Jingsheng, and so Zhang was not a "Chinese Kinsey" but Kinsey was a "Western Zhang."[58] *Sex Histories* was, as stated on the dust jacket of Dala's 2006 reprint, a book that "sent the souls of the Chinese people half-way up to heaven eighty years ago" and today it challenged the state's boundaries on censorship and obscenity and pushed Taiwanese society's tolerance of sexual expression. The People's Republic of China edition of *Sex Histories* was not released until 2014, and Zhang Jingsheng was hailed in the popular media as a misunderstood, heroic prophet who attempted to free the Chinese people's innermost yearnings and to channel them toward productive ends with the help of Western sexological science. These discourses appropriated *Sex Histories* for contemporary China, as they argued for an "honest" narrativization of sexual subjectivities in the midst of China's postsocialist "economic miracle" and its concomitant sexual revolution.

Conclusion

By contrasting two seemingly obscure texts from early twentieth-century China, Ye Dehui's *Shadow of the Double Plum Tree Anthology* and Zhang Jingsheng's *Sex Histories*, this chapter has shown the complex role of translation as a negotiator of scientific knowledge and cultural identity. It has demonstrated that there exist two radically different "Chinese sexologies," which are both products of the global translation and circulation of sexological knowledge.

For Ye Dehui, European and American sexology was merely "old news from afar," and he responded to his encounters with European and American texts on reproduction and eugenics by turning inward and constructing an "indigenous," Chinese sexology based on classical sources recorded in Japanese texts. By trying to embargo Western knowledge and attacking literati influence, he aimed to save Confucianism and resist modernization. Ye's carefully constructed "Chinese sexology" would eventually influence the shaping of modern sexuality studies in the West as it was misidentified as the Chinese *ars erotica*, which, for Foucault and others, was fundamental to the distinction between "Western" and "Eastern" discourses about sex. In contrast, Zhang Jingsheng embraced the cross-cultural exchange of ideas. Like many of his fellow May Fourth intellectuals, he argued that the ideas put forward by English sexual reformers had never existed in Chinese history. He turned to the works of sexologists such as Havelock Ellis and Marie Stopes to fashion his own idiosyncratic brand of "eugenic sex." Zhang's work, then, adapted some of the European scientific racism to demolish what he regarded as the repressive, traditional, Confucian sexual conventions. Yet while he thought his work new, his opponents argued that he was merely recycling older ideas about sex.

Considering the translations of *The Shadow of the Double Plum Tree Anthology* and *Sex Histories* thus reveals the important yet contradictory currency of "sex" in debates about modern China. Such a translation approach makes clear that "sex" was used to argue both for the existence of a Chinese erotic tradition and for the need to adapt Western ideas to forge a new sexual politics in the Sinophone world.

NOTES

1. Meng Zhaochen, *Zhongguo jindai xiaobao shi* [The modern history of tabloids in China] (Beijing: Shehui Kexue Wenxian Chubanshe, 2005), 27–34; Hong Yu, *Jindai Shanghai xiaobao yu shimin wenhua yanjiu* [Tabloids in modern Shanghai and research in civic culture 1897–1937] (Shanghai: Shanghai Shiji Chuban Jituan, 2007).

2. Ye Dehui, *Shuangmei jing'an congshu* [Shadow of the double plum tree anthology] (Changsha: Yeshi Xiyuan, 1903–1917), Needham Research Institute, Rare Books Collection, 809.30011 YDH (RBR); Zhang Jingsheng, *Xingshi* [Sex histories] (Taipei: Dala, 2006, and Beijing: Shijie Tushu Chuban Gongsi, 2014), originally published in Shanghai in 1926.

3. Du Maizhi and Zhang Chengzong, *Ye Dehui pingzhuan* [Critical biography of Ye Dehui] (Changsha: Yuelu Shushe, 1986); Zhang Jingping, *Ye Dehui shengping ji xueshu sixiang yanjiu* [Research on Ye Dehui's life, scholarship, and thought] (Changsha: Hunan Shifan Daxue Chubanshe, 2008); Wang Yiming, ed., *Ye Dehui ji* [Ye Dehui's collected writings], 4 vols. (Beijing: Xueyuan Chubanshe, 2007).

4. Joseph W. Esherick, *Reform and Revolution in China: The 1911 Revolution in Hunan and Hubei* (Berkeley: University of California Press, 1976), 125–126.

5. *Juan* is a difficult unit of measurement, not quite the same as "volumes." See Robert E. Hegel, *Reading Illustrated Fiction in Late Imperial China* (Stanford, CA: Stanford University Press, 1998), 74–76; Joseph P. McDermott, *A Social History of the Chinese Book: Books and Literati Culture in Late Imperial China* (Hong Kong: Hong Kong University Press, 2006), 49; Li Xuemei, *Jindai Zhongguo cangshu wenhua* [The culture of book collection in modern China] (Beijing: Xiandai Chubanshe, 1999); Ren Jiyu, ed., *Zhongguo cangshu lou* [Book collections in China] (Shenyang: Liaoning Renmin Chubanshe, 2001); Wei Li, "Lingering Traces: In Search of China's Old Libraries," trans. Duncan Campbell, *China Heritage Quarterly*, no. 18 (2009), available at http://www.china heritagequarterly.org/scholarship.php?searchterm=018_oldlibraries.inc&issue=018; Wei Li, "Further Lingering Traces: China's Traditional Libraries," trans. Duncan Campbell, *China Heritage Quarterly*, no. 20 (2009), available at http://www.chinaheritage quarterly.org/features.php?searchterm=020_wei_li.inc&issue=020.

6. Su Yu, ed., *Yijiao congbian* [Collected essays on defending Confucianism], 6 vols. (Taipei: Wenhai Chubanshe, 1971 [1898]).

7. Kang Youwei, *Xinxue weijing kao* [An exposé of the forged classics] (Beijing: Zhonghua Shuju, 2012 [1891]); Kang Youwei, *Kongzi gaizhi kao* [Confucius as a reformer] (Beijing: Zhonghua Shuju, 2012 [1892–1898]).

8. See Anne Cheng, "Nationalism, Citizenship, and the Old Text / New Text Controversy in the Late Nineteenth Century," in *Imagining the People: Chinese Intellectuals and the Concept of Citizenship 1890–1920*, ed. Joshua A. Fogel and Peter G. Zarrow (Armonk, NY: Sharpe, 1997), 61–81; Hans van Ess, "The Old Text / New Text Controversy: Has the Twentieth Century Got It Wrong?" *T'oung Pao* 80 (1994): 146–170; Peter Zarrow, "The Political Movement, the Monarchy, and Political Modernity," in *Rethinking the 1898 Reform Period: Political and Cultural Change in Late Qing China*, ed. Rebecca E. Karl and Peter Zarrow (Cambridge, MA: Harvard University Press, 2002), 17–47; Peter Zarrow, *After Empire: The Conceptual Transformation of the Chinese State, 1885–1924* (Stanford, CA: Stanford University Press, 2012), 24–55.

9. See, for example, Ye Dehui, *Xiyuan xiaoxue sizhong* [Four works on elementary studies by Xiyuan] (Nanyang: Ye Shi Guangu Tang, 1931).

10. Ye Dehui, *Shulin qinghua* [Plain talks on the forest of books] (Beijing: Guji Chubanshe, 1957 [1911]); Ye Dehui, *Cangshu shiyue* [*Bookman's Decalogue*], trans. Achilles Fang, in *Harvard Journal of Asiatic Studies* 13 (1950): 132–173, originally published in 1911; McDermott, *Social History of the Chinese Book*, 263; Cynthia J. Brokaw, "On the History of the Book in China," in *Printing and Book Culture in Late Imperial China*, ed. Cynthia J. Brokaw and Kai-wing Chow (Berkeley: University of California Press, 2005), 3–54.

11. Leon Antonio Rocha, "Sex, Eugenics, Aesthetics, Utopia in the Life and Work of Zhang Jingsheng (1888–1970)" (Ph.D. diss., University of Cambridge, 2010); Charles L. Leary, "Sexual Modernism in China: Zhang Jingsheng and 1920s Urban Culture" (Ph.D. diss., Cornell University, 1994). My biographical account is informed by Peng Hsiao-yen, "Sex Histories: Zhang Jingsheng's Sexual Revolution," *Critical Studies* 18 (1999): 159–177; Jiang Xiaoyuan, "Zhang Jingsheng qiren qishi" [Zhang Jingsheng's life and deeds], in Zhang, *Xingshi*, 9–23; Jiang Zhongxiao, "Xu er Zhang Jingsheng de sheng-ping sixiang he zhushu" [Preface II: Zhang Jingsheng's life, thought, and work], in Zhang Jingsheng, *Zhang Jingsheng wenji* [The collected works of Zhang Jingsheng], ed. Jiang Zhongxiao, 2 vols. (Guangzhou: Guangzhou Chubanshe, 1998), 1:11–23; Zhang Jingsheng, *Fusheng mantan Zhang Jingsheng suibi xuan* [Reveries on a floating life: Zhang Jingsheng's selected miscellaneous essays], ed. Zhang Peizhong (Beijing: Sanlian Shudian, 2008); Zhang Peizhong, *Wenyao yu xianzi Zhang Jingsheng chuan* [The monster and the prophet: A biography of Zhang Jingsheng] (Beijing: Sanlian Shudian, 2008).

12. Jiang, "Zhang Jingsheng qiren qishi," 9. On Stratz, see Irvin C. Schick, *The Erotic Margin: Sexuality and Spatiality in Alteritist Discourse* (London: Verso, 1999); Michael Hau, *The Cult of Health and Beauty in Germany: A Social History, 1890–1930* (Chicago: University of Chicago Press, 2003), 82–100.

13. Hau, *Cult of Health and Beauty in Germany*, 225n37.

14. Lai Shu-ching, "Minchu jixunju yu jixun liuxuesheng de paiqian" [The 1912–1913 Bureau of Merits of the Nanking provisional government and the sending of merit students studying abroad], in *Guoshi guan guankan* [Academia Historica Journal] 22 (2009): 57–96; Ye Weili, *Seeking Modernity in China's Name: Chinese Students in the United States, 1900–1927* (Stanford, CA: Stanford University Press, 2001).

15. K. S. Tchang [Zhang Jingsheng], *Les sources antiques des théories de J.-J. Rousseau sur l'éducation* (Lyon: Roudil, 1919).

16. Jean-Jacques Rousseau, *Lusao chanhui lu* [The confessions], trans. Zhang Jingsheng (Shanghai: Mei De Shudian, 1928); Zhang Jingsheng, *Meng yu fangzhu* [Dreams and exile], abridged Chinese translation of Rousseau's *Reveries of a Solitary Walker* and Victor Hugo's *Actes et paroles—pendant l'exil* (Shanghai: Shijie Shuju, 1929).

17. Sanger's visit was meticulously documented in Beijing's *Chenbao fukan* [Morning Daily Supplement], April 22–25, 1922.

18. On Zhang Jingsheng's participation in the so-called Rules of Love debate in 1923, see Zhang Peizhong, ed., *Aiqing dingze: Xiandai Zhongguo diyi ci aiqing da taolun* [The rules of love: The first major debate on love in modern China] (Beijing: Sanlian Shudian, 2011); Haiyan Lee, *Revolution of the Heart: A Genealogy of Love in China, 1900–1950* (Stanford, CA: Stanford University Press, 2007), 140–185.

19. The May Fourth historiography is being increasingly critiqued in China studies: Milena Doleželová-Velingerová and Oldřich Král, eds., *The Appropriation of Cultural*

Capital: China's May Fourth Project (Cambridge, MA: Harvard University Press, 2001); Kai-wing Chow et al., eds., Beyond the May Fourth Paradigm: In Search of Chinese Modernity (Lanham, MD: Lexington Books, 2008).

20. Lydia H. Liu, Translingual Practice: Literature, National Culture, and Translated Modernity—China, 1900–1937 (Stanford, CA: Stanford University Press, 1995).

21. Leo Ou-fan Lee, Shanghai Modern: The Flowering of a New Urban Culture in China, 1930–1945 (Cambridge, MA: Harvard University Press, 1999), 43–81.

22. Susan Mann, Precious Records: Women in China's Long Eighteenth Century (Stanford, CA: Stanford University Press, 1997), 121–142; Catherine Yeh, Shanghai Love: Courtesans, Intellectuals, and Entertainment Culture, 1850–1910 (Seattle: University of Washington Press, 2006).

23. Among the vast literature on Daoism, I found the following sources particularly useful: Sumiyo Umekawa, "Sex and Immortality: A Study of Chinese Sexual Activities for Better-Being" (Ph.D. diss., School of Oriental and African Studies, University of London, 2004); Yoshinobu Sakade and Sumiyo Umekawa, "Ki" no shiso kara miru dokyo no bochujutsu: Ima ni ikiru kodai Chugoku no seiai chojuho [Ideas on "qi" in Daoist art of the bedchamber: Sexual cultivation techniques in ancient China] (Tokyo: Goyo Shobo, 2003).

24. Douglas Wile, Art of the Bedchamber: The Chinese Sexual Yoga Classics Including Women's Solo Meditation Texts (Albany: State University of New York Press, 1992), 94–100.

25. Sumiyo Umekawa, "Tiandi yinyang jiaohuang dalefu and the Art of the Bedchamber," in Medieval Chinese Medicine: The Dunhuang Medical Manuscripts, ed. Vivienne Lo and Christopher Cullen (London: Routledge, 2004), 252–277.

26. Leon Antonio Rocha, "The Way of Sex: Joseph Needham and Jolan Chang," Studies in the History and Philosophy of Biological and Biomedical Sciences 43, no. 3 (2012): 611–626.

27. Rudolf Pfister, "Gendering Sexual Pleasures in Early and Medieval China," Asian Medicine 7 (2012), 34–64; Gao Wenzhu et al., Yixinfang jiaozhu yanjiu [Studies on the collation and annotation of The Core Prescriptions of Medicine] (Beijing: Huaxia Chubanshe, 1996).

28. Ye Dehui, "Sunü jing xu" [Preface to The Classic of the Plain Girl], in Shuangmei jing'an congshu [Shadow of the double plum tree anthology], 2.

29. Charlotte Furth, "Rethinking van Gulik: Sexuality and Reproduction in Traditional Chinese Medicine," in Engendering China: Women, Culture, and the State, ed. Christina K. Gilmartin et al. (Cambridge, MA: Harvard University Press, 1995), 130.

30. The book's full title continues as follows: Love, Its Laws, Power, etc.: Selection, or Mutual Adaptation: Courtship, Married Life, and Perfect Children: Their Generation, Endowment, Paternity, Maternity, Bearing, Nursing and Rearing; Together with Puberty, Boyhood, Girlhood, etc.; Sexual Impairments Restored, Male Vigour and Female Health and Beauty Perpetuated and Augmented etc. as Taught by Phrenology and Physiology. A Canadian version is available online via the John Robarts Library, University of Toronto, available at https://archive.org/details/creativesexualsc00fowluoft.

31. Orson Squire Fowler, Danjo kogo shin ron [New theories on sexual intercourse], trans. Hashizume Kanichi (Tokyo: Shunyodo Shoten, 1878). Partial translation of Creative and Sexual Science (Philadelphia: Jones, 1875).

32. Fawuluo [Orson Squire Fowler], *Nannü jiaohe xinlun* [New theories on sexual intercourse], trans. Youyazi (place and publisher unknown, around 1880s).

33. Carl Frederick Schmidt, *The Octagon Fad* (New York: privately printed, 1958).

34. Y. Yvon Wang, "Whorish Representation: Pornography, Media, and Modernity in Fin-de-Siècle Beijing," *Modern China* (2013), available at http://mcx.sagepub.com/content/early/2013/08/24/0097700413499732.abstract.

35. Matsumoto Yasuko, *Danjo seishoku kenzenho* [Methods for strengthening male and female reproduction] (Tokyo: Chuo Kangofukai, 1900).

36. Matsumoto Yasuko, *Hunyin weisheng xue* [The hygiene of marriage]. Translation of Youminzi, *Danjo seishoku kenzenho* (Yokohama: Kingsell, 1902).

37. Henry Hartshorne, *Tsuzoku seishoku ron* [Easy to understand theories of genitalia], trans. Hasegawa Tai (Tokyo: Sakagami Hanshichi, 1878). Partial translation of *A Conspectus of the Medical Sciences: Comprising Manuals of Anatomy, Physiology, Chemistry, Materia Medica, Practice of Medicine, Surgery and Obstetrics for the Use of Students* (Philadelphia: Lea, 1874), available at https://archive.org/details/aconspectus medi00hartgoog.

38. Kang Youwei, *Riben shumu zhi* [Bibliography of Japanese books], in *Kang Nanhai xiansheng yizhu huikan* [The collected writings of Master Kang Nanhai], ed. Jiang Guilin, 22 vols. (Taipei: Hongye, 1976 [1898]), vol. 11; Wang, "Whorish Representation," 13.

39. Michael Lackner, "*Ex Oriente Scientia*? Reconsidering the Ideology of a Chinese Origin of Western Knowledge," *Asia Major* 21, no. 1–2 (2008): 183–200.

40. Zhang, *Fusheng mantan Zhang Jingsheng suibi xuan*, 154.

41. Zhang, *Xingshi*, 80–84.

42. Marie Stopes, *Married Love: A New Contribution to the Solution of Sex Difficulties*, ed. Ross McKibbin (Oxford: Oxford University Press, 2004 [1918]), 54.

43. Ibid., 55.

44. Annamarie Jagose, *Orgasmology* (Durham, NC: Duke University Press, 2013), 40–77.

45. Margaret Jackson, *The Real Facts of Life: Feminism and the Politics of Sexuality 1850–1940* (London: Routledge, 1994), 138–139; David Bennett, "Burghers, Burglars, and Masturbators: The Sovereign Spender in the Age of Consumerism," *New Literary History* 30 (1999): 275.

46. Zhang Jingsheng, "Disanzhongshui yu luanzhu ji shengji de dian he yousheng de guanxi huo mei de xingyu" [The relationship between the third kind of water and the ovum, and vital electricity and eugenics, or, Beautiful sexual desire] in *Xin wenhua* [New Culture] 1, no. 2 (1927): 23–48 at 30.

47. Michael Gordon, "From an Unfortunate Necessity to a Cult of Mutual Orgasm: Sex in American Marital Education Literature, 1830–1940," in *Studies in the Sociology of Sex*, ed. James M. Heslin (New York: Appleton-Century-Crofts, 1971), 53–77; Angus McLaren, *Twentieth-Century Sexuality: A History* (Oxford: Blackwell, 1999), 52; Angus McLaren, *Impotence: A Cultural History* (Chicago: University of Chicago Press, 2007), 171.

48. Angus McLaren, *Reproductive Rituals: The Perception of Fertility in England from the Sixteenth Century to the Nineteenth Century* (London: Methuen, 1984), 19–20.

49. McLaren, *Twentieth-Century Sexuality*, 46–63.

50. On Zhou Jianren and Pan Guangdan, see Sakamoto Hiroko, "The Cult of 'Love and Eugenics' in May Fourth Movement Discourse," *positions: east asia cultures critique* 12 (2004): 329–376; Leon Antonio Rocha, "Quentin Pan in *The China Critic*," *China Heritage Quarterly*, no. 30–31 (2012), available at http://www.chinaheritagequarterly .org/features.php?searchterm=030_rocha.inc&issue=030. On the *Sex Histories* debates, see Charles L. Leary, "Intellectual Orthodoxy, the Economy of Knowledge and the Debate over Zhang Jingsheng's *Sex Histories*," *Republican China* 18, no. 2 (1993): 99–137; Lee, *Revolution of the Heart*, 186–219; Wendy Larson, *From Ah Q to Lei Feng: Freud and Revolutionary Spirit in Twentieth-Century China* (Stanford, CA: Stanford University Press, 2009), 55–59.

51. Henry Havelock Ellis, *The Dance of Life* (Boston: Houghton Mifflin, 1923), 17, 33.

52. Joseph Needham, with Lu Gwei-Djen, *Science and Civilisation in China, Volume V: Chemistry and Chemical Technology, Part 5: Spagyrical Discovery and Invention: Physiological Alchemy* (Cambridge: Cambridge University Press, 1985), 201.

53. Ibid.

54. Leon Antonio Rocha, "*Scientia Sexualis* versus *Ars Erotica*: Foucault, van Gulik, Needham," *Studies in the History and Philosophy of Biological and Biomedical Sciences* 42, no. 3 (2011): 328–343.

55. Robert H. van Gulik, *Sexual Life in Ancient China: A Preliminary Survey of Chinese Sex and Society from ca. 1500 BC till 1644 AD* (Leiden, Netherlands: Brill, 2003 [1961]). French translation by Louis Évrard titled *La vie sexuelle dans la Chine ancienne* (Paris: Gallimard, 1971).

56. Interview with Dala spokesperson Wu Hsin-wen on TVBS National Evening News (Taiwan), July 17, 2006.

57. TVBS National Evening News (Taiwan), July 17, 2006.

58. Promotional materials from Dala Publishers blog, available at http://blog.yam .com/dala.

III

Dis/Identifications

How were the new sexological ideas received? One of the most troubling questions in the history of sexuality is about how to make sense of the relationship between discourse and subjectivity, or, between texts and the lives they describe and categorize. Some scholars have answered this question by describing the flow of information between sexology and its audiences as a form of "reverse discourse," meaning that they focus on how the subjects of sexology adapted and transformed the newly coined scientific vocabulary that classified their desires. Other scholars have, however, pointed out that "reverse discourse" insufficiently explains both sexual discourse formation and its reception, not least because writers, philosophers, literary critics, and other "lay people" played an important role in coining the terms and concepts that have come to be associated with sexual subjectivities and identities. The chapters in this final part of the collection pay fresh attention to the ways in which sexological knowledge was received and transmitted. They turn to issues of translation to gain a better understanding of the "dis/identifications"—or the psychic and political issues—that shaped the reception and transformation of modern sexuality in terms of both individual and collective responses.

This part begins with two chapters—Jennifer Fraser's study of the gendered literary reception of scientific sexual discourse in Peru and Michiko Suzuki's analysis of the Japanese reception of Edward Carpenter's *Intermediate Sex*—that bridge the focus in Part II on different national sexologies and the concerns with the reception of sexual ideas that lies at the core of this final part of the collection. While Fraser's examination of the transformations of scientific positivism into a feminist discourse about desire also speaks to the concerns with the conceptualization of sexuality that is the focus of Part I, it is included here for its emphasis on the literary reception of scientific ideas about sex. Fraser examines how two Peruvian writers struggled against the exclusion of women from the scientific and political spheres because of their gender. By tracking the ways in which their novels translated scientific ideas into a feminist discourse about desire and the self, Fraser shows how these women received scientific ideas about "sex" and adapted them to intervene in exclusive male-oriented discourses about science, citizenship, and the emerging Peruvian nation. Suzuki's chapter is similarly framed in national terms, but its focus on the Japanese reception of Carpenter's work allows her to pay attention to the structural similarities in the global development of modern sexuality. She shows that *The Intermediate Sex* was translated in a way that deliberately adapted its take on same-sex sexuality to fit existing Japanese norms about desire and the body. However, Suzuki also demonstrates that the feminist and socialist receptions of Carpenter's work in Japan reveal some of the coeval aspects of sexual modernity: that despite the culturally specific reception of the "English" sexual discourse in Japan, same-sex sexuality occupied similar discursive and political spaces in Japan and England.

Whereas both Fraser and Suzuki are concerned in different ways, then, with the feminist reception of sexual science in (trans)national contexts, the final two chapters of this part explore the relationship between sexology and the formation of same-sex identities and subjectivities. James Wilper examines the transformations that occurred when the American writer Edward Prime-Stevenson translated a selection of case studies taken from Richard von Krafft-Ebing's *Psychopathia Sexualis* into his own study of what he called *The Intersexes*. Wilper's comparison between the two texts provides specific insights into how Prime-Stevenson, who was himself attracted to other men, received the sexological writings and adapted them to develop a theory of same-sex sexuality that sought to "rectify" what he considered the negative stereotyping and misrepresentations of same-sex desire found in Krafft-Ebing's influential sexological work. Heike Bauer also examines the negative aspects of modern same-sex history and the ways in which sexology absorbed or challenged them. Her chapter flips the focus of the other studies in this part, which are all in different ways concerned with how sexology was received. Instead Bauer explores how the work of one of the best-known sexologists, Magnus Hirschfeld, was influenced by his encounters with homosexual suicide. While her chapter thus also addresses larger concerns about the formation of sexology, she here turns to translations between German and English in Hirschfeld's work specifically to examine the affective underpinnings of modern sexology. She shows how negative social norms and discriminatory medical practices had a real impact not only on (the negation of) individual lives but also on the shaping of Hirschfeld's reform-oriented sexual science.

The attention to the receptions of sexology and its audiences in this part indicates the complex ways in which scientific ideas about "sex" were absorbed into political debates that ranged from feminism to homosexual rights politics and that reached across national boundaries even if their focus was on specific national concerns. But here we also find evidence of a particular kind of discursive flow: the impact of encounters with the difficult realities of same-sex existence and non-normative feelings, bodies, and desires on the shaping of reform-oriented sexual science. By examining how the sexual discourses and ideas were received, both by individual women and men and in the context of larger political movements, then, the chapters brought together in this final part complicate understanding of the issues at stake in the shaping and transmission of sexual discourses in political, disciplinary, and subcultural contexts. They provide new insights into the relationship between sexual discourses, lives, and politics, demonstrating that attention to translation deepens understanding of the subjective and collective concerns that shaped the "dis/identifications" with modern sexuality by the subjects who inhabit the sexological archive.

9

Novel Translations of the Scientific Subject

Clorinda Matto de Turner, Margarita Práxedes Muñoz,
and the Gendered Shaping of Discourses of Desire in
Nineteenth-Century Peru

JENNIFER FRASER

> You know the struggle which I had to insist on with my
> family, who did not understand that a weak girl would dream
> of decorating her chest with Minerva's laurels, which is the
> exclusive patrimony of the strong sex, and you were not ig-
> norant of how bitter my existence was before achieving the
> satisfaction of my legitimate aspirations.[1]
> —MARGARITA PRÁXEDES MUÑOZ, *La evolución de Paulina*

Unlike in Europe and other parts of the world, which saw the emergence of a medico-forensic sexology—or the science of sex—in the
nineteenth century, many discussions about "sex" in Peru were located in positivist scientific discourses about society, citizenship and the
modern nation.[2] Many of these discourses, which focused on issues of gender, specifically the social role of women and the regulation of their bodies
and behaviors, were the product of a predominantly male scientific sphere
from which women were, in the main, excluded other than as recipients
of the ideas and social regulations. Fiction was a space in which women
writers were able to respond and engage with these ideas by producing literary works that moved these debates out of a narrow "expert" realm into
a broader public discourse. This chapter examines the work of two writers—Clorinda Matto de Turner (1852–1909) and Margarita Práxedes Muñoz
(1862–1909)—to demonstrate that Peruvian women writers translated

scientific ideas into fiction. It shows that their writings challenged male scientific authority and developed women's engagement with issues of science
and the state more broadly. The chapter argues that attention to issues of
translation—understood here in terms of the migration of ideas between
disciplines and genres—provides fresh insights into gendered issues at stake
in Peruvian debates about society and the nation, as well as deepening understandings of the relationship between authors and readers, discourses
and lives, in the shaping of "sex" and citizenship in modern Peru.

Contexts

From 1879 to 1883 Peru was involved in the economically, politically, and
socially disastrous War of the Pacific, with the result that in all sectors of
Peruvian society the postwar years were marked by discussions about national reconstruction and great debate about why Peru suffered such devastating losses. In effect, the war prompted a severe crisis of moral and political
hegemony for the different sectors of Peru's elite. As Peter Flindell Klarén
outlines, depending on the political and economic positions that the elites
occupied, they placed the blame and explanation for the losses suffered on
different sectors of Peruvian society.[3] The losses were attributed to factors
that ranged from social and political factionalism to the Indigenous population and its lack of integration into the social body and to the power of
the Catholic Church. Importantly, as different actors emerged and contributed to the debate, the postwar crisis also opened new discursive spaces for
imagining what Peru's future as a viable modern nation might look like. The
answers to the crisis were as varied as the arguments for why it had come
about. This chapter will focus on those elites who turned to science, specifically Comtian positivism, and who would change the terms of the debate
by bringing the questions of a secular scientific understanding to the social,
economic, and political problems facing Peru.

For many of these liberal and reform-oriented elites, positivism became
the answer for establishing political order, economic development, and social regeneration after the war because it permitted them to situate Peruvian
history and society within a recuperative framework of progress.[4] This was
particularly important at this time because it allowed them to find rational
and scientific reasons for Peru's losses and to suggest that the way forward
was under the positivist banner of "order and progress." As a philosophy,
positivism also appealed to elites who were looking for a more secular approach to explaining their worlds. Methodologically, positivism's focus on
scientific observation and its emphasis on understanding cause and effect
allowed elites to find apparently objective, scientific, and thus "natural" laws
for governance of both the state and the social body.[5] The literary community

actively participated in these debates and sought to change the values and narratives constituting Peruvian national identity through newspapers, family journals, and novels. Print media provided reformers with a broad audience to whom they could make their bids for interpretative power to reorder the existing hierarchy of social values governing the national body, such that the power balance could shift from the Catholic Church and the values of the traditional oligarchy toward science and a reformed family.

Questions about what was socially and educationally appropriate for a young woman occupied many writers in late nineteenth-century Peru. How should a woman behave? What sort of education should she receive? Who should she socialize with? Who should she marry? And, of fundamental importance, how should these choices be made? These questions fill the pages of novels, family journals, and guides to good conduct. As many scholars have argued, the emphasis on women and their behavior was very much linked to concerns about nation-building and citizenship.[6] As mothers, women were tasked with the care of the private sphere and the raising of citizens. The debates covered many positions from liberal through conservative, but there was agreement that these "angels of the house," whatever the political and social leanings of their families, were tasked with the formation of a new generation of citizens. Thus, their education and training for this role were of the utmost importance. This led to powerful normative models of femininity based around the home, childcare, and their duties as wives. While women's channeling of their desires in other directions was seen to contest the established social order, women nevertheless played an important role in shaping the debates around their place in a modernized nation.[7] From the mid-1870s in Peru, women began to participate openly in the literary community through fiction, journalism, and literary societies.[8] In fact, during the postwar period women were among the most prolific and prominent novelists. Between 1884 and 1895 thirty novels were written by Peruvians and published in Peru, while a further eight were published by Peruvians abroad and read in Peru. Nineteen of these novels were authored by women.[9]

Despite their remarkable literary activities, women had extremely limited access to the institutionalized realms of science. Scientific theories were circulated and debated in the literary community, but women generally could not undertake a scientific education or be members of scientific societies.[10] Nonetheless, at the margins of other debates the questions of whether and how women might engage with the emerging fields of positivist science began to appear. These questions were much more fraught as they broke with the normative social models for young women as well as threatened to displace the traditional power of the Catholic Church in favor of scientific ways of understanding the social body. Clorinda Matto de Turner and Margarita

Práxedes Muñoz both wrote novels that had explicitly scientific frames and were written to provide exemplary models for young women of scientifically informed citizenship. They engaged with questions of science and citizenship for women as well as explicitly constructing an active space for women in the modern scientifically understood nation state. This work differed from most novels authored by women, which, although concerned with the roles of women in a modernized nation, tended to a have a moralistic tone and showed little concern with science and its relationship to the social body.[11] In contrast, Práxedes Muñoz's *La evolución de Paulina* (Paulina's evolution) (Santiago, 1893, and Buenos Aires, 1897) and Matto de Turner's *Herencia* (Inheritance) (Lima, 1895) brought together the practices of scientific observation with writing fiction, thus contributing to new ways of imagining a secular modernity.

In what follows, I will show that in writing novels that engage readers overtly with scientific theories and their social and political applications, Matto de Turner and Práxedes Muñoz negotiate the gap between a widening acceptance of women as writers and their absence in the field of science. Fiction offers them a space for engaging with and promoting scientific ideas outside the male domain, even as their novels also contest narratives about normative models of femininity through their characterizations of female protagonists and their overt and covert representations of female desires. I will examine the strategies they used to translate emerging ideas about science into fiction and in doing so engaged their audiences and asked them to read against the grain of their regular reading practices and established genres. In so doing, the chapter will also consider how the socially transgressive act of being a woman writing about science also required translating and justifying non-normative social selves.

Reading, Writing, and Knowing:
(New) Religions and Literary Sciences

Attention to translation, as this section will show, allows us to begin to explain what was at stake for these writers. By paying attention to their distinct critical engagements with religion as the pervasive frame for structuring social knowledge, we can see how they challenged norms about femininity, family, and desire. Both Práxedes Muñoz and Matto de Turner occupy interesting places in Peruvian history. Although Práxedes Muñoz led an exceptional and path-breaking life, both she and her work are relatively unknown in Peru.[12] After receiving special permission to attend university, she became the first woman to graduate from Lima's Universidad Nacional Mayor de San Marcos with a bachelor of science degree in 1890. Afterward she was unable to study medicine in Peru, so she was given a special scholarship by President Andrés Avelino Cáceres to study in Chile. She went on to practice medicine in Chile and then to establish a reputation as a positivist writer in Argentina. In Buenos Aires she became part of a group of politically nonconforming Peruvian writers living in exile that included Matto de Turner. While Práxedes Muñoz's departure from Peru was not originally due to political exile, we can see that it was a type of social exile. Her desire to study science and practice medicine went too far against the social norms for young women living in Lima. It is easy to imagine that the words of her autobiographical fictional heroine Paulina, which are the epigraph to this chapter, echo her experiences in Peru and resulted in an educational and social exile.

In contrast to Práxedes Muñoz, Matto de Turner is one of Peru's most well-known nineteenth-century writers.[13] She was an active journalist, the editor of a prominent weekly newspaper, the author of three novels, and an outspoken political supporter of the campaigns and presidencies of Andrés Avelino Cáceres (1886–1890, 1894–1895). In 1895, when she published her final novel *Herencia*, she was forced into exile, already having been excommunicated and burned in effigy, and her first novel, *Aves sin nido* (*Birds without a Nest*) (1889), was placed on the Catholic Church's list of prohibited books. What could a woman writing at the end of the nineteenth century do to earn such a controversial place in Peruvian society? Certainly her political journalism gave her a powerful adversary in a new president and could lead to exile, but to make such enemies in the Church so as to be excommunicated would probably require something beyond political allegiances.[14] It is likely that various factors contributed, not the least of which was her iconoclastic first novel. However, another significant cause may have been her portrayal of modern citizenship in which the Catholic Church is pushed to the margins of social and political power, while science becomes the frame for understanding the nation and citizenship. Nowhere is this as evident as in her last novel, and it is this frame that links *Herencia* to Práxedes Muñoz's *La evolución de Paulina*.

Herencia recounts the lives of two young women in Lima, Margarita Marín and Camila Aguilera, as they come out into society, find husbands, and begin families. Margarita's family is part of the liberal reforming elite, while Camila is a member of the traditional landed elite. At the end of the novel the Maríns are celebrating Margarita's successful marriage to Ernesto, while Camila, who falls pregnant without her parents' knowledge and before she is married, lies on her bed physically beaten by a gambling and corrupt husband who brings no wealth or actual social standing to their marriage. The girls' parallel lives model the differences between a family that values moderation and sound fiscal and physical economies and one that is given over to excess and maintaining appearances and that is morally, financially, and physically bankrupt despite their social standing as members of the oligarchy. Underlying the Marín and Aguilera families' approaches to moral and fiscal economies is a difference in orientation toward science or traditional Catholicism. As a result each girl and her family serve to model the paths open to Peruvians as they attempt to bring Peru into a new century, with the clear message that if they want a sustainable modern future, then social and economic moderation, national investment, and a scientific understanding of citizenship and family is the desirable path. As I have argued elsewhere, in *Herencia* Matto de Turner challenges the existing hierarchy of values to model new social and economic knowledges that rest on a frame of secular and scientific understandings of family, citizenship, and the state.[15]

Like *Herencia*, *La evolución de Paulina* tells the story of a young Limeñan woman and her love affair. This account, however, is framed quite differently than the lives of Margarita and Camila. Paulina's life story takes place outside the normative family relations that shape the other girls' experiences. She is an orphan of independent means who lives alone and spends her days studying science. While her social independence has been hard won, it allows her to dedicate her time to study and to engage in a love relationship of choice with another young scientist, Alberto. Ultimately, the relationship leads to heartbreak for Paulina, and she leaves Lima for Colombia, where she finds a society more open to her nonconforming social and political beliefs. While there she comes to adopt *la religión de la humanidad*, which is based in Comtian philosophy.

The narrative of *La evolución de Paulina* is framed as a letter from Paulina to her childhood friend Estela and provides readers with the apparent intimacy of a first-person female narration. This feature makes it unique among Peruvian novels of its time. In the first part of the letter Paulina recounts for Estela the events in her life since they last saw one another. This section also serves as a place for Paulina to reflect on her journey toward a scientific education and outlines the struggles she had to establish herself as a scientist. When Paulina is explaining to Estela the most recent events of her life, including her move to Colombia, her narrative voice is interrupted by a lecture from a Jesuit priest, Father Esteban, who recounts the scientific principles on which her new religion is based. Afterward, the letter returns to Paulina as she provides Estela with her own explanation of *la religión de la humanidad* and the hope for society that she finds in it. The novel is not without its problems in terms of form and messages, but, like *Herencia*, it contains a clear message about the possibilities contained in scientific understandings of society for bringing about necessary social and political changes.[16]

In both texts we can see how ideas are migrated from scientific spheres into social ones through the medium of fiction. On one level this is a relatively smooth transition between disciplines as it brings new and complex ideas to readers in a more accessible form. As we will see, on other levels, these acts of translation are highly charged and transgressive. Paying attention to the implications of translating scientific ideas into fiction reveals some of the gendered politics of access to knowledge, knowing, and who can speak about science.

As Matto de Turner alludes to in her prologue, the scientific messages of these texts purposefully disrupt established ways of knowing. This is especially the case when we consider how the texts' heroines, like their authors, do not fit normative social models of femininity. The choices that Margarita and Paulina make, with or without their families' approval, go against the grain of the social worlds that they live in. For instance, Paulina's overt pursuit of science, her rejection of Catholicism, her advocacy of civil marriage, and her embrace of a religion based in positivist science mark her as clearly different from her friend Estela and other young women of her milieu. While Margarita does not openly speak of science, the choices she makes for her marriage partner—with the clear approval of her father, who does voice his scientific opinion on the matter—are framed within a discourse of science and fiscal moderation. These two factors set her apart from the other young women in Lima, something that the narrator and Margarita's admirers comment on in the novel's opening scene.[17] These narratives are presented to readers in forms that make them seem less transgressive. For instance, Paulina recounts her story to Estela in the form of an intimate letter, and Margarita is not required to take personal responsibility for the science that frames her choices. Nonetheless, the messages in these texts interrupt established ways of knowing and the paths that are available to young women. This meant that work needed to be done to translate both the science and the social selves (of the heroines and authors alike) into something that their audiences could relate to, or, at least, be open to reading and considering. In a social and political environment in which women were predominantly seen as domestic angels linked to private spheres of influence, writing— especially writing about science—became a transgressive act that needed to be managed carefully.

Paratexts, Writers, and Readers

Translation also allows us to conceptualize the relationship between author(ship) and reader(ship) in these texts. As other critics of nineteenth-century Latin American literature have argued, the relationships between these two constituencies were fundamental in projects of nation-building, especially with regard to the educational role that literature played in the production of citizenship.[18] For women who were marginalized in terms of finding socially sanctioned political spaces in which to act, the relationships they could construct with readers became spaces in which to influence national politics and ideas about modern citizenship. In the case of authors who were also seeking to engage with and change the terms through which citizenship was constructed, for instance using scientific knowledge as opposed to Catholic values, their relationships with readers become even more significant.

In both of the novels we can see how the relationship of a female author to her reading public is cultivated through not only the novels themselves but also the communications that open the texts. These come in a variety of forms, including dedications and prologues, and serve as introductions to the novels and to the author's social and political projects. These pieces or, as Gérard Genette has called them, *paratexts*, provide the opening frames for the novels. They influence the reception of the texts and provide a set of reading instructions and a space of transition between readers' actual lives and the imagined worlds of the novels. They do the work of presenting the novel or "*make present*, to ensure the text's presence in the world, its 'reception' and consumption in the form . . . of a book" (italics in original).[19] In other words, they do the work of facilitating a text's reception. The paratexts of both of these novels build bridges from the non-normative lives of their authors and protagonists to their readers. They work to establish an understanding of why Práxedes Muñoz and Matto de Turner are writing, to show what they are asking of readers, and, crucially, to open a conversation between authors and readers.

Before the start of the main narrative of Matto de Turner's novel, there are two notes. The first dedicates the book to Nicanor Bolet Peraza, who was a Venezuelan political writer based in New York, while the second announces the renaming of the book from *Cruz de agata* (Cross of agate) to *Herencia* and discusses the reasons for and significance of this change. Similarly, Práxedes Muñoz's text contains a dedication, this one to Andrés Avelino Cáceres, who had helped fund her study of medicine. It also includes a letter ("Dos palabras a nuestros lectores" [Two words to our readers]) explaining her reasons for writing the novel. The second edition (1897) contains a relatively long prologue by an Argentine author and positivist, M. S. Victoria, which is framed as an introduction to the text and its author for readers in Buenos Aires.[20] Both Matto de Turner and Práxedes Muñoz address their readers directly in the paratexts and provide instructions or guidance for reading.

These paratexts are significant for how they open dialogues with readers by addressing them directly and before the confines of the different narrative voices of the novels. Both authors use a conversational, yet instructive, tone. In the "Rebautizo" (Rechristening), Matto de Turner refers directly to her readers in the prologue and suggests that they are accustomed to her writing and "el terreno" (the terrain) of her work.[21] The direct address and invocation of a prior relationship differs from the voice of the third-person-omniscient narration of the text that follows. It is this ongoing conversation that Matto de Turner suggests prepares readers for "la dureza de mi pluma" (the hardness of my pen).[22] She can also directly own the ideas presented in the novel because the "Rebautizo" effectively creates a clear link between the author, the ideas of the novel, and the readers. There is no pretense that Matto de Turner is testing ideas. Nor does she hide from readers that the material may provoke discomfort. The implicit message is that the novel is not simply about pleasure but also about learning, and Matto de Turner is openly engaging readers in a conversation that has already begun in her previous novels and will continue in future publications.

Práxedes Muñoz also clearly directs her work at readers with the title of her paratext, "Dos palabras a nuestros lectores." One of the features of this paratext is the use of the collective voice "we" and the references to "todos sentimos" (we all feel) and "[n]uestro presente" (our present time).[23] This goes beyond being a grammatically polite construction to send a message of collectivism. Through using a plural voice, Práxedes Muñoz brings readers into her paratext to convey a shared problem and a solution. It relies on an affective connection to a community in which both readers and author participate and is important because affect or sentiment is one of the areas in which female authors could participate in a socially sanctioned way. As long as authors remained within the confines of the domestic or sentimental romance, they were participating through a set of values conceived of as feminine and were not overly disrupting the established social order.[24]

The dialogue that these paratexts establish permits the work of transition for the reader, especially the nineteenth-century reader addressed by the authors, between the worlds that they inhabit and the new worlds and ideas that the authors present in their novels. Ultimately, they also begin the project of translating ideas that normally were debated outside the domestic and feminine spheres into these spaces. Indeed, as Genette suggests, paratexts are "a zone not only of transition but also of *transaction* . . . [that] is at the service of a better reception for the text and a more pertinent reading of it."[25] This work of transition and transaction is necessary to establish Práxedes Muñoz and Matto de Turner's authority to write generally and to write about topics considered beyond the realm of female authors. It is also what permits readers to make a transition with them into a world in which women have the authority to write about what they want to and to desire identities beyond normative models of feminine citizenship.

As an overt space of conversation between authors, editors, and readers, the paratexts sit outside the "official" fiction of the novel while they also produce their own fictions of authority and acceptance. This means that an important part of this dialogue is that they establish something about who the readers are and give them instructions for reading, as well as establishing who the authors are and what their authority is. In fact, the paratexts authorize a double transgression from the normative role of women. By establishing the authors as possessing the authority to write about science, they also provide models of scientific citizenship, which is significant if we consider the role of the paratexts in creating a better reception of the ideas in the texts. The novels ask readers to engage in a scientific understanding of themselves as citizens. Establishing themselves authoritatively and as scientific citizens by providing evidence of their suitability, the authors provide models for readers, and readers in turn agree to read what might be controversial and possibly transform themselves in the process.

The paratexts show, then, that Matto de Turner and Práxedes Muñoz navigated the often conflicting roles they occupied within the social body, providing us with a different account of women's experiences than the stereotypes and conventions included within the main text of the novels. Matto de Turner's paratexts relay an educated, politically astute, and scientifically fluent voice that contrasts with the novel's domestic angels, who, though educated, have lives that are limited to the domestic sphere and its concerns. Likewise, Práxedes Muñoz's paratexts suggest that she is no angel of the house who writes in her spare time but is a professional scientist. In this way the paratexts become historical traces that tell alternative narratives about what these women were attempting to do. They reveal how the authors positioned themselves, as well as the frames that they give to the politics of walking the tension between normative expectations of them as domestic angels and their professions as writers and scientists.

Writing to Claim Scientific Authority and New Forms of Citizenship

What, then, constitutes the transformation of science into literature? And what spaces does this transformation offer for sociopolitical critique, particularly for altering the horizons of possibility for women as writers and citizens? Práxedes Muñoz and Matto de Turner engage different tactics for establishing their scientific and authorial legitimacy. Much of Matto de Turner's authority is based on her standing as an established literary figure, and this helps her push the boundaries of possibility in her writing. At the same time, her established position in the literary community and her career in journalism contrast with the roles that her female characters play as guardians of the domestic realm as daughters, wives, and mothers. By contrast, Práxedes

Muñoz has no such reputation and her protagonist does not easily fit a normative subjectivity. On the title page of *La evolución de Paulina*, directly under Práxedes Muñoz's name, readers see that she holds a bachelor of science degree and worked previously as an assistant in Dr. Augusto Orrego Lugo's clinic in Santiago.[26] This underscoring of her scientific training is important because she does not have a long-standing relationship with readers to invoke when entering a difficult topic. In fact, she is at pains to point out to readers that what motivates her is moral necessity and social good and that her skill lies in the area of being able to explain positivist ideas to readers, albeit in the form of a novel.[27] These are clearly contestatory narratives that are also strategically engaged in a conciliatory dance. In this way science becomes what both legitimizes Práxedes Muñoz's intervention and excuses any failings of the novel. It also demonstrates why she chooses this medium to write about science. The novel form seems to offer a more permissible space to work in than public- or university-based science. So it becomes a safer space for women writing to locate themselves to do reforming work while it also reaches a broader audience through a more accessible form.

While fiction might have provided a slightly safer space to write about science, the novels still make clear both authors' intention to engage in social and political critique through a scientifically informed lens. Read together, the texts create the subgenre of the *novela sociológica* (sociological novel). Práxedes Muñoz does this in naming her novel *La evolución de Paulina, novela sociológica*, while Matto de Turner employs sociology as her methodology for engaging in social analysis. If the paratexts function as a space of conversation between authors and readers, then what this type of novel might contain and what its purposes are can be negotiated here. In effect, the paratexts, and subsequently the novels, translate scientific concepts, specifically sociology, to the reading public. Omar de Lucia traces the ways that Argentine writers used the *novela sociológica* as a way of bringing ideas, such as those of positivist philosophy, to a greater number of readers.[28] In Peru, unlike in some European countries such as France or England, the *novela sociológica* did not develop and, other than these two novels, it was not taken up as its own genre. However, as a subgenre it brings two novels, which are very different stylistically, together with specific reforming motivations while highlighting the emerging science of sociology and its ways of understanding social reform.

Práxedes Muñoz is clear about the purpose of her text, its scientific basis, and the intervention she wants to make. In the paratext she writes, "By bringing the principles of positivism to the public today in the clothing of a novel, we believe we have fulfilled a social duty at the same time as satisfying a moral necessity."[29] Although she employs very broad terms to discuss her audience and those affected by the problems she discusses, the focus of the novel is Peru and the moral and political crisis affecting the country after the War of the Pacific. She frames the crisis as a "pathological state that has reached a maximum intensity" whose answer lies in the re-ordering of religion and science.[30] Práxedes Muñoz argues that "it is necessary that Christian idealism is substituted with scientific reality, and that it regulate our conduct and authorize our actions."[31] Práxedes Muñoz emphasizes the importance of the "here and now" of science in the achievement of human happiness. She distinguishes this from the "vague and pompous promises toward an uncertain and doubtful future" offered by religion.[32] However, she is not advocating the wholesale rejection of religion for Comtian science. Instead she is interested in using elements of positivism to further social change. She argues that Auguste Comte's structure

> contains the precious seed of our future glory; for this reason we de-
> sire that it be spread and that all enlightened men that are currently
> interested in solving large social problems, study and meditate hard
> on this massive creation of the most immense and profound genius
> of our century.[33]

These passages from the paratext reveal a clear message from Práxedes Muñoz to readers not only about her understanding of science and Comtian positivism, but also the importance of science for understanding social problems. It raises science as the most significant lens through which readers can understand their present moment.

For Matto de Turner, the novel provides a didactic space for educating citizens in their proper comportment within the national body. In the pro-logue to *Aves sin nido* she argues that "the task of the novel is to be the pho-tograph that captures the vices and virtues of a people, censuring the former with the appropriate moral lesson and paying its homage of admiration to the latter."[34] In *Herencia* she goes further to declare that the novel is "fruit of my sociological observations and my daring to critique society's evils, to bring about good in a widespread way."[35] In both novels, Matto de Turner uses scientific knowledge and methods to further her goal of creating new social knowledge that will provide Peruvians with the necessary tools to move forward into the twentieth century.

Práxedes Muñoz engages far more overtly in a social analysis through the lenses of positivist philosophy and science than Matto de Turner. By including specific and detailed commentary on positivism, and Comtian ideas in particular, she engages directly with the ideas while suggesting how to reorganize moral and social ways of knowing. This difference is in part stylistic, but it also reflects Práxedes Muñoz's training in science and the progressive nature of her university studies.[36] In arguing that social change will be brought about by examining positivism or Comte's ideas, Práxedes Muñoz states in explicit terms what Matto de Turner reveals implicitly: as the fruits of sociological studies, these novels can address social problems and offer a remedy, positivism, to cure these ills.

Framing their fictions in the scientific terms of sociology achieves several things for these authors in terms of their relationships to readers. First, they advise readers that these are not purely fictions but are also rigorous scientific studies. This is meant to give legitimacy to their observations because the science of sociology was understood to rely on classifiable and provable observation and cause and effect. This could cut through gendered critiques of women writing and allow readers to focus on the content of the arguments.[37] It also meant that readers could be assured that the social arguments, although presented in a fictional form, were grounded in scientific reasoning and could thus be verified. Second, by bringing science explicitly into the frame, readers are exposed to the emerging vocabularies of science and the practices of citizenship that are grounded in secular and scientific ways of organizing social knowledge. This is especially important as both novels break with established modes of citizenship and models of femininity. Finally, the form of these texts is important. By writing novels, these authors could reach a broad readership, including women who might have access to novels but not to scientific texts. Furthermore, by cloaking their scientific theories in fictional characters, the authors could allow readers to identify differently with the heroines.

As we have seen, the discourses around gender, science, and nationhood intersect in different ways to create pedagogic models for citizenship. These both conform to and contest normative models of femininity and the shape that female protagonists' and authors' desires for science could take. While an analysis of the actual novels is not the focus of this chapter, it is worth noting here that the two authors deploy science within their texts quite differently. A significant feature that separates the texts is which characters are given a voice with which to speak about science in the novels themselves. In *La evolución de Paulina*, both Father Esteban and Paulina discuss science, but the ways they do so differ. In the first part of the text Paulina narrates her personal desires for scientific knowledge to Estela and, in the third part, the impact that *la religión de la humanidad* could have for the social body. The explanation of the tenets of positivism as a "hard" science is left to Father Esteban in the second part of the text. This apparent contradiction between Paulina's desires, her realities, and what Práxedes Muñoz appears to advocate for other women creates a tension for readers that other critics have noted.[38] However, this complication is not as strong as the contradiction in Matto de Turner's text. In *Herencia* the lives and choices of the female characters that readers are meant to emulate are all framed within a scientific discourse, but they never speak a word of science. This is left to the male characters, who explain to readers and the female characters the importance of science and what its impact is on modern understandings of citizenship. These differences make the paratexts all the more important in terms of the authors stating their claim to science and the validity of their engagements with positivism. They are also important for us to be able to see the tensions and contradictions that the authors were navigating.

The authors further navigate the tensions that arise between their incursions into the world of science and their gender by framing their texts within a language of doing the work of "social good." For example, Práxedes Muñoz adopts an apologetic tone regarding the quality of her writing so as to deflect any possible literary criticism and refocus the reader's attention on her social and scientific aims. Her paratext closes with the following:

> To work for the good of our brothers has always been the supreme aspiration of our spirit, and it is only with such an elevated proposition that we have undertaken, without any talent for this literary genre, a work that is above our weak skills. We hope, nevertheless, that all of the defects of this narration will be forgiven in light of the good intentions that motivate us.[39]

Práxedes Muñoz claims no literary talents, only social commitment. This claim mirrors Matto de Turner's that she writes to "critique society's evils, to bring about good in a widespread way."[40] Both paratexts set out projects of working toward some sort of social good that assert a new type of scientifically informed morality. However, this also displaces any responsibility the authors have for naming their own contestatory desires in the process. Nevertheless, these desires come through, both in the paratexts and in the novels, because they cannot be contained within normative models of femininity. The good that the authors call upon appears to be one thing, while a closer reading of the texts reveals it to be slightly different than readers might first expect. For instance, Margarita turns out to be racially and socially of a group that readers would be likely to reject outright if this had been revealed to them at the beginning of the text.[41] Ultimately, then, readers are asked to read against the grain of their expectations and identify with characters that they may not recognize themselves in, and this makes these novels more interesting than they might appear at a first reading.

Conclusion

Historical evidence shows that the project of postwar reform was complex and fraught with tensions. By 1895 a new extremely conservative and

Catholic presidency no longer permitted a space for Matto de Turner and Práxedes Muñoz to express their radical ideas in Peru, and both were living in exile in Argentina. While they both deftly navigated the problems of gender and science during the postwar years, their life stories together with what is hinted at in the paratexts make clear that the act of writing about science and expressing desire for non-normative choices was both transgressive and dangerous. Matto de Turner and Práxedes Muñoz embrace positivism in their novels as a method to resolve political, social, and economic problems. They show that, contrary to conservative elites' concerns, secularization through scientific principles will not destabilize society.

The novels of Matto de Turner and Práxedes Muñoz engage in acts of translation in a number of ways. On one level they translate science into a wider sphere so that a broader audience can engage with it and, on another level, the novels translate the non-normative selves and desires of the female authors into socially palatable forms for readers. Attention to these forms of translation thus offers vital insights into the ways in which access to science and naming a desire for knowledge about science was gendered. Furthermore, attention to translation also reveals the novelists' contributions to the shaping of the intersecting sexual and national discourses in nineteenth-century Peru, making clear that unlike in the European *scientia sexualis*, the discussions about desire here focused more specifically on issues of scientific knowledge and authority. In these ways the novels of Matto de Turner and Práxedes Muñoz played a significant role in the debates around social reform projects: they translated science into the home and the intimate lives of readers and attempted to authorize women to write about science, and non-normative desires and subjectivities.

NOTES

1. "Sabías la lucha en que me había visto empeñada con mi familia, que no comprendía que una débil niña soñara engalanar sus sienes con los laureles de Minerva, patrimonio exclusivo del sexo fuerte, y no ignorabas cuán acribada había sido mi existencia antes de alcanzar la satisfacción de mis legítimas aspiraciones." Margarita Práxedes Muñoz, *La evolución de Paulina: Novela sociológica*, 2nd ed. (Buenos Aires: La Elzeviriana, 1897), 14. All translations from *La evolución de Paulina* are mine.

2. See María Emma Mannarelli, *Limpias y modernas: Género, higiene y cultura en la Lima del novecientos* (Lima: Ediciones Flora Tristán, 1999).

3. Peter Flindell Klarén, *Peru: Society and Nationhood in the Andes* (Oxford: Oxford University Press, 2000).

4. Marcos Cueto, *Excelencia científica en la periferia: Actividades científicas e investigación biomédica en el Perú—1890-1950* (Lima: CONCYTEC, 1989), 51–55.

5. Oscar R. Martí, "Positivist Thought in Latin America," in *Routledge Encyclopedia of Philosophy*, ed. Edward Craig (New York: Routledge, 1998), 7:565–570.

6. See, for example, Francesca Denegri, *El abanico y la cigarrera: La primera generación de mujeres ilustradas en el Perú* (Lima: IEP and Flora Tristán Centro de la Mujer Peruana, 1996); Mannarelli, *Limpias y modernas*; Mary Louise Pratt, "Las mujeres y el imaginario nacional en el siglo XIX," *Revista de Crítica Literaria Latinoamericana* 19, no. 38 (1993): 51–62; Maritza Villavicencio, *Del silencio a la palabra: Mujeres peruanas en los siglos XIX y XX* (Lima: Flora Tristán Centro de la Mujer Peruana, 1992).

7. See Villavicencio, *Silencio a la palabra*, for an analysis of the ways in which women writers both played into and contested these norms.

8. For women's participation in the Peruvian literary scene see, for example, Denegri, *Abanico y la cigarrera*, and Villavicencio, *Silencio a la palabra*.

9. Jorge Basadre, *Introducción a las bases documentales para la historia de la República del Perú* (Lima: Villanueva, 1971).

10. A career in science or medicine became possible for women after a 1908 reform that opened university studies to women. Some women practiced obstetrics before then, largely in rural locations, and often trained abroad. See Judith Prieto de Zegarra, *Mujer, poder y desarrollo en el Perú*, vol. 2 (Callao, Peru: DORHCA, 1980).

11. See Mercedes Cabello de Carbonera, *Sacrificio y recompensa: Novela* (1886), *Los amores de Hortensia: Novela* (1887), *Eleodora: Novela* (1887), *Blanca Sol* (1889), *Las consecuencias: Novela* (1889), and *El conspirador: Autobiografía de un hombre público: Novela político-social* (1892); Carolina Freyre de Jaimes, *El regalo de bodas* (1887), and *Memorias de una reclusa* (1887); Teresa González de Fanning, *Ambición y abnegación* (1886), *Regina* (under the pseudonym María de la Luz) (1886), and *Lucecitas* (1893); Lastenia Larriva de Llona, *Un drama singular: Historia de una familia* (1888), *Luz: Novela* (1890), *Oro y escoria* (1889), and *Oro y escoria (segunda parte)* (1890); and María Nieves y Bustamante, *Jorge o el hijo del pueblo: Novela* (1892).

12. Práxedes Muñoz's work received relatively little critical attention at the time of publication, and it is also largely absent from current critical engagements with Peruvian women's writing, yet her work was considered important enough to merit a one-page entry in what is considered the most comprehensive history of Peru (Basadre, *Introducción*). See also Magdalena Chocano, "Lima, Masónica: Las logias simbólicas y su progreso en el medio urbano a fines del siglo XIX," *Revista de Indias* 70 (2010): 409–444; Isabelle Tauzin Castellanos, "El positivismo peruano en versión femenina: Mercedes Cabello de Carbonera y Margarita Práxedes Muñoz," *Boletín de la Academia Peruana de la Lengua* 27 (1996): 79–100.

13. For studies of Matto de Turner, see Catherine Bryan, "Making National Citizens: Gender, Race, and Class in Two Works by Clorinda Matto de Turner," *Cincinnati Romance Review* 15 (1996): 113–118; Antonio Cornejo Polar, *Clorinda Matto de Turner, novelista* (Lima: Lluvia, 1992); Sara Beatriz Guardia, "En nombre del otro desvalido y excluido por el poder: La escritura de Clorinda Matto y Laura Riesco," *Mujeres que escriben en América Latina* (Lima: Centro de Estudios La Mujer en la Historia de América Latina, 2007), 265–278; Mariselle Meléndez, "Obreras del pensamiento y educadoras de la nación: El sujeto femenino en la ensayística femenina decimonónica de transición," *Revista Iberoamericana* 64 (1998): 573–586; Ana Peluffo, *Lágrimas andinas: Sentimentalismo, género y virtud republicana en Clorinda Matto de Turner* (Pittsburgh: University of Pittsburgh Press, 2005); Joan Torres-Pou, "Clorinda Matto de Turner y el ángel del hogar," *Revista Hispanica Moderna* 43 (1990): 3–15.

14. For a synthesis of the reactions to Matto de Turner's first novel and the subsequent events that contributed to her exile, see Sara Beatriz Guardia, "Escritura femenina del siglo XIX: Voces de ruptura y cambio en nombre del desvalido y excluido por el poder," in *Cien años después: La literatura de mujeres en América Latina: El legado de Mercedes Cabello de Carbonera y Clorinda Matto de Turner*, ed. Claire Emilie Martin (Lima: Universidad de San Martín Porres, 2010), 67–78.

15. Jennifer Fraser, "Clorinda Matto de Turner's *Herencia* as the Creation of an Alternative Social Knowledge," *Bulletin of Hispanic Studies* 88, no. 1 (2011): 97–112.

16. I have addressed these issues of form and content elsewhere. See Jennifer Fraser, "'That Women's Writing Thing You Do': Reflections on Silence, Writing and Academic Spaces," *Modern Languages Open* (2014), available at http://www.modernlanguageso pen.org/index.php/mlo/article/view/7/17; Jennifer Fraser, "'Con el ropaje de la novela': Margarita Práxedes Muñoz's *La evolución de Paulina* as an Attempt to (Re)negotiate Literary Forms and Contest Normative Subjectivities," *Journal of Romance Studies* 15, no. 1 (2015).

17. Clorinda Matto de Turner, *Herencia* (Lima: Masias, 1895), 1–16.

18. See Doris Sommer, *Foundational Fictions: The National Romances of Latin America* (Berkeley: University of California Press, 1991); Fernando Unzueta, "Scenes of Reading: Imagining Nations / Romancing History in Spanish America," in *Beyond Imagined Communities: Reading and Writing the Nation in Nineteenth-Century Latin America*, ed. Sara Castro-Klarén and John Charles Chasteen (Baltimore: Johns Hopkins University Press, 2003), 115–160.

19. Gérard Genette, *Paratexts: Thresholds of Interpretation*, trans. Jane E. Lewin (Cambridge: Cambridge University Press, 1997), 1.

20. It has not been possible to locate a copy of the first edition in any public or university libraries and archives. This makes it difficult to know what it might contain, if anything, instead of the prologue by M. S. Victoria. Presumably this prologue is absent in the first (1893) edition from Santiago.

21. Matto de Turner, *Herencia*, viii.

22. Ibid.

23. Práxedes Muñoz, *Evolución de Paulina*, 5–6.

24. Denegri, *Abanico y la cigarrera*, 41.

25. Genette, *Paratexts*, 2.

26. Orrego Luco (1849–1933) was a Chilean psychiatrist and politician known for his liberal and secular politics.

27. Práxedes Muñoz, *Evolución de Paulina*, 1, 9.

28. Daniel Omar de Lucia, "Margarita Práxedes Muñoz, visión del alba y el ocaso," *El Catoblepas: Revista Crítica del Presente* 83 (2009): 13, available at http://www.nodulo.org/ec/2009/n083p13.htm.

29. "Al presentar hoy al público los principios de la escuela positivista con el ropaje de la novela, hemos creído cumplir un deber social á [sic] la vez que satisfacer una necesidad moral." Práxedes Muñoz, *Evolución de Paulina*, 5.

30. "un estado patológico que ha llegado al máximum de intensidad." Ibid., 6.

31. "preciso es que el idealismo cristiano sea sustituído [sic] por la realidad científica, que dé norma á [sic] nuestra conducta y sanción á [sic] nuestros actos." Práxedes Muñoz, *Evolución de Paulina*, 6.

32. "vagas y pomposas promesas respecto de un futuro incierto y dudoso." Ibid., 7.

33. "encierra el germen precioso de nuestro futuro engrandecimiento; por eso deseamos se difunda y que todos los hombres ilustrados que al presente se interesan por solucionar los grandes problemas sociales, examinen y mediten con empeño esta monumental creación del más vasto y profundo genio de nuestro siglo." Ibid., 7.

34. Clorinda Matto de Turner, *Birds without a Nest*, trans. John H. R. Polt (Oxford: Oxford University Press, 1998), 3. "la novela tiene que ser la fotografía que estereotipe los vicios y las virtudes de un pueblo, con la consiguiente moraleja correctiva para aquéllos y el homenaje de admiración para éstas." Clorinda Matto de Turner, *Aves sin nido* (Mexico City: Colofón, 1996 [1889]), 51.

35. "fruto de mis observaciones sociológicas y de mi arrojo para fustigar los males de la sociedad, provocando el bien en la forma que se ha generalizado'" Matto de Turner, *Herencia*, v. All translations from *Herencia* are mine.

36. See Augusto Salazar Bondy, *Historia de las ideas en el Perú contemporáneo: El proceso del pensamiento filosófico*, 2nd ed., 2 vols. (Lima: Moncloa, 1967).

37. Other critics have traced the ways in which male writers of the time attacked Matto de Turner publically in very personal terms for her writing. For instance, Pedro Paz Soldán y Unanue, writing under the pseudonym Juan de Arona, called her, among other things, a *marimacho* or a "butch" woman. See Beatriz Guardia, "Escritura femenina del siglo XIX"; Villavicencio, *Silencio a la palabra*.

38. Tauzin Castellanos, "Positivismo peruano en versión femenina."

39. "Trabajar por el bien de nuestros hermanos, fue siempre la suprema aspiración de nuestro espíritu, y solo con tan levantado propósito, hemos emprendido, sin dote alguna para este género literario, una obra superior a nuestras débiles fuerzas. Esperamos, sin embargo, nos sean perdonados todos los defectos de esta narración en gracia a los buenos propósitos que nos animan." Práxedes Muñoz, *Evolución de Paulina*, 9.

40. "fustigar los males de la sociedad, provocando el bien en la forma que se ha generalizado." Matto de Turner, *Herencia*, v.

41. Fraser, "Clorinda Matto de Turner," 97–112.

10

The Translation of Edward Carpenter's *The Intermediate Sex* in Early Twentieth-Century Japan

MICHIKO SUZUKI

The story of translations in the early twentieth century—the movement of texts, terms, and ideas around the globe—is a story of unexpected events and unforeseen effects. Often, a translation was understood or used in its new context in a manner quite different from how it was used in the original work. "Translation" also included such things as synopses, adaptations, and condensed versions; moreover, texts were not always translated directly from the original language. Such aspects of translation during this period complicate the view that sexological texts and ideas were disseminated from the Western "center" to the Asian "periphery" in a predictable, more or less straightforward fashion. Furthermore, the complex processes of transmission do not simply reinforce expected differences and gaps with regard to language and cultural context. They also reveal the realities of a dynamic, coeval modernity in which individuals deployed similar strategies to articulate and circulate new vocabulary, concepts, and ideology about the science of sex.

This chapter examines from several different perspectives the first Japanese translation of Edward Carpenter's (1844–1929) *The Intermediate Sex* (1908), serialized in 1914 and published in book form in 1919. First, I will focus on specific issues regarding these publications, the context of translation, and the choices that were made in translating terms such as "intermediate sex." In the latter part of the chapter, I explore some unexpected ways in which Carpenter's ideas were used in Japan. Differences and similarities between the original and its Japanese translations (both textual and conceptual) afford important insight into the development of sexological discourses in a global framework.

Edward Carpenter in Japan

Since the mid-nineteenth century, Japan's drive to become a modern empire necessitated a rapid absorption of all things Western. In this context, sexology played an important role in creating new views of gender, sexuality, and national identity. By 1894, an abridged translation of Richard von Krafft-Ebing's *Psychopathia Sexualis* (4th ed.) had already been published, and it was retranslated in a more complete form in 1913 after prominent intellectuals endorsed its importance as a work presenting "new Western knowledge."[1] Indeed, during the 1910s–1920s, there was a sexology boom in Japan: works by Western and Japanese sexologists were widely published and read by both intellectual and popular audiences in a variety of venues, and sexological ideas quickly spread within the cultural imaginary.

Edward Carpenter, though not a medical sexologist, contributed significantly to what Heike Bauer calls "literary sexology,"[2] especially with regard to discussions of homosexuality. Although various aspects of Carpenter's thought were influential in Japan, his association with socialism originally facilitated the rapid introduction of his works by Japanese socialists and democracy activists. Many of his works, such as *Civilisation: Its Cause and Cure* (1889; trans. 1893), were translated soon after their publication.[3] Socialist Ishikawa Sanshirō (1876–1956) played a critical role in promoting Carpenter as one of the great thinkers of the day, publishing in 1912 *Tetsujin Kaapentaa* (Carpenter the sage), a work discussing Carpenter's ideas.[4] Later Carpenter also became recognized for works on love and sexuality, and his *Love's Coming of Age* (1896) especially reached a wide audience; different abbreviated translations circulated, and a full translation was published in 1921.[5] In this way, Carpenter came to be considered an important contributor to discourses about sexology and love, as well as social transformation and progress in early twentieth-century Japan.

The Intermediate Sex: A Study of Some Transitional Types of Men and Women is Carpenter's collection of essays treating different topics regarding inversion and same-sex relationships. Although it was published in 1908, the essays themselves were written (and some published) over a decade earlier.[6] Despite controversy, the English-language text went through many editions. Sheila Rowbotham notes that it was "remarkable in addressing a general readership and thus breaking the taboo on how ideas about homosexuality could be communicated."[7] Carpenter not only presented a positive genealogy of same-sex sexuality to combat degeneration discourse but also suggested that those of the "intermediate sex" served a critical role in the advancement of society.[8] In communicating these radical ideas, Carpenter used certain textual strategies. He framed the text as part of scientific, scholarly knowledge, making references to "untranslated European texts throughout" and including "a long bibliographical appendix"; he also skillfully used a style of writing that "made it exceedingly difficult to pin down his precise meaning." As Rowbotham puts it, what Carpenter said in this text "might appear perfectly clear; what he *meant* was frequently opaque."[9] By sustaining multi-layered levels of meaning in his work, Carpenter was able to navigate the restrictions of his day.

In discussing same-sex intimacy in these essays, Carpenter focuses on male–male relationships.[10] Although the work presents some notions of female inversion and same-sex attachments, they are not discussed with as much detail and enthusiasm. Although Carpenter was known for his concern for feminist issues, girls and women are secondary (and at times negatively presented) in these discussions.[11] In Japan, however, it was women who translated and published this work amid growing interest in female same-sex love and sexuality. In addition to Carpenter's bona fides in Japan as a "sage," the discussion of recent Western sexological ideas relevant to female–female sexuality, combined with an opaque and sexually nonexplicit style of writing, made *The Intermediate Sex* an attractive and relevant text for translation.

The Intermediate Sex and Female Same-Sex Love in Japan

The Intermediate Sex was translated by socialist feminist Yamakawa (Aoyama) Kikue (1890–1980) with the title *Chūseiron* (Theories about the intermediate sex) and serialized in *Safuran* (Saffron, 1914), a short-lived journal published by the feminist artist Otake Kōkichi (1893–1966).[12] Later the translation was changed in some parts, retitled *Dōseiai* (Same-sex love) and printed in book form together with a translation of a section of Lester Ward's (1841–1913) *Pure Sociology* (1903) in 1919. The excerpt from Ward's work, titled *Josei chūshinsetsu* (Gynæcocentric theory), discusses the idea that the female sex, rather than the male, is the primary, originary sex. *Dōseiai* was probably published together with this text because both translators were socialist activists, and both works addressed the evolution of society and the changing aspects of sex/gender as critical manifestations of modernity.[13]

Although Carpenter's *The Intermediate Sex* primarily featured male identity, in Japan its publication was imbricated with various issues and questions about modern female sexual identity and the development of feminist movements. During the 1910s there were many discussions and reports in the media about the new, "modern" phenomenon of female same-sex love, particularly among schoolgirls. Especially following a high-profile love suicide in 1911, there was much debate regarding the true nature of female–female love, whether it was sexual and abnormal (or platonic but emotionally excessive), innate or temporary, and how it related to questions of masculinity and femininity, as well as sexual identity and gender roles.[14] Proliferating images of the so-called New Woman rebelling against traditional Confucian values also led to widespread interest in various forms of "new" female identities and their impact on society.

Western sexological discourse on female same-sex intimacy and the identity of the female invert had already been introduced to Japan through texts such as *Psychopathia Sexualis* and Havelock Ellis's *Studies in the Psychology of Sex* (1897). In 1914, *Seitō* (Bluestocking, 1911–1916), the first Japanese feminist journal, published a condensed translation of "Sexual Inversion in Women," a chapter from *Studies in the Psychology of Sex*.[15] Historian Gregory Pflugfelder has suggested that the translation of *The Intermediate Sex* in *Safuran* may have been a response to the Ellis translation, involving some personal issues between feminists and/or a challenge to "Ellis's somewhat less positive evaluation of 'same-sex love.'"[16]

In *Safuran*'s editorial notes, feminist Kamichika Ichiko (1888–1981) explains that the Carpenter translation came about as a result of a conversation she had with Yamakawa, who explained that Carpenter believed "same-sex love (*dōsei ren'ai*)" was "of a more spiritual nature than the [love] between men and women, and if steered in a good direction, there was no limit as to how one could influence and direct the other [person] [in a good way]." This grabbed Kamichika's attention, and she asked Yamakawa to translate the work. Kamichika also suggests that Carpenter's text is valuable because "in Japan too there are men and women of the intermediate sex (*chūsei*) who have begun appearing these days."[17] But despite this reference to both genders, it seems that the focus is on the phenomenon of female same-sex intimacy as opposed to that between men. The usage of the term *dōsei ren'ai*, strongly associated with female–female love and often considered nonsexual in nature, additionally underscores the spiritual aspects of this love as the main point of interest.[18]

The translation of *The Intermediate Sex* was one of the earliest publications by Yamakawa, who would later become an important socialist feminist.[19] She would also publish the full translation of *Love's Coming of Age* in 1921.[20] In an interview published in 1979, Yamakawa explained that Carpenter, "a minister who never married," recognized that there were many "great geniuses who remained single," and examined "the important achievements of single people (*dokushinsha*) for society and humanity." The term "single people" is gender and sexuality neutral (used either inadvertently or strategically), but Yamakawa makes it clear that she wanted to present such positive views in order to combat the "traditional prejudice against unmarried women" that was still present even among male socialist activists.[21] Whether the Japanese translation of *The Intermediate Sex* was the result of personal issues between individual women, rivalry between two feminist journals, an attempt to present differing views about female same-sex love, or a feminist defense of spinsterhood, it is important to view it as part of a greater exploration of "new" female sexualities, relationships, and identities.

Translating the Term "Intermediate Sex"

Carpenter's text was certainly read by those interested in male–male sexuality,[22] but its translation emerged in the context of widespread concerns of and about women. This likely influenced some choices made in translation; through use of certain words and selective excising, the Japanese version highlights temperament and emotion rather than sexuality. This was no doubt part of a strategy to prevent censorship, and it also helped feminists associated with the text avoid being personally linked with sexual perversity considered the subject of sexological inquiry.[23]

In *The Intermediate Sex*, Carpenter focuses on erasing associations of pathology and degeneration with inversion, and promoting ideal aspects of same-sex attachments in general. He is grappling with the realities of censorship while working simultaneously to "rebrand" homosexuality. Thus, already in the original text, special care is taken with wording and language. For example, Carpenter often legitimates same-sex sexuality by, ironically, undermining sexual desire or practice; he tends to emphasize inverted characteristics or temperament, and the notion of love is presented mainly as "the inner devotion of one person to another."[24] These rhetorical strategies were especially crucial for presenting a nonthreatening, less sexualized perspective of male inversion and relationships. In the Japanese translation, such "sanitizing" is further heightened so that love, as opposed to sexuality, is underscored.

Carpenter discusses various ideas about homosexuality by drawing on a range of terms, such as "Urning," "Uranian" and "intermediate sex." The word "Urning," coined by Karl Heinrich Ulrichs in 1864,[25] was already in use by Japanese intellectuals during the early twentieth century, translated phonetically as *ūruningu*.[26] Probably because in Japan this word already had negative associations as a medico-scientific term for a perverse sexual phenomenon/identity, the translation of *The Intermediate Sex* uses the term only once (in English) when discussing inverts specifically in relation to sexual practices.[27] "Uranian," a less known term, also associated with abnormal same-sex sexuality, is never used. Japanese sexological texts usually rendered this word as *uranisumusu* (Uranismus), and later on often differentiated

"Urning" and "Uranian" as male and female, respectively.[28] In either case, usage of such words clearly associated with abnormal same-sex sexuality would not have been desirable for Carpenter's positive presentation of inverts and same-sex love. Thus, in the Japanese translation of *The Intermediate Sex*, these terms ("Urning," "Uranian" and "intermediate sex") are generally all translated using the single neologism *"chūseisha"* (intermediate-sex person, or middle-sex person). This decision was most likely a conscious effort by the translator to eschew known sexological terms with possible negative associations, and use instead *"chūseisha,"* unassociated with overt negative meaning.

Rowbotham notes that "in using the term the 'intermediate sex' Carpenter was adapting a concept which was already in circulation."[29] Bauer also comments that "the notion of the 'intermediate sex' aligned Carpenter's theories more closely with the German activist strand of sexology derived from Ulrichs' inversion theory and further developed by [Magnus] Hirschfeld's *Zwischenstufenlehre*, which is perhaps most accurately translated into English as the theory of intermediate sexes."[30] For certain readers even in Japan, the term "intermediate sex" may have evoked associations with German terminology and also with Hirschfeld's ideas. In a 1916 article in the socialist journal *Shin Shakai* (New society) that introduces Carpenter's ideas from *The Intermediate Sex*, the term "intermediate [sex]" or *"intaamejieeto"* is explained as corresponding to *"'die sexuellen Zwischenstufen'* in German" and "should be translated as *chūsei.*"[31] Hirschfeld's Scientific-Humanitarian Committee, as well as ideas from its annual publication, the *Jahrbuch für sexuelle Zwischenstufen*, had already been introduced to Japan by the early twentieth century.[32] Sexologists and intellectuals with specialized knowledge were likely to have made this connection between Carpenter's term and the earlier German concept, as well as other related terms.[33]

Judging from the translator's decision to erase earlier terminology from the text, however, I would suggest that the goal was not to emphasize connections between Carpenter's term and prior sexological discourse. Although in the Western context various terms had emerged from efforts to acknowledge homosexuality as natural and legitimate, words such as Urning in Japan implied for most readers a non-normative sexuality newly defined by the scientific language of sexology. The author of the 1916 article in *Shin Shakai* clearly understood that Carpenter's representation shows homosexuality in a positive light and that in Carpenter's view, the intermediate identity is "congenital." He discusses Carpenter's idea that "men and women of the intermediate sex express to varying degrees the tendency towards same-sex love" and that these people "fulfill a productive and important function in the social evolution of humanity."[34] The terms *chūsei* (intermediate sex) and *chūseisha* (intermediate-sex person) function well in supporting this argument and also helped protect the translator and publisher: these words did not have prior "baggage" semantically and they also conveyed a unique nuance in Japanese.

Since the late nineteenth century a great many Japanese words and meanings were created or transformed through Western influences, and it is often difficult to trace the earliest usage and changing definitions. The term *chūsei* is in current use and has a wide range of meanings, although nuances were somewhat different during the early twentieth century. "*Chū*" means "middle," and in a 1921 dictionary, we see "*sei*" defined as "character," "quality," "life," "sex," or "gender" (in terms of grammar).[35] This dictionary defines "*chūsei*" as (1) "a quality of being in between something," (2) equivalent to the English phrase "neutral gender" (in terms of grammar), and (3) equivalent to the English word "neutrality" (in terms of science, being neither acid nor alkaline).[36] These definitions point to the term's emergence from grammatical or scientific concepts of being in-between and neutral.

In contemporary Japanese, *chūsei* has additionally come to mean "lacking pronounced male or female characteristics"[37] or "a state in which sexual characteristics are not taken as either male or female."[38] Although these definitions are not yet found in the 1921 dictionary, it is likely that the sense of sexual neutrality in a broader sense had already become a part of the term's nuance. Thus, *chūsei* was perceived not only as a "middle sex" but also as a kind of "neutral sex" that may harbor certain tendencies or desires but does not express them through actual sexual activity. In a 1924 article in a popular women's magazine, for example, the word *chūseika* (becoming *chūsei*) is used to explain that women who become too educated will lose their sexual drive, become asexual, and abandon the inclination to marry or reproduce. *Chūsei* is also used in this article to describe biological organisms such as worker bees and ants. The writer suggests that they are of a neutral sex and their only function is to work and not reproduce; thus, humans who work too much are likened to these insects because of their diminishing sexual drives. Such usage emphasizes neutralization in terms of loss of sexual desire and lack of sexual activity.[39]

Chūsei worked well as a Japanese translation for Carpenter's "intermediate sex" because it suggested a distinct "middle sex" different from male and female sexes. Furthermore, the additional nuance of neutrality or asexuality that did not exist in English (intermediate) or German (*Zwischen*) helped to underscore Carpenter's "sanitized" representation, highlighting the idea that same-sex love can be a spiritual expression or desire, not necessarily "degenerate" sexual acts. Ultimately, however, neither *chūsei* nor *chūseisha* really became a featured or foundational component of early twentieth-century Japanese sexological vocabulary. Perhaps this was due to the fact that inversion theory and the terminology of *seiteki tentōsha* (sex-inverted person) were already quite prevalent. And despite the usefulness of the vague meaning of *chūsei* and its "neutral" nuance for translators in this case, the term may have been *too* vague or confusing for use in other sexological contexts.

When the Japanese book version of *The Intermediate Sex* came out in 1919, the title had been changed from *Chūseiron* (Theories about the intermediate sex), used in the serialization, to *Dōseiai* (Same-sex love). The new title used the term originally associated with female same-sex intimacy, considered more spiritual and less sexual than male homosexuality. *Dōseiai* as a word first appeared in the 1910s and became standardized as a term during the 1920s.[40] Ultimately, it became the generic word for both male and female same-sex love and sexuality. Furukawa Makoto discusses the intense media focus on female same-sex love during the 1910s–1930s and suggests there was a need for a term that defined homosexuality as both a male and female phenomenon, unlike earlier terms such as *nanshoku* that only referred to male–male sexuality/eroticism. Rather than vocabulary that alluded to male–male intercourse and erotic desire, the rise of female–female love, which was believed to be basically nonsexual, led to the eventual adoption of *dōseiai* as the standard term for male and female same-sex love.[41] It can be argued that in 1919, the word would have been flexible enough to suggest both female same-sex attachments and/or same-sex relationships for both sexes with an emphasis on love (*ai*).

The title of Carpenter's text was doubtless changed for purposes of clarity (that the work was not about pH balance or the grammatical neuter), but the new title could also have been a way to suggest that its content focused on female same-sex love, a popular topic in the media, published as it was together with Lester Ward's sociological work on the female sex. The changed title also worked well with another publishing trend of the day, in which works about love in general were becoming extremely important. Carpenter's text, with its stress on emotional attachment that nurtures human and social development, could have been categorized not only as a work of sexology but also as one of many Western and Japanese works on theories about love. Indeed, texts that discussed love as a sign of advancement and a means to achieve male–female equality were becoming widely consumed at the time, and the new title might have been a means to tap into multiple publication trends of the day.[42]

It is difficult to draw an overarching conclusion about all of the different choices made in translating Carpenter's text and the terminology of the "intermediate sex." Translations are often arbitrary and contain mistakes; they also reflect unintended results that stem from quirks of the particular language. However, the fact that the Japanese translation systematically eliminates various sexological terms suggests intent to create distance from prior sexual associations. This, coupled with the unique nuances of the Japanese word *chūsei*, resulted in further deemphasizing sexual practice and high-lighting emotional intimacy and spiritual love. Perhaps it was important for the women who produced this work to distance themselves from medical sexology (a field dominated by men and perceived as focusing on pathology) even as many of Carpenter's essays engaged with sexological ideas. Certainly, the representation of the content as being about broader expressions and experiences of same-sex love helped protect the translator and publisher.[43] It bolstered Carpenter's original strategy for "rebranding" male–male inti-macy, while reinforcing the existing image of female same-sex love as pre-dominantly nonsexual in nature. In this way, the work ultimately added to the defense of same-sex relationships, particularly as positive means to de-velop female identity.

Translating "Affection in Education" in Japan

To show how Carpenter's ideas were used in broader Japanese discourses about female same-sex relationships and its positive, spiritual qualities, I will focus on how the famous Japanese popular fiction writer Yoshiya Nobuko (1896–1973) used one particular essay in *The Intermediate Sex* titled "Affection in Education."[44] This essay by Carpenter focuses not on the iden-tity of the intermediate sex but examines same-sex relationships that have been denigrated or viewed with suspicion. He defends same-sex friendships in schools, particularly between older and younger boys and in the mentor-ing between teachers and pupils; he also critiques the British school system's lack of open discussion and education about sexual matters. Carpenter uses the model of ancient Greece to suggest that affection in schools is critical for successful human development and social progress, and he criticizes educa-tors who see only sexual dangers in such relationships. He argues that for op-timal physical and mental growth, "purity (in the sense of continence) *is* of the first importance to boyhood" and suggests that ideal affection, "whether to the one sex or the other—springs up normally in the youthful mind in a quite diffused, ideal, emotional form—a kind of longing and amazement as at something divine—with no definite thought of distinct consciousness of sex in it."[45] By emphasizing innocence, Carpenter is able to promote male bonding. His main focus is male–male relationships, but he suggests at the end of the essay that prejudicial views toward such attachments also exist in girls' schools. Unlike boys, girls are "encouraged by public opinion" to cultivate friendships, but due to similar repressive elements in schools, these friendships "are for the most part . . . of a weak and sentimental turn, and not very healthy either in themselves or in the habits they lead to."[46]

This essay is very much part of the broader sexological inquiry regard-ing the distinction between what is normal and abnormal for same-sex attachments. In terms of emotional and/or physical intimacy and questions of inversion, adolescence was particularly a difficult time about which to make a definite determination. Carpenter validates innocent "healthy affection" in youth as "the basis of education" and an important component for maturation for both the individual and society at large.[47] This argument in "Affection in Education" contributes to Carpenter's broader aim: to elevate male same-sex relationships, often through evocation of Hellenic civilization and Greek love.[48]

It may be, therefore, quite surprising and unexpected that in Japan this work was used to defend schoolgirl same-sex intimacy. Similar to the many other kinds of female romantic friendships around the world, such manifestations in Japan were linked to the emergence of single-sex schools. Sexologists worldwide discussed the nature of such relationships in adolescence as platonic or sexual, as positive or harmful, as temporary or terminal, as an essential part of femininity (such as affection and nurturing impulse) or an inverted expression of masculinity. Although it is difficult to generalize, many sexologists viewed these romantic friendships as "normal." Havelock Ellis determines in his study of sexual inversion that such relationships are temporary and platonic and do not count as "congenital perversion," and Japanese sexologist Habuto Eiji notes in his 1920 *Ippan seiyokugaku* (General sexology) that this type of same-sex attachment in adolescence is a normal part of the growth process toward heterosexual maturation.[49]

Such "scientific" determination about female same-sex intimacy helped add legitimacy to a thriving world of girls' culture, represented by popular girls' magazines and the literary genre of "girls' fiction" (*shōjo shōsetsu*), featuring female–female romance often set in schools. This is not to say that all sexological discourse saw such adolescent affection as normal, platonic, or harmless, but sexology's views of such intimacy as "normal" provided yet another level of sanction to female same-sex love already associated with innocence and emotional closeness. Girls' culture in general emphasized purity, as can be seen in girls' magazines, generic plots of girls' fiction, and even in the famous motto of Takarazuka, the all-female revue troupe: "pure, righteous and beautiful" (*kiyoku, tadashiku, utsukushiku*).[50]

Yoshiya Nobuko, a successful popular literature writer, was at the heart of this girls' culture.[51] By the late 1910s and early 1920s she was already well established as a best-selling author of girls' fiction. Because of her "unusual" lifestyle (not marrying but living with a lifelong female partner) and her exceptional literary and financial success, Yoshiya remained a prominent figure into the 1970s. Although often viewed only as a "popular writer," she actively engaged with important areas of cultural knowledge such as sexology and feminist debates while working within a variety of literary genres.[52]

Hanamonogatari (Flower tales, 1916–1924), Yoshiya's representative best-selling girls' fiction, featured romantic friendships between girls and/ or women. These short melodramatic stories are not simply a reiteration of broader girls' culture (or a reflection of Yoshiya's own identity and values), they are also complex cultural expressions that explore various views and discourses about girlhood, including sexology.[53] A typical plot revolves around a student–student or student–teacher romance or crush often in a school setting; the stories are sentimental, usually featuring unrequited love or a melancholic end to relationships through death, illness, physical separation, marriage, or graduation. Because of their focus on pure, emotional intimacy and the containment of same-sex love as only a girlhood phenomenon, these stories can be read as part of acceptable mainstream values, stressing girlhood romance as innocent, beautiful, and ultimately ephemeral. On the other hand, they can also be interpreted as having radical implications, expressing resistance to mandated maturity into heterosexuality and rejecting the ideal identity of Good Wife, Wise Mother that was common currency in Japan at this time.[54] It is important to note that these stories are quite varied in terms of setting and tone; some are simple decorative vignettes, while others seem to have a deeper message. Some persuade girls to be virtuous and pure; others challenge social conventions of marriage and express desire for a same-sex partnership.[55] While keeping the broad range of explorations of same-sex intimacy in *Hanamonogatari* in mind, it is important to see that these stories actively negotiate complicity and resistance in their content and literary style, questioning the status quo but at the same time reiterating the idea of a "pure," nonsexual expression of youthful same-sex love.

Yoshiya also wrote essays about girlhood and was regularly interviewed in the media as an important advocate for girls and the world of girls' culture. In a 1921 essay titled "Aishiau kotodomo" (What it means to love each other), she specifically discusses her views on female same-sex love.[56] There is also a longer version of this essay titled "Dōsei o aisuru saiwai" (The happiness of loving another of the same sex), published in *Akogare shiru koro* (A time of knowing longing), a 1923 collection of Yoshiya's early writings.[57] In both the 1921 and 1923 versions of the essays, Yoshiya defends same-sex romantic friendships in schools as an important element of girls' education and development, using ideas from Carpenter's "Affection in Education"; in the 1921 essay, she specifically mentions Carpenter's name and his work.[58] As someone who had studied English texts in her youth, it is possible she read the original, but it is more likely that she had access to the Japanese translation (either through *Safuran* or the book version), titled "Aijō no kyōiku" (The education of love).[59]

In the 1921 essay "What it means to love each other," Yoshiya explains Carpenter's views on "*yūai*" (love between friends), applying them directly to the specific context of girls' schools in Japan: "When it happens between an older girl and a younger girl, or when it happens between a teacher and student, it is extremely beneficial in terms of educational value and its worth is immeasurable." The youth worships the elder and copies her actions, and the older individual is moved by this to become her "protector and helper"; such a relationship is important for developing "a beautiful, moral, social and non-self-centered character." Also, following Carpenter's lead, Yoshiya criticizes educators who reject such relationships as "unnatural" or "the first step to corruption," and who are unable to see the benefit of such love as "a glorious foundation" of human development. Such suppression by educators, Yoshiya explains, makes girls "doubt their own love" and contributes negatively to their growth as individuals.[60] In the longer 1923 version, direct reference to Carpenter is erased, but Yoshiya uses his strategy of drawing on the ancient Greeks, saying that this love was legally protected and acknowledged by them. She then adds a rather interesting twist, suggesting that such protection must have been afforded to others, "not just to groups of young girls."[61] In other words, she takes Carpenter's use of ancient Greek love to legitimate male–male intimacy and knowingly "translates" this tactic in a context where female–female love was very much in the media spotlight. Carpenter's primary focus and message are transformed, while his arguments and rhetoric to defend same-sex relationships are directly utilized.

In both essays, Yoshiya does not touch upon the negative elements of female attachments mentioned by Carpenter. Actually, the Japanese translation of *The Intermediate Sex* shows some change from the 1914 serialized journal version to the 1919 book version; the earlier translation of Carpenter's criticism of friendships in girls' schools is fairly close to the original, but in the book version, which would have reached a broader audience (and perhaps would have been subject to greater scrutiny by the censors), the translation is more vague, avoiding the earlier definition of these relationships and their results as being "unable to be called very healthy"[62] and only elusively stating that they are "unable to be called quite perfect."[63] But even if Yoshiya was not aware of such translation issues, it is clear that she ignored Carpenter's negative presentation of female–female intimacy and instead adapted his positive arguments about male–male attachments. In both the 1921 and 1923 essays, Yoshiya's fundamental premise is that girls' school relationships are nonphysical and beneficial; Yoshiya expresses her wish that these emotions of love, intrinsic to virginal purity, be recognized and valued by society.[64]

To be clear, Yoshiya was not burdened with the need to defend same-sex intimacy in schools with the same sort of vigilance and care required of Carpenter writing about similar male relationships. During the early twentieth century, some girls' schools specifically discouraged friendships between older and younger students, but by the 1920s many educators and sexologists suggested that love between schoolgirls was harmless, in distinction to the immoral sexual practices between boys.[65] In many ways, schoolgirl same-sex romance became an accepted part of girls' culture, particularly if it manifested itself through girlhood-associated virtues of selflessness and purity. Yet this did not mean that it was never viewed with suspicion or worry, as something that could be pure but dangerous (leading to suicide or eventual manifestation as inversion), or an extension of the disease that was female adolescence itself. Sexologists and educators throughout the prewar period extensively discussed what was normal or abnormal in girlhood same-sex relationships, as they tried to understand identity in terms of gender, sexuality, developmental stage, class, and social context—a whole new realm of categories with which to conceptualize the modern Japanese.

In her essays, Yoshiya uses Carpenter's authority as a known theorist of love, adapting his argument in order to enhance legitimacy for same-sex love. In effect, she defends her own melodramatic literary productions that dramatize these relationships; she is suggesting that her own works are not vacuous or detrimental but have educational value for teaching girls about this innocent love suitable in their stage of maturity. In her girls' fiction, Yoshiya consistently emphasizes the fundamental nature of this love as transitional, terminal, and "pure"—ideas enhanced by the authoritative worldview of sexology—and in this way she enabled herself to explore themes that otherwise would have been viewed with disapproval or suspicion, including the rejection of marriage and the prioritizing of same-sex relationships. Later, she would go on to use sexological terminology and ideas in examining adult inversion in the context of nonsexual romance in her privately published magazine for a select, older readership.[66]

Conclusion

Yoshiya's use of Carpenter shows how the transformation and dissemination of Western sexological concepts often occurred in unexpected ways. This was, as demonstrated, also very much the case for the Japanese translation and publication of *The Intermediate Sex*. In translating this collection of Carpenter's essays, the primary motivating factor was not to advocate for inverts or to promote male–male relationships, but most likely to present a work by a British socialist well known in Japan and to address the rising interest in female same-sex love. The way in which most of the established sexological terms for inversion were erased in the translation, and the emphasis on purity or asexuality created by the neologism *chūsei*, also underscore the different concerns and nuances of the Japanese text. However, despite such differences, these examples of Carpenter's translation and transmission very much highlight the notion of a coeval modernity. Here, we see how similar ideas and methods were used in both the West and Japan to articulate and defend same-sex relationships through the limited vocabulary and venues of the times.

Just as Carpenter relied on the notions of love and intimacy to create new positive ways of articulating inversion as well as male–male camaraderie, Yoshiya emphasized the purity and positive aspects of female–female romance, successfully establishing its key role for the development of modern female identity during the period. If we approach *The Intermediate Sex* from a twenty-first-century perspective, the erasure or undermining of physical sexuality is one-sided, but we can see how ideas of love and affection, and proscribed values such as purity and sexual innocence, were deployed in ways to speak in code about same-sex relationships, transform established negative notions, and create resistant viewpoints. Yoshiya also strategically used the notion of a pure, nonsexual intimacy to question and challenge the status quo in a variety of ways. This is a powerful reminder that sexological views were influential not only in examining the "abnormal," but also in establishing "normal" spaces from which to safely articulate unexplored identities, lifestyles, and relationships.

In this chapter, then, I have examined the translation and uses of *The Intermediate Sex* in Japan, not only to show the unexpected ways in which sexology traveled around the globe, but also to demonstrate how similar practices and challenges were part of creating legitimacy for same-sex love and developing gender identities. By pursuing the specificities of the transmission and adaptation of Carpenter's text beyond Euro-American boundaries, we can consider new possibilities in mapping the development of sexological discourse and knowledge during the early twentieth century.

NOTES

All Japanese translations are mine. Cited Japanese publications are published in Tokyo.

1. Saitō Hikaru, "*Hentai seiyoku shinri* kaisetsu," in *Hentai seiyoku to kindai shakai* 1, vol. 2 of *Kindai Nihon no sekushuariti*, ed. Saitō Hikaru (Yumani Shobō, 2006), 4–6. According to Saitō (6), the 1913 translation was probably based on the 12th, 13th, or 14th edition.

2. Heike Bauer, *English Literary Sexology: Translations of Inversion, 1860–1930* (Basingstoke, UK: Palgrave Macmillan, 2009), esp. 73–81. For Carpenter's biographical information, see Edward Carpenter, *My Days and Dreams* (London: Allen and Unwin, 1916); Sheila Rowbotham, *Edward Carpenter: A Life of Liberty and Love* (London: Verso, 2008); Sheila Rowbotham, "Edward Carpenter: Prophet of the New Life," in *Socialism and the New Life: The Personal and Sexual Politics of Edward Carpenter and Havelock Ellis*, ed. Sheila Rowbotham and Jeffrey Weeks (London: Pluto Press, 1977), 25–138; Chushichi Tsuzuki, *Edward Carpenter 1844–1929: Prophet of Human Fellowship* (Cambridge: Cambridge University Press, 1980).

3. See Chushichi Tsuzuki, "'My Dear Sanshiro': Edward Carpenter and His Japanese Disciple," *Hitotsubashi Journal of Social Studies* 6, no. 1 (whole number 6) (1972): 1; Rowbotham, *Edward Carpenter*, 348.

4. Ishikawa Sanshirō, *Tetsujin Kaapentaa* (Tōundō, 1912), 1–300, facsimile reprint in *Ishikawa Sanshirō senshū*, vol. 5 (Kokushoku Sensensha, 1983). The correspondences between Ishikawa and Carpenter (from 1909) are collected in *Ishikawa Sanshirō chosakushū*, vol. 7 (Seidosha, 1979). On their relationship, including meetings in London and Millthorpe, see "Ishikawa Sanshirō nenpu," in *Ishikawa Sanshirō chosakushū*, 7:406–408; Tsuzuki, "'My Dear Sanshiro,'" 1–9; Rowbotham, *Edward Carpenter*, 348–350, 399; Carpenter, *My Days and Dreams*, 276–279.

5. Japanese translations of *Love's Coming of Age* that I have been able to examine (including the 1921 version) do not include the essay "The Intermediate Sex," first included in the 1906 Swan Sonnenschein edition. On this 1906 edition, see Rowbotham, *Edward Carpenter*, 281.

6. Edward Carpenter, "Prefatory Note to First Edition," in *The Intermediate Sex: A Study of Some Transitional Types of Men and Women* (London: Allen and Unwin, 1930), 7.

7. Rowbotham, *Edward Carpenter*, 282.

8. Bauer, *English Literary Sexology*, 78; Rowbotham, *Edward Carpenter*, 283.

9. Rowbotham, *Edward Carpenter*, 283.

10. Rowbotham, "Edward Carpenter," 98.

11. See Bauer, *English Literary Sexology*, 79.

12. Edowaado Kaapentaa [Edward Carpenter], "Chūseiron," trans. Aoyama Kikue, is serialized in *Safuran* 1, no. 3 (1914): 1–22; no. 4 (1914): 130–153; no. 5 (1914): 55–76. Facsimile reprints appear in *Safuran*, 2 vols. (Fuji Shuppan, 1984).

13. The book's foreword explains that both Ward's and Carpenter's texts are "materials with which to study the problem of both sexes." Sakai Toshihiko, "Hashigaki," in Resutaa Wōdo [Lester Ward] and Edowaado Kaapentaa [Edward Carpenter], *Josei chūshinsetsu to Dōseiai*, trans. Sakai Toshihiko and Yamakawa Kikue (Arususha, 1919), 2.

14. For English-language discussions of female same-sex love and sexology discourse in this period in Japan, see, for example, Gregory M. Pflugfelder, "'S' Is for Sister: Schoolgirl Intimacy and 'Same-Sex Love' in Early Twentieth-Century Japan," in *Gendering Modern Japanese History*, ed. Barbara Molony and Kathleen Uno (Cambridge, MA: Harvard University Asia Center, 2005), 133–190; Jennifer Robertson, "Dying to Tell: Sexuality and Suicide in Imperial Japan," *Signs: Journal of Women in Culture and Society* 25, no. 1 (1999): 1–35; Michiko Suzuki, "Writing Same-Sex Love: Sexology and Literary Representation in Yoshiya Nobuko's Early Fiction," *Journal of Asian Studies* 65, no. 3 (2006): 575–599; Michiko Suzuki, *Becoming Modern Women: Love and Female Identity in Prewar Japanese Literature and Culture* (Stanford, CA: Stanford University Press, 2010), 23–33.

15. Erisu [Ellis], "Joseikan no dōsei ren'ai," trans. Nomo, foreword by Hiratsuka Raichō, *Seitō* 4, no. 4 (1914): furoku 1–24. For the original English text, see Havelock Ellis, *Studies in the Psychology of Sex* (New York: Random House, 1942), 1:195–263.

16. Pflugfelder, "'S' Is for Sister," 169. See also 165–169.

17. "Henshūshitsu nite," *Safuran* 1, no. 3 (1914): 157–158, facsimile reprint in *Safuran*, vol. 1. Also see Pflugfelder's translations and discussion in "'S' Is for Sister," 168–169.

18. For this term, see Furukawa Makoto, "Dōsei 'ai' kō," *Imago* 6, no. 12 (1995): 205–207.

19. See "Yamakawa Kikue chosaku mokuroku," in *Yamakawa Kikue no kōseki: Watashi no undōshi to chosaku mokuroku*, ed. Sotozaki Mitsuhiro and Okabe Masako (Domesu Shuppan, 1979), 99.

20. See Edowaado Kaapentaa [Edward Carpenter], *Ren'ai ron*, trans. Yamakawa Kikue (Daitōkaku, 1921), facsimile reprint as Mizuta Tamae, ed., *Sekai joseigaku kiso bunken shūsei (Meiji Taishō hen)*, vol. 13 (Yumani Shobō, 2001).

21. *Rekishi hyōron* henshūbu, ed., *Kindai Nihon joseishi e no shōgen: Yamakawa Kikue, Ichikawa Fusae, Maruyama Hideko, Tatewaki Sadayo* (Domesu Shuppan, 1979), 26–29. From the context of the interview, it is unclear which particular text she is discussing when she talks about Carpenter's general views and ideas.

22. For some examples, see Gregory M. Pflugfelder, *Cartographies of Desire: Male-Male Sexuality in Japanese Discourse 1600–1950* (Berkeley: University of California Press, 1999), 307.

23. We see a similar strategy in the 1914 translation of Ellis's "Sexual Inversion in Women," in *Seitō*. The Japanese title is rendered broadly as "Same sex love between women" (*Joseikan no dōsei ren'ai*) rather than using the specific sexological terminology of "sexual inversion" (*seiteki tentō*). This term is used in the text, but not in the title. For the 1913 editorial comment about censorship concerns regarding this text, see Yoshikawa Toyoko, "*Ren'ai to kekkon* (Ellen Key) to sekusorojii," in *Seitō o yomu*, ed. Shin feminizumu hihyō no kai (Gakugei Shorin, 1998), 257.

24. Carpenter, "Introductory," in *The Intermediate Sex*, 15.

25. Bauer, *English Literary Sexology*, 4.

26. For more on this term in Japan, see Pflugfelder, *Cartographies of Desire*, 259; Furukawa, "Dōsei 'ai' kō," 206.

27. Kaapentaa, "Chūseiron," *Safuran* 1, no. 4 (1914): 139; Kaapentaa, *Dōseiai*, in *Josei chūshinsetsu to Dōseiai*, 207.

28. Habuto Eiji, an important Japanese sexologist of the early twentieth century, differentiates the two terms for male and female in *Hentai seiyoku no kenkyū* (Gakugei Shoin, 1921), 193. Facsimile reprint in *Hentai seiyoku to kindai shakai* 2, vol. 3 of *Kindai Nihon no sekushuariti*, ed. Saitō Hikaru (Yumani Shobō, 2006). See also the explanations on *ūruningu* and *uranisumusu* that focus on sexuality and perversity in Satō Kōka, ed., "Seiyokugaku goi: Gekan," *Hentai shiryō*, vol. rinji tokubetsu gō (1927): 90–92. Facsimile reprint in *Hentai shiryō*, vol. 3, ed. Shimamura Teru (Yumani Shobō, 2006).

29. Rowbotham, *Edward Carpenter*, 283.

30. Bauer, *English Literary Sexology*, 75. She explains that Carpenter viewed "love between men or between women in Ulrichsian terms as an inversion of the soul" (73).

31. Kuzumi Kesson, "Kaapentaa shi no chūseikan," *Shin Shakai* 2, no. 5 (1916): 22.

32. See Pflugfelder, *Cartographies of Desire*, 249–250. For more on the Japan-Hirschfeld connection, see also 250, 259–260.

33. Perhaps another related term would have been *das dritte Geschlecht* (the third sex). See Furukawa, "Dōsei 'ai' kō," 202; Carolyn J. Dean, *Sexuality and Modern Western Culture* (New York: Twayne, 1996), 24.

34. Kuzumi, "Kaapentaa shi no chūseikan," 22.

35. *Gensen: Nihon daijiten*, vol. 3 (Ōkura Shoten, 1921), s.v. "sei."

36. Ibid., s.v. "chūsei."

37. *Kōjien*, 5th ed. (Iwanami Shoten, 2005), s.v. "chūsei." Additional meanings here also include "same as *kansei* (intersex)" and "nature that is neither positive nor negative in terms of electrical charge."

38. *Meikyō kokugo jiten* (Taishūkan Shoten, 2002–2004), s.v. "chūsei."

39. Kagawa Toyohiko, "Kyōyō aru fujin to kekkon nan no mondai: 1. Chūseika no kiken," *Fujin Kōron* 9, no. 6 (1924): 22–27.

40. Pflugfelder, "'S' Is for Sister," 141, 157.

41. Furukawa Makoto, "Sekushuariti no henyō: Kindai Nihon no dōseiai o meguru mittsu no kōdo," *Nichibei Josei Jaanaru* 17 (1994): 44; Furukawa, "Dōsei 'ai' kō," 206–207. Also see Pflugfelder for discussions of earlier male-oriented terms such as *nanshoku*. Pflugfelder, *Cartographies of Desire*, 23–44.

42. For more on such texts, see Suzuki, *Becoming Modern Women*.

43. The foreword to *Dōseiai* notes that translator Yamakawa does not necessarily agree with all the theories discussed in Carpenter's text. Sakai Toshihiko, "Hashigaki," 2. Pflugfelder notes this caveat in "'S' Is for Sister," 168. Although it is difficult to reconstruct Yamakawa's personal views, this can also be considered part of a strategy to avoid censorship and association with sexual pathology or homosexual activism.

44. Carpenter, "Affection in Education," in *The Intermediate Sex*, 83–106.

45. Ibid., 93.

46. Ibid., 105.

47. Ibid.

48. For Carpenter's and other writers' use of the idea of Greek love and civilization see Bauer, *English Literary Sexology*, 7, 77–78.

49. Havelock Ellis, *Sexual Inversion*, 3rd ed., revised and enlarged, vol. 2 of *Studies in the Psychology of Sex* (Philadelphia: Davis, 1924), 374; Habuto Eiji, *Kyōiku shiryō: Ippan seiyokugaku* (Jitsugyō No Nipponsha, 1921), 354. For more on the bifurcation of adolescent "pure" female same-sex love and adult "abnormal" female same-sex love, see Suzuki, "Writing Same-Sex Love"; Suzuki, *Becoming Modern Women*, 23–33.

50. On this motto, see Jennifer Robertson, *Takarazuka: Sexual Politics and Popular Culture in Modern Japan* (Berkeley: University of California Press, 1998), 151. For discussions of some areas of prewar Japanese girls' culture and notions of purity, see Kawamura Kunimitsu, *Otome no inori: Kindai josei imeeji no tanjō* (Kinokuniya Shoten, 1993); Kawamura Kunimitsu, *Otome no shintai: Onna no kindai to sexuariti* (Kinokuniya Shoten, 1994); Kume Yoriko, "Kōsei sareru 'shōjo': Meijiki 'shōjo shōsetsu' no janru keisei," *Nihon Kindai Bungaku* 68 (2003): 1–15; Satō (Sakuma) Rika, "'Kiyoki shijō de gokōsai o': Meiji makki shōjo zasshi tōshoran ni miru dokusha kyōdōtai no kenkyū," *Joseigaku* 4 (1996): 129–131; Watanabe Shūko, *'Shōjo' zō no tanjō: Kindai Nihon ni okeru 'shōjo' kihan no keisei* (Shinsensha, 2007); Suzuki, *Becoming Modern Women*, 34–42; Deborah Shamoon, *Passionate Friendship: The Aesthetics of Girls' Culture in Japan* (Honolulu: University of Hawai'i Press, 2012), 29–57.

51. For some recent works in English on Yoshiya Nobuko, see, for example, Suzuki, "Writing Same-Sex Love"; Suzuki, *Becoming Modern Women*, 23–62; Suzuki, *"The Husband's Chastity*: Progress, Equality, and Difference in 1930s Japan," *Signs: Journal of Women in Culture and Society* 38, no. 2 (2013): 327–352; Sarah Frederick, "Not That Innocent: Yoshiya Nobuko's Good Girls," in *Bad Girls of Japan*, ed. Laura Miller and

Jan Bardsley (New York: Palgrave Macmillan, 2005), 65–79; Hitomi Tsuchiya Dollase, "Early Twentieth Century Japanese Girls' Magazine Stories: Examining *Shōjo* Voice in *Hanamonogatari* (Flower Tales)," *Journal of Popular Culture* 36, no. 4 (2003): 724–755; Shamoon, *Passionate Friendship*, 58–81; Jennifer Robertson, "Yoshiya Nobuko: Out and Outspoken in Practice and Prose," in *The Human Tradition in Modern Japan*, ed. Anne Walthall (Wilmington, DE: Scholarly Resources, 2002), 155–174.

52. Suzuki, "Writing Same-Sex Love"; Suzuki, *Becoming Modern Women*, 23–62; Suzuki, *"Husband's Chastity."*

53. See Suzuki, "Writing Same-Sex Love," 575–586; Suzuki, *Becoming Modern Women*, 34–42.

54. For some examples of Japanese scholarship that initially pointed out the resistant or liberating aspect of *Hanamonogatari*, see Honda Masuko, *Ibunka to shite no kodomo* (Chikuma Shobō, 1992), 202–219; Kurosawa Ariko, "Shōjotachi no chikadōmei: Yoshiya Nobuko no *Onna no yūjō* o megutte," in *Onna to hyōgen: Feminizumu hihyō no genzai*, vol. 2 of *Nyū feminizumu rebuyū*, ed. Mizuta Noriko (Gakuyō Shobō, 1991), 87–88; Yoshitake Teruko, *Nyonin Yoshiya Nobuko* (Bungei Shunjū, 1982), 12; Komashaku Kimi, *Yoshiya Nobuko kakure feminisuto* (Liburoporto, 1994), 24–30.

55. See Yoshiya Nobuko, "Hanamonogatari," in *Yoshiya Nobuko zenshū*, vol. 1 (Asahi Shinbunsha, 1975), 3–356. "Kibara" (Yellow rose), from *Hanamonogatari*, has been translated into English. Yoshiya Nobuko, *Yellow Rose*, trans. Sarah Frederick (Expanded Editions, 2014), Kindle e-book. For discussion on this particular story, see Frederick's "Translator's Introduction," as well as Suzuki, "Writing Same-Sex Love," 583–586; Suzuki, *Becoming Modern Women*, 39–42.

56. Yoshiya Nobuko, "Aishiau kotodomo," *Shin Shōsetsu* (January 1921): 78–80, facsimile reprint in *Senzenki Dōseiai kanren bunken shūsei*, ed. Furukawa Makoto and Akaeda Kanako (Fuji Shuppan, 2006), 3:151. See Pflugfelder's analysis in "'S' Is for Sister," 163–165. This essay was also reprinted in Yoshiya Nobuko, *Shojo dokuhon* (Kenbunsha, 1936), 101–105, facsimile reprint as Yamazaki Tomoko, ed., *Shojo dokuhon*, vol. 35 of *Sōsho Joseiron* (Ōzorasha, 1997).

57. Yoshiya Nobuko, "Dōsei o aisuru saiwai," in *Akogare shirukoro* (Kōransha, 1923), 14–21.

58. See Yoshiya, "Aishiau kotodomo," 151; Yoshiya, *Shojo dokuhon*, 103. In the 1921 essay Yoshiya calls Carpenter's work "Ai no kyōiku" (The education of love). The use of Carpenter here has been noted in Pflugfelder, "'S' Is for Sister," 171; Suzuki, "Writing Same-Sex Love," 582; Suzuki, *Becoming Modern Women*, 37.

59. Kaapentaa, "Chūseiron," *Safuran* 1, no. 5 (1914): 55–65; Kaapentaa, *Dōseiai*, 227–241.

60. Yoshiya, "Aishiau kotodomo," 151; Yoshiya, *Shojo dokuhon*, 103–105.

61. Yoshiya, "Dōsei o aisuru saiwai," 19. The discussion about Greece is in Carpenter, "Affection in Education," 89–90; Kaapentaa, "Chūseiron," *Safuran* 1, no. 5 (1914): 58; Kaapentaa, *Dōseiai*, 231.

62. Kaapentaa, "Chūseiron," *Safuran* 1, no. 5 (1914): 65. For the original, see Carpenter, "Affection in Education," 105.

63. Kaapentaa, *Dōseiai*, 240.

64. For a different take on modern female same-sex love and its role in education (as essentially nonphysical in nature but something to be neither encouraged nor discour-

aged), see Furuya Toyoko, "Dōseiai no joshi kyōikujō ni okeru shin'igi," *Fujin Kōron* (August 1922): 24–29, facsimile reprint in *Senzenki Dōseiai kanren bunken shūsei*, 3:174–175. This essay by a female educator mentions Carpenter by name and engages with his ideas. See Pflugfelder, "'S' Is for Sister," 170–172.

65. See Numata Rippō, *Gendai shōjo to sono kyōiku* (Dōbunsha, 1916), 47–50, facsimile reprint as *Kindai Nihon joshi kyōiku bunkenshū*, vol. 15 (Nihon Tosho Sentaa, 1984); Sabine Frühstück, *Colonizing Sex: Sexology and Social Control in Modern Japan* (Berkeley: University of California Press, 2003), 70; Pflugfelder, "'S' Is for Sister," 148.

66. See Suzuki, "Writing Same-Sex Love," 586–593; Suzuki, *Becoming Modern Women*, 54–60.

II

Translation and the Construction of a "Uranian" Identity

Edward Prime-Stevenson's [Xavier Mayne's]
The Intersexes *(1908)*

JAMES P. WILPER

This chapter examines the role of translation in *The Intersexes: A History of Similisexualism as a Problem in Social Life* (1908). The study was written by one of the often-overlooked pioneers in the early twentieth-century homosexual rights movement, the American writer Edward Prime-Stevenson (1858–1942), who published it under the pseudonym Xavier Mayne.[1] Translation played an indispensable role in *The Intersexes*, which draws on and partly reproduces a wide range of cultural and scientific texts about sex. Margaret Breen, in a recent analysis of Prime-Stevenson's contribution to sexology, has turned to the role of translation in the work to argue that *The Intersexes* is "a mediating text" between the lay reader and the field of sexological research. "*The Intersexes* is not, from a medical or scholarly point of view, a significant study," she argues. "Taken as a cultural document, it is, however, useful," she continues, "because it offers insight into the importance of translation for late nineteenth- and early twentieth-century conceptualizations of homosexuality. As a metaphor, process, and act, translation not only facilitates but proves to be integral to Prime-Stevenson's discussion of homosexuality."[2]

This chapter extends Breen's research by paying closer attention to the actual translations of sexology in the study and exploring what they can tell us about Prime-Stevenson's own (dis)identifications with sexological literature. Following George Steiner, it conceptualizes the translation between languages that characterizes *The Intersexes* as an aggressive act, an "incursive and extractive" undertaking in which "the translator invades, extracts, and brings home" meaning.[3] In Steiner's reading, the translator is a sort of pillaging invader and the translated text is the spoils of war. This conception is useful for understanding the role of translation in *The Intersexes*, where Prime-Stevenson translated excerpts from a variety of Continental sexological texts on homosexuality: invading, extracting, and bringing home this knowledge, but selecting to represent only that which would further his liberationist aims. I argue that this often-overlooked text provides important insights into the ways in which sexological ideas were received and disseminated by laymen whose bodies and desires formed the subject of the *scientia sexualis*.

In what follows, I will explore the ways in which Prime-Stevenson transforms rather than translates German sexological research in a bid to defend "homosexualism" and construct a Uranian identity. I will focus here on the relationship between *The Intersexes* and Richard von Krafft-Ebing's *Psychopathia Sexualis* (first edition 1886), which is the text from which *The Intersexes* takes the most material. I show that the way in which Prime-Stevenson transforms rather than translates Krafft-Ebing's study is twofold: first, he extracts Krafft-Ebing's case histories from the theoretical framework of his study, and second, he produces what, in many cases, can only be described as highly selective translations of the case histories themselves, even by the standards of translation of the day. I argue that these translations of Krafft-Ebing's case histories can be characterized as an aggressive undertaking, in Steiner's terms, in that Prime-Stevenson reappropriates Krafft-Ebing's work for his own means. In the role of translator, Prime-Stevenson "invades, extracts, and brings home" that which will support his defense of homosexuality.[4] After a critical introduction, the chapter will consider Prime-Stevenson's writings and politics, briefly comparing them to similar efforts in Britain by John Addington Symonds and Edward Carpenter. I will then discuss Krafft-Ebing and his theories in order to highlight the ways in which Prime-Stevenson disregards these theories as he sources case histories from *Psychopathia Sexualis*, before concluding with a more detailed examination of those cases that demonstrate the greatest reworking. This analysis will show that translation played a crucial role in Prime-Stevenson's liberationist politics, enabling him to represent the "Uranian" affirmatively to the general public and to emerging homosexual communities themselves in an effort to contradict prevailing stereotypes by mobilizing the authority of Continental medical science. The chapter thus extends the boundaries of existing histories of sexology by revealing the important role played by Prime-Stevenson in shaping an affirmative male same-sex discourse.

Translation and Prime-Stevenson's Third Sex

Historians of sexology have paid considerable attention to the development of the *scientia sexualis* in Europe, including its relationship to issues of modern homosexual identity formation. Scholars have shown that modern ideas about sexuality were shaped as much in and through literary and cultural texts as they were the products of distinct scientific ventures. Because the pioneers of sexology in Britain, as Heike Bauer argues, "approached the study of sex exclusively or at least partially from non-scientific backgrounds," they were able to enrich sexological discourse by fusing it with cultural-historical discourses.[5] And yet relatively few literary texts and figures are discussed in this context, most frequently John Addington Symonds, Edward Carpenter, and Havelock Ellis. Prime-Stevenson's *The Intersexes* substantively extends understanding of male same-sex discourse formation and its reception. The work was first published in Naples, Italy, in a small run of 125 copies; Prime-Stevenson took it upon himself to distribute his defense of homosexuality, sending copies to many of Europe's and America's most important libraries, including the Library of the British Museum and Magnus Hirschfeld's *Institut für Sexualwissenschaft* (Institute for Sexual Science).[6] A writer and music critic, he lived in Europe, in self-imposed exile from America, from around 1900. In 1906, also as Xavier Mayne, he privately published *Imre: A Memorandum*, one of the first novels to treat love between two men openly and end happily for its two gay protagonists, Oswald and Imre. It is a novel that, similarly to the study *The Intersexes*, translates sexological terms, concepts, and knowledge selectively for nonscientific audiences.

The Intersexes was not highly regarded by contemporary reviewers. Havelock Ellis, for instance, writing in *Sexual Inversion*, deemed it "subjective and scarcely scientific."[7] For my inquiry here, it is precisely the novel's subjective and nonscientific aspects that are of interest. The scope of *The Intersexes* is broad to the point of being somewhat dilettantish. The preface to the work presents it as making research into homosexuality accessible to an English-speaking, nonspecialist readership, as these studies "are not primarily in English."[8] Prime-Stevenson, though, considered his project "a very full, carefully systematized, minutely complete History of Homosexualism." In 1906, in a letter to his friend and literary executor, Paul Elmer More, he writes:

> There is nothing of the sort in English—in spite of numerous contributions towards this or that aspect, by English-writing psychiaters of more of less weight. For, such larger things as those by Havelock Ellis and John Addington Symonds, or the late Dr. Hammond are far from adequate; dealing with pathologic conditions, with only

limited "typic" aspects, and are too much from and for exclusively a professional-psychiatric standpoint. Even in German, French, Italian, Russian, etc., where the literature of homosexual study is enormous nowadays, there is no work covering the scope of my book.[9]

This passage indicates that while Prime-Stevenson certainly knew about Ellis and Symonds's *Sexual Inversion* (1897), the study's liberationist bent was lost on him. As well, it shows that he was not acquainted with Carpenter's writings. Despite there being distinct parallels observable between Prime-Stevenson's study and Carpenter's *The Intermediate Sex* (also published in 1908), it is unlikely that the former had read the earlier work of the latter. Sean Brady writes that until "Homogenic Love" was published as a chapter in *Love's Coming of Age* in 1906, Carpenter's explicitly homosexual writings would have been unavailable to those outside his circle.[10] Both Prime-Stevenson's *The Intersexes* and Carpenter's *The Intermediate Sex* translate the concept of the third sex into English as a same-sex gender and sexual orientation, citing and reprinting excerpts from many of the same sources, including Karl Heinrich Ulrichs, Otto de Joux, Hirschfeld, Krafft-Ebing, and others. Carpenter had read *Imre* and quotes it in the appendix of *The Intermediate Sex*.[11] The similarity between the two activists, as I argue elsewhere, is likely due to the fact that they were drawing similar conclusions from the same body of sources.[12]

What is distinct about Prime-Stevenson's contribution compared to the work of Carpenter and others is that Prime-Stevenson extensively reworked existing sexological literature. As he was not a physician, he did not possess the necessary credentials to be taken seriously as a sexologist. Ivan Crozier writes that in the early years of the discipline "there was a necessity to be a doctor to speak about sex credibly." He explains that Ellis, for instance, "became a doctor specifically so he could write about sex."[13] Thus, unlike other studies, which Prime-Stevenson writes "are too much from and for exclusively a professional-psychiatric standpoint," his *Intersexes*, like Symonds's *A Problem in Modern Ethics* (1891) and Carpenter's *The Intermediate Sex*, would move sexology beyond the medical sphere. *The Intersexes* does include seven full and five partial original case histories of homosexual and bisexual men and women, which Prime-Stevenson collected or which were offered to him, so he states, by practicing physicians. There is no reason to doubt Prime-Stevenson's assertion that these are genuine case histories. Therefore it is unfortunate that he is not given credit for this modest but real contribution to sexual science.

The Intersexes shows that Prime-Stevenson was well read in sexological research. For instance, in chapter 2, which explains the foundation for this study, he discusses a theory of gender/sexuality that clearly draws from Hirschfeld's theory of sexual intermediaries. Sex is not determined by the body, argues Prime-Stevenson, but rather "sex is determined by the sexual instinct; by the desire physical and psychical, of one human being for another, no matter what his or her body aspect and other endowment" (18). Although, he writes, sexologists have charted subtle grades of sexuality, he proposes for the purposes of his study four distinct sexes: those of man, woman, Uranian, and Uraniad, the latter two being homosexual men and women, respectively (18–19). *The Intersexes* is clearly indebted to Ulrichs and Hirschfeld for its conceptual foundation, and yet it is not from these two theorists that Prime-Stevenson sources and translates the most material, but rather from Krafft-Ebing's *Psychopathia Sexualis*. Attention to Prime-Stevenson's reappropriation of Krafft-Ebing's work shows that the American author deliberately reworked Krafft-Ebing's scientific case studies into narratives that fit better his own liberationist conception of male same-sex sexuality.

Pillaging Krafft-Ebing's *Psychopathia Sexualis*

Psychopathia Sexualis is the single largest source of sexological material for *The Intersexes*. Prime-Stevenson attributes fourteen of the case histories to Krafft-Ebing: ten men and four women. Eleven of those can be found in the twelfth edition of *Psychopathia Sexualis*, the final edition to be edited by Krafft-Ebing personally.[14] While, in twenty-first-century terms, Prime-Stevenson's debts to Krafft-Ebing may seem close to plagiarism, early twentieth-century sexologists typically borrowed and reworked each other's ideas and sources. It was not uncommon, for example, for sexologists, particularly in the early years of the discipline, to reprint case histories published by other researchers.[15] Hence, similarity is a reflection of the fact that early sex research drew on similar sources and ideas. However, *The Intersexes* is unusual in that it borrows a particularly large amount of material from *Psychopathia Sexualis*. Prime-Stevenson himself acknowledged this debt, noting that he had discussed his project with Krafft-Ebing.[16] While Prime Stevenson acknowledged Krafft-Ebing's influence by dedicating *The Intersexes* to the sexologist, the work itself for the most part disregards Krafft-Ebing's theoretical framework for the study of homosexuality.

Krafft-Ebing developed a distinct, binary understanding of sexual behaviors, which helped him make a case for the "naturalness" of some sexual acts while dismissing others. In *Psychopathia Sexualis* he draws a distinction between *Perversität* (perversity) and *Perversion* (perversion), the former being a form of acquired vice, whereas the latter was an inborn form of non-normative sexuality. Early in his career, Krafft-Ebing regarded congenital homosexuality as "a functional sign of degeneration" that was linked to other manifestations of hereditary degeneration, such as various neuroses, psychoses, and illnesses.[17] But, as Harry Oosterhuis, Heike Bauer, and Heinrich Ammerer have shown in their work on Krafft-Ebing, as he began to have contact with a broader range of homosexual individuals, he eventually came to view same-sex sexuality as a natural anomaly.[18] Heinrich Ammerer explains: "Krafft-Ebing's relationship with homosexuality transformed between his first treatise in 1877 and his death. From an interested, but clinically neutral, observer, he became an advocate for homosexuals who campaigned with a great deal of empathy for their exemption from punishment."[19] Krafft-Ebing signed Magnus Hirschfeld's petition to amend laws forbidding sex between men, and, in his last piece of writing on homosexuality, which was published in the third edition of Hirschfeld's *Jahrbuch für sexuelle Zwischenstufen* in 1901, he rejected his earlier degenerative hypothesis, arguing that same-sex desire was a fixed orientation that should be viewed neither as vice nor as sickness.[20] Despite the more progressive attitude the Austrian psychiatrist adopted, his is not the theory of homosexuality presented by Prime-Stevenson in his book.

When comparing *The Intersexes* against *Psychopathia Sexualis* it is difficult to tell at first why Prime-Stevenson chose some case histories over others. He draws his case histories of men from the homosexual and effeminate subcategories, while, for women, he draws one from psychical hermaphroditism, two from homosexuality, and one from gynandry. However, Prime-Stevenson largely disregards Krafft-Ebing's distinctions, and the similarities between the two texts become apparent only on close comparison. For instance, a minor similarity is that Prime-Stevenson tends toward shorter case histories. Those that are longer, for instance three of the four case histories of women that he selects and translates, appear abridged in a manner that emphasizes certain aspects of the histories, which support the claims that he makes at the particular point in the study in which these cases fit. The longest and most detailed cases in his study are his original contributions. The average length of the case histories from *Psychopathia Sexualis* is 350 words, the shortest being 160 and the longest 530, whereas his original cases are more than twice that in length. Hence, it seems that Krafft-Ebing's cases act as supporting or backup material for his own contributions. This is further reinforced by the order in which he presents his evidence. In chapter 5, in which he treats homosexuality in men, he presents the case of B. R—— (89–96), which is then immediately followed by four cases attributed to Krafft-Ebing (97–100). Chapter 6, in which he discusses female homosexuality, is similar in format: he first presents the case of Miss A—— (129–133), which is followed directly by three cases from other sources, one of which is from Krafft-Ebing, the case of S. J—— (133–134). Prime-Stevenson thus selects a supporting cast of homosexual men and women, recruiting their life stories in his effort to bring about social change.

The greatest similarity between the cases that Prime-Stevenson sources from *Psychopathia Sexualis* (*PS*) is that they all represent some of the "healthiest" and most "normal" of Krafft-Ebing's subjects. For example, Mr. Z—— (533–534), which is observation 138 in *PS* (260–261 [German edition]; 242 [English edition]) is described by Krafft-Ebing as "an intellectual man and a fine-feeling one; outwardly thoroughly manly, of normal education" (534).[21] The case of another example, Mr. E—— (99–100), observation 147 in *PS* (271–272 [German edition]; 254–255 [English edition]), demonstrates that Uranians aspire to mainstream norms, domesticating the homosexual couple via their emulation of heterosexual ideals: "He lives now, since some time back, with a man of like age, the two keeping house together as 'man and wife'" (100).[22] Even a case that Prime-Stevenson meant to represent degenerate forms of homosexuality, that of Mr. C—— (106–107), which is observation 148 in *PS* (272–273 [German edition]; 255 [English edition]), is that of a man who, although he is nervous and effeminate and has a family history of mental illness, possesses considerable aesthetic endowments: "C—— was talented in music, poetry, and interested himself in the theater" (116).[23] Bias in *The Intersexes* takes the form of Prime-Stevenson's preference for those who would reiterate rather than contradict his claims that Uranians are not degenerates, that they represent "a super-virile, not sub-virile, sex" (187). And, as I demonstrate in the next section, when a useful case deviated from normality, Prime-Stevenson as translator brought the subject back to the straight and narrow.

From *Psychopathia Sexualis* to *The Intersexes*

Apart from the selective nature of his translations and his strategic omissions, Prime-Stevenson's German may not have been up to the task of translating accurately the case studies from *Psychopathia Sexualis*. For instance, among other small errors, on a few occasions he mistranslates the German word *Geschwister*, which means "sibling(s)," as "sister" (which is actually *Schwester*). In this case, the error is certainly the result of mistake. However, with some instances of small omissions and errors, it is not clear whether or not they are intentional. For instance, in the case of Mr. E—— (99–100), which is observation 147 in *PS* (271–272 [German edition]; 254–255 [English edition]), he mistranslates the Latin in a passage. The source reads that the subject was "*Sohn eines potator strenuus*" (271), whereas Prime-Stevenson writes that E—— "is the son of a father exceedingly potent sexually" (99), which is translated more accurately by Franklin Klaf as "son of an inveterate drunkard" (254). Either Prime-Stevenson was unfamiliar with this Latin expression or he wished to disassociate this subject from alcoholism and its association with hereditary degeneration. The same might be the case for a mistranslation in the case of B—— (117–119), which is observation 149 in *PS* (273–274 [German edition]; 255–257 [English edition]), where he renders the term "*mannsüchtig*" (273) as "a sexual aversion to men" (118) when it actually means the exact opposite. It may have been more acceptable, in light of the emancipationist aim of the study, for the subject to have a "frigid" sister rather than one who was a "nymphomaniac." These and other minor deviations may be, or may not be, the result of mere human error on Prime-Stevenson's part. Greater discrepancies emerge at other points, however, that cannot be written off as mere error. In what follows I discuss four case histories, those of Mr. P—— (534–535), Mrs. R—— (550–551), B—— (117–119), and Mrs. M—— (551–552), which show, I argue, that Prime-Stevenson deliberately transformed Krafft-Ebing's text.

According to information provided in the case study, Mr. P——, observation 144 in *PS* (264–265 [German edition]; 246 [English edition]), was a thirty-seven-year-old man who married to try to "re-orientate" himself toward women. In order to consummate his marriage, he would imagine he was with a young man, but after two years his imagination began failing him, and he "returned to his homosexual intimacies" (535).[24] Prime-Stevenson translates the case history accurately, with two notable exceptions. First, while Krafft-Ebing recounts in German that P—— enjoyed seeing other men's genitals ("beim Anblick ihrer Genitalien sich sehr aufgeregt" [264]), Prime-Stevenson renders the fact in Latin in his English version as follows: "With adspic. genitalia much excitement" (534). While this keeps the meaning of the German sentence, the addition of Latin here disrupts the narrative at the point when the sexual transgression is mentioned. The use of Latin is one of the generic conventions of sexological literature. It is typically deployed by sexologists such as Krafft-Ebing to describe explicit sexual acts, ostensibly to make them less accessible to lay readers, although, as Renate Hauser and others have pointed out, this strategy proved to be ineffective.[25] Given that Prime-Stevenson's work aimed to make sexology more accessible to an English-speaking, nonscientific readership, it seems odd that he mostly leaves untranslated Krafft-Ebing's Latin expressions. I argue that Prime-Stevenson's use of Latin had a deliberate function that was distinct from Krafft-Ebing's exclusive scientific project. Where Krafft-Ebing used Latin to obscure his ideas for a lay readership, Prime-Stevenson's use of Latin distanced the reader from the actual practice in a bid to make the case seem more presentable and thus better fit to an overtly reform-driven study.

The second change occurs at the end of the case where Prime-Stevenson makes some changes and omissions that markedly affect the tone of the case, specifically in the account of how P——was apprehended by the police for an act of mutual masturbation with another man in public. Krafft-Ebing writes:

> For two years he avoided coitus, resumed his homosexual practices and was apprehended by the police in the act of mutual masturbation with a young man. He pleaded that prolonged sexual abstinence had unduly excited him when he saw the genitals of a man and in his confusion he had yielded to the impulse. There was no amnesia. Thoroughly virile. Decent appearance. (246)[26]

In contrast, Prime-Stevenson renders this passage as follows:

> After two years, he has now returned to his homosexual intimacies, such as masturb. mut. with a young man (in a public place!). He excuses this last incident by the fact that through his long abstinence from homosexual relations he was wholly thrown off his guard by adspic. genitalia ...... Mr. P—— has a thoroughly virile exterior, a decorous personality; genitalia normal. (535)

While the differences between these two accounts are not huge, they are effective. Prime-Stevenson once again renders in Latin what Krafft-Ebing's German observation on what happens when P—— sees male genitals. Furthermore, although he does not omit that P—— engaged in masturbation with another man in public, the way in which he presents this information seems to deemphasize it. Not only does Krafft-Ebing's Latin expression remain untranslated, but he abbreviates it: "masturb. mut." versus "inter masturbationem mutuam." Prime-Stevenson brackets the location where the act was committed in parenthesis, adding an exclamation mark that emphasizes the unacceptable public nature of the place where P—— chose to masturbate. Prime-Stevenson entirely omits the fact that this act of public indecency led to a *"Kurze Freiheitsstrafe"* (short prison sentence). These changes make the account of the case fit better Prime-Stevenson's liberationist project, for one of his main aims was to alter public opinion and achieve penal reform. Admitting that Uranians did even occasionally have such scrapes with the law might jeopardize this aim, and his addition of brackets and an exclamation mark seems to visually highlight the danger of such public transgression.

That Prime-Stevenson was invested in a politics of positive representation of same-sex sexuality is further indicated by his translation of the case of Mrs. R——, which is observation 157 (290–291 [German edition]; 271–273 [English edition]), a thirty-five-year-old woman who was unhappily married to a man. Owing to the latter fact, Prime-Stevenson includes her case history in chapter 11 of *The Intersexes*, "The Uranian and Uraniad in Relation

to Marriage as a 'Cure' for Similisexualism." In Prime-Stevenson's translation, she comes across as an intelligent woman, who, because of her talent
in music and languages, became a governess. At age twenty-eight, she met
a woman five years younger than herself with whom she began a sexual
relationship that lasted four years and ended when the younger partner was
married off. She then entered into a marriage with a wealthy man who loved
her, but without knowing what she was getting herself into. "The result has
been unfortunate. She grew deeply depressed, morally, by coitus. She had
never supposed marriage to 'mean' this phase. Weariness of life, etc., ensued.
The husband could not comprehend her riddlesome demeanour, and really
loving his wife, did his best to calm her" (550–551).[27] Mrs. R—— gained a
respite from her depression when, while traveling, she encountered her former lover. Her husband separated the two women, though, finding their
friendship "peculiar." When he found their correspondence, it "was exactly
like that between a pair of lovers" (551).[28]

   Prime-Stevenson abridges the case history in his translation. Some of
what he omits are minor details and superfluous information that does not
overtly affect the history, but a great deal of it describes the patient's history
of mental instability. "At the consultation the patient gave the impression
of a very neuropathic, tainted person" (272).[29] Prime-Stevenson omits the
details about the family history of depression and that Mrs. R—— suffered
several serious nervous breakdowns, one at age seventeen, another brought
on by overwork while working as a governess, one after the marriage of her
lover, and another before her own marriage. These omissions by the translator skirt around the nature and profundity of Mrs. R——'s chronic depression, removing what was believed to be a manifestation of degeneration, and
thereby making her a more model example. So why include this case history at all? The case of Mrs. R—— importantly supports Prime-Stevenson's
argument that marriage is not a viable solution for eradicating same-sex
desires but can only lead to immense unhappiness for both of the partners.
While certain aspects of Mrs. R——'s life story were problematic for Prime-
Stevenson—chiefly, her history of depression, since one supposed sign of
degeneration, the depression, might point to another, her lesbianism—
Mrs. R——'s story nevertheless compellingly illustrates that marriage is no
"cure" for same-sex desire. By abridging the case history in such a way as to
eliminate the troubling facts of her psychosexual life, Prime-Stevenson thus
presented the salient facts of Mrs. R——'s suffering in a way that problema-
tized Krafft-Ebing's account of her suffering.

   That Prime-Stevenson amended Krafft-Ebing's words to fit his own reform aims is further indicated by the case histories of B—— and Mrs. M——.
B——'s case (*PS* 273–274 [German edition]; 255–257 [English edition]), appears in chapter 5 of *The Intersexes*, where Prime-Stevenson presents his case

histories of homosexual men. It demonstrates that homosexuality is not con-
fined to the upper classes—an assumption that held a particular currency
in Germany at the time, as the so-called Eulenburg affair, a scandal where
members of Wilhelm II's entourage were accused of homosexuality, was still
fresh in the public mind.[30] Most of the cases Prime-Stevenson presents in
this chapter are of exceptionally well-traveled and well-educated, leisure-
and professional-class men. Indeed, *The Intersexes* shares this class bias with
Psychopathia Sexualis. As Oosterhuis points out, most cases of patients in
Psychopathia Sexualis were upper and middle class,[31] and, as Crozier argues, "framing the patient as respectable, intelligent, or a professional" was
a way by which sexologists could establish the credibility of their cases.[32]
In contrast, Prime-Stevenson argued that "exhibitions of [homosexuality]
occur in humbler as well as exalted ranks" (117). This directly challenges
the assumption that homosexuality is the product of either lower-class degeneration or upper-class vice, an assumption that had gained great public
currency via fin-de-siècle scandals, such as the trials of Oscar Wilde or the
Eulenburg affair, which was widely reported in America and Britain.[33] The
case of B—— challenges the classed misconceptions in a number of ways including in terms of gender. He is a waiter who enjoys feminine occupations
but is in other ways masculine "except as to a slightly wavering walk nothing betrays his womanish nature" (119).[34] His "feminine" nature is manifest
sexually in that "he feels inclined always to the passive role in his perverted
sexuality," but "Pederasty (coitus analis) is disgusting to him, in the highest degree, and he has never allowed it" (118).[35] B—— is a healthy, although
femininely natured, man from a working-class background who seems not
to practice any "baser" sexual acts; his case thus seems exemplary to support
Prime-Stevenson's arguments about the third- or intermediate-sex theory.
However, the changes and omissions Prime-Stevenson made in translating
the case indicate that he shaped B——'s story to fit his own sexual politics.

For instance, Prime-Stevenson omits the nature of B——'s sexual awakening with a discreet ellipsis. *Psychopathia Sexualis* explains it as follows:

> His sexual life awoke at the age of eight. He began to masturbate and
> derive much pleasure from stimulating the penis of other boys in his
> mouth. At the age of twelve he began to fall in love with men, prefer-
> ring those in the thirties and with moustaches. (256)[36]

The Intersexes significantly shortens this account: "His sexual life began at
eight years. . . . At twelve years, he began falling in love with men, mostly
those in the thirties and with mustaches" (118). The translation excludes the
detail that at age eight B—— began masturbating and enjoyed administering oral sex on other boys. Furthermore, Prime-Stevenson omits that B——

"had an irresistible desire to loiter about W.C.'s in order to get a look at the men's genitals" (257).[37] These aspects of B——'s sexual life are problematic for Prime-Stevenson's study because, as he argues elsewhere:

> Nude embracements and close contact genitally as a rule suffice for all the pleasurable sensations of normal sexual intercourse. Mere close embraces, or coit[us] inter fem[ora] is usually adequate toward complete orgasm by him. Often less than that is needed. For, one must remember that the Uranian passion is informed much by a sort of idealism, far more vivid and nervous than the sensation of normalists. (115)

Prime-Stevenson argues that practices such as oral and anal sex "are not invariably instinctive to the Uranian" (115). He thus distances the Uranian from all but certain forms of sexual expression, those that, from the outside, might be considered less noxious. As a consequence, for his homosexual readers, he proscribes particular acts. Chief among these forbidden practices is anal intercourse. So, why, then, did he include the case study of B——? His translation suggests that there are two different political aims in conflict. On the one hand Prime-Stevenson sought to show that homosexuality is found at every level of society, which B——'s case, unlike so many others, appositely shows. On the other hand, however, he aimed to uphold his claim that homosexual men and women are "healthy," "normal," and "valuable" members of society. In order to reconcile these two viewpoints, therefore, Prime-Stevenson selectively translated the case history, omitting the passages that would contradict his reform aims.

The case history of Mrs. M—— further illustrates that Prime-Stevenson edits out key aspects of Krafft-Ebing's work, adapting the case studies of *Psychopathia Sexualis* for his own reform goals in ways that sometime denied the sexuality of the subjects under discussion. The case of Mrs. M——, which is observation 154 in *PS* (285–287 [German edition]; 266–268 [English edition]), is the story of a forty-four-year-old woman from an artistically gifted family who had been married twice and had four children. As with the cases of Miss X—— (139–140) and Mrs. R——, which Prime-Stevenson sources from Krafft-Ebing, this one is highly abridged but is mostly accurately translated, except for a mistake and a few omissions. Most strikingly, it includes a decisive departure from the original that pertains to M——'s relation to one of her daughters, the awakening of the child's sexuality, and how this impacted that of the mother. *Psychopathia Sexualis* presents the case as follows:

> Three years after her second husband's death, she discovered that her daughter by the first husband, now nine years of age, was given

to masturbation and going into decline. She read an article about this vice in the *Enclopaedia* [*sic*], and now could not resist the temptation to try it herself and thus became an onanist. She hesitated to give a full account of this period of her life. She stated, however, that she became sexually so excited that she had to send her two daughters away from home in order to preserve them from something "terrible." The two boys could remain at home. (267)[38]

This account is shortened in *The Intersexes*, which reads:

> Her own nine-year old daughter now began to show signs of sexual insubordination, and it greatly distressed her mother. A terrible period for Mrs. M—— ensued; what with her anxieties, violent sexual desires that almost distracted her, etc. (552)

Again we can see that Prime-Stevenson omitted those parts of a case history that troubled his own views on homosexual politics. Clearly the full case history in *Psychopathia Sexualis* is not the picture of a "Uraniad" that would support Prime-Stevenson defense of homosexuality. When he writes that Mrs. M—— was subject to "anxieties, violent sexual desires that almost distracted her," his are considerably toned down compared to Krafft-Ebing's, which describe how a mother learned how to masturbate from her daughter and was forced to send the two girls away for fear that, overcome by her desires, she might sexually molest one or both of her daughters.

Whereas Prime-Stevenson distances his male Uranians from only certain practices—mostly anal sex and some forms of oral sex—his account of the female Uraniad is marked by a negative view of her sexuality. He writes, for instance, that "the physical rapports of Uraniadism, as contrasted with male similisexual relations, do not allow the bodily satisfactions of the Uraniad to be organically so vivid as the man's. Man's seminal system and its ejaculative process make his pleasure more acutely physical" (128). Not only are women, in Prime-Stevenson's view, barred from the joys of sexual intercourse experienced by their male counterparts, because of what he considers their "inferior" sexual body, but he also suggests that sex between women could actually be detrimental to their mental health. "The Uranian embraces are not necessarily at all dangerous to his nervous system," he writes, continuing, "but the nervous demands on the Uraniad frequently make the gratification of her desires pernicious; disturbing gravely her intellectual and nervous poise" (128). While in the original case history of Miss A——, he describes her as sexually active—"Masturb. mut. sapphism. mut." (131)—and while he does not omit that Miss X—— had had a love relationship that "had not been wholly platonic" (140),[39] the case history of

Mrs. M—— suggests that for Prime-Stevenson the Uraniad was decidedly nonsexual.

Conclusion: Translation and Homosexual Liberation

The comparison between *The Intersexes* and *Psychopathia Sexualis* thus reveals Prime-Stevenson's gendered sexual reform politics, which insisted on representing same-sex sexuality in a way that he thought least offensive to the general public. While Prime-Stevenson's study is not a translation of Krafft-Ebing's work—which had been translated into English by Charles Gilbert Chaddock and F. J. Rebman—his engagement with the German text nevertheless went beyond mere referential or intertextual links. Instead Prime-Stevenson's translations of the case studies reveal that he deliberately adapted the original text to fit his own reform politics. The changes he made are not simply examples of "bad" translation, but they indicate that his translations were politically motivated, aiming to "bring home," to use Steiner's words, only that which supported Prime-Stevenson's own views and goals. *The Intersexes* thus demonstrates how Prime-Stevenson used translation as a tool for transforming negative sexological representations into narratives that fitted his own ideas about gender, sex, and social change. The work indicates the important role that translation played in early homosexual identity construction.

In its preface, *The Intersexes* announces itself a summary of the field of sexological research for an English-speaking readership, but it is actually a great deal more than that. It mines sexological studies, those of Krafft-Ebing, Hirschfeld, Ulrichs, and others, while at the same time putting forward original case histories of homosexual individuals. It presents a narrative of homosexual history as well as an exploration and anthology of homosexuality in world literature. It seeks to defend the homosexual man and woman against religious and legal condemnation as well as to contradict the degenerative hypothesis prevalent in sexology at the time. It forges a Uranian sexual identity, providing the homosexual reader with the tools he or she would need to assign meaning to his or her desires and to make sense of his or her sexual subjectivity, while at the same time proscribing behaviors and practices, such as certain forms of sexual expression. There is a great deal of affinity between Prime-Stevenson's efforts in this direction and those of John Addington Symonds and Edward Carpenter: they utilized scientific knowledge, despite their standing as amateurs, and fused it with cultural and historical discourses of same-sex love to offer homosexual men and women positive images of themselves and ultimately to achieve homosexual liberation. Paying attention to the role of translation in *The Intersexes* thus adds to research on the cultural archive of sexology-specific insights into the extent to which Prime-Stevenson identified with as well as rejected and transformed scientific ideas about sex.

NOTES

1. In this chapter, I refer to the writer and activist as Edward Prime-Stevenson rather than by his nom de plume, Xavier Mayne.

2. Margaret S. Breen, "Homosexual Identity, Translation, and Prime-Stevenson's *Imre* and *The Intersexes*," *CLCWeb: Comparative Literature and Culture* 14, no. 1 (2012): 5.

3. George Steiner, *After Babel: Aspects of Language and Translation*, 3rd ed. (Oxford: Oxford University Press, 1998), 313–314.

4. Ibid., 314.

5. Heike Bauer, *English Literary Sexology: Translations of Inversion, 1860–1930* (Basingstoke, UK: Palgrave Macmillan, 2009), 52. See also Sean Brady's discussion of Edward Carpenter and John Addington Symonds in *Masculinity and Male Homosexuality in Britain, 1861–1913* (Basingstoke, UK: Palgrave Macmillan, 2009).

6. Of the original 125 copies, 34 are accounted for. James Gifford, "What Became of the Intersexes?" *The Gay and Lesbian Review Worldwide* (September–October 2011), para. 18, available at http://www.glreview.com/article/what-became-of-the-intersexes/.

7. Havelock Ellis, *Studies in the Psychology of Sex*, vol. 2, *Sexual Inversion*, 3rd ed., revised and enlarged (Philadelphia: Davis, 1924), 72.

8. Edward Prime-Stevenson, *The Intersexes: A History of Similisexualism as a Problem in Social Life* (Naples: privately printed, 1908), x. Hereafter cited parenthetically in the text.

9. Edward Prime-Stevenson, "Letter to Paul Elmer More, 10–12 March 1906," in *Imre: A Memorandum*, ed. James Gifford (Orchard Park, NY: Broadview Press, 2003), 135.

10. Brady, *Masculinity and Male Homosexuality*, 202.

11. Edward Carpenter, *The Intermediate Sex: A Study of Some Transitional Types of Men and Women* (London: Swan Sonnenschein, 1908), 167–169.

12. See James Wilper, "Sexology, Homosexual History, and Walt Whitman: The 'Uranian' Identity in *Imre: A Memorandum*," *Critical Survey* 22, no. 3 (2010): 52–68.

13. Ivan Crozier, "Pillow Talk: Credibility, Trust and the Sexological Case History," *History of Science* 46, no.4 (2008): 391.

14. Three of the cases that Prime-Stevenson attributes to the Austrian psychiatrist are not in the later editions of *Psychopathia sexualis*, *Neue Forschungen auf dem Gebiet der Psychopathia Sexualis* [New research in the field of psychopathia sexualis] (1890), or *Der Conträrsexuale vor dem Strafrichter* [The homosexual before the criminal court] (1894).

15. Borrowing case histories from other studies was by no means uncommon practice in sexology. Krafft-Ebing, himself, borrowed 11 of the 179 case histories of contrary sexual feeling. Harry Oosterhuis, *Stepchildren of Nature: Krafft-Ebing, Psychiatry, and the Making of Sexual Identity* (Chicago: University of Chicago Press, 2000), writes that "initially the majority of the cases were borrowed from other physicians" (152); see table 4, p. 153.

16. On the dedication page appears: "To the memory of the pioneer in dispassionate, humane, scientific study of similisexualism, Dr. Richard von Krafft-Ebing" without

whose "suggestion and aid it would never have been begun nor carried on to its close." Additionally, Prime-Stevenson's novel, *Imre: A Memorandum*, features a tribute to Krafft-Ebing in "one eminent Viennese specialist" who "had not a little comforted and strengthened Imre morally; warning him away from despising himself: from thinking himself alone, and a sexual pariah; from over-morbid sufferings; from that bitterness and despair which year by year all over the world can explain, in hundreds of cases, the depressed lives, the lonely existences, the careers mysteriously interrupted—broken" (118–119).

17. Richard von Krafft-Ebing, *Psychopathia Sexualis, with Especial Reference to the Antipathic Sexual Instinct: A Medico-Forensic Study*, trans. from the 12th German edition by Franklin S. Klaf (London: Staples Press, 1965), 242. Hereafter cited parenthetically in the text. "Ein funktionelles Degenerationszeichen." Richard von Krafft-Ebing, *Psychopathia Sexualis, mit besonderer Berücksichtigung der conträren Sexualempfindung: Eine medicinisch-gerichtliche Studie für Ärzte und Juristen*, 12th ed. (Stuttgart: Enke, 1903), 233. Hereafter cited parenthetically in the text.

18. Heike Bauer, "'Not a Translation but a Mutilation': The Limits of Translation and the Discipline of Sexology," *Yale Journal of Criticism* 16, no. 2 (2003): 386–387; Bauer, *English Literary Sexology*, 33; Oosterhuis, *Stepchildren of Nature*, esp. pt. 3, "Articulate Sufferers: Perversion and Autobiography," 127–208.

19. Heinrich Ammerer, *Am Anfang war die Perversion: Richard von Krafft-Ebing: Psychiater und Pionier der modernen Sexualkunde* (Vienna: Styria, 2011), 283. "Krafft-Ebings Verhältnis zur Homosexualität wandelte sich zwischen seiner ersten Abhandlung 1877 und seinem Tod. Aus einem interessierten, aber nüchternen Beobachter wurde ein Fürsprecher der Homosexuellen, der sich mit großer Empathie für deren Straffreiheit einsetzte." The translation of the quotation is my own.

20. Robert Beachy, "The German Invention of Homosexuality," *Journal of Modern History* 82, no. 4 (2010): 819.

21. "Ich fand in Z. einen geistig hochstehenden feinfühligen, in seinem Aeuseren durchaus virilen, normal gebildeten Menschen vor" (*PS* 261).

22. "Er lebt seit einiger Zeit mit einem gleichaltrigen Mann in gemeinsamem Haushalte wie Mann und Frau" (*PS* 272).

23. "C. war talentirt für Musik, Dichtkunst, interessiert sich früh für's Theater" (*PS* 272).

24. "wandte sich wider dem homosexualen Verkehr zu" (*PS* 265).

25. See Renate Hauser, "Krafft-Ebing's Psychological Understanding of Sexual Behaviour," in *Sexual Knowledge, Sexual Science: The History of Attitudes to Sexuality*, ed. Roy Porter and Mikulás Teich (Cambridge: Cambridge University Press, 1994), 212.

26. "Er mied seit 2 Jahren den Coitus maritalis, wandte sich wider dem homosexualen Verkehr zu und liess sich kürzlich an einem öffentlichen Orte inter masturbationem mutuam mit einem jungen Manne betreten. Er entschuldigt dies damit, dass er durch längere Abstinenz sehr libidinös, beim Anblick der Genitalien eine Mannes in einen förmlichen Affekt gerathen sei 'wie berauscht' und sich in einer Art Sinnesverwirrung damals befunden habe. Amnesie für diesen Zeitraum bot er nicht. Kurze Freiheitsstrafe. Durchaus virile, decente Persönlichkeit. Genitalien normal" (*PS* 265).

27. "Am 6. Juni 1886 erster Coitus. Sie war davon moralische tief deprimirt. So hatte sie sich die Ehre nicht gedacht! Anfangs war sie von heftigem Taedium vitae geplagt. Der

Mann, welcher seine Frau aufrichtig liebte, that sein Möglichstes, um sie zu beruhigen" (*PS* 290).

28. "Gelegentlich überzeugte er sich durch die Correspondenz seiner Frau mit dieser 'Freundin', dass der Briefwechsel genau dem zweier Liebenden entsprach" (*PS* 291).

29. "Patientin machte bei der Consultation der Eindruck einer höchst belasteten neuropathischen Persönlichkeit" (*PS* 291).

30. For Eulenburg, see Heike Bauer, "'Race,' Normativity and the History of Sexuality: Magnus Hirschfeld's Racism and Early Twentieth-Century Sexology," *Psychology and Sexuality* 1, no. 3 (2010): 239–249.

31. See Oosterhuis, *Stepchildren of Nature*, table 1, p. 151.

32. Crozier, "Pillow Talk," 392.

33. For a detailed examination of the impact of the affair both in and outside Germany, see James D. Steakley, "Iconography of a Scandal: Political Cartoons and the Eulenburg Affair in Wilhelmine Germany," in *Hidden from History: Reclaiming the Gay and Lesbian Past*, ed. Martin B. Duberman, Martha Vicinus, and George Chauncey Jr. (London: Penguin, 1991), 233–257.

34. "Sein Aeusseres, ausgenommen leicht wiegender Gang, bietet nichts, was auf eine weibliche Natur hindeuten würde" (*PS* 274).

35. "Offerte zur Päderastie, die ihm sowohl aktiv als passiv höchst ekelhaft sei, habe er nie acceptirt. Beim perversen Geschlechtsakte habe er sich immer in der Rolle des Weibes gedacht" (*PS* 273).

36. "Schon mit 8 Jahren sei sein Geschlechtsleben erwacht. Er habe masturbiert und sei auf die Idee verfallen, penem aliorum puerorum in os arrigere, was ihm grossen Genuss gewährt habe. Mit 12 Jahren fing er an, sich in Männer zu verlieben, am meisten in solche in den 30er Jahren mit Schnurrbart" (*PS* 273).

37. "konnte oft dem Drange nicht widerstehen, in Pissoirs herumzulungern, um männlicher Genitalien ansichtig zu werden" (*PS* 274).

38. "Drei Jahre nach dem Tode des zweiten Mannes machte Patientin die Entdeckung, dass ihre 9jährige Tochter aus erster Ehe der Masturbation ergeben war und dahinsiechte. Patientin las im Conversationslexikon über diese Laster nach, konnte dem Drange nicht widerstehen, es auch zu versuchen und wurde Onanistin. Ueber diese Periode ihres Lebens kann sie sich nicht entschliessen, ausführlich zu berichten. Sie versichert, dass sie sexuell schrecklich erregt wurde, eines Tages ihre beiden Mädchen aus dem Hauses geben musste, um sie vor 'Schrecklichem' zu bewahren, während sie ihre beiden Knaben daheim behalten konnte!" (*PS* 286–287).

39. "in einem jeden falls nicht rein platonischen Liebesverhältnisse" (*PS* 300).

12

Suicidal Subjects

Translation and the Affective Foundations
of Magnus Hirschfeld's Sexology

HEIKE BAUER

A ttention to translation between languages can offer glimpses at the elusive evidence of past emotions and the circumstance in which they are formed. Or, to phrase this differently, we might say that the process of translation has a vital dimension that links texts to bodies, and representation to subjectivity, and that can reveal some of the feelings and experiences that occurred when particular ideas were formulated. Judith Butler has pointed out that "the notion of the human will only be built over time in and by the process of cultural translation."[1] The accounts of human bodies and experiences found in the sexological archive can similarly be understood as cultural translations that reveal not only how sexual subjects are produced but how they are denied and come undone across time. This chapter turns to translation to examine the writings on homosexual death and suicide by the Jewish sexologist and homosexual rights activist Magnus Hirschfeld (1868–1935) and what they can tell us about both individual feelings of queer unlivability and their collective impact. It is prompted by the realization that while we know of many queer lives that have ended tragically as a result of legal persecution, violent attack, or the inability to cope with heteronormative social and emotional pressures, we know surprisingly little about the traumatic impact of these deaths on the lives of their contemporaries, and on the shaping of modern queer culture more broadly.[2] I use the word "trauma" here in the specific sense articulated by Ann Cvetkovich. She understands trauma "as a name for experiences of politically situated social violence [that] forges overt connections between politics and the emotions."[3]

This conception provides a useful framework for an investigation of the impact of homosexual death, including suicide. It draws attention to the links between the social denial of homosexuality and the violence experienced by women and men whose desires were, or were seen to be, oriented away from the heterosexual norm.

Cvetkovich's concern with the relationship between feeling and politics allows us to think about homosexual suicide not merely in terms of individual suffering but as a collective experience. Hirschfeld's writings on homosexual death reveal some of the intersections between sex research and popular and cultural discourses about sexuality, and how they are linked to the lives of women and men who inhabit this archive. A second-generation sexologist famous for his homosexual rights activism, attention to transgender, and opening of the world's first Institute of Sexual Sciences in Berlin, Hirschfeld was also a chronicler of hate and violence against lesbians and homosexual men.[4] His famous writings on homosexuality, for example, which were mainly written in German but occasionally also in English, include statistical surveys of lesbian and homosexual suicide. This material has received little critical attention. Yet it extends in specific ways our understanding of the fact that, to borrow the words of Heather Love, "the history of Western representation is littered with the corpses of gender and sexual deviants."[5] It shows not only that the sociopolitical, legal, and discursive denial of homosexuality profoundly shaped the lives of many individuals who felt, in Hirschfeld's words, "different from the others" (*anders als die anderen*), but that there is a tangible collective shape to this suffering. By paying attention to Hirschfeld's writings in German and English on homosexual suicide, its causes, and its reception, this chapter will show that lesbian and homosexual suffering caused emotional shock waves that rippled far across the geopolitical boundaries of the modern world.

Translating Suicidal Subjects

Reading the translations of queer existence in sexological texts and related writings on sexuality is often difficult. This is partly because of the elusive nature of contextual evidence about the lives of the women and men who inhabit the sexological archive, and partly because the emotional threads running through modern queer lives are frequently bleak. They describe feelings of despair and rejection as well as suicidal thoughts and evidence that these thoughts are sometimes acted upon. This material thus constitutes a problematic archive for queer historiography because it predominantly testifies to the negative experiences of women and men whose genders and desires did not fit the heterosexual mold and who were frequently persecuted, discriminated against, and rejected as a result.[6] Such an archive is problematic not only because it describes experiences that caused hurt and upset, but also because it associates same-sex sexuality with inevitable, abject misery. This damaging form of stereotyping has a great deal of currency in popular culture and the scientific and political efforts that shaped modern Western societies. It is therefore no surprise that lesbian and gay history and historiography has spent considerable effort on countering the pervasive and pernicious image of inevitable homosexual suffering. Scholars have both deconstructed the structures of oppression and excavated affirmative evidence of queer lives across time and space, evidence that shows how nonnormative forms of existence can thrive even in hostile social conditions.[7] However, while the importance of such recuperative scholarship cannot be overstated, it is equally important to acknowledge that the excavation of affirmative histories alone cannot account for the full range of feelings and experiences that shape queer existence, nor can it explain fully the conditions that make possible the negation of same-sex life. Hirschfeld's writings on homosexual death are a poignant reminder that queer existence is subjected to real and imagined attacks, attacks that can be lethal.

Hirschfeld was by his own account prompted to switch from general medical practice to sexology after "the suicide of a young officer who shot himself on the eve of his marriage, bequeathing . . . Hirschfeld many of his notes and drawings."[8] He repeatedly returned to this traumatic event in his writings, both to validate his sexology and to let speak the voice of a "*Selbstmörder*."[9] The German word *Selbstmörder* has no single English equivalent, translating literally as "someone who murders himself," thus overtly casting the person in criminal terms. This linguistic particularity draws attention to the fact that suicide, not unlike homosexuality, occupies a stigmatized and criminalized role in Western history.[10] Countries as politically diverse as the United States, England, Russia, and the German nations all had antisuicide laws that enabled posthumous punishment of a person who takes his or her own life, for instance by the annulment of the dead person's will.[11] In addition, Christian churches treated harshly those who had committed the "sin" of suicide, often denying the dead person conventional burial rites.[12] While over the course of the nineteenth century some of these laws were repealed—the German Penal Code of 1871 decriminalized unassisted suicide—and while religious attitudes softened, suicide remained a social taboo. One of the earliest histories of modern suicide by the English observer Henry Romilly Fedden illustrates this point. When "the comforts of Victorianism overlay the primitive horror of suicide and blunt the precise dogmatic teaching of the Church," he noted, "it [was] no longer the thing in itself that create[d] the scare, so much as what other people [thought] of it . . . [as] loss of fortune [was] substituted with the scourge of gossip."[13] Fedden's observations on gossip chime with the tone of the suicide letter written by

Hirschfeld's patient, which emphasizes the desperate unspeakability of the man's suffering. The man explains that he will kill himself because he lacks "the strength" (*die Kraft*) to tell his parents "the truth" (*die Wahrheit*) and stop a marriage "against which nothing could be said in and of itself."[14] Hoping that his parents will never learn about "that which nearly strangled my heart," an expression that, like the remainder of the letter, avoids giving "it" a name, the man implies that law, marriage, and family instituted heterosexual norms that made his life unlivable.[15]

The suicide letter suggests that unlivability and unspeakability are closely linked. Hirschfeld's choice of words further indicates that he did not consider the young man's suicide to be a voluntary act. For while *Selbstmörder* is the common German term for a man who committed suicide (a woman would be a *Selbstmörderin*), by the turn of the century the word had come to compete in critical and philosophical debates with Friedrich Nietzsche's recent conception of the "*Freitod*."[16] Nietzsche celebrated "the free death, which occurs because I want it" (*den freien Tod, der mir kommt, weil ich will*), arguing that the ability to choose death is one of the characteristic features of the super-man.[17] Hirschfeld was familiar with Nietzsche's work, considering him one of the thinkers "who at least theoretically fully understood homosexual love."[18] This makes it all the more significant that he ignored Nietzsche's notion of the freely chosen death. The insistence on describing the suicide of his patient in the older language of *Selbstmord* reinforces that Hirschfeld did not consider this particular death a heroic choice but an act of despair.

Yet if for the young man naming his feelings was an unspeakable act, his letter nevertheless also conveys an awareness that there are others who feel the same way. Entreating Hirschfeld to listen to the "outcry of a desolate man" (*Aufschrei eines Elenden*), the man's final words implore his physician to dedicate his life to the homosexual cause: "the thought that you [Hirschfeld] could contribute to a future when the German fatherland will think of us in more just terms sweetens my hour of death."[19] These concluding words alert us to the fact that suicide is only a "final" act for the person who takes his or her life. Its impact continues to be felt by others, a fact that is grammatically underscored in the suicide note by the use of the subjunctive, which turns the man's final wish into a command that will bind Hirschfeld's future.[20]

The sense of connection between the suicidal man and his doctor is reinforced by the ambiguous demand for justice "for us" in the "fatherland." The word "us" evokes both a larger group of people and closeness between Hirschfeld and the man. By his own account, Hirschfeld was treating the young officer for severe depression around the time of this death. We cannot know for certain if the closeness evoked by the young officer refers to

an actual friendship between him and his doctor. However, this seems unlikely given the overall tone of the letter and the formal address of "*Sie.*"
The psychic, emotional, and social pressures that led to the young officer's
suicide are ultimately unknowable to us, in the same way that there is no
hard "proof" that the man's posthumous opening up to Hirschfeld is linked
to a recognition that Hirschfeld was himself attracted to men. Yet if the
"truth" of events appears elusive partly because we have to rely entirely on
Hirschfeld's narration of events, this narrative nevertheless tells a particular
story about the conditions that contributed to the end of a young man's life.
It constitutes, in Cvetkovich's terms, a repository "of feelings and emotions,
which are encoded not only in the content of the texts themselves but in
practices that surround their production and reception."[21] The poignancy of
the story lies in the fact that the young man literally bestows on Hirschfeld
a material record of the fears and unfulfilled desires that he is unable to
discuss in their face-to-face meetings. The man's unspeakable life is thus
transformed into an articulate death, a death that would provide an affective
motor for Hirschfeld's subsequent professional practice.

Death and Professional Life

The narrative of the young officer's suicide gained a relatively prominent role
in Hirschfeld's vast oeuvre due to the fact that he included it in various autobiographical reflections published over the course of his life.[22] Hirschfeld
used the story to legitimize his sexological practice, aiming to give it an
emotional credibility and a political urgency that would distinguish his work
from that of his colleagues. The 1922–1923 account of events, which was published in the homosexual journal *Die Freundschaft* (The friendship), shows
that Hirschfeld used the suicide narrative in an attempt to gain professional
credibility among the competing factions of early twentieth-century homosexual culture. Here he mentions the suicide in an article about the history
of the Wissenschaftlich-humanitäres Komittee (Scientific-Humanitarian
Committee; WhK), which was directed specifically at a homosexual audience and sought to promote Hirschfeld's many reform activities. The WhK
was cofounded by Hirschfeld in May 1897, shortly before Oscar Wilde's release from prison, with the aim to increase public knowledge about, and
acceptance of, homosexuality. Its best-known campaign was the petition for
the revocation of Paragraph 175 of the German Penal Code, which attracted
many famous signatories. The WhK also played a key role in the publication of new sexuality research, competing with and overlapping with other
journals in complicated ways. For instance, Sigmund Freud explained in
a letter to Carl Jung in 1908 that an article of his had appeared in the new
Zeitschrift für Sexualwissenschaften (Journal of sexual sciences) due to "a

bit of skullduggery on the part of the editors [who had] originally solicited the piece for the *Jahrbuch für sexuelle Zwischenstufen* [Yearbook of sexual intermediaries]." "I was not told until several months later," he continues, "that it was to be published in the *Zeitschrift für Sexualwissenschaft* which was just being founded. I asked for a guarantee that this new organ was not to be a chronicle of the W.h. Committee [WhK] in which case I preferred to withdraw my contribution, but received no answer."[23] Freud's words indicate the sometimes rapidly shifting allegiances of the early sex researchers. He had originally submitted his work to the *Jahrbuch*, knowing that it was closely aligned with the WhK. Shortly afterward, however, Freud turned his back on the WhK in a row over Hirschfeld's use of a questionnaire to assess homosexual life. Freud's article, meanwhile, in all likelihood as a response to the methodological quarrel, was passed from the editors of the *Jahrbuch* to the editors of the newly founded *Zeitschrift*, who then contacted Freud with their editorial queries.

The episode, which is barely more than a footnote in the history of sex research, nevertheless serves to illustrate how a complex web of professional disputes and personal rivalries shaped modern sexology. By the time Hirschfeld wrote his short history of the WhK in 1922, the organization had undergone further transformations as it became closely associated with the broader activities of the Institute of Sexual Sciences. The institute, which had been founded by Hirschfeld in 1919, had a significant popular reach, successfully drawing in large audiences through initiatives such as the Marriage Consultation Department and so-called Questionnaire Evenings where members of the public could anonymously deposit questions in a box, which were then answered by an institute physician.[24] If the popularity of these kinds of initiatives furthered Hirschfeld's fame, they did not make him immune to competition from other homosexual organizations. Hirschfeld's greatest rival in Berlin's homosexual subculture was the so-called Gemeinschaft der Eigenen, another homosexual society, which was led by Adolf Brand and Benedict Friedländer and heavily influenced by the anarchist writings of John Henry Mackay.[25] Founded in 1903, the Gemeinschaft der Eigenen supported Hirschfeld's fight for the abolition of anti-homosexuality legislation but rejected his theorization of sexual intermediaries. Instead, Brand and Friedländer adapted the masculine ideals of Hellenic revivalism that had gained such popularity in nineteenth-century England, combining them with the physical pursuits of outdoor culture and an affirmative focus on homosexual virility that stood in stark contrast to Hirschfeld's ideas about the infinite variations of gender and sexuality. Hirschfeld's description of homosexual suicide implicitly counters the image of strong, masculine homosexuality with a reminder that there are many unhappy men whose lives end prematurely because they are unable to free themselves from social constraint.

If the suicide of his patient had a traumatic impact on Hirschfeld, the telling of the story indicates how cultural conventions work themselves into the representation of his memory of the event. Cathy Caruth has argued that it is difficult to listen and respond "to traumatic stories in a way that does not lose their impact, reduce them to clichés or turn them all into versions of the same story."[26] Hirschfeld's repeated return to the suicide suggests that the event retained a haunting presence in his work, which reached beyond the realm of the well-rehearsed anecdote even as it was shaped by narrative conventions. Hirschfeld's final mention of the suicide occurs in one of the last pieces he wrote, an "autobiographical sketch" published posthumously in 1936.[27] Unlike the 1922 account, the later "autobiographical sketch" was written in English. The two pieces tell a slightly different story about the events of the suicide. According to Hirschfeld's 1922 version, the man died "immediately *after* his wedding."[28] There is something particularly poignant about the idea that the young man went through the rituals of a wedding before he committed suicide, especially because this chain of events goes against the conventional conception of "wedding nerves," which locates the moment of crisis *before* the wedding.[29] When Hirschfeld returns to the event at the end of his life, the conventional time frame is restored: here he writes that the man killed himself on the "eve of his marriage."[30] Given the absence of other sources we cannot know the actual time of the death, but the temporal slippage in Hirschfeld's accounts of the suicide alerts us to the ease by which cliché attaches itself to the narration of traumatic events.

Hirschfeld wrote the "autobiographical sketch" in English for the *Encyclopedia Sexualis* (1936), a compendium of key themes and figures in the sexual sciences edited by the American physician and historian of medicine Victor Robinson. Robinson had a particular interest in the stories that shaped scientific development, an interest that defined how he approached and wrote "history." His subsequent account of *The Story of Medicine* (1943), for instance, which makes no mention of Hirschfeld or homosexuality, begins with the imaginative assertion that "the first cry of pain through the primitive jungle was the first call for a physician."[31] Robinson's editorship may play a role in the conventionalized temporality of Hirschfeld's English account of the suicide. However, even as the English narrative might suggest that the details of the event faded over the course of Hirschfeld's life, the fact he repeatedly returned to the suicide over three decades also indicates the degree of traumatic stasis by which this tragic death retained a presence in Hirschfeld's writings.

Suicide's Statistical Ends

Where, then, does this single death fit into Hirschfeld's work and the history of sexuality more broadly? For some critics, the question of whose life counts in the narratives that modern society tells about itself can inevitably be answered with reference to what they consider the seismic impact of nineteenth-century sciences on the regulation and expression of intimacy, desire, and the vagaries of identity. Karma Lochrie, for instance, takes for granted what she calls "the installation of norms first in statistical science and second in sexology."[32] She argues that the emergence of these sciences marks a fundamental distinction between "normal" modernity and a premodernity, which, according to Lochrie, "is neither hopelessly utopian nor inveterately heteronormative."[33] Lochrie distills the complex observations on the institution of normativity articulated in the works of Michel Canguilhelm and Michel Foucault into a neat narrative about statistics and sexology. According to her, these disciplines function as the harbingers of medico-scientific reductiveness, legal persecution, and related social norms that bring an end to the anormality she accords to premodernity. It is not difficult to find evidence of the damage caused by the process of disciplining sex—including in terms of its problematic conceptual and scientific legacies and the physical and psychic suffering caused by practitioners who actively tried to "cure" their homosexual or transgendered "patients"—and it is vital that we take account of this damage.[34] Yet I am uneasy about histories such as Lochrie's, which hinge on a clearly identifiable modern "invention" of sexual norms. The attribution of seismic structural shifts in power to one or two scientific developments problematically smooths over many of the edges that delineate the process of "disciplining sex," a process that sharpened queer lives across time and space. We therefore need histories that acknowledge that the grand narratives of oppression and liberatory struggle that frame queer history and historiography intersect with countless personal and fictional life stories, confused cultural fantasies, and fragmentary evidence of intimate relationships that sometimes support and sometimes undermine our understanding of their historical context.

Hirschfeld's complex role as a homosexual sexologist is a case in point. While he singles out the transformative power of the suicide of the young German officer, he also notes in his account of the event in 1922 that he had received countless other "farewell letters" (Abschiedsbriefe) in the intervening years.[35] If these words create a certain distance between Hirschfeld and the young officer who seems to slip into the realm of statistics, it would be mistaken to read Hirschfeld's evocation of the large number of queer suicides as an expression of a detached scientific concern. The tragic deaths and the socioscientific arguments Hirschfeld and others constructed around them complicate the taxonomic efforts with which sexology is primarily associated today. The collation of statistics about homosexual suicide at the turn of the last century both raises awareness of the suffering of homosexuals at the time and flags up that as a group homosexuals were excluded from the burgeoning scientific literature on suicide.

From the later nineteenth century, suicide had begun to garner considerable and sustained interest in scientific and philosophical investigations. In Berlin, psychiatrists began to collect a huge archive of case studies of women and men who killed themselves.[36] The most famous and influential work on the topic would be Émile Durkheim's large-scale study *Le Suicide*, which was first published in 1897, around the same time that Hirschfeld published his first book, *Sappho und Sokrates*. *Le Suicide* is commonly seen as one of the founding texts of modern sociology. Durkheim conducted a comparison of the suicide rates among Catholics and Protestants, classifying four different "types" of suicide that according to him all originated from social factors.[37] Ian Marsh and others who have traced the shifting historical conceptions of suicide and its etiologies have shown that Durkheim's rejection of pathological models of suicide was not unique. Over the course of the nineteenth century, philosophers and thinkers increasingly turned attention to the social conditions that prompt suicide.[38] Karl Marx, for instance, had already noted in 1846 that suicide constitutes "one of the thousand and one symptoms of the general social struggle ever fought out on new ground."[39] It is not my concern here to trace the complex history of suicide or critique the methods by which it has been studied and "treated" by medical practitioners, psychologists, and lawmakers. Instead I want to pick up on a queer absence in nineteenth-century debates about suicide: the fact that before Hirschfeld began to count homosexual suicide—and despite the explosion of discourses around "sex" at the time—the "act whose author is also the sufferer" was rarely considered in relation to homosexuality.[40]

The discursive absence of homosexuality in "mainstream" discussions of suicide reinforces how easily heteronormative assumptions work themselves into the fabric of social research. Karl Marx and Friedrich Engels, for instance, who so famously sought to challenge the gendered as well as classed boundaries of modern society, also expressed strong anti-homosexual sentiments that seem at odds with their politics.[41] In a letter to Marx written on June 22, 1869, Engels employed a derogatory older sexual vocabulary to discredit the emerging emancipatory efforts of men who love and desire other men. He observed that

> the paederasts are beginning to count themselves and discover that they are a power in the state. Only power was lacking, but according to this source [Karl Heinrich Ulrichs's pro "Urning" pamphlets],

it apparently already exists in secret . . . *Guerre aux cons, paix aus trous-de-cul* [War on cunts, peace for arseholes[42]] will now be the slogan. It is a piece of luck that we, personally, are too old to fear that when this party wins, we shall have to pay physical tribute to the victors. But the younger generation![43]

These words were prompted by Engels's encounter with the work of the lawyer and homosexual rights activist Karl Heinrich Ulrichs, who in the lead-up to the unification of the German states was campaigning for adoption of an antidiscriminatory penal code in the new state.[44] Engels's expressed loathing for "paederasty" refuses to acknowledge Ulrichs's new terminology of "Urningism," which conceptualized love between men in affirmative terms, as a natural phenomenon with a long and positive cultural history. Anticipating the generic conventions of first-generation sexology, Engels turns to a foreign language—in this case French—to articulate what is otherwise unspeakable to him.[45] His outrage against the fact that "paederasts" are beginning to "count themselves" indicates the powerful sway of numbers, if not statistics, through which the emerging homosexual movement came to impact on the existing political landscape.

The unspeakability of homosexuality generally alerts us more specifically to the complicated place of both sexuality and suicide in defining a collective identity, even as the absence of studies of homosexual suicide raises questions about whose lives counted in the modern state. Katrina Jaworski has argued that "in relation to suicide, death is not power's limit, since norms, meanings and assumptions and the processes that are part of making sense of suicide will constitute knowledge before, during and after the act of taking one's life."[46] For Jaworski this realization is closely tied in to the difficult question of agency, which in her reading is overshadowed by the fact that "dead or alive, it may not be possible to be free of the operations of power."[47] With this in mind, Hirschfeld's attempt to draw statistical attention to homosexual suicide can be understood as a protest against the negation of homosexuality in life as well as death. It speaks to Judith Butler's concern with "the terms that govern reality," which allow or deny a sense of self.[48] Homosexual suicide statistics raise questions about the flip side of heteronormative political power: the negation of women and men whose sexuality discounts their existence socially and politically, with the effect that many of them felt that they had to end their life. Hirschfeld's collation of statistics on homosexual suicide, then, makes a real intervention in social matters. "Without doubt a large number of homosexuals feel prompted by their sexual particularity to voluntarily end their life," writes Hirschfeld in his magnum opus *Die Homosexualität des Mannes und des Weibes* (The homosexuality of man and woman), which was published in 1914.[49] While he claims that one of the reasons for suicide is the universal problematic of unrequited love, he also points out that homosexual suicides should not be seen as "voluntary" acts but as products of social rejection and legal persecution, caused by feelings of upset about homosexuality as well as by both active persecution and a pronounced fear of blackmail and scandal.[50]

When Walter Benjamin looked back to the economic crises of 1840, he noted that it was during this time that "the idea of suicide became familiar to the working masses" who "despair(ed) of earning a living."[51] He observed that suicide gained a degree of cultural capital at the time, as indicated by the popular circulation of a lithograph depicting a suicidal unemployed English worker whose fate, according to Benjamin, provided inspiration to many others who, finding themselves in similarly hopeless financial straits, followed suit.[52] Hirschfeld in turn suggested that homosexuality can similarly create feelings of hopelessness, emphasizing that "homosexuals don't suffer because of their homosexuality, but because of the false judgement passed upon them by themselves and others."[53] Hirschfeld thus argues that homosexual suicide is not the result of an inherent "defect" but that it is the product of the social pressures that attack and negate this "disqualified identity."

Gendered Sexology

Hirschfeld's intervention has its own, gendered, blind spots. While he ostensibly discussed both homosexual and lesbian suicide, his focus clearly lies on men who kill themselves. The only examples of women taking their lives appear in a section on unhappy love. Here he mentions the unsuccessful double suicide attempt of two young female factory workers whose relationship was threatened by the interference of their parents, and the successful suicide of two married women who shot each other, leaving a note asking, "please do not search for the reason behind this deed."[54] Hirschfeld's gendered evidence base indicates how closely the analysis of suicide remained tied in to conventional debates about sexuality and citizenship, debates that tended to marginalize women. Hirschfeld himself does not reflect on the fact that while lesbianism, unlike male homosexuality, was not criminalized, the social taboo of love between women and the pressures exercised on women to make them conform to heterosexual norms, created difficult living conditions for lesbians—to the extent that some women felt unable to continue their lives in this context. While Hirschfeld acknowledges the social factors of lesbian suicide, his focus on issues of unfulfilled love and tragic relationships does not address in any detail the gendered circumstance that doomed the lives of these women. Adrienne Rich has argued that "the destruction of records and memorabilia and letters documenting the realities of lesbian existence must be taken very seriously as a means of keeping heterosexuality compulsory for women, since what has been kept from our knowledge is joy, sexuality, courage, and community, as well as guilt, self-betrayal and pain."[55] There is no evidence that Hirschfeld actively destroyed lesbian archives—and it is worth noting that he wrote about both female and male same-sex sexuality. Yet his relatively limited analysis and superficial treatment of lesbian suicide nevertheless illustrates what Rich has identified as the historical deprival of lesbian "political existence through 'inclusion' as female versions of male homosexuality."[56]

Hirschfeld's gender bias indicates the manifold ways in which women were pushed to the side lines of popular, professional, and political debates even by men such as Hirschfeld who supported the feminist movement. It also indicates that Hirschfeld heavily drew on personal experience in his work. When it comes to male homosexual suicide, Hirschfeld is explicit about his own personal involvement. Writing in 1914, he claims to have known personally over half of the one hundred homosexual suicides that had taken place in recent years. He explains that an analysis of the responses to his questionnaire, which was completed by around ten thousand homosexual women and men and their families, led him to estimate that around three in every one hundred "Urnings" successfully commit suicide. Of all the homosexuals alive, he claims, about a quarter attempt suicide while the remaining three-quarters have suicidal thoughts at some point in their lives.[57] In short, then, according to Hirschfeld's findings homosexual existence is at least *felt* to be unlivable at some point. If this paints a grim picture, Hirschfeld also mentions that the figures are not necessarily accurate. He cites the work of a Dutch physician who had undertaken a similar survey and arrived at slightly lower numbers.[58] The figures are further compromised by the fact that they are based largely on accounts of visitors to the institute, many of whom had come to seek help in dealing with feelings of isolation, rejection, and despair. But the statistical accuracy of this data and the methodology that framed the investigation are not the main points of interest here. More significant is that Hirschfeld spoke publicly about the unlivability of queer existence (especially in relation to men); and that he did so at a time when homosexuality lacked rights, and, in the case of lesbianism—as Hirschfeld's own work shows—recognition and visibility.

Words Attack Lives

It is, of course, important to note that not all homosexuals, female or male, in the early twentieth century killed themselves or even led lives that were full of suffering. Affirmative lesbian and gay histories have importantly recuperated evidence of happy and fulfilled lives in the past, not least to counter prevailing stereotypes of miserable, lonely homosexuality. While the political—and often personal—importance of this affirmative scholarship cannot be overestimated, it is equally important to acknowledge that for some queer people unhappiness and suffering are the formative aspects of their lives. If it is ultimately impossible to explain why someone takes her or his life while someone else lives in circumstance that appear akin, we can nevertheless construct archives around negated identities that allow us to identify some of the terms that make these lives precarious. Thinking collectively about homosexual suicide makes graspable the force of heteronormative ideals and expectations.

Translations between languages are productive sites for investigating the very real and dangerous impact words can have on individual lives.[59] This is well illustrated by Hirschfeld's observations on the "consequences of persecution" (*Folgen der Verfolgung*), where he offsets German and English expressions against each other to critique the transmission of anti-homosexuality sentiments by the medical profession. He describes an encounter with an American patient who had told him that when he had asked his doctor back home in Philadelphia for advice about his homosexuality, the physician had responded that the man could only deal with his homosexuality in three possible ways: masturbation, voluntary commitment to a lunatic asylum, or suicide.[60] My choice of words for translating the three options offered to the man—masturbation, voluntary commitment to a lunatic asylum and suicide—provides a fairly literal rendering of Hirschfeld's German words, employing English terms that would have been in circulation in early twentieth-century North America.

However, the way Hirschfeld records the incident in the German text makes clear that issues of translation are crucial to the way he tells this story. He explains that the Philadelphian doctor had told his patient that there are only three options for the dealing with the man's homosexuality: "*Selbstbefriedigung* (use his right hand), *freiwilliger Aufenthalt in einer Irrenanstalt* (place himself in a madhouse) *oder Selbstmord* (or better commit suicide)."[61] The passage includes the English expressions used by the Philadelphia-based physician. Set apart from Hirschfeld's own words by being reproduced in brackets, these English words tell their own story of the doctor's negative stance toward homosexuality. According to this information, the doctor had advised his patient to "use his right hand," employing a slang term for masturbation, which was a social taboo.[62] Next, the patient was offered the option "to place himself in a madhouse," a choice of words that reinforces the derogatory tone of the doctor's advice as the clinical terminology of the "psychiatric hospital" had long since replaced the term "madhouse."[63] Most chillingly, the physician emphasized that the preferred cause of action for his homosexual patient would be to "*better* commit suicide." Hirschfeld does not translate the emphatic "better." However, his decision to include the doctor's English words ensures that their devastating implications are not missed. From contextual evidence we know that Hirschfeld wrote for an educated audience that would have been able to read both German and English. By presenting alongside each other the original English words and their German translation, the sexological text here draws attention to the deadly climax of the Philadelphian doctor's words. Recording in parallel the German and English text, the passage undermines the professional objectivity of the Philadelphian doctor, alerting us to the complicity of certain medical discourses and certain doctors in perpetuating violence against homosexuals.

If the Philadelphian example constitutes a clear attack on homosexual life, the archive of suicide that can be found in Hirschfeld's writings is often difficult not simply because it contains evidence of such persecution, but because it shows that in a considerable number of successful suicides the social rejection that prompted them was imagined rather than real. Hirschfeld recounts, for example, the "unnecessary" suicide of a man from Baden in south Germany who had been arrested for homosexual conduct while on holiday in Berlin. The man hanged himself in his cell shortly after his arrest, without awaiting replies to the letters he had sent to Hirschfeld, his family, and the company that employed him, in which he notified them of his arrest. Hirschfeld notes that the bureaucratic process of sending the letters out of prison fatally delayed their receipt by five days, a time span that proved too long for the man who killed himself believing that "outside nobody wants to know him any longer."[64] Hirschfeld points out that this death is particularly tragic because the man's sense of rejection was unfounded: both his family and his employer immediately sent supportive replies, and the company further emphasized that the man could return to his post "even if he was found guilty."[65] In other words, while the man clearly suffered from legal persecution, the sense of isolation and social rejection that motivated his suicide was not borne out by the support expressed by his family and workplace.

By bringing together these tragic narratives and giving them a statistical frame, Hirschfeld's writings present individual suffering in collective terms. His work shows that homosexual persecution creates despair and shame that can make queer lives feel unlivable even if they are not overtly rejected. Hirschfeld mentions elsewhere that he often encountered on the bodies of his patients "scars left by suicide attempts" (*Suizidialnarben*).[66] The image of the scars indicates how the damage caused by social norms touched Hirschfeld's sexological practice in real terms, while his collection of data on homosexual suicide in turn helps to make visible the queer scar tissue that marks modern homosexuality.

Translation as a Vital Textual Politics

From our vantage point today, in an age of discursive explosions around difficult events and emotions, it is easy to forget that both extreme emotional experience and "everyday" suffering have not always been publicly speakable.[67] Hirschfeld's archive of homosexual suicide serves as a poignant reminder that discursive realities have a real impact on whether or not lives are felt to be (un)livable. Gayatri Spivak, in her examination of translation as a tool for understanding the relationship between representation, the self, and the social, has argued that "language is not everything. It is only a vital *clue* to where the self loses its boundaries."[68] However, for an investigation such as my own, which is concerned with the less tangible, emotional aspects of queer history, this linguistic body is often the only evidence we have of the thoughts, feelings, and experiences that shaped identities and subjectivities in the past. In this chapter I have therefore shifted around the emphasis of Spivak's words to argue that while language is indeed not everything, translation can provide vital insights into the way homosexual lives and discourses are connected across national boundaries.

By turning attention to the translations of (unlivable) lives in Hirschfeld's work, this chapter has demonstrated that there are real links between popular discourses about sexuality and the lives of the women and men who inhabit the sexological archive. This examination is not about recuperating the *scientia sexualis* or about denying the damage caused by sexological norms and the devastating practices of doctors who tried to "cure" others of their unspeakable desires. Instead I have considered the translations in Hirschfeld's work to address the difficult question of how we might understand emotional upset caused in relation to an identity—in this case homosexuality—that is discursively extremely restricted because of its lack of public legitimacy. My aim has been to pursue what I think of as a "vital textual politics," a reading strategy inspired by Judith Butler's concern with what she calls the "terms that govern reality." In *Undoing Gender*, Butler writes about the importance of considering "how to create a world in which those who understand their gender and their desire to be nonnormative can live and thrive not only without the threat of violence from the outside but without the pervasive sense of their own unreality, which can lead to suicide or a suicidal life."[69] Attention to translation in Hirschfeld's suicide narratives helps to make visible the social norms that prompted many women and men to end their life because of the sense that their homosexual feelings and desires fundamentally "disqualified" them from living. These writings and their translations thus provide vital insights into the damaging terms that governed queer reality in the early twentieth century as they reveal the powerful impact homosexual persecution and social rejection had on individual lives at the time.

NOTES

1. Judith Butler, *Undoing Gender* (New York: Routledge, 2004), 38.

2. For excellent histories of violent queer histories, see Gail Mason, *The Spectacle of Violence: Homophobia, Gender and Knowledge* (New York: Routledge, 2002); Carolyn J. Dean, *The Frail Social Body: Pornography, Homosexuality and Other Fantasies in Interwar France* (Berkeley: University of California Press, 2000); Lisa Duggan, *Sapphic Slashers: Sex, Violence, and American Modernity* (Durham, NC: Duke University Press, 2000); Günter Grau and Claudia Schoppmann, eds., *Hidden Holocaust: Gay and Lesbian Persecution in Germany 1933–45* (New York: Routledge, 1995); Erwin J. Haeberle, "Swastika, Pink Triangle and Yellow Star: The Destruction of Sexology and the Persecution of Homosexuality in Nazi Germany," *Journal of Sex Research* 17, no. 3 (1981): 270–287; Dagmar Herzog, ed., *Sexuality and German Fascism* (Oxford: Berghahn, 2005); David K. Johnson, *The Lavender Scare: The Cold War Persecution of Gays and Lesbians in the Federal Government* (Chicago: University of Chicago Press, 2004); Lucy Bland and Laura Doan, eds., *Sexology in Culture: Labelling Bodies and Desires* (Cambridge: Polity, 1998).

3. Ann Cvetkovich, *An Archive of Feelings: Trauma, Sexuality and Lesbian Public Cultures* (Durham, NC: Duke University Press, 2003), 3.

4. See, for instance, Elena Mancini, *Magnus Hirschfeld and the Quest for Sexual Freedom* (Basingstoke, UK: Palgrave Macmillan, 2010); Susan Stryker, *Transgender History* (Berkeley, CA: Seal Press, 2008); Charlotte Wolff, *Magnus Hirschfeld: A Portrait of a Pioneer in Sexology* (London: Quartet, 1986).

5. Heather Love, *Feeling Backward: Loss and the Politics of Queer History* (Cambridge, MA: Harvard University Press, 2007), 1.

6. See Love, *Feeling Backward*; Cvetkovich, *Archive of Feelings*. Judith Halberstam's more recent *The Queer Art of Failure* (Durham, NC: Duke University Press, 2011) challenges the alignment of failure with miserableness.

7. As examples of the range of this scholarship, see, for instance, Lisa Duggan, *Sapphic Slashers: Sex, Violence, and American Modernity* (Durham, NC: Duke University Press, 2001); Judith Halberstam, *Female Masculinity* (Durham, NC: Duke University Press, 1998); Omise'eke Natasha Tinsley, *Thiefing Sugar: Eroticism between Women in Caribbean Literature* (Durham, NC: Duke University Press, 2010); Martha Vicinus, *Intimate Friends: Women Who Loved Women, 1778–1928* (Chicago: University of Chicago Press, 2004).

8. Magnus Hirschfeld, "Autobiographical Sketch," in *Encyclopedia Sexualis: A Comprehensive Encyclopedia-Dictionary of Sexual Sciences*, ed. Victor Robinson (New York: Dingwall-Rock, 1936), 318.

9. Magnus Hirschfeld, "Die Gründung des WhK und seine ersten Mitglieder," reprinted in *Magnus Hirschfeld, Von Einst bis Jetzt: Geschichte einer homosexuellen Bewegung 1897–1922*, ed. James Steakley (Berlin: Rosa Winkel, 1986), 48.

10. For an innovative rethinking of the disciplining of criminality and sexuality, see Regina Kunzel, *Criminal Intimacy: Prison and the Uneven History of Modern American Sexuality* (Chicago: University of Chicago Press, 2008).

11. See Émile Durkheim, *Suicide: A Study in Sociology*, ed. George Simpson, trans. John A. Spaulding and George Simpson (New York: Free Press, 1979 [1897]), 326–360; Richard Bell, *We Shall Be No More: Suicide and Self-Government in the Newly United States* (Cambridge, MA: Harvard University Press, 2012); Ron Brown, *Art of Suicide* (London: Reaktion Books, 2001), 146–193; Barbara Gates, *Victorian Suicide: Mad Crimes and Sad Histories* (Princeton, NJ: Princeton University Press, 1988); Olive Anderson, *Suicide in Victorian and Edwardian England* (Oxford: Clarendon, 1987); Howard Kushner, *American Suicide* (New Brunswick, NJ: Rutgers University Press, 1991); Irina Paperno, *Suicide as a Cultural Institution in Dostoevsky's Russia* (Ithaca, NY: Cornell University Press, 1997); Kevin Grauke, "'I Cannot Bear to Be Hurted Anymore': Suicide as Dialectical Ideological Sin in Nineteenth-Century American Realism," in *Representations of Death in Nineteenth-Century US Writing and Culture*, ed. Lucy Frank (Aldershot, UK: Ashgate, 2007), 77–88; Helmut Thome, "Violent Crime (and Suicide) in Imperial Germany, 1883–1902," *International Criminal Justice Review* 20, no. 1 (2010): 5–34; Thomas Joiner, *Myths about Suicide* (Cambridge, MA: Harvard University Press, 2010).

12. A good overview of English suicide laws and their Christian underpinnings can be found in Norman St. John-Stevas, *Life, Death and the Law: Law and Christian Morals in England and the United States* (Washington, DC: Beard Books, 2002 [1961]), 233–241.

13. Henry Romilly Fedden, *Suicide: A Social and Historical Study* (London: Davies, 1938), 247–248.

14. "gegen die an sich nicht das mindeste einzuwenden war." Hirschfeld, "Die Gründung des WhK," 48.

15. "was mir fast that Herz abdrücken wollte." Ibid.

16. Friedrich Nietzsche, *Also Sprach Zarathustra? Ein Buch für Alle und Keinen* (Chemnitz, Germany: Schmeitzner, 1883).

17. Ibid., 109.

18. "der mindestens theoretisch volles Verständnis für die homosexuelle Liebe besaß." Magnus Hirschfeld, *Die Homosexualität des Mannes und des Weibes*, Nachdruck der Erstauflage von 1914 mit einer kommentierten Einleitung von E. J. Haeberle (Berlin: de Gruyter, 1984), 421.

19. "Der Gedanke, daß sie dazu beitragen könnten, daß auch das deutsche Vaterland über uns gerechter denkt, verschönt meine Sterbestunde." Ibid.

20. *Oxford English Dictionary*, 2nd ed., s.v. "conjunctive."

21. Cvetkovich, *Archive of Feelings*, 7.

22. Reiner Herrm, in conversation with me at the Dartmouth Humanities Institute 2013, has said that this particular suicide is an invention, a rhetorical means by which Hirschfeld justifies his sexology. If this view may seem supported by the fact that Hirschfeld published his first study under a pseudonym, it is difficult to establish the facts of the matter. More interesting to me is precisely the fact that Hirschfeld presents the tragic subject of homosexual suicide central to the justification for his sexological reform project.

23. Sigmund Freud to C. G. Jung, February 25, 1908. Reprinted in *The Freud-Jung Letters: The Correspondence between Sigmund Freud and C. G. Jung*, ed. William McGuire, trans. Ralph Mannheim and R. F. C. Hull (London: Hogarth, 1974), 125–127.

24. Hirschfeld, "Autobiographical Sketch," 319.

25. Yvonne Ivory, "The Urning and His Own: Individualism and the Fin-de-Siècle Invert," *German Studies Review* 26, no. 2 (2003): 333–352 (esp. 338); James D. Steakley, *The Homosexual Emancipation Movement in Germany* (Salem, NH: Ayer, 1975).

26. Cathy Caruth, preface to *Trauma: Explorations in Memory* (Baltimore: Johns Hopkins University Press, 1995), vii.

27. Hirschfeld, "Autobiographical Sketch," 317–321.

28. "unmittelbar *nach* seiner Hochzeit." Hirschfeld, "Die Gründung des WhK," 48. My emphasis.

29. Peter Cryle, in an extensive survey of eighteenth- and nineteenth-century French literature, has shown that male anxieties about the wedding night are deeply entrenched in the cultural imagination. Peter Cryle, *The Telling of the Act: Sexuality as Narrative in Eighteenth- and Nineteenth-Century France* (London: Associated University Press, 2001).

30. Hirschfeld, "Autobiographical Sketch," 318.

31. "The first cry of pain through the primitive jungle was the first call for a physician," begins Victor Robinson's *The Story of Medicine* (New York: New Home Library, 1943), 1.

32. Karma Lochrie, *Heterosyncracies: Female Sexuality When Normal Wasn't* (Minneapolis: University of Minnesota Press, 2005), 24–25.

33. Ibid.

34. See, for example, Janice M. Irvine's excellent dissection of the issues at stake in *Disorders of Desire: Sexuality and Gender in Modern American Sexology* (Philadelphia: Temple University Press, 2005); Jennifer Terry, "Lesbians under the Medical Gaze: Scientists Search for Remarkable Differences," *Journal of Sex Research* 27, no. 3 (1990): 317–339; Jennifer Terry, *An American Obsession: Science, Medicine, and Homosexuality in Modern Society* (Chicago: University of Chicago Press, 1999).

35. Hirschfeld, "Die Gründung des WhK," 49.

36. Thank you to Reiner Herrn for bringing this to my attention.

37. See Émile Durkheim, *Le Suicide* (Paris: n.p., 1897).

38. Ian Marsh, *Suicide: Foucault, History and Truth* (Cambridge: Cambridge University Press, 2010), 77–192; Robert D. Goldney, Johann A. Schioldann, and Kirsten I. Dunn, "Suicide before Durkheim," *Health and History* 10, no. 2 (2008): 73–93.

39. Karl Marx, "Peuchet on Suicide," in *Marx on Suicide*, ed. and trans. Eric A. Plaut, Gabrielle Edgcomb, and Kevin Anderson (Evanston, IL: Northwestern University Press, 1999), 51.

40. Durkheim uses the expression "the act whose author is also the sufferer" in his *Suicide: A Study in Sociology*, 42.

41. Hubert Kennedy traces their anti-homosexuality stance in "Johann Baptist von Schweitzer: The Queer Marx Loved to Hate," *Journal of Homosexuality* 29, no. 2–3 (1995): 69–96.

42. The English and French translations are available at http://www.marxists.org/archive/marx/works/cw/volume43/index.htm. The translation captures the older connotations of the term "cons," which is derived from the Latin *cunnus* and was used in de Sade's work with the sense and the force of "cunt." Its strength was eroded in the course of the nineteenth and twentieth centuries as it came to be used as a common disparaging expression for stupid people. I am grateful to Peter Cryle for explaining this linguistic change to me.

43. Friedrich Engels to Karl Marx, June 22, 1869, in *Marx and Engels Collected Works*, 43:295, available in English at http://www.marxists.org/archive/marx/works/cw/volume43/index.htm.

44. See Heike Bauer, *English Literary Sexology: Translations of Inversion, 1860–1930* (Basingstoke, UK: Palgrave Macmillan, 2009), 23–29.

45. Early sexologists such as, famously, Richard von Krafft-Ebing in the twelve editions of his *Psychopathia Sexualis*, published between 1886 and 1902, turned to Latin when describing the details of "abnormal" and "unnatural" sexual practices.

46. Katrina Jaworski, "The Author, Agency and Suicide," *Social Identities* 14, no. 4 (2010): 677.

47. Ibid.

48. Butler, *Undoing Gender*, 31.

49. "Daß eine große Anzahl Homosexueller sich im Zusammenhange mir ihrer geschlechtlichen Eigenart veranlaßt sieht, ihrem Leben ein freiwilliges Ende zu bereiten, steht außer Zweifel." Hirschfeld, *Homosexualität des Mannes und des Weibes*, 902.

50. Ibid., 905.

51. Cited in Kevin Anderson, "Marx on Suicide in the Context of His Other Writings on Alienation and Gender," in Plaut, Edgcomb, and Anderson, *Marx on Suicide*, 7.

52. Ibid.

53. "Die Homosexuellen leiden nicht an der Homosexualität, sondern an ihrer unrichtigen Beurteilung durch sich und andere." Hirschfeld, "Die Gründung des WhK," 49.

54. "Bitte, nach den Motiven unserer Tat nicht zu forschen." Hirschfeld, *Homosexualität des Mannes und des Weibes*, 914.

55. Adrienne Rich, "Compulsory Heterosexuality and Lesbian Existence," *Signs: Journal of Women in Culture and Society* 5, no. 4 (1980): 649.

56. Ibid.

57. Hirschfeld, *Homosexualität des Mannes und des Weibes*, 902.

58. Ibid.

59. Ibid., 899.

60. I discuss the episode more fully in "Staging Un/Translatability: Magnus Hirschfeld Encounters Philadelphia," in *Un/Translatables*, ed. Catriona McLeod (Evanston, IL: Northwestern University Press, forthcoming).

61. "Der Arzt, den er in Philadelphia seiner homosexuellen Leiden halber um Rat gefragt habe, ihm geantworted hätte: 'es gäbe für ihn nur drei Möglichkeiten: Selbstbefriedigung (use his right hand), freiwilliger Aufenthalt in einer Irrenanstalt (place himself in a madhouse) oder Selbstmord (or better commit suicide).'" Hirschfeld, *Homosexualität des Mannes und des Weibes*, 899.

62. Paula Bennett and Vernon Rosario, eds., *Solitary Pleasures: The Historical, Literary and Artistic Discourses of Autoeroticism* (New York, Routledge, 1995), 1–19. See also Thomas Laqueur, *Solitary Sex: A Cultural History of Masturbation* (New York: Zone Books, 2003).

63. Andrew Scull, *Social Order / Mental Disorder: Anglo-American Psychiatry in Historical Perspective* (Berkeley: University of California Press, 1989), 96–118.

64. "draußen niemand mehr etwas von ihm wissen wollte." Hirschfeld, *Homosexualität des Mannes und des Weibes*, 906.

65. "selbst im Falle seiner Verurteilung." Ibid.

66. Ibid., 903.

67. Ann E. Kaplan, *Trauma Culture: The Politics of Loss and Terror in Media and Literature* (New Brunswick, NJ: Rutgers University Press, 2005), 2.

68. Gayatri Spivak, *Outside in the Teaching Machine* (New York: Routledge, 1993), 179–200.

69. Butler, *Undoing Gender*, 219.

Selected Bibliography

Listed here are key critical and further reading sources available in English. Full references to the primary sources can be found in the individual chapters.

Aldrich, Robert. *The Seduction of the Mediterranean: Writing, Art, and Homosexual Fantasy.* London: Routledge, 1993.

Altman, Dennis. *Global Sex.* Chicago: University of Chicago Press, 2001.

———. "Rupture or Continuity? The Internationalization of Gay Identities." *Social Text* 14 (1996): 77–94.

Ang, Ien. *On Not Speaking Chinese: Living between Asia and the West.* New York: Routledge, 2001.

Apter, Emily. *The Translation Zone: A New Comparative Literature.* Princeton, NJ: Princeton University Press, 2006.

Babayan, Kathryn, and Afsaneh Najmabadi, eds. *Islamicate Sexualities: Translations across Temporal Geographies of Desire.* Cambridge, MA: Harvard University Press, 2008.

Bachmann-Medick, Doris. "Introduction: The Translational Turn." *Translation Studies* 2, no. 1 (2009): 2–16.

Baker, Mona, ed. *Critical Readings in Translation Studies.* New York: Routledge, 2010.

Baron, Beth, and Nikki R. Kedie, eds. *Women in Middle Eastern History: Shifting Boundaries in Sex and Gender.* New Haven, CT: Yale University Press, 1991.

Bassnett, Susan, and André Lefevere, eds. *Constructing Cultures: Essays on Literary Translation.* Clevedon, UK: Multilingual Matters, 1998.

Bauer, Heike. *English Literary Sexology: Translations of Inversion, 1860–1930.* Basingstoke, UK: Palgrave Macmillan, 2009.

———. "'Not a Translation but a Mutilation': The Limits of Translation and the Discipline of Sexology." *Yale Journal of Criticism* 16, no. 2 (2003): 381–405.

——. "'Race,' Normativity and the History of Sexuality: Magnus Hirschfeld's Racism and Early Twentieth-Century Sexology." *Psychology and Sexuality* 1, no. 3 (2010): 239–249.

——. "Sexology Backward: Hirschfeld, Kinsey and the Reshaping of Sex Research in the 1950s." In *Queer 1950s: Rethinking Sexuality in the Postwar Years*, edited by Heike Bauer and Matt Cook, 133–149. Basingstoke, UK: Palgrave Macmillan, 2012.

Bauer, Heike, and Matt Cook, eds. *Queer 1950s: Rethinking Sexuality in the Postwar Years*. Basingstoke, UK: Palgrave Macmillan, 2012.

Beachy, Robert. "The German Invention of Homosexuality." *Journal of Modern History* 82, no. 4 (2010): 801–838.

Beccalossi, Chiara. *Female Sexual Inversion: Same-Sex Desires in Italian and British Sexology, c. 1870–1920*. New York: Palgrave Macmillan, 2012.

——. "Madness and Sexual Psychopathies as the Magnifying Glass of the Normal: Italian Psychiatry and Sexuality, c. 1880–1910." *Social History of Medicine* 27, no. 2 (2014): 303–325.

Beer, Gillian. *Open Fields: Science in Cultural Encounter*. Oxford: Oxford University Press, 1999.

Bennett, Judith M. "Confronting Continuity." *Journal of Women's History* 9, no. 3 (1997): 73–94.

——. "'Lesbian-Like' and the Social History of Lesbianism." *Journal of the History of Sexuality* 9 (2000): 1–24.

Bennett, Paula, and Vernon Rosario, eds. *Solitary Pleasures: The Historical, Literary and Artistic Discourses of Autoeroticism*. New York: Routledge, 1995.

Berlant, Lauren. "On the Case." *Critical Inquiry* 33, no. 4 (2007): 663–672.

Bhabha, Homi. *The Location of Culture*. New York: Routledge, 1994.

Birken, Lawrence. *Consuming Desire: Sexual Science and the Emergence of a Culture of Abundance, 1871–1914*. Ithaca, NY: Cornell University Press, 1988.

Blackwood, Evelyn. "Transnational Discourses and Circuits of Queer Knowledge in Indonesia." *GLQ: A Journal of Lesbian and Gay Studies* 14 (2008): 481–507.

Bland, Lucy. *Banishing the Beast: Sexuality and the Early Feminists*. London: Penguin, 1995.

Bland, Lucy, and Laura Doan, eds. *Sexology in Culture: Labelling Bodies and Desires*. Cambridge: Polity, 1998.

Bleys, Rudi. *The Geography of Perversion: Male-to-Male Sexual Behaviour outside the West and the Ethnographic Imagination, 1750–1918*. New York: New York University Press, 1995.

Blowers, Geoffrey, and Shelley Wang Xuelai. "Gone with the *West Wind*: The Emergence and Disappearance of Psychotherapeutic Culture in China, 1936–68." In *Psychiatry and Chinese History*, edited by Howard Chiang, 143–160. London: Pickering and Chatto, 2014.

Brady, Sean, ed. *John Addington Symonds (1840–1893) and Homosexuality: A Critical Edition of Sources*. Basingstoke, UK: Palgrave Macmillan, 2012.

——. *Masculinity and Male Homosexuality in Britain, 1861–1913*. Basingstoke, UK: Palgrave Macmillan, 2009.

Breen, Margaret. "Homosexual Identity, Translation, and Prime-Stevenson's *Imre* and *The Intersexes*." *CLCWeb: Comparative Literature and Culture* 14, no. 1 (2012): 1–9.

Breger, Claudia. "Feminine Masculinities: Scientific and Literary Representations of 'Female Inversion' at the Turn of the Twentieth Century." *Journal of the History of Sexuality* 14, no. 1–2 (2005): 76–106.

Bristow, Joseph. *Sexuality.* 2nd ed. New York: Routledge, 2011.

———. "Symonds' History, Ellis' Heredity: Sexual Inversion." In *Sexology in Culture: Labelling Bodies and Desires,* edited by Lucy Bland and Laura Doan, 79–99. Cambridge: Polity, 1998.

Brook, Timothy. *The Confusions of Pleasure: Commerce and Culture in Ming China.* Berkeley: University of California Press, 1999.

Bryan, Catherine. "Making National Citizens: Gender, Race, and Class in Two Works by Clorinda Matto de Turner." *Cincinnati Romance Review* 15 (1996): 113–118.

Bullough, Vern L., ed. *Before Stonewall: Activist for Gay and Lesbian Rights in Historical Context.* Binghamton, NY: Haworth, 2002.

Butler, Judith. *Undoing Gender.* New York: Routledge, 2004.

Castle, Terry. *The Apparitional Lesbian: Female Homosexuality and Modern Culture.* New York: Columbia University Press, 1993.

Castro-Klarén, Sara, and John Charles Chasteen, eds. *Beyond Imagined Communities: Reading and Writing the Nation in Nineteenth-Century Latin America.* Baltimore: Johns Hopkins University Press, 2003.

Chauncey, George, Jr. "From Sexual Inversion to Homosexuality: Medicine and the Changing Conceptualisation of Female Deviance." *Salmagundi* 58–59 (1982–1983): 114–146.

Chiang, Howard. "The Conceptual Contours of Sex in the Chinese Life Sciences: Zhu Xi (1899–1962), Hermaphroditism, and the Biological Discourse of *Ci* and *Xiong,* 1920–1950." *East Asian Science, Technology and Society: An International Journal* 2, no. 3 (2008): 401–430.

———. "(De)Provincializing China: Queer Historicism and Sinophone Postcolonial Critique." In *Queer Sinophone Cultures,* edited by Howard Chiang and Ari Larissa Heinrich, 19–51. London: Routledge, 2013.

———. "Double Alterity and the Global Historiography of Sexuality: China, Europe, and the Emergence of Sexuality as a Global Possibility." *e-pisteme* 2, no. 1 (2009): 33–52.

———. "Epistemic Modernity and the Emergence of Homosexuality in China." *Gender and History* 22, no. 3 (2010): 629–657.

———. "Liberating Sex, Knowing Desire: *Scientia Sexualis* and Epistemic Turning Points in the History of Sexuality." *History of the Human Sciences* 23, no. 5 (2010): 42–69.

———, ed. "Queer Transnationalism in China." Topical cluster, *English Language Notes* 49, no. 1 (2011): 109–144.

———. "Rethinking 'Style' for Historians and Philosophers of Science: Converging Lessons from Sexuality, Translation, and East Asian Studies." *Studies in History and Philosophy of Biological and Biomedical Sciences* 40 (2009): 109–118.

Chiang, Howard, and Ari Larissa Heinrich. *Queer Sinophone Cultures.* London: Routledge, 2013.

Chou Wah-shan. *Tongzhi: Politics of Same-Sex Eroticism in Chinese Societies.* New York: Haworth, 2000.

Cook, Matt. *London and the Culture of Homosexuality, 1885–1914.* Cambridge: Cambridge University Press, 2003.

Crozier, Ivan. "Havelock Ellis, Eonism and the Patient's Discourse; or, Writing a Book about Sex." *History of Psychiatry* 11 (2000): 125–154.

———. "Nineteenth-Century British Psychiatric Writing about Homosexuality before Havelock Ellis: The Missing Story." *Journal of the History of Medicine and Allied Sciences* 63, no. 1 (2008): 65–102.

———. "Pillow Talk: Credibility, Trust and the Sexological Case History." *History of Science* 46, no. 4 (2008): 375–404.

———, ed. *Sexual Inversion: A Critical Edition.* Basingstoke, UK: Palgrave Macmillan, 2007.

Cryle, Peter. *The Telling of the Act: Sexuality as Narrative in Eighteenth- and Nineteenth-Century France.* London: Associated University Press, 2001.

Cryle, Peter, and Christopher Forth, eds. *Sexuality at the Fin de Siècle: The Makings of a "Central Problem."* Newark: University of Delaware Press, 2008.

Cvetkovich, Ann. *An Archive of Feelings: Trauma, Sexuality and Lesbian Public Cultures.* Durham, NC: Duke University Press, 2003.

Damousi, Joy, Birgit Lang, and Katie Sutton, eds. *Cases and the Dissemination of Knowledge.* New York: Routledge, 2015.

Davidson, Arnold. *The Emergence of Sexuality: Historical Epistemology and the Formation of Concepts.* Cambridge, MA: Harvard University Press, 2001.

Dean, Carolyn J. "The Productive Hypothesis: Foucault, Gender and the History of Sexuality." *History and Theory* 33, no. 3 (1994): 271–296.

———. *Sexuality and Modern Western Culture.* New York: Twayne, 1996.

D'Emilio, John, and Estelle B. Freedman. *Intimate Matters: A History of Sexuality in America.* New York: Harper and Row, 1988.

Dickinson, Edward R., and Richard F. Wetzell. "The Historiography of Sexuality in Modern Germany." *German History* 23, no. 3 (2005): 291–305.

Dikötter, Frank. *Sex, Culture, and Modernity in China: Medical Science and the Construction of Sexual Identities in the Early Republican Period.* Honolulu: University of Hawai'i Press, 1995.

Dinshaw, Carolyn. *Getting Medieval: Sexualities and Communities, Pre-and Postmodern.* Durham, NC: Duke University Press, 1999.

Dizdar, Dilek. "Translational Transitions: 'Translation Proper' and Translation Studies in the Humanities." *Translation Studies* 2, no. 1 (2009): 89–102.

Doan, Laura. *Disturbing Practices: History, Sexuality, and Women's Experience of Modern War.* Chicago: University of Chicago Press, 2013.

———. *Fashioning Sapphism: The Origins of a Modern English Lesbian Culture.* New York: Columbia University Press, 2001.

Dollase, Hitomi Tsuchiya. "Early Twentieth Century Japanese Girls' Magazine Stories: Examining *Shōjo* Voice in *Hanamonogatari* (Flower Tales)." *Journal of Popular Culture* 36, no. 4 (2003): 724–755.

Dose, Ralf. *Magnus Hirschfeld: The Origins of the Gay Liberation Movement.* New York: Monthly Review Press, 2014.

Dowling, Linda. *Hellenism and Homosexuality in Victorian Oxford.* Ithaca, NY: Cornell University Press, 1994.

Downing, Lisa. *The Cambridge Introduction to Michel Foucault*. Cambridge: Cambridge University Press, 2008.

Drucker, Peter, ed. *Different Rainbows*. London: Gay Men's Press, 2000.

Duberman, Martin B., Martha Vicinus, and George Chauncey Jr., eds. *Hidden from History: Reclaiming the Gay and Lesbian Past*. New York: New American Library, 1989.

Duggan, Lisa. "From Instincts to Politics: Writing the History of Sexuality in the U.S." *Journal of Sex Research* 27, no. 1 (1990): 95–109.

———. *Sapphic Slashers: Sex, Violence, and American Modernity*. Durham, NC: Duke University Press, 2001.

Dyer, Richard. "Less and More than Women and Men: Lesbian and Gay Cinema in Weimar Germany." *New German Critique*, no. 51 (1990): 5–31.

Eder, Franz X., Lesley A. Hall, and Gert Hekma, eds. *Sexual Cultures in Europe: National Histories*. Manchester, UK: Manchester University Press, 1999.

El-Rouayheb, Khaled. *Before Homosexuality in the Arab-Islamic World, 1500–1800*. Chicago: University of Chicago Press, 2005.

El-Shakry, Omnia. "Barren Land and Fecund Bodies: The Emergence of Population Discourse in Interwar Egypt." *International Journal of Middle East Studies* 37 (2005): 360–361.

Exner, Lisbeth. *Leopold von Sacher-Masoch*. Reinbek, Germany: Rowohlt, 2003.

Farquhar, Judith. *Appetites: Food and Sex in Post-Socialist China*. Durham, NC: Duke University Press, 2002.

Faulkner, Evelyn. "'Powerless to Prevent Him': Attitudes of Married Working-Class Women in the 1920s and the Rise of Sexual Power." *Local Population Studies* 49 (1992): 51–61.

Ferguson, Roderick. *Aberrations in Black: Towards a Queer of Colour Critique*. Minneapolis: University of Minnesota Press, 2004.

Fisher, Kate, and Jana Funke. "'Let Us Leave the Hospital [. . .]; Let Us Go on a Journey around the World': Sexual Science and the Global Search for Variation and Difference." In *Towards a Global History of Sexual Science, 1880–1950*, edited by Veronika Fuechtner, Douglas E. Haynes, and Ryan Jones. Forthcoming.

Foucault, Michel. *The Archeology of Knowledge and the Discourse on Language*. Translated by A. M. Sheridan Smith. New York: Pantheon, 1972 [1969].

———. *The History of Sexuality*. Vol. 1: *An Introduction*. Translated by Robert Hurley. London: Penguin, 1990.

Fradenberg, Louis, and Carla Freccero, eds. *Premodern Sexualities*. London: Routledge, 1996.

Fraser, Jennifer. "Clorinda Matto de Turner's *Herencia* as the Creation of an Alternative Social Knowledge." *Bulletin of Hispanic Studies* 88, no. 1 (2011): 97–112.

———. "'Con el ropaje de la novela': Margarita Práxedes Muñoz's *La evolución de Paulina* as an Attempt to (Re)negotiate Literary Forms and Contest Normative Subjectivities." *Journal of Romance Studies* 15, no. 1 (2015).

———. "'That Women's Writing Thing You Do': Reflections on Silence, Writing and Academic Spaces." *Modern Languages Open* (2014). Available at http://www.modern languagesopen.org/index.php/mlo/article/view/7/17.

Frederick, Sarah. "Not That Innocent: Yoshiya Nobuko's Good Girls." In *Bad Girls of Japan*, edited by Laura Miller and Jan Bardsley, 65–79. New York: Palgrave Macmillan, 2005.

Freidenreich, Harriet Pass. "Jewish Women Physicians in Central Europe in the Early Twentieth Century." *Contemporary Jewry* 17 (1996): 79–105.

Frühstück, Sabine. *Colonizing Sex: Sexology and Social Control in Modern Japan.* Berkeley: University of California Press, 2003.

Fuechtner, Veronika, Douglas E. Haynes, and Ryan Jones, eds. *Towards a Global History of Sexual Science, 1880–1950.* Forthcoming.

Funke, Jana. "Navigating the Past: Sexuality, Race and the Uses of the Primitive in Magnus Hirschfeld's World Journey of a Sexologist." In *Sex, Knowledge and Receptions of the Past,* edited by Kate Fisher and Rebecca Langlands. Oxford: Oxford University Press, forthcoming.

———. "'We Cannot Be Greek Now': Age Difference, Corruption of Youth and the Making of *Sexual Inversion.*" *English Studies* 94, no. 2 (2013): 139–153.

Furth, Charlotte. "Rethinking van Gulik: Sexuality and Reproduction in Traditional Chinese Medicine." In *Engendering China: Women, Culture, and the State,* edited by Christina K. Gilmartin, Gail Hershatter, Lisa Rofel, and Tyrene White, 125–146. Cambridge, MA: Harvard University Press, 1995.

Garber, Linda. "Where in the World Are the Lesbians?" *Journal of the History of Sexuality* 14 (2005): 28–50.

Genette, Gérard. *Palimpsests: Literature in the Second Degree.* Translated by Channa Newman and Claude Doubinsky. Lincoln: University of Nebraska Press, 1998.

Giffney, Noreen, Michelle Sauer, and Diane Watt, eds. *The Lesbian Premodern.* New York: Palgrave Macmillan, 2011.

Gifford, James. *Dayneford's Library: American Homosexual Writing, 1900–1913.* Amherst: University of Massachusetts Press, 1995.

Gilman, Sander L. *Differences and Pathology: Stereotypes of Sexuality, Race and Madness.* Ithaca, NY: Cornell University Press, 1985.

Gluckman, Catherine Bailey. "Constructing Queer Female Identities in Late Realist German Fiction." *German Life and Letters* 65, no. 3 (2012): 318–332.

Gordon, Michael. "From an Unfortunate Necessity to a Cult of Mutual Orgasm: Sex in American Marital Education Literature, 1830–1940." In *Studies in the Sociology of Sex,* edited by James M. Heslin, 53–77. New York: Appleton-Century-Crofts, 1971.

Grau, Günter, and Claudia Schoppmann, eds. *Hidden Holocaust: Gay and Lesbian Persecution in Germany 1933–45.* New York: Routledge, 1995.

Grewal, Inderpal, and Caren Kaplan. "Global Identities: Theorizing Transnational Studies of Sexuality." *GLQ: A Journal of Lesbian and Gay Studies* 7, no. 4 (2001): 663–679.

Grosskurth, Phyllis. *Havelock Ellis: A Biography.* New York: Knopf, 1980.

Grossmann, Atina. *Reforming Sex: The German Movement for Birth Control and Abortion Reform, 1920–1950.* Oxford: Oxford University Press, 1995.

Hacking, Ian. *Scientific Reason.* Taipei: National Taiwan University Press, 2008.

———. *The Social Construction of What?* Cambridge, MA: Harvard University Press, 1999.

Haeberle, Erwin J. "Swastika, Pink Triangle and Yellow Star: The Destruction of Sexology and the Persecution of Homosexuality in Nazi Germany." *Journal of Sex Research* 17, no. 3 (1981): 270–287.

Halberstam, Judith. *Female Masculinity*. Durham, NC: Duke University Press, 1998.

Hall, Lesley A. "Hauling Down the Double Standard: Feminism, Social Purity and Sexual Science in Late Nineteenth-Century Britain." *Gender and History* 16 (2004): 36–56.

———. "Impotent Ghosts from No Man's Land, Flappers' Boyfriends, or Crypto-Patriarchs? Men, Sex and Social Change in 1920s Britain." *Social History* 21 (1996): 54–70.

———. "'Somehow Very Distasteful': Doctors, Men and Sexual Problems between the Wars." *Journal of Contemporary History* 20 (1985): 553–574.

Hall, Lesley A., and Roy Porter. *The Facts of Life: The Creation of Sexual Knowledge in Britain, 1650–1950*. New Haven, CT: Yale University Press, 1995.

Halley, Janet, and Andrew Parker, eds. *After Sex? On Writing since Queer Theory*. Durham, NC: Duke University Press, 2011.

Halperin, David M. *How to Do the History of Homosexuality*. Chicago: University of Chicago Press, 2002.

———. *One Hundred Years of Homosexuality and Other Essays on Greek Love*. New York: Routledge, 1990.

Hau, Michael. *The Cult of Health and Beauty in Germany: A Social History, 1890–1930*. Chicago: University of Chicago Press, 2003.

Hauser, Renate. "Krafft-Ebing's Psychological Understanding of Sexual Behaviour." In *Sexual Knowledge, Sexual Science: The History of Attitudes to Sexuality*, edited by Roy Porter and Mikulás Teich, 210–230. Cambridge: Cambridge University Press, 1994.

Healey, Dan. *Homosexual Desire in Revolutionary Russia: The Regulation of Sexual and Gender Dissent*. Chicago: University of Chicago Press, 2001.

Herzog, Dagmar, ed. *Sexuality and German Fascism*. Oxford: Berghahn, 2005.

Hinsch, Bret. *Passions of the Cut Sleeve: The Male Homosexual Tradition in China*. Berkeley: University of California Press, 1990.

Hirsch, Dafna. "Zionist Eugenics, Mixed Marriage, and the Creation of a 'New Jewish Type.'" *Journal of the Royal Anthropological Institute* 15 (2009): 592–609.

Ho, Loretta Wing Wah. *Gay and Lesbian Subculture in Urban China*. London: Routledge, 2010.

Irvine, Janice M. *Disorders of Desire: Sexuality and Gender in Modern American Sexology*. Philadelphia: Temple University Press, 2005.

Ivory, Yvonne. "The Urning and His Own: Individualism and the Fin-de-Siècle Invert." *German Studies Review* 26, no. 2 (2003): 333–352.

Jackson, Margaret. *The Real Facts of Life: Feminism and the Politics of Sexuality 1850–1940*. London: Routledge, 1994.

Jackson, Peter A. "Capitalism and Global Queering: National Markets, Parallels among Sexual Cultures, and Multiple Queer Modernities." *GLQ: A Journal of Lesbian and Gay Studies* 15 (2009): 357–395.

Jacob, Wilson Chacko. "Overcoming 'Simply Being': Straight Sex, Masculinity and Physical Culture in Modern Egypt." *Gender and History* 22 (2010): 658–676.

———. *Working Out Egypt: Effendi Masculinity and Subject Formation in Colonial Modernity, 1870–1940*. Durham, NC: Duke University Press, 2011.

Jagose, Annamarie. *Orgasmology*. Durham, NC: Duke University Press, 2013.

Jiménez-Lucena, Isabel. "Gender and Coloniality: The 'Moroccan Woman' and the 'Spanish Woman' in Spain's Sanitary Policies in Morocco." *Historia, Ciencias, Saude Manguinhos* 13 (2006): 33–54.

Jingsheng, Zhang. *Sex Histories (Xingshi)*. Taipei: Dala, 2006.

Johnson, Mark. "Transgression and the Making of 'Western' Sexual Sciences." In *Transgressive Sex: Subversion and Control in Erotic Encounters*, edited by Hastings Donnan and Fiona Magowan, 167–189. New York: Berghahn, 2009.

Kang, Wenqing. "Male Same-Sex Relations in Modern China: Language, Medical Representation, and Law, 1900–1949." *positions: east asia cultures critique* 18, no. 2 (2010): 489–510.

———. *Obsession: Male Same-Sex Relations in China, 1900–1950*. Hong Kong: Hong Kong University Press, 2009.

Katz, Jonathan Ned. *The Invention of Heterosexuality*. Chicago: University of Chicago Press, 2007.

Keller, Richard C. *Colonial Madness: Psychiatry in French North Africa*. Chicago: University of Chicago Press, 2007.

Kholoussy, Hanan. *For Better, for Worse: The Marriage Crisis That Made Modern Egypt, 1898–1936*. Stanford, CA: Stanford University Press, 2010.

———. "Monitoring and Medicalising Male Sexuality in Semi-Colonial Egypt." *Gender and History* 22 (2010): 677–691.

Ko, Dorothy. *Teachers of the Inner Chamber: Women and Culture in Seventeenth-Century China*. Stanford, CA: Stanford University Press, 1995.

Koestenbaum, Wayne. *Double Talk: The Erotics of Male Literary Collaboration*. New York: Routledge, 1989.

Kong, Travis. *Chinese Male Homosexualities: Memba, Tongzhi, and Golden Boy*. London: Routledge, 2010.

Kozma, Liat. *Policing Egyptian Women: Sex, Law and Medicine in Egypt 1850–1882*. Syracuse, NY: Syracuse University Press, 2011.

———. "Sexology in the Yishuv: The Rise and Decline of Sexual Consultation in Tel Aviv, 1930–39." *International Journal of Middle East Studies* 42, no. 2 (2010): 231–249.

———. "'We, the Sexologists . . .': Arabic Medical Writing on Sexuality, 1879–1943." *Journal of the History of Sexuality* 22, no. 3 (2013): 426–445.

Kunzel, Regina. *Criminal Intimacy: Prison and the Uneven History of Modern American Sexuality*. Chicago: University of Chicago Press, 2008.

Kuzniar, Alice. *The Queer German Cinema*. Stanford, CA: Stanford University Press, 2000.

Lackner, Michael. "*Ex Oriente Scientia?* Reconsidering the Ideology of a Chinese Origin of Western Knowledge." *Asia Major* 21, no. 1–2 (2008): 183–200.

Lalo, Alexei. *Libertinage in Russian Culture and Literature: A Bio-History of Sexualities at the Threshold of Modernity*. Leiden, Netherlands: Brill, 2011.

Lang, Birgit. "The Shifting Case of Masochism: Leopold von Sacher-Masoch's *Venus in Furs*." In *Making the Case: The Case Study Genre in Sexology, Psychoanalysis and Literature*, by Birgit Lang, Joy Damousi, and Alison Lewis. Manchester, UK: Manchester University Press, forthcoming.

Laqueur, Thomas. *Making Sex: Body and Gender from the Greeks to Freud*. Cambridge, MA: Harvard University Press, 1990.

Larson, Wendy. *From Ah Q to Lei Feng: Freud and Revolutionary Spirit in Twentieth-Century China*. Stanford, CA: Stanford University Press, 2009.

Leary, Charles L. "Intellectual Orthodoxy, the Economy of Knowledge and the Debate over Zhang Jingsheng's *Sex Histories*." *Republican China* 18, no. 2 (1993): 99–137.

———. "Sexual Modernism in China: Zhang Jingsheng and 1920s Urban Culture." Ph.D. diss., Cornell University, 1994.

Lee, Haiyan. *Revolution of the Heart: A Genealogy of Love in China, 1900–1950*. Stanford, CA: Stanford University Press, 2007.

Leung, Helen. "Archiving Queer Feelings in Hong Kong." *Inter-Asia Cultural Studies* 8 (2007): 559–571.

Liu Jen-peng and Ding Naifei. "Reticent Poetics, Queer Politics." *Inter-Asia Cultural Studies* 6, no. 1 (2005): 30–55.

Liu, Lydia H., ed. *Tokens of Exchange: The Problem of Translation in Global Circulations*. Durham, NC: Duke University Press, 1999.

———. *Translingual Practice: Literature, National Culture, and Translated Modernity—China, 1900–1937*. Stanford, CA: Stanford University Press, 1995.

Livesey, Matthew J. "From This Moment On: The Homosexual Origins of the Gay Novel in American Literature." Ph.D. diss., University of Wisconsin, 1997.

Lochrie, Karma. *Heterosyncracies: Female Sexuality When Normal Wasn't*. Minneapolis: University of Minnesota Press, 2005.

Looby, Christopher. "The Gay Novel in the United States, 1900–1950." In *A Companion to the Modern American Novel 1900–1950*, edited by John T. Matthews, 414–436. Oxford: Wiley-Blackwell, 2009.

Lorcin, Patricia M. E. *Imperial Identities: Stereotyping, Prejudice and Race in Colonial Algeria*. London: Tauris, 1995.

Love, Heather. *Feeling Backward: Loss and the Politics of Queer History*. Cambridge, MA: Harvard University Press, 2007.

Lybeck, Marti M. "Gender, Sexuality, and Belonging: Female Homosexuality in Germany 1890–1933." Ph.D. diss., University of Michigan, 2007.

Mackintosh, Jonathan D. *Homosexuality and Manliness and Postwar Japan*. Abingdon, UK: Routledge, 2010.

Mann, Susan. *Precious Records: Women in China's Long Eighteenth Century*. Stanford, CA: Stanford University Press, 1997.

Marsh, Ian. *Suicide: Foucault, History and Truth*. Cambridge: Cambridge University Press, 2010.

Martin, Biddy. *Femininity Played Straight: The Significance of Being Lesbian*. New York: Routledge, 1996.

Martin, Fran, and Ari Larissa Heinrich, eds. *Embodied Modernities: Corporealities, Representation, and Chinese Cultures*. Honolulu: University of Hawai'i Press, 2006.

Martin, Fran, Peter A. Jackson, Mark McLelland, and Audrey Yue, eds. *AsiaPacifiQueer: Rethinking Genders and Sexualities*. Urbana: University of Illinois Press, 2008.

Mason, Gail. *The Spectacle of Violence: Homophobia, Gender and Knowledge*. New York: Routledge, 2002.

Massad, Joseph. *Desiring Arabs*. Chicago: University of Chicago Press, 2007.

———. "Re-Orienting Desire: The Gay International and the Arab World." *Public Culture* 14, no. 2 (2002): 361–385.

Matte, Nicholas. "International Sexual Reform and Sexology in Europe, 1897–1933." *Canadian Bulletin of Medical History* 22, no. 2 (2005): 253–270.

Matzner, Sebastian. "From Uranians to Homosexuals: Philhellenism, Greek Homoeroticism and Gay Emancipation in Germany 1835–1915." *Classical Receptions Journal* 2, no. 1 (2010): 60–91.

McClintock, Anne. *Imperial Leather: Race, Gender and Sexuality in Colonial Contest.* New York: Routledge, 1995.

McLaren, Angus. *Impotence: A Cultural History.* Chicago: University of Chicago Press, 2007.

———. *Twentieth-Century Sexuality: A History.* Oxford: Blackwell, 1999.

McMahon, Keith. *Polygamy and Sublime Passion: Sexuality in China on the Verge of Modernity.* Honolulu: University of Hawai'i Press, 2009.

McMillan, Joanna. *Sex, Science and Morality in China.* New York: Routledge, 2006.

Meijer, Marinus J. "Homosexual Offences in Ch'ing Law." *T'oung Pao* 71 (1985): 109–133.

Miller, Martin. *Freud and the Bolsheviks: Psychoanalysis in Imperial Russia and the Soviet Union.* New Haven, CT: Yale University Press, 1998.

Mizielinska, Joanna, and Robert Kulpa, eds. *De-Centring Western Sexualities: Central and Eastern European Perspectives.* Farnham, UK: Ashgate, 2011.

Molony, Barbara, and Kathleen Uno, eds. *Gendering Modern Japanese History.* Cambridge, MA: Harvard University Asia Center, 2005.

Montgomery, Scott L. *Science in Translation: Movements of Knowledge through Cultures and Time.* Chicago: University of Chicago Press, 2000.

Mort, Frank. *Dangerous Sexualities: Medico-Moral Politics in England since 1830.* London: Routledge and Kegan Paul, 1987.

Mosse, George L. *Nationalism and Sexuality: Respectability and Abnormal Sexuality in Modern Europe.* New York: Fertig, 1985.

Najmabadi, Afsaneh. "Beyond the Americas: Are Gender and Sexuality Useful Categories of Analysis?" *Journal of Women's History* 18 (2006): 11–21.

———. *Professing Selves: Transsexuality and Same-Sex Desire in Contemporary Iran.* Durham, NC: Duke University Press, 2013.

———. *Women with Mustaches and Men without Beards: Gender and Sexual Anxieties of Iranian Modernity.* Berkeley: University of California Press, 2005.

Nappi, Carla. "The Global and Beyond: Adventures in the Local Historiographies of Science." *Isis* 104, no. 1 (2013): 102–110.

Ng, Vivian. "Homosexuality and State in Late Imperial China." In *Hidden from History: Reclaiming the Gay and Lesbian Past,* edited by Martin B. Duberman, Martha Vicinus, and George Chauncey Jr., 76–89. New York: New American Library, 1989.

———. "Ideology and Sexuality: Rape Laws in Qing China." *Journal of Asian Studies* 46 (1987): 57–70.

Nye, Robert A. "The History of Sexuality in Context: National Sexological Traditions." *Science in Context* 4, no. 2 (1991): 387–406.

Oosterhuis, Harry. "Sexual Modernity in the Works of Richard von Krafft-Ebing and Albert Moll." *Medical History* 56, no. 2 (2012): 133–155.

———. *Stepchildren of Nature: Krafft-Ebing, Psychiatry, and the Making of Sexual Identity.* Chicago: University of Chicago Press, 2000.

Pande, Ishita. *Medicine, Race and Liberalism in British Bengal: Symptoms of Empire.* New York: Routledge, 2012.

Peakman, Julie, ed. *A Cultural History of Sexuality.* 6 vols. London: Berg, 2010.

Peng, Hsiao-yen. "Sex Histories: Zhang Jingsheng's Sexual Revolution." In *Feminism/ Femininity in Chinese Literature,* edited by Peng-hsiang Chen and Whitney Crothers Dilley, 159–177. Critical Studies 18. Amsterdam: Rodopi, 1999.

Pflugfelder, Gregory M. *Cartographies of Desire: Male–Male Sexuality in Japanese Discourse 1600–1950.* Berkeley: University of California Press, 1999.

Pollard, Lisa. "From Husbands and Housewives to Suckers and Whores: Marital-Political Anxieties in the 'House of Egypt,' 1919–48." *Gender and History* 21 (2009): 647–669.

———. *Nurturing the Nation: The Family Politics of Modernizing, Colonizing and Liberating Egypt, 1805–1923.* Berkeley: University of California Press, 2005.

Povinelli, Elizabeth A., and George Chauncey Jr. "Thinking Sexuality Transnationally: An Introduction." *GLQ: A Journal of Lesbian and Gay Studies* 5, no. 4 (1999): 439–449.

Puar, Jasbir. "Rethinking Homonationalism." *International Journal of Middle East Studies* 45 (2013): 336–339.

Pym, Anthony. *Exploring Translation Theories.* London: Routledge, 2012.

Rich, Adrienne. "Compulsory Heterosexuality and Lesbian Existence." *Signs: Journal of Women in Culture and Society* 5, no. 4 (1980): 631–660.

Robertson, Jennifer. *Takarazuka: Sexual Politics and Popular Culture in Modern Japan.* Berkeley: University of California Press, 1998.

———. "Yoshiya Nobuko: Out and Outspoken in Practice and Prose." In *The Human Tradition in Modern Japan,* edited by Anne Walthall, 155–174. Wilmington, DE: Scholarly Resources, 2002.

Rocha, Leon Antonio. "Quentin Pan in *The China Critic.*" *China Heritage Quarterly,* no. 30–31 (2012). Available at http://www.chinaheritagequarterly.org/features .php?searchterm=030_rocha.inc&issue=030.

———. "*Scientia Sexualis* versus *Ars Erotica*: Foucault, van Gulik, Needham." *Studies in History and Philosophy of Biological and Biomedical Sciences* 42, no. 3 (2011): 328–343.

———. "Sex, Eugenics, Aesthetics, Utopia in the Life and Work of Zhang Jingsheng (1888–1970)." Ph.D. diss., University of Cambridge, 2010.

———. "The Way of Sex: Joseph Needham and Jolan Chang." *Studies in History and Philosophy of Biological and Biomedical Sciences* 43, no. 3 (2012): 611–626.

Rofel, Lisa. *Desiring China: Experiments in Neoliberalism, Sexuality, and Public Culture.* Durham, NC: Duke University Press, 2007.

Rohy, Valerie. *Anachronism and Its Others: Sexuality, Race, Temporality.* New York: State University of New York Press, 2009.

Rosario, Vernon A. *The Erotic Imagination: French Histories of Perversity.* Oxford: Oxford University Press, 1997.

———, ed. *Science and Homosexualities.* New York: Routledge, 1997.

Rowbotham, Sheila. *Edward Carpenter: A Life of Liberty and Love.* London: Verso, 2008.

Rowbotham, Sheila, and Jeffrey Weeks, eds. *Socialism and the New Life: The Personal and Sexual Politics of Edward Carpenter and Havelock Ellis.* London: Pluto, 1977.

Rupp, Leila. *Sapphistries: A Global History of Love between Women.* New York: New York University Press, 2009.

Ryan, Paul. *Asking Angela Macnamara: An Intimate History of Irish Lives.* Dublin: Irish Academic Press, 2011.

Said, Edward. *Orientalism.* London: Penguin, 1978.

Sakai, Naoki. "How Do We Count a Language? Translation and Discontinuity." *Translation Studies* 2, no. 1 (2009): 71–88.

Sakai, Naoki, and Yukiko Hanawa, eds. *Traces 1: Spectres of the West and the Politics of Translation.* Hong Kong: Hong Kong University Press, 2001.

Sakai, Naoki, and Jon Solomon. *Translation, Biopolitics and Colonial Difference.* Hong Kong: Hong Kong University Press, 2006.

Sakamoto, Hiroko. "The Cult of 'Love and Eugenics' in May Fourth Movement Discourse." *positions: east asia cultures critique* 12, no. 2 (2004): 329–376.

Sang, Tse-Lan. *The Emerging Lesbian: Female Same-Sex Desire in Modern China.* Chicago: University of Chicago Press, 2003.

Schaffner, Anna Katharina. *Modernism and Perversion: Sexual Deviance in Sexology and Literature, 1850–1930.* Basingstoke, UK: Palgrave Macmillan, 2012.

Schick, Irvin C. *The Erotic Margin: Sexuality and Spatiality in Alteritist Discourse.* London: Verso, 1999.

Schulte, Rainer, and John Biguenet, eds. *Theories of Translation: An Anthology of Essays from Dryden to Derrida.* Chicago: University of Chicago Press, 1992.

Scott, Joan. "The Evidence of Experience." *Critical Inquiry* 17, no. 4 (1991): 773–797.

Sedgwick, Eve Kosofsky. *Between Men: English Literature and Male Homosocial Desire.* New York: Columbia University Press, 1985.

———. *Epistemology of the Closet.* Berkeley: University of California Press, 1990.

———. *Tendencies.* Durham, NC: Duke University Press, 1993.

Sengoopta, Chandak. "Glandular Politics: Experimental Biology, Clinical Medicine, and Homosexual Emancipation in Fin-de-Siècle Central Europe." *Isis* 89 (1998): 445–473.

Shamoon, Deborah. *Passionate Friendship: The Aesthetics of Girls' Culture in Japan.* Honolulu: University of Hawai'i Press, 2012.

Sirotkina, Irina. *Diagnosing Literary Genius: A Cultural History of Psychiatry in Russia, 1880–1930.* Baltimore: Johns Hopkins University Press, 2002.

Solomon, Jon. "Translation, Violence, and the Heterolingual Intimacy." *eipcp* 9 (2007): n. 16. Available at http://eipcp.net/transversal/1107/solomon/en/#_ftnref16.

Somerville, Siobhan B. *Queering the Color Line: Race and the Invention of Homosexuality in American Culture.* Durham, NC: Duke University Press, 2000.

Sommer, Doris. *Foundational Fictions: The National Romances of Latin America.* Berkeley: University of California Press, 1991.

Sommer, Matthew. *Sex, Law, and Society in Late Imperial China.* Stanford, CA: Stanford University Press, 2000.

Sonbol, Amira El Azhary. *The Creation of the Medical Profession in Egypt.* Syracuse, NY: Syracuse University Press, 1991.

Spector, Scott, Helmut Puff, and Dagmar Herzog, eds. *After* The History of Sexuality: *German Genealogies with and beyond Foucault.* Spektrum: Publications of the German Studies Association. New York: Berghahn, 2012.

Spivak, Gayatri. *Outside in the Teaching Machine*. New York: Routledge, 1993.

Steakley, James D. *The Homosexual Emancipation Movement in Germany*. Salem, NH: Ayer, 1975.

Steiner, George. *After Babel: Aspects of Language and Translation*. 3rd ed. Oxford: Oxford University Press, 1998.

Stevens, Hugh, and Caroline Howlett, eds. *Modernist Sexualities*. Manchester, UK: University of Manchester Press, 2000.

Stoler, Ann Laura. *Carnal Knowledge and Imperial Power: Race and the Intimate in Colonial Rule*. Berkeley: University of California Press, 2002.

———. *Race and the Education of Desire: Foucault's History of Sexuality and the Colonial Order of Things*. Durham, NC: Duke University Press, 2005.

Storr, Merl. "Transformations: Subjects, Categories and Cures in Krafft-Ebing's Sexology." In *Sexology in Culture: Labelling Bodies and Desires*, edited by Lucy Bland and Laura Doan, 11–26. Cambridge: Polity, 1998.

Stryker, Susan. *Transgender History*. Berkeley, CA: Seal Press, 2008.

Studer, Nina Salouâ. "'Pregnant with Madness': Muslim Women in French Psychiatric Writing about Colonial North Africa." *Maghreb Review* 35 (2010): 439–452.

Sutton, Katie. "'We Too Deserve a Place in the Sun': The Politics of Transvestite Identity in Weimar Germany." *German Studies Review* 35, no. 2 (2012): 335–354.

Suzuki, Michiko. *Becoming Modern Women: Love and Female Identity in Prewar Japanese Literature and Culture*. Stanford, CA: Stanford University Press, 2010.

———. "'The Husband's Chastity': Progress, Equality, and Difference in 1930s Japan." *Signs: Journal of Women in Culture and Society* 38, no. 2 (2013): 327–352.

———. "Writing Same-Sex Love: Sexology and Literary Representation in Yoshiya Nobuko's Early Fiction." *Journal of Asian Studies* 65, no. 3 (2006): 575–599.

Tamale, Sylvia, ed. *African Sexualities: A Reader*. Cape Town: Pambazuka, 2011.

Terry, Jennifer. *An American Obsession: Science, Medicine, and Homosexuality in Modern Society*. Chicago: University of Chicago Press, 1999.

———. "Lesbians under the Medical Gaze: Scientists Search for Remarkable Differences." *Journal of Sex Research* 27, no. 3 (1990): 317–339.

Tinsley, Omise'eke Natasha. *Thiefing Sugar: Eroticism between Women in Caribbean Literature*. Durham, NC: Duke University Press, 2010.

Tougaw, Jason Daniel. *Strange Cases: The Medical Case History and the British Novel*. New York: Routledge, 2006.

Toulalan, Sarah, and Kate Fisher, eds. *The Routledge History of Sex and the Body, 1500 to the Present*. Abingdon, UK: Routledge, 2013.

Traub, Valerie. "The New Unhistoricism in Queer Studies." *PMLA* 128, no. 1 (2013): 21–38.

———. "The Present Future of Lesbian Historiography." In *A Companion to Lesbian, Gay, Bisexual, Transgender, and Queer Studies*, edited by George E. Haggerty and Molly McGarry, 124–145. Malden, MA: Blackwell, 2007.

Tsuzuki, Chushichi. *Edward Carpenter 1844–1929: Prophet of Human Fellowship*. Cambridge: Cambridge University Press, 1980.

Umekawa, Sumiyo. "Sex and Immortality: A Study of Chinese Sexual Activities for Better-Being." Ph.D. diss., School of Oriental and African Studies, University of London, 2004.

Usborne, Cornelie. *The Politics of the Body in Weimar Germany: Women's Reproductive Rights and Duties*. Basingstoke, UK: Macmillan, 1992.

Vanita, Ruth, ed. *Queering India: Same-Sex Love and Eroticism in Indian Culture and Society*. New York: Routledge, 2002.

Venuti, Lawrence. *The Translator's Invisibility: A History of Translation*. 2nd ed. Abingdon, UK: Routledge, 2008.

Vicinus, Martha. *Intimate Friends: Women Who Loved Women, 1778–1928*. Chicago: University of Chicago Press, 2004.

Vitiello, Giovanni. *The Libertine's Friend: Homosexuality and Masculinity in Late Imperial China*. Chicago: University of Chicago Press, 2011.

Voloshinov, V. N. *Freudianism: A Critical Sketch*. Translated by I. R. Titunik. Bloomington: Indiana University Press, 1976.

Volpp, Sophie. "The Discourse on Male Marriage: Li Yu's 'A Male Mencius's Mother.'" *positions: east asia cultures critique* 2 (1994): 113–132.

Wang, Y. Yvon. "Whorish Representation: Pornography, Media, and Modernity in Fin-de-Siècle Beijing." *Modern China* (2013). Available at http://mcx.sagepub.com/content/early/2013/08/24/0097700413499732.abstract.

Warner, John Harley. *Against the Spirit of System: The French Impulse in Nineteenth-Century American Medicine*. Princeton, NJ: Princeton University Press, 1998.

Waters, Chris. "Sexology." In *Palgrave Advances in the Modern History of Sexuality*, edited by Harry G. Cocks and Matt Houlbrook, 41–63. Basingstoke, UK: Palgrave, 2005.

Weikart, Richard. *From Darwin to Hitler: Evolutionary Ethics, Eugenics, and Racism in Germany*. New York: Palgrave Macmillan, 2004.

White, Chris, ed. *Nineteenth-Century Writings on Homosexuality: A Sourcebook*. London: Routledge, 1999.

Wile, Douglas. *Art of the Bedchamber: The Chinese Sexual Yoga Classics Including Women's Solo Meditation Texts*. Albany: State University of New York Press, 1992.

Wilper, James. "Sexology, Homosexual History, and Walt Whitman: The 'Uranian' Identity in *Imre: A Memorandum*." *Critical Survey* 22, no. 3 (2010): 52–68.

Wolff, Charlotte. *Magnus Hirschfeld: A Portrait of a Pioneer in Sexology*. London: Quartet, 1986.

Wu, Cuncun. *Homoerotic Sensibilities in Late Imperial China*. London: Routledge Curzon, 2004.

Wu, Cuncun, and Mark Stevenson. "Male Love Lost: The Fate of Male Same-Sex Prostitution in Beijing in the Late Nineteenth and Early Twentieth Centuries." In *Embodied Modernities: Corporeality, Representation, and Chinese Cultures*, edited by Fran Martin and Ari Larissa Heinrich, 42–59. Honolulu: University of Hawai'i Press, 2006.

———. "Speaking of Flowers: Theatre, Public Culture, and Homoerotic Writing in Nineteenth-Century Beijing." *Asian Theatre Journal* 27, no. 1 (2010): 100–129.

Yeh, Catherine. *Shanghai Love: Courtesans, Intellectuals, and Entertainment Culture, 1850–1910*. Seattle: University of Washington Press, 2006.

Ze'evi, Dror. *Producing Desire: Changing Sexual Discourse in the Ottoman Middle East, 1500–1900*. Berkeley: University of California Press, 2006.

Zito, Angela. "Queering Filiality, Raising the Dead." *Journal of the History of Sexuality* 10, no. 2 (2001): 195–201.

Zou, John. "Cross-Dressed Nation: Mei Lanfang and the Clothing of Modern Chinese Men." In *Embodied Modernities: Corporeality, Representation, and Chinese Cultures*, edited by Fran Martin and Ari Larissa Heinrich, 79–97. Honolulu: University of Hawai'i Press, 2006.

Contributors

Brian James Baer is Professor of Russian and Translation Studies at Kent State University. He is author of *Other Russias: Homosexuality and the Crisis of Post-Soviet Identity* (2009), editor of the volume *Contexts, Subtexts and Pretexts: Literary Translation in Eastern Europe and Russia* (2011), and co-editor of the volumes *Beyond the Ivory Tower: Re-thinking Translation Pedagogy* (2003) and *Russian Writers on Translation: An Anthology* (2013). He is founding editor of the journal *Translation and Interpreting Studies* (Benjamins) and co-editor of the book series *Literatures, Cultures, Translation* (Bloomsbury). He is currently completing a monograph titled *Translation and the Making of Modern Russian Literature*.

Heike Bauer is Senior Lecturer in English and Gender Studies at Birkbeck, University of London. She has published widely on the history of sexuality, on nineteenth- and twentieth-century literary culture, and on translation. Her books include *English Literary Sexology, 1860–1930* (2009), the three-volume edited anthology *Women and Cross-Dressing, 1800–1939* (2006), and a collection of essays co-edited with Matt Cook, *Queer 1950s: Rethinking Sexuality in the Postwar Years* (2012). She co-edited with Churnjeet Mahn "Transnational Lesbian Culture," a special issue of the *Journal of Lesbian Studies* 18, no. 3 (2014), and is currently completing the AHRC-funded study *A Violent World of Difference: Magnus Hirschfeld and the Shaping of Queer Modernity*.

Howard Chiang is Assistant Professor of Modern Chinese History at the University of Warwick, UK. He is a General Editor of *Cultural History* and the editor of *Transgender China* (2012), *Queer Sinophone Cultures* (2013, with Ari Larissa Heinrich), *Psychiatry and Chinese History* (2014), and *Historical Epistemology and the Making of Modern*

Chinese Medicine (2015). His forthcoming monograph is tentatively titled *After Eunuchs: Science and the Transformations of Sex in Modern China.*

Peter Cryle is Emeritus Professor of French at the Centre for the History of European Discourses at the University of Queensland. His has published numerous books including *The Thematics of Commitment: The Tower and the Plain* (Princeton University Press, 1985), *Geometry in the Boudoir: Shifting Positions in Classical French Erotic Narrative* (Cornell University Press, 1994), and *The Telling of the Act: Eroticism as Narrative in French Fiction of the Eighteenth and Nineteenth Centuries* (University of Delaware Press, 2001). He is co-editor, with Lisa O'Connell, of *Libertine Enlightenment: Sex, Liberty, and License in the Eighteenth Century* (Palgrave, 2003) and, with Christopher Forth, of *Sexuality at the Fin de Siècle: The Makings of a "Central Problem"* (University of Delaware Press, 2008).

Kate Fisher is Professor of Social and Cultural History at the University of Exeter. She has written four books: *Birth Control, Sex and Marriage in Britain 1918–1960* (Oxford University Press, 2006), *Sex before the Sexual Revolution* (with Simon Szreter) (Cambridge University Press, 2010), *Bodies, Sex and Desire from the Renaissance to the Present* (co-edited with Sarah Toulalan) (Palgrave, 2011), and *The Routledge History of Sex and the Body 1500 to the Present* (co-edited with Sarah Toulalan) (Routledge, 2013). With Dr. Rebecca Langlands (University of Exeter) she directs the *Sex and History* project, which uses objects from past cultures as a stimulus for discussing issues relating to sex, sexuality, and relationships. In collaboration with the Relationship and Sexuality Education Hub, they have developed a new resource for schools.

Jennifer Fraser works at the Centre for Transformative Practice in Learning and Teaching at Birkbeck, University of London. Her research interests are at the intersections of critical and queer pedagogies and gender studies. She completed a Ph.D. at the University of London on the role of literature in constructing social knowledge and educating the national citizenry in nineteenth-century Peru. Parts of this research have been published in the *Bulletin of Hispanic Studies* and *Modern Languages Open.*

Jana Funke is an Advanced Research Fellow in the English Department at the University of Exeter. She is contributing co-editor of *Sex, Gender and Time in Fiction and Culture* (Palgrave, 2011) and editor of *The World and Other Unpublished Works of Radclyffe Hall* (Manchester University Press, 2015). She has published journal articles and book chapters on late nineteenth- and early twentieth-century literature and culture, the history of sexuality, and uses of the past and historiography.

Liat Kozma is a Senior Lecturer at the Department of Islamic and Middle Eastern Studies at Hebrew University, Jerusalem. She is the author of *Policing Egyptian Women: Sex, Law, and Medicine in Khedival Egypt* (Syracuse University Press, 2011). Her research interests include feminism in the Middle East and the history of drug traffic and traffic in women in the region, as well as the League of Nations' interest in social questions.

Birgit Lang is Senior Lecturer in German Studies at the University of Melbourne. She has published widely on the case study genre, literary modernism, the history of sexuality/sexology and exile and contemporary German and Austrian migrant literature. She is co-editor of *Limbus: Australian Yearbook for German Literary and Cultural Studies* (2008–).

Leon Antonio Rocha is Lecturer in Chinese Studies at the Department of History, University of Liverpool. His current book projects include *Harnessing Pleasure: Imagining and Transforming Chinese Sexuality in the Twentieth Century* and *Needham Questions*. He is co-editor, with Robbie Duschinsky, of *Foucault, the Family and Politics* (Palgrave Macmillan 2012).

Katie Sutton is a Lecturer in German and Gender Studies at the Australian National University. Her current research focuses on the historical relationships between sexology and psychoanalysis, building on work undertaken as an Australian Research Council postdoctoral fellow at the University of Melbourne. There she formed part of a research team investigating the interdisciplinary history of the case study genre, with Birgit Lang and Joy Damousi. She has published on interwar German popular culture and sex/gender subcultures, including *The Masculine Woman in Weimar Germany* (Berghahn Books, 2011).

Michiko Suzuki is Associate Professor in the Department of East Asian Languages and Cultures at Indiana University. She specializes in modern Japanese literature and culture with a focus on issues such as gender, sexuality, sexology, and material culture. Her works include *Becoming Modern Women: Love and Female Identity in Prewar Japanese Literature and Culture* (Stanford University Press, 2010) and articles in *Signs: Journal of Women in Culture and Society*, *Journal of Asian Studies*, *Journal of Japanese Studies*, and *U.S.-Japan Women's Journal*. In addition to research on early twentieth-century popular fiction, sexology, and notions of male–female difference, she is currently writing on postwar representations of kimono in Japanese literature and film.

James P. Wilper holds a Ph.D. in comparative literature and culture, which was awarded by Birkbeck, University of London, in 2013. He is currently completing a monograph on the emergence of the gay novel genre in English and German, which will be published by Purdue University Press in 2016. His articles include "Wilde and the Model of Homosexuality in Mann's *Tod in Venedig*" in *CLCWeb: Comparative Literature and Culture* (2013) and "Sexology, Homosexual History, and Walt Whitman: The 'Uranian' Identity in *Imre: A Memorandum*" in *Critical Survey* (2010). He currently teaches at Queen Mary, University of London, and the University of Westminster.

Index